DATE DUE

Antonio Caldara

Antonio
Caldara
Essays on
his life
and times

edited by
BRIAN W. PRITCHARD

Scolar Press

First published 1987 by
Scolar Press
Gower Publishing Company Limited
Gower House, Croft Road
Aldershot GU11 3HR
England

U.S.A.
Gower Publishing Company
Old Post Road
Brookfield
Vermont 05036

British Library Cataloguing in Publication Data

Antonio Caldara: essays on his life and
    times.
    1. Caldara, Antonio   2. Composers—Italy
    —Biography
    I. Pritchard, Brian
    780'.92'4   ML410.C26

    ISBN 0-85967-720-6

Published with the assistance of the
LUCIE L. D. SMITH
Fund

Typeset by Saba Graphics, Christchurch, New Zealand
and printed in Great Britain by
Redwood Burn Limited
Trowbridge, Wiltshire

Contents

Illustrations

Abbreviations

Instrumental designations

acc.	accompanying instruments	org.	organo
b.c.	basso continuo	thb.	theorbo
bn.	bassoon	timp.	timpani
btn.	baryton	trb.	trombone
cl.	clarino	trp.	trumpet
ct.	cornetto	va.	viola
gmb.	gamba	vc.	violoncello
hn.	horn	vgr.	violone grosso
hp.	harpsichord	vn.	violin
lt.	lute	vne.	violone
ob.	oboe	vni unis.	violins unison

Pitch notation

Middle C is c^{I}; octaves above are indicated c^{II}, c^{III} etc. Octaves are based on C.

Library sigla

A: Austria

A-GÖ	Furth bei Göttweig, Benediktinerstift
A-H	Herzogenburg, Chorherrenstift
A-KR	Kremsmünster, Benediktinerstift
A-M	Melk an der Donau, Benediktinerstift
A-Wgm	Vienna, Gesellschaft der Musikfreunde
A-Wn	Vienna, Österreichische Nationalbibliothek (Musiksammlung)

B: Belgium

B-Bc	Brussels, Conservatoire Royal de Musique

Cs: Czechoslovakia

Cs-Bm	Brno, Moravské Muzeum, Hudebněhistorické Oddělení
Cs-K	Český Krumlov, Pracoviště Státního Archívu Třeboň
Cs-N	Nitra, Státní Archív
Cs-Pnm	Prague, Národní Muzeum, Hudební Oddeliní

D: Germany

D-brd-B	Berlin, Staatsbibliothek Preussischer Kulturbesitz
D-brd-DO	Donaueschingen, Fürstlich Fürstenbergische Hofbibliothek
D-brd-DS	Darmstadt, Hessische Landes- und Hochschülbibliothek
D-ddr-Bds	Berlin, Deutsche Staatsbibliothek, Musikabteilung
D-ddr-Dlb	Dresden, Sächsische Landesbibliothek
D-ddr-MEi	Meiningen, Staatliche Museen

GB: Great Britain

GB-Er	Edinburgh, Reid Music Library of the University of Edinburgh
GB-Ge	Glasgow, Euing Music Library
GB-Lam	London, Royal Academy of Music
GB-Lbl	London, British Library

I: Italy

I-Fc	Florence, Conservatorio di Musica Luigi Cherubini
I-Fm	Florence, Biblioteca Marucelliana
I-Mb	Milan, Biblioteca Nazionale Braidense
I-OS	Ostiglia, Biblioteca Musicale Greggiata
I-PAc	Parma, Conservatorio di Musica Arrigo Boito

S: Sweden

S-St	Stockholm, Kungliga Teaterns Bibliothek

US: United States of America

US-CA	Cambridge, Harvard University Music Libraries
US-LAu	Los Angeles, University of California, Walter H. Rubsamen Music Library
US-Pu	Pittsburgh, University of Pittsburgh, Theodore Finney Music Library
US-Wc	Washington, DC, Library of Congress, Music Division

Acknowledgements

While not without difficulties, the preparation and production of this volume have been realized because of the strong support that has come from many scholars in the international community. Above all, I am indebted to the contributors for their faith in this project: their generous responses to suggestions have been greatly appreciated.

Professor Michael Talbot, Music Department, University of Liverpool, Dr Otto Biba, Archivist, Gesellschaft der Musikfreunde in Vienna, and Dr Rosemary Moravec, Österreichische Nationalbibliothek (Musiksammlung) Vienna, have willingly provided information and, in particular, Professor F. W. Riedel, Musikwissenschaftliches Institut, Johannes Gutenberg-Universität, Mainz, Univ.-Dozent Dr Herbert Seifert, Institut für Musikwissenschaft, Universität Wien, and Dr Colin Timms, Department of Music, University of Birmingham, have all encouraged this volume at various times. Special thanks must be extended to Dr Hermine Williams, Hamilton College, Clinton, U.S.A., who placed her extensive knowledge of musical activity at the Viennese court in the early eighteenth century at my disposal. The co-operation of many libraries has been essential. I would record the kind help of the Österreichische Nationalbibliothek (Musiksammlung), the Gesellschaft der Musikfreunde, the Glasgow University Library (Euing Music Library), The British Library, The Library of Congress (Music Division), Harvard University Library, the Sächsische Landesbibliothek, Dresden, and the Moravské Muzeum, Brno.

The unenviable task of preparing the typescript was undertaken by Susan Wallis; all music examples were computer-set by Timothy Bell. Saba Graphics, Christchurch, type-set a complex text with remarkable patience, and James Price, Editor of Scolar Press, guided proceedings. Professor Emeritus T. E. Carter, Dr R. W. Fisher and Dr U. Bartholomae, all of the German Department, University of Canterbury, provided translations for many of the Abstracts, and shared the proof-reading with Jenny Pickering. John M. Jennings of the School of Music, University of Canterbury, offered much advice, both literary and musical, and assumed responsibility for the Index.

On a personal note it remains to thank the DAAD, Bonn, whose award of a study grant facilitated the initial preparations for this volume, and the University of Canterbury, which, for many years, has supported my research on Antonio Caldara.

University of Canterbury   B.W.P.
Christchurch
August, 1986

Editor's preface

On 27 December, 1736, Antonio Caldara, *Vizekapellmeister* at the Imperial court in Vienna for two decades, died at the age of 66 years. Two days later, to the tolling of a *Fürstengeläut* he was interred in the crypt of the city's cathedral. His death, and that of Prince Eugene of Savoy in the preceding April, marked the beginning of the end of a glorious period in Vienna's musical and political history. If the Prince had been the architect of the Habsburg empire's military strength, security and prosperity, Caldara had been the provider of so many of the compositions, sacred and secular alike, that in their own way epitomized the assurance and confidence of those early decades of the eighteenth century.

Within another four years the Emperor, Charles VI, who had presided over this *Blütezeit* also was dead, and with the demise of the court's long-serving *Kapellmeister*, Johann Joseph Fux, in 1741, the final link with the golden decades was broken. The Pragmatic Sanction which put Maria Theresa on the throne in 1740 was bitterly contested, the empire's boundaries contracted as a result of military defeats, economic recession severely reduced ceremonial and cultural activities, and the composers who took over the leading positions at court could scarcely compare with the men they succeeded. But perhaps most devastating of all was the radical shift away from the style that had prevailed in all spheres of artistic endeavour. For Vienna, the baroque was over. In music, the 1740s saw the dissolution of the huge structures of Caldara and Fux, and their contemporaries such as Francesco Conti; it also marked a hiatus in the emergence of a new, clearly defined and unified style. Fate, it seemed, was to deal Caldara a double blow; his pen was still forever, and now that sympathetic *milieu* in which his works were esteemed and their particular virtues extolled, was steadily demolished. Charles VI need scarcely have lamented the passing of the *Vizekapellmeister* whom he esteemed above all other composers — the era itself was about to be swept away.

Caldara's eclipse, however, was not total. Certainly he had not secured the immediate immortality that *Gradus ad Parnassum* brought to Fux, but throughout the eighteenth century a few of his compositions continued to be performed at the *Hofkapelle*, and rather more were used in abbeys and churches throughout the empire and beyond. Early lexicographers[1] included him in their dictionaries, albeit often with erroneous details; by the end of the century he was represented by an occasional extract in treatises on composition.[2]

Rehabilitation gained momentum in the nineteenth century. Although initially it stemmed largely from the personal quirks and enthusiams of a few connoisseurs and dilettanti, nevertheless it produced the first substantial biography of Caldara,[3] public performances of his music,[4] and the growing preparation and dissemination of copies of his scores.[5]

At the end of the century Caldara entered the academic world. In his pioneering dissertation of 1894, Felix von Kraus provided both a biography and thematic catalogue,[6] which even today still prove valuable sources of information. Kraus's efforts scarcely unleashed a flood of investigations into Caldara's life and works but the present century has seen a deepening of our knowledge of the late-baroque composer.

No one would dispute that Ursula Kirkendale's *Antonio Caldara: sein Leben und seine venezianisch-römischen Oratorien*, first published in 1966, has been a landmark. The frequent references made to it by contributors to this volume are a sure sign that it has yet to be displaced from its pre-eminent position.[7] With painstaking detail she has provided an authoritative account of Caldara's career and established beyond question the framework of his working life: the apprenticeship years in Venice to 1699; the appointment to the court at Mantua to 1707; the years in Rome to 1716, broken by a visit to Spain in 1708; and the final two decades spent at Vienna.

Within this framework our knowledge of Caldara, 250 years after his death, remains incomplete. On the one hand we have a number of intensive analytical studies of aspects of his output; on the other, we still await a life-and-works study that allows us to grasp, readily and comprehensively, his whole career. We have records of the payments made to the copyists who prepared scores of Caldara's music during his Roman period — yet the exact date and place of his birth remain a mystery. We can assign a date of composition and dates of performances to many of his compositions — yet his total output has to be precisely defined. We have Caldara's petitions to Charles VI for increases in salary — yet we have still to determine his part in the celebrations which marked Charles's return from Spain *via* Milan to his coronation in Frankfurt. We have many of the compositions Caldara wrote during the six months he spent in Vienna in 1712 — yet his sojourn in that city remains undocumented. We have the operas he wrote for the Archbishop's court at Salzburg between 1716 and 1727 — yet the connection remains unexplored. We know that Donberger was Caldara's pupil, but we can only conjecture that he himself received instruction from Giovanni Legrenzi.

These *lacunae* are not addressed in this volume. The present essays — analytical, documentary and sociological — attempt to widen further our understanding of Caldara's compositions and working methods, the environments in which he moved, and the resources available to him whether of heritage, style or local instrumental and vocal forces.

A. Peter Brown discusses Caldara's response to very particular demands of style and occasion at Vienna — a response quite different from that seen in Reinhard G. Pauly's study of one composition produced for the court of Mantua. In Hisako Serizawa's survey of the overtures to secular compositions, the fusion of Italian with local Viennese traits not only highlights Caldara's adaptability but also emphasizes one of the most important characteristics of all his Viennese compositions, whether sacred or secular — the assimilation of conventions into a personal style.

Caldara's ability to make the most effective use of the resources available at any one time or place is demonstrated in Eleanor Selfridge-Field's discussion of the instrumental situation pertaining at Venice, Rome, and Vienna, while the specific background to one aspect of Caldara's output — the cantatas written at Vienna — is analysed by Lawrence E. Bennett. The importance of Caldara's compositions in the repertoires of institutions beyond Vienna is described by both Robert N. Freeman and Wolfgang Horn, whose essays also raise the issue of the reworkings and adaptations of Caldara's music by his contemporaries as well as by later composers. Jiří Sehnal documents the wider dissemination of Caldara's music. In a study of one province of the Habsburg empire, he places it within the context of compositions by local musicians and local opportunities for musical performances. The identification of so-called 'anonymous' and/or misattributed compositions is the subject of Glennys Ward's essay which also brings to light the most distant distribution of Caldara's music in the eighteenth century.

Three essays are devoted to aspects of baroque opera. Through Andrew D. McCredie's survey, the ballet music to Caldara's Viennese operas is seen to be no mere appendage, but emerges as an art-form in its own right. Olga Termini explores one of the principal working methods of baroque opera composers — the *rifacimento* process — opening out a *modus operandi* which Caldara himself may have used or to which his own operas very possibly were subjected. Frauke Gerdes traces the evolution of the art of stage and design in Italy up to the point where the early achievements of the Galli Bibiena family and their contemporaries formed the settings for Caldara's first operas.

If Caldara could be characterized by one word, it must be 'pragmatic'. Even in an age noted for mobility among musicians engaged in a constant search for positions that brought security and reward, there could be few composers who achieved so much in such contrasted situations. Thus the diversity of this volume seems a particularly appropriate tribute to a composer who chameleon-like, adapted so successfully to widely differing environments and emphases.

Notes

[1] The earliest reference appears in Johann Gottfried Walther *Musicalisches Lexicon* (Leipzig, 1732). See also the list of dictionaries which concludes Ursula Kirkendale 'Caldara, Antonio' *Dizionario Biografico degli Italiani* (Roma, 1973) 16, p. 566.

[2] For example, in Giuseppe Paolucci *Arte Pratica di Contrappunto* (Venezia, 1765) and Johann Georg Albrechtsberger *Gründliche Anweisung zur Komposition* (Leipzig, 1790).

[3] [Franz Sales Kandler] 'Caldara' *Allgemeine Musikalische Zeitung, mit besonderer Rücksicht auf den österreichischen Kaiserstaat* Jg. 1820, cols 485–488.

[4] For example those performed at Raphael Georg Kiesewetter's house-concerts in Vienna. From *c*1817 to 1834, ten of Caldara's sacred compositions were performed. See Herfrid Kier *Raphael Georg Kiesewetter (1773–1850): Wegbereiter des musikalischen Historismus* (Regensburg, 1968) pp. 62–3 and 179.

[5] Particularly through the efforts of Kandler, Kiesewetter and Fortunato Santini.

[6] 'Biographie des k.k. Vize-Hofkapellmeisters Antonio Caldara' (D.Phil., Universität Wien).

[7] Further biographical studies by Ursula Kirkendale appeared as 'La Vita' *Chigiana XXVI–XXVII* (1971) pp. 223–346, and in the *Dizionario Biografico* . . . . . . pp. 556–66.

Caldara's trumpet music
for the Imperial celebrations of
Charles VI and Elisabeth Christine

A. Peter Brown

Zusammenfassung

Die Trompetenmusik Caldaras für die Reichsfeier Karls VI und Elisabeth Christines

Der erste teil dieses Beitrags, der Kilian Reinhardts *Rubriche Generali* von 1727, den *Hof- und Ehren-Calender*, die *Hof-Statt*, das *Wienerische Diarium*, und Urkunden des *Haus-, Hof-, und Staatsarchiv* verwertet, behandelt die Verwaltung und die Verwendung von Trompeten und Pauken bei Kirchen- und Reichsfeierlichkeiten. Ein Verzeichnis der Trompeter und Pauker, die von 1715 bis 1736 sowohl den *Musikalischen Trompetern und Pauckern* wie auch den *Hof- und Feld-Trompetern* angehörten, wird beigegeben. Der zweite Teil wendet sich einem Teilgebiet der Trompetenmusik Caldaras zu: den Trompetenouvertüren und Arien aus Opern und Oratorien, die für die Namens- und Geburtstage des Kaisers und der Kaiserin sowie für andere Feste komponiert wurden. Im letzten Teil wird darauf hingedeutet, daß die Sätze für doppelte Trompeten- und Paukenchöre eine musikalische Äußerung des kaiserlichen Spruchs *Fortitudine & Constantia* darstellen, und daß die für diese Feste komponierten Opern nicht nach dem Maßstab der Oper als dramatischer Form zu beurteilen sind, sondern eher nach dem Gesichtspunkt einer dynastischen Offenbarung.

Caldara's trumpet music for the Imperial celebrations of Charles VI and Elisabeth Christine

A. Peter Brown

THE FIFTY-SEVEN YEARS from the defeat of the Turks in 1683 until the death of Charles VI in 1740, were an era of unknown peace and security for the city of Vienna. But this was not only a period without threat: it was a true *Blütezeit*. The ruins of the final two-month siege by the Turkish forces soon were replaced by magnificent structures designed by the Fischer von Erlachs and Johann Lucas von Hildebrand, which brought to the city those unified façades later dubbed the *Reichsstil*.[1] Music also flourished: the *Hofmusikkapelle* at the Imperial seat grew to a size previously unrivaled[2] and J. J. Fux and Antonio Caldara were appointed to direct and compose the Imperial music. All this was promulgated by the Emperors themselves — Leopold I, Joseph I, and Charles VI — each one an accomplished performer, composer and conductor.[3] As early as Leopold's reign, a strict musical protocol of activities for the Imperial celebrations, including regular operatic performances, was established.

During the reigns of Joseph and Charles, music provided a clear signal as to the type and character of the events in the liturgical/imperial year. Prolonged ringing of church bells indicated that the immediate surviving relatives of the deceased Emperor, Leopold I, had entered the Capuchin crypt to pray at the coffin on the anniversary of the death of husband and father. Just as cannons were fired to commemorate military encounters, so trumpets heralded joyous feasts and celebrations. Thus the yearly refrains of sound made every citizen of Vienna aware of the character of the day marked, whether or not they possessed the court calendars that specifically chronicled each event.

In 1715, almost from the commencement of Charles's reign, the court began to print calendars of varying detail which contained such diverse information as the days of the saints, long-range weather forecasts and the phases of the moon, as well as every anniversary imaginable from the founding of the university to the birthdays and namedays of the members of the Imperial clan, whether they were situated in or far from Vienna. Some calendars were published in octavo format and included a listing of the *Hof-Statt* from *Obrister Hof-Kanzler* to *Zuckerbacher*; others were small directories that would fit nicely into a pocket.[4]

The educated class also could learn of the court's activities from the official newspaper, the *Wienerisches Diarium*. Here, too, the yearly cycle could be generally ascertained, but without the systematic detail of the calendars. While the *Diarium* may not have mentioned every event listed in the *Calender*, very often it named the special guests and the music performed, together with the composer, librettist, and performers for each celebration it reported.[5]

The indispensible guide for the precise musical requirements of the events of the yearly cycle is Kilian Reinhardt's

> *RUBRICHE GENERALI Per le Funzioni Ecclesiastiche Musicali di tutto l'Anno. Con un'Appendice in fine dell'Essenziali ad Uso, e Servizio dell' August*[issi]*ma Austriaca, ed Imp*[eria]*le. Capella.*

Extant in a fair copy dated 1727, it records the court practices established over the preceding decades.[6] As the title implies, the *Rubriche* are in two parts: the first deals with liturgical feasts (*Festtage der Heiligen*), the second with court feasts (*Hof-Feste*). Nevertheless, the court feasts should not be viewed strictly as secular because liturgical and court celebrations were closely bound with one another.

Both the *Hof-Calender* and the *Rubriche* ranked the *Hof-Feste* according to three levels. The highest feasts were the *Gala-Tage* which included the birth- and namedays as well as betrothals and weddings of the Emperor, the Empress, and their family. A second level, the *Toison-Feste*, were attended by members of the Order of the Golden Fleece. (In 1729 some 40 of the Viennese nobility were so honoured.)[7] The lowest level of the *Hof-Feste* comprised the *Gewöhnliche Andachten und Solennitäten*; these included saints' days, such as that of St Joannis de Matha (8 February), in addition to a series of processions to, and devotions in, various Viennese cloisters and churches. In the liturgical sphere, the so-called *Toison-Feste* were accorded the highest rank. These included the Marian and Apostolic feasts (both the first Vesper Service and High Mass) which, except for those that occurred during spring and summer, also were attended by the members of the Order of the Golden Fleece.[8] At the second level came the *Pontifical* feasts, encompassing all the remaining high feast-days, first and second Vespers, and Compline on the eve of certain feasts, as well as the celebrations on Good Friday, the other services of Holy Week, and marriages, baptisms, etc. The third level included celebrations of Mass and Vespers for the remaining Sundays and the more austere services during Advent and Lent.

Trumpet and timpani choirs played a prominent part in the music performed at the feasts of the first and second levels in both types.[9] They either functioned within the instrumental ensemble during Mass and

Vespers in varying degrees of exposure, and/or provided *Intraden* (fanfares) prior to, during, or after the service. Sometimes *Intraden* alternated with appropriate chant verses and they also were performed before the Mass itself; before, during, and after the *Te Deum*; for Litanies; and in processions.[10]

The trumpet and timpani choirs were made up of four trumpeters, often used in pairs, and a single timpanist. One pair of trumpets, termed *clarini*, were given intricate and demanding lines in a high *tessitura*. The other pair, dubbed *trombe*, and with their parts notated in the alto clef, functioned in what is commonly called the 'principale'; that is, they played in the lower register with the upper *tromba* providing an harmonic 'filler', and the lower *tromba* usually doubling the timpani at the octave. Although its make-up is not specified, this seems to be the scoring Reinhardt means when he refers to 'pleni chor'. Trumpets were also used in double choirs, occasionally in triple complement, and rarely in a quadruple setting (e.g., for the Festival of the Holy Name of Mary, where the *Ave maris stella* was performed in procession alternating with trumpet interludes).

From the pattern of activity presented in the above-mentioned documents and the surviving music, there seems to have been a hierarchical association with the number of choirs used. For example, within the *Gala-Tage* for the birth- and namedays of the members of the Imperial family, double-choir scorings seem to have been reserved (if not always used) for the Emperor, and very occasionally for the Empress, for the birth of an heir to the throne and, in 1736, for the nuptials of Maria Theresa.[11]

This plethora of trumpeting in both the court and liturgical realms was realized by several groups of players in the Imperial employ during the reign of Charles VI. According to the *Hof-Statt*,[12] there were at least five divisions of the court where trumpeters were active. Presumably, the most prestigious was that which went under the title of *Musikalische Trompeter und Hör-Paucker* and formed part of the *Kaiserliche Hof- und Kammer-Musici* (Table 1). During Caldara's service as *Vizekapell-meister*, this group grew from fourteen in 1715 to a maximum of eighteen in 1721. A second administrative unit consisted of the *Hof- und Feld-Trompeter und Hör-Paucker* (Table 2). While the *Musikalische Trompeter* were under the jurisdiction of the *Hof-Kapellmeister*, this latter group was under the *Obrist-Stallmeister-Staab und Hof-Futter Amt*. Yet the trumpeters and timpanists seemingly had a small degree of independence for they had their own *Ober-Trompeter* (O.T.). The size of this unit varied from a maximum of twenty-six in 1716, 1717 and 1721 to only seventeen in 1735. However, Tables 1 and 2 reveal that a large number of the *Hof- und Feld-Trompeter* also belonged to the *Musikalische Trompeter*. In addition, there were six trumpeters and one timpanist who, dressed in mail (*Hartschieren*), belonged to the *Kaiserliche Leib-Garde*. As these players cannot now be identified we are unable to tell if they were drawn from the already-resident trumpeters. However, the six trumpeters and the timpanist listed[13] in the *Hof-Statt* for 1715

Table 1. Musikalische Trompeter und Paucker during *Caldara's years in Vienna*

Note: For 1719, 1724, 1729, and 1732 the *Hof-Calender* are either no longer extant or do not contain a listing of the *Hof-Statt.*

Trompeter	1715	1716	1717	1718	1720	1721	1722	1723	1725	1726	1727	1728	1730	1731	1733	1734	1735	1736
Küffel (Küfel), Franz Anton	x	x	x	x	x	x	x	x	x	x	x	x	x	x	x	x	x	x
Wlach, Thomas	x	x	x	x	x	x	x	x	x	x	x	x	x	x	x	x	x	x
Zischeck (Czizek), Johann	x	x	x	x	x	x	x	x	x	x								
Zechart (Sechart), Andreas	x	x	x	x	x	x	x	x	x	x	x							
Schmidt, Matthias	x	x	x	x	x	x	x	x	x	x	x	x	x	x	x	x	x	x
Bonn, Thomas	x	x	x															
Nosotto, Sebastian	x	x	x	x	x	x	x	x	x	x	x	x	x	x				
Jesorka, Nicolaus	x	x	x	x	x	x	x	x	x	x	x	x	x	x	x	x	x	x
Gorscheck (Gortschek), Georg	x	x	x	x	x	x	x	x	x	x	x	x	x					
Pernember (Pernebmer), Tobias Andreas	x	x	x	x	x	x	x	x	x									
Turnowsky, Franz	x	x	x	x	x	x	x	x	x	x	x	x	x	x	x	x	x	x
Holland, Joseph	x	x	x	x	x	x	x	x	x	x	x	x	x	x	x	x	x	x
Hien (Hein), Rudolf		x	x	x	x	x	x	x	x	x	x	x	x	x	x	x	x	x
Koch, Matthias		x	x	x	x	x	x	x	x	x	x	x	x	x	x	x	x	x
Rebhindl (Rebhendl), Johann Michael		x	x	x	x	x	x	x										
Schön, Franz						x	x	x	x	x	x	x	x	x	x	x	x	x
Koberer, Rudolph											x	x						
Greinauer (Grünauer), Christian						x												
Sessler, Jacob Ernst										x	x	x	x	x	x	x	x	x
Bonn, Franz Joseph													x	x	x	x	x	x
Hainisch (Heinisch), Johann														x	x	x	x	x
Peyer (Payer, Bayer), Johann Ernst															x	x	x	x
	12	15	15	14	14	16	15	15	14	14	14	13	13	13	13	13	13	13
Paucker																		
Hellmann, Maximilian	x	x	x	x	x	x	x											
Mayr, Heinrich	x																	
Hellmann, Jacob Leopold														x		x	x	x
Denck (Tenck), Johann Gottfried			x	x	x	x	x	x	x	x	x	x	x	x	x			
Vogel, Leopold Philipp																x	x	x
	2	1	2	2	2	2	2	1	1	1	1	1	1	2	1	2	2	2

and mentioned there as 'mit Ihre Käyserl. Majest. der Kayserin seynd nachfolgende Trompeter und Paucker ankommen', subsequently appeared in the two main groups. This does suggest that at least some of the *Musikalische Trompeter* and the *Hof- und Feld-Trompeter* served their apprenticeships in such positions as the *Leib-Garde*, although a few of their number came *via* the more prestigious *Kaiserliche-Musikalische Hof-Scholaren*. Finally, there were trumpeters assigned to the *Hof-Statt* of the widowed *Kaiserin*, Wilhelmine Amalie, as part of her *Leib-Garde* (*Hartschieren*) and, for a few years, those who performed as *Exercitien* (that is, for parade drills).

It has been a correctly accepted truism that the Imperial trumpeters obtained a prestige and a degree of self-governance that would not have been tolerated for any other group of employees at the European courts. A guild of trumpeters and timpanists was first established by Imperial privilege granted by Ferdinand II in 1623, and continued at the Habsburg court well into the nineteenth century.[14] In the first forty years of the eighteenth century, a school of *clarino* playing that was unrivalled by any equivalent in Italy, North-Central Germany, or England, established itself in Vienna.

Although we know of him only from the *Hof-Statt* and other court documents, one of these legendary players must have been Franz Küffel who, as the *Ober-Trompeter* from 1711 to 1754, dominated the entire period of Caldara's Imperial service. Another virtuoso of the first rank was certainly Franz Josef Holland (1687–1747), whose compensation was comparable to Küffel's and who established a trust (*Stiftung*) for his survivors.[15] Yet the player most often mentioned is Johann Hainisch (Heinisch) who served at the court from 1730 to 1750. Regarding his rendition of an obbligato to an aria from Bernasconi's *Artaserse* performed in October, 1746, the Kremsmünster monk, Pater Heinrich Pichler, reported in his diary:

> Nach dieser kam eine andere, welche erst kürzlich aus Venedig ist kommen. Diese hat eine Arie adagio gesungen, wie ein Engel, wann so zu sagen erlaubt ist. Herr Heinisch der berühmte Trompeter hat ein Solo zu dieser Arie geblasen, so künstlich und hoch, dass es menschlicher Weis fast nicht möglich sein hätte können, denn es ging die Trompete wie ein Flötel. Zum End dieser Arie schlug dieses Weibsbild einen so langen und lieblichen Triller, dass ich wirklich geglaubt, der Atem werde ihr nicht mehr kommen; und also machte auch einen ebenso langen und noch längeren Triller Herr Heinisch auf der Trompete mit ihr.[16]

Hainisch's fame spread far beyond Vienna. In speaking of Caspar Köstler, a Salzburg trumpeter, Hammerle wrote: 'Er ist ein Schüler des so sehr behrühmten seel. Hrn. Heinisch in Wien; gibt der Trompete einen feinen, gar angenehmen singbaren Ton ... '[17]

It was for this environment, full of accomplishment and potential, that Caldara, Fux, Reutter, Bonno and others produced a series of impressive works, both sacred and secular, in which the scorings for

Table 2. Hof- und Feld-Trompeter und Paucker *during Caldara's years in Vienna*

Note: for 1719, 1724, 1729, and 1732 the *Hof-Calender* are either no longer extant or do not contain a listing of the *Hof-Statt.*
OT = Ober-Trompeter, S = Scholar

Trompeter	1715	1716	1717	1718	1720	1721	1722	1723	1725	1726	1727	1728	1730	1731	1733	1734	1735	1736
Küffel (Küefel), Franz Anton	OT	OT	OT	OT	OT	OT	OT	OT	OT	OT	OT	OT	OT	OT	OT	OT	OT	OT
Kortscheck, Gerog	x	x	x	x														
Wlach, Thomas	x	x	x	x	x	x	x	x	x	x	x	x	x	x	x	x	x	x
Fehringer, Lorenz	x	x	x	x	x	x	x	x	x	x	x	x	x	x	x	x	x	x
Jesorka, Nicholaus	x	x	x	x	x	x	x	x	x	x	x	x	x	x				
Zischeck (Cizek), Johann	x	x	x	x	x													
Schwarz, Andre	x	x	x	x	x	x	x	x										
Zechart (Sechart), Andreas	x	x	x	x	x	x	x	x	x	x	x	x	x					
Bonn, Thomas	x	x	x															
Timthl (Tunckl), Bartholome	x	x	x	x	x	x	x	x	x	x	x	x	x	x	x	x	x	x
Schmidt, Matthias	x	x	x	x	x	x	x	x	x	x	x	x	x	x	x	x	x	x
Pernember (Pernebmer), Tobias Andreas	x	x	x	x	x	x	x	x	x	x	x	x	x	x				
Turnowsky, Franz	x	x	x	x	x	x	x	x	x	x	x	x	x	x	x	x	x	x
Schön, Franz	x	x	x	x	x	x	x	x	x	x	x	x	x	x	x	x	x	
Nosoto, Sebastian	x	x	x	x	x	x	x	x	x	?	x	x	x	x	x			
Promb, Ferdinand	x	x	x	x	x													
Holland, Joseph	x	x	x	x	x	x	x	x	x	x	x	x	x	x	x	x	x	x
Schilling, Florian	x																	
Puchmeister (Buchmeister), Paul	x	x	x	x	x	x	x	x	x	x	x	x	x	x	x	x	x	x
Hien (Hein), Rudolf		x	x	x	x	x	x	x	x	x	x	x	x	x	x	x	x	x
Zeillinger, Paul			x	x	x	x	x	x										
Koch, Matthias		x	x	x	x	x	x	x	x	x	x	x	x	x	x	x	x	x
Rebhindl (Rebhendl), Johann [Joseph Michael]	x	x	x	x	x													

Table 2. (contd)

Trompeter	1715	1716	1717	1718	1720	1721	1722	1723	1725	1726	1727	1728	1730	1731	1733	1734	1735	1736
Bonn, Franz		x	x	x	x	x	x	x	x	x	x	x	x	x	x	x	x	x
Zürnich, Caspar		x	x	x	x	x	x	x	x	x	x	x	x	x	x	x	x	x
Namiesky, Maximilian					x	x	x	x	x	x	x	x	x	x				
Greinauer (Grünauer), Christian						x							x	x				
Kogerer, Rudolph						x	x	x	x	x	x	x	x	x				
Sessler, Jacob Ernst						x	x	x	x	x	x	x	x	x				
Hainisch (Heinisch), Johann									x	x	x	x	x	x	x	x	x	x
Peyer (Payer, Bayer), Johann Ernst										S	S	S	S	x	x	x	x	x
Turnovsky, Joseph												S	S	S				
Hölzl, Ferdinand																x	x	x
Kreibich (Kreybich), Franz															x	x	x	x
	19	24	24	23	21	24	23	20	20	18	19	19	19	18	15	16	15	15
Paucker																		
Hellmann, Maximilian	x	x	x	x	x	x	x											
Mayr, Heinrich	x																	
Hellmann, Jacob Leopold		x	x	x	x	x	x	x	x	x	x	x	x	x				
Denck (Tenck), Johann Gottfried										x	x	x	x	x	x	x	x	x
Vogel, Leopold Philipp																x	x	x
	2	2	2	2	2	2	2	1	1	2	2	2	2	2	1	2	2	2

brass ranged from a solo trumpet to full double-choirs. This present survey is concerned more especially with Caldara's trumpet writing found in the non-liturgical music performed for the *Hof-Fest Gala-Tage*: the Emperor Charles VI's birthday on 1 October and his nameday on 4 November, and the Empress Elisabeth Christine's birthday on 28 August and her nameday on 19 November.

These days were, of course, marked by liturgical and secular celebrations. In his *Rubriche*, Reinhardt laid out the appropriate musical genres for both types of celebrations and defined the manner in which they were to be set[18] (Plate 1). The secular festivities, the evening entertainments styled 'Gala Grande', were similarly designed for both the Emperor and the Empress:

for the birthday of the Empress:

> Il Giorno feliciss.^{mo} Natalizio della Ces.^{a}
> R.^{le} Catt.^{ca} M'tà dell'Imperatrice Elisabetta
> Christina. Gala Grande.
> Servizio di Cam.^{ra} overo Opera, secondo
> il Commando Aug.^{mo}

for the birthday of the Emperor:

> Servizio di Tavola la Mattina, e sera per tutti
> li Musici, con opera, overo Servizio di Cam.^{a},
> secondo il commando della S.^{a} Ces.^{a} e R.^{le} Catt.^{ca} M'tà.

for the nameday of the Emperor:

> Gala grande. Servizio di Tavola Mattina, e
> sera, per essere il giorno glor.^{mo} del Nome di
> S:M:C:C: Carlo VI. Sifà Opera, overo
> servizio di Cam.^{a}

for the nameday of the Empress:

> Gala Grande. Servizio di Tavola mattina,
> e sera per tutti. Servizio di Cam.^{a} overo Opera.

The *servizio di camera* was a relatively small and intimate piece (rarely with trumpets) akin to an extended cantata. The operas, on the other hand, invariably were of great length (three or five acts, with ballet music, and concluding with a laudatory *Licenza*) and employed all the musical, literary and architectural capabilities of the Imperial court.[19] In two decades of service, Caldara alone contributed some forty works for these secular festivities (Plate 2). The majority were operas and it is among these (but also in a few oratorios and occasionally in smaller festive pieces), in the 'trumpet' overtures (Table 3) and the arias designated 'con tromba' or 'trombe' (Table 4), that his most sustained and notable writing for the Imperial trumpeters can best be observed.

However, a brief mention must first be made of the trumpet parts in some of the compositions which resulted from Caldara's initial encounter with Charles VI. This apparently occurred in 1708, during

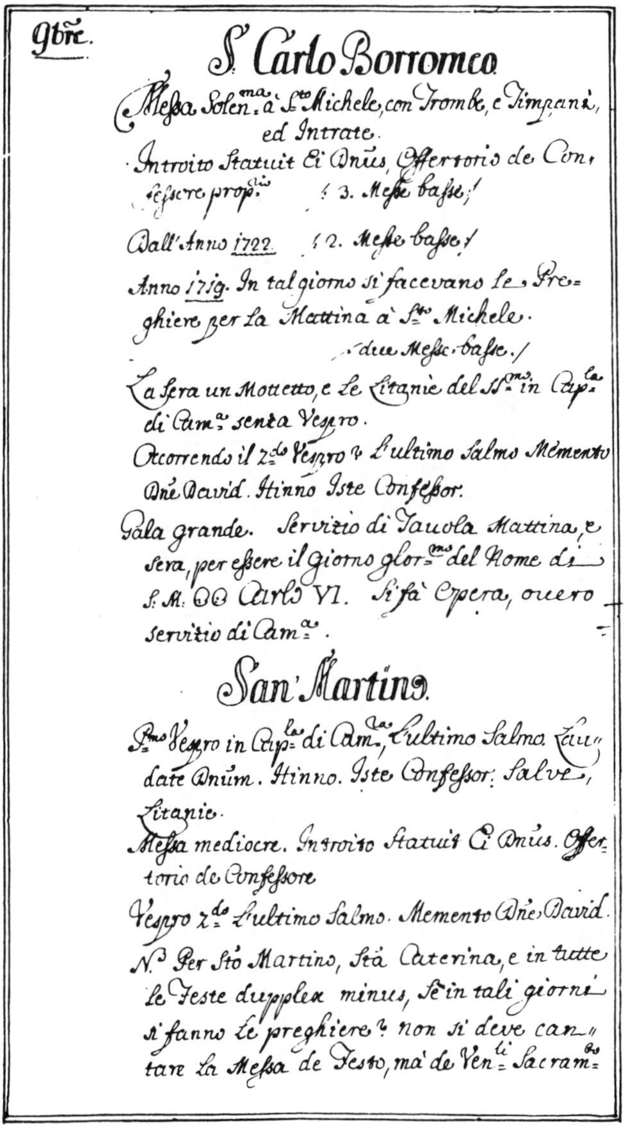

9bre.

S. Carlo Borromeo

Messa Solen.ma à S.to Michele, con Trombe, e Timpani, ed Intrate.

Introito Statuit Ei Dnus, Offertorio de Confessore prop.cio   / 3. Messe basse /

Dall'Anno 1722   / 2. Messe basse /

Anno 1719. In tal giorno si facevano le Preghiere per la Mattina à S.to Michele.
                    / due Messe basse /

La sera un Mottetto, e Le Litanie del SS.mo in Cap.la di Cam.a senza Vespro.

Occorrendo il 2.do Vespro ? L'ultimo Salmo Memento Dne David. Hinno Iste Confessor.

Gala grande. Servizio di Tavola Mattina, e sera, per essere il Giorno glor.mo del Nome di S.M. CC Carlo VI. Si fà Opera, ouero servizio di Cam.a.

San Martino.

P.mo Vespro in Cap.la di Cam.a, L'ultimo Salmo Laudate Dnum. Hinno. Iste Confessor: Salve, Litanie.

Messa mediocre. Introito Statuit Ei Dnus. Offertorio de Confessore

Vespro 2.do L'ultimo Salmo. Memento Dne David.

N.B Per S.to Martino, S.ta Caterina, e in tutte le Feste dupplex minus, Se in tali giorni si fanno le preghiere? non si deve cantare la Messa de Festo, ma de Ven.ti Sacram.to

Plate 1. Kilian Reinhardt *Rubriche Generali*. Specifications for the celebration of the Feast-day of St Karl Borromeus (4 November), the nameday of the Emperor, Charles VI. (A-Wn: S.m. 2503)
Reproduced by permission of the Österreichische Nationalbibliothek, Musiksammlung, Vienna

Plate 2. Caldara *Cajo Fabbricio*. Title-page of the full score prepared for the Imperial
collection. (A-Wn: Mus.Hs. 17150)
*Reproduced by permission of the Österreichische Nationalbibliothek,
Musiksammlung, Vienna*

the eleven-year period when, as Charles III, the future Emperor laid claim to the Spanish throne and held court in Barcelona. In that year Caldara produced, among other works, *Il più bel nome*, a *componimento da camera* with a libretto by Pariati, that was to celebrate Charles's marriage to Elisabeth Christine of Braunschweig as well as the bride's nameday. In the following year Caldara composed another *componimento* (again to a text by Pariati), *Il nome più glorioso*.[20] This time it was for the nameday of the King himself. Charles must have not been displeased with the result, for it was revived in Vienna for the same *Gala-Tag* in 1718.

The extensive role of the trumpets in this work — the *sinfonia*, an aria, and the final chorus are all scored for *due trombe* — is of particular interest. The D-major *sinfonia* is in full concerto style with ritornelli, fanfare-like themes, driving rhythms, and sequences. The trumpets are held in reserve until after the opening ritornello and make their first entry, unaccompanied, in duet style, followed by a dialogue (Ex. 1). A brief *Adagio* for strings, concluding on the dominant of the relative minor, leads directly into another concerto-styled movement (*Allegro 3/8*) which commences with a two-trumpet fanfare. The aria itself is in much the same vein, with unaccompanied duet fanfares and hyper-energized rhythms. The return of the trumpets for the final chorus results in a framing of sound that was to become almost a commonplace in Caldara's Viennese operas. While *Il nome più glorioso* had little

Example 1. *Introduzione* to *Il nome più glorioso* bars 1–18

Ex. 1 (contd)

connection with the musical style of the composers then resident in the *Hofburg,* both it and its companion foreshadowed one of Caldara's main duties after his appointment to the Imperial court — the composition of music for the Emperor's and Empress's personal *Gala-Tage.*

The overtures

Caldara's first contribution to the Imperial *Gala-Tage* was a setting of Pariati's *Cajo Marzio Coriolano* for the Empress's birthday in 1717. Here the two-movement *Introduzione* opens with a brilliant fanfare for a quartet of trumpets with timpani (Ex. 2). No distinction is made between 'clarino' and 'principale' styles; all four players go beyond the restricted function of the latter. At times the quartet is treated antiphonally, but perhaps more important is Caldara's exploitation of the different timbres of his instrumental choirs in successive passages: trumpets and timpani, oboes and bassoons, and strings with *basso continuo* are heard in turn. The fanfare itself serves as a ritornello, resounding at the beginning,

Example 2. *Introduzione* to *Cajo Marzio Coriolano* bars 1–5

Table 3. *Caldara's* Introduzioni *with trumpet(s)*

Operas

1709 *Il nome più glorioso* (for the nameday of Charles III)
2 trombe, 2 oboes, (bassoons?), strings à 4, basso continuo

1717 *Cajo Marzio Coriolano* (for the birthday of the Empress)
4 trombe, timpani, 2 oboes, bassoon, strings à 4, basso continuo

1721 *Ormisda, re di Persia* (for the nameday of the Emperor)
2 choirs of 2 clarini, 2 trombe and timpani, 2 oboes, bassoon, strings à 4, basso continuo

1723 *La concordia de'pianeti* (for the nameday of the Empress)
2 clarini, 2 trombe, timpani, (oboes, bassons?), strings à 4, basso continuo

1724 *Gianguir* (for the nameday of the Emperor)
2 choirs of 2 clarini, 2 trombe and timpani, 2 oboes, bassoon, string à 4, basso continuo

1725 *Il Venceslao* (for the nameday of the Emperor)
2 choirs of 2 clarini, 2 trombe and timpani, (oboes, bassoons?), strings à 4, basso continuo

1727 *Ornospade* (for the nameday of the Emperor)
2 choirs of 2 clarini, 2 trombe and timpani, (oboes?), strings à 4, basso continuo

1728 *La forza dell'amicizia ossia Pilade ed Oreste** (for the birthday of the Empress)
2 choirs of 2 clarini, 1 tromba and timpani, (oboes, bassoons?), strings à 4, basso continuo

1728 *Mitridate* (for the nameday of the Emperor)
2 choirs of 2 clarini, 2 trombe and timpani, (oboes, bassoons?), strings à 4, basso continuo

1729 *Cajo Fabbricio* (for the nameday of the Emperor)
2 choirs of 2 clarini, 2 trombe and timpani, (oboes, bassoons?), strings à 4, basso continuo (revived 1730)

1732 *Adriano in Siria* (for the nameday of the Emperor)
2 choirs of 2 clarini, 2 trombe and timpani, (oboes and bassoons?), strings à 4 (solo violin, cello and bass), basso continuo

1734 *Enone* (composed 1728) (for the birthday of the Empress)
2 clarini, 2 trombe, timpani, (oboes, bassoons?), strings à 4, basso continuo

1736 *Ciro riconosciuto* (for the birthday of the Empress)
2 choirs of 2 clarini, 2 trombe and timpani, (oboes and bassoon?), strings à 4, basso continuo

1736 *Achille in Sciro* (for the wedding of the Archduchess Maria Theresa and Franz Stephan von Lothringen)
2 choirs of 2 clarini, 2 trombe and timpani (oboes, bassoons?), strings à 4, basso continuo

Oratorios

1720 *Assalonne*
2 clarini, 2 trombe, timpani (oboes?), bassoon, strings à 4 (solo violin and cello), basso continuo

1723 *Ester*
tromba, (oboes and bassoon?), strings à 4, basso continuo

1725 *Il trionfo della religione, e dell'amore***
2 clarini, 2 trombe, timpani, 2 oboes, bassoon, strings à 4, basso continuo

*The attribution of the overture to Caldara is doubtful; according to the title page, Reutter composed Act 1, Caldara Acts II and III and the *Intermezzi*.
**This oratorio is also described as a 'Theatral Festin', 'Serenata' and 'Festa sacra'.

middle, and end of the *Allegro*. At each return it is enhanced by thicker textures and more active rhythms. After a terse but harmonically rich *Adagio* for strings, the trumpets reappear for the opening chorus of the first act.

Only two other opera overtures call for a quartet of trumpets — those to *La concordia de'pianeti* and *Enone*. Unlike *Coriolano*, the scoring of *La concordia* possibly was dictated by the circumstances of the first performance which took place in Znojmo (Moravia) on November 19, 1723,[21] during the Imperial couple's return from Prague where, only a few weeks earlier, they had been crowned as monarchs of Bohemia. There, as part of the festivities, Caldara had directed the performance of Fux's *Costanza e Fortezza*.[22] *La concordia's* première was reported in the *Wienerisches Diarium*:

> [Nach 5. Uhr] kamen zum Kaiserl. Quartier zwey auf das herzlichste ausgezierte und jeder von 8 Pferden 4. und 4. neben einander gezogne sehr hohe Triumph-Wägen: die Pferde waren mit kostbaren Schabracken und Feder-Buschen aufgeputzet; und die Wägen mit sher [sic] schönen von Gold und Silber untermischten Mahlereyen gezieret wie auch mit vielen Fahnen und unterschiedlichen Triumph-Zeichen um und um behangen; auf welchen Wägen die Kaiserl. Vocal und Instrumental-Music davon die Personen in Opera-Kleidern sehr proper angezogen waren eine unter der Direction des Kaiserl. Obristen Directors Musices (Tit.). Herrn Prinssen Pio, &c. sehens würdigste Serenata, unter dem Titel: *La Concordia de Pianeti*. Die Übereinstimmung deren Planeten produciret wurde: die Poesie davon ware von Herrn Pariati, Kaiserl. Poeten gemacht diese aber von dem Herrn Anton Caldara, Kaiserl. Vice-Cappell-Meistern in die Music gebracht worden. Um denen 2. Wägen herum stunden eine Menge in alt-Romanischen Kleidern angethane Personen weisse Wachs-Fackeln in Handen habend: und weilen die meisten aldortigen Juwohnern [sic] dergleichen herzliche Vorstellung niemalen ihr Lebenlang gesehen ware der Zulauf dermassen häuffig dass die sonst grosse Stadt ihnen fast zu klein worden und die höchsten Dächer besetzet gewesen haben dann die Hamiltonischen Soldaten genug zu thun hatten um alle Unordnungen zu verhüten. Diese Bewunderns-würdige Vorstellung hatte sich mit allerhöchsten contento beider Kaiserl. Majestäten und aller hohen und niedern zustehenden Stands-Personen gegen 9. Uhr geendiget nach welchem das Abendmal eingenommen und also dieser erwünschte und beglückte Tag vollendet worden.

As the *Wienerisches Diarium* noted, Pariati created the libretto for both Caldara's *La concordia* and Fux's *Costanza*. Despite their different dimensions both operas begin with similar music/poetic structures: a 'trumpet' overture is linked to an opening chorus with a refrain in which the trumpets are ever prominent:

Costanza e Fortezza	*La concordia*
Overture	Overture
Allegro 4/4	*Allegro* 4/4
Andante 3/4	*Largo* 3/2
Allegro 4/4- 3/4	

Scene 1

Allegro 4/4	Tarquinio, Porsenna, Chorus 1		
Allegro 3/4	Duet — Tarquinio, Porsenna		
Allegro 4/4	Chorus 1		
Allegro 4/4	Duet — Erminio, Valeria, Chorus		
Allegro 4/4	Chorus 1		
Andante 4/4	Aria — Porsenna		
Allegro 4/4	Chorus 1		
Andante 4/4	Valeria, Erminio, Chorus		
Allegro 4/4	Chorus 1		
4/4	Recitative — Erminio, Porsenna, Valeria, Tarquinio		
Allegro 4/4	Chorus 1		
[*Allegro*] 4/4	Duet — Valerio Erminio, Chorus		
[*Allegro*] 4/4	Recitative — Porsenna		
Allegro 4/4	Chorus 1		
4/4	Recitative — Erminio, Tarquinio, Valeria, Porsenna		
Allegro 4/4	Chorus 1		
	(429 bars)		

Scene 1

[*Allegro*] 2/4	Chorus
3/8	Duet — Diana, Apollo
2/4	Chorus
3/8	Duet — Venere, Giove
2/4	Chorus
2/4	Trio — Marto, Mercur, Saturno
2/4	Chorus
4/4	Recitative — Mercur
2/4	Chorus
	(251 bars)

However, unlike *Coriolano*, the four trumpets in *La concordia* are divided into a pair of *clarini* and a pair of *trombe*. Each pair follows its particular role which, as we observed earlier, was customary in such scorings — the *clarini* here continuing the activity of the violins, and the *trombe* providing harmonic support (Ex. 3). Although the first movement is rooted once again in the structure and style of the concerto, characteristics associated with an Imperial or *Reichsstil* are now observable. The traditional fanfares and passages built on dotted rhythms are augmented by three brief fugal expositions, to the last of which is added a statement of the subject by the *clarino primo*. Such episodes call attention to the contrapuntal style that remained in favour with the Habsburgs for more than a century, from Leopold I to Joseph II.

The *Introduzione* to Caldara's setting of Apostolo Zeno's *Enone* (first performed in 1734) is scored for the same setting as *La concordia* and uses the same Imperial style. *Enone*, however, does not begin with a blare of trumpets or even a tutti; rather, a tight fugal exposition for the strings is presented in two duets interrupted by the quartet of trumpets. The trumpets nearly always follow each subsequent fugal exposition, but as the texture and material is varied with each reappearance, the expected sequence of events remains unfulfilled and, instead, a feeling of anticipation is built up. Unlike the previous two-movement overtures, the *Introduzione* to *Enone* is a full-fledged three-movement sinfonia (*Allegro*; a *Largo* interlude in the relative minor ending on its dominant;

Allegro 3/8) whose style anticipates the mid-century symphony but whose sound is sheer Baroque grandeur.

Although these three overtures together powerfully state the main aspects of the Imperial style, their scoring for trumpets is restricted. In contrast, the nine remaining opera *introduzioni* are set for full double-choirs of trumpets and timpani. Such polychoral writing by Caldara (as well as by Fux) has been attributed to the Venetian tradition. Certainly

Example 3. *Introduzione* to *La concordia de'pianeti* bars 1–10

Ex. 3 (contd)

Caldara spent most of his first thirty years in Venice; for Fux it has been hypothesized, but still not proven, that he may have been in Italy before his documented presence in Vienna.[23] Nevertheless, to declare this polychoral writing as Venetian in origin despite the fact that it had become common practice in the courts and chambers north of the Alps several generations earlier, seems ahistorical.

Except for the overture to *Adriano in Siria*, in which the slow movement is followed by a chorus of soldiers, and that to *Il Venceslao*, in which the finale is an aria scored for the same instruments as the opening movement, all double-choir overtures are in three full movements — an initial *Allegro* in C major; a central movement in the relative minor (excepting the use of the tonic minor in *Achille in Sciro*) concluding on its dominant; and a finale in the tonic major.

The opening movements are again compact but elaborate concerto-styled pieces which often provide solos not only for the trumpets but also occasionally for the concertmaster, the principal cello, and a trio of two oboes and bassoons. The first movement of *Gianguir* (1724) serves to illustrate the general shape of these opening allegros (Fig. 1). Typical is the double statement of the fanfare at the beginning, and the ensuing series of fugal expositions and episodes. Each of the exposition/episode pairs ends with a climactic passage: trumpets against oboes, oboes against violins, antiphonal solo trumpets and a tutti cadence. The occasional *stretto* is not used strategically, but ornamentally. The key scheme is unremarkable. More peculiar to *Gianguir* is the return in the tonic of the fanfare played not, as we would expect, by the trumpets, but by the oboes and bassoons. The brass are held in reserve for the last exposition and final cadences.

Figure 1. *Introduzione* to *Gianguir*

area:	Fanfare choir 1	Fanfare choir 2	Fugal Expos. 1 strings Sub: vn 1, 2, va, vc, vn 1	Stretto vn 1, 2
key:	C			
bar:	1		7	
	Episode 1	choir 1 + 2 vs obs	Expos. 2 strings Sub: vn 2, vc, basso	Episode 2 plus trps
		G	a	
	17	20	22	26
	obs vs vn	Expos. 3/Stretto strings + obs Sub: vn. 1 + 2 stretto, vc + vne stretto	Episode 3 strings alone	choir 1 + 2 2 solo trps
		F	d	e
	28	31	34	35
	Fanfare obs + bn	Expos. 4 Sub: choir 1, choir 2	tutti cadence	Coda
	C			
	40	42	45	46-49

The middle movements provide a stark contrast with their minor mode, string scoring, soft dynamics, and restrained effect. Solemnity is often underlined by imitative entries, dotted rhythms and final Phrygian cadences. It is not until the 1730s that this style for the middle movements is cast aside: *Adriano in Siria* (1732) substitutes an *Allegretta* 2/4 with binary repeats followed by a *Grave* 2/4 cadence, and *Achille in Sciro* (1736) not only uses binary form but also disposes of the four-part texture (the violins play in unison) and replaces the usually solemn cadence with a *reprisa* of the last four measures. Such changes push these later movements from a high-Baroque into a mid-century idiom.[24]

With the exception of two *minuets* (in *Mitridate* and *Achille in Sciro*), the finales of the *introduzioni* are *alla breve* marches in which the trumpets and other instrumental choirs share the material and conclude with a tutti. In all the double-trumpet-choir pieces, apart from the overtures to *Ormisda* and *La forza dell'amicizia*, the two brass groups combine into a single unit and no longer perform antiphonally in the third movement. The trumpet writing, too, is far less idiomatic.

It should be emphasized that the scoring of an *introduzione* has no effect on the instrumentation for the remainder of the opera. Brilliant trumpet writing may occur within a work whose overture calls only for woodwind, strings and continuo (as in *Il Temistocle*), while even a double-trumpet-choir overture can head an opera (for example, *Adriano in Siria*) in which the aria accompaniments are entirely for strings, doubling woodwind and continuo.

We should note in passing that the three 'trumpet' overtures to the oratorios listed in Table 3 are definitely anomalies within the context of the Viennese oratorio tradition. This, of course, was a genre reserved for performance during Lent. Instrumental colouring was attained by the diverse obbligato instruments of the aria accompaniments and not by bold ceremonial statements. In both *Assalonne* and *Ester* the texts of the opening numbers account for trumpets in the overtures. *Il trionfo della religione, e dell'amore* also is based on a subject appropriate to a trumpet scoring, but there is some doubt as to whether this work, performed on 22 April, 1725, (that is, *after* Lent) can be classified as an oratorio.[25]

Two of the 'trumpet' overtures also survive in altered versions that make no reference to their origins in opera or oratorio:

> *Sonata* (A-Kr: 21.90) is the overture to *Il trionfo della religione* (A-Wn: Mus.Hs. 18144). The Kremsmünster source reduces the scoring from 2 *clarini* and 2 *trombe* to just 2 *clarini* and deletes several repetitious measures.

> *Sonata* (A-Wn: S.m. 3617) is the overture to *Cajo Fabbricio*. This version reduces the double-choir to one, and after the slow movement replaces the original finale with a *da capo* of the first movement. The envelope containing the extant performance material records performances in 1750, 1751 and 1752.

The independent existence of these pieces, presumably for use in liturgical or para-liturgical contexts, suggests that other trumpet overtures also may have been adapted for such purposes.[26] Certainly Reinhardt's *Rubriche* provides occasions on which these pieces might have been performed — for example, the ceremonial events in the *Ritterstuben*, such as the oath of allegiance to the Emperor; the ceremonial meal for the Emperor's and Empress's Hungarian coronation; as part of the various 'Servizio di Tavola con Ouverture di Trombe e Timpani, e senza'; during the Easter liturgy; for the introit and offertory during Epiphany; for the feast of the Annunciation of the Blessed Virgin;[27] and for the feast-days of St Paul and St Andrew. Indeed, in an engraving portraying an event from 8 November, 1712 (the day on which the members of the Order of the Golden Fleece paid homage to the Emperor) entitled '*Die Kayserl Taffel in der Ritterstuben*', an orchestra that contains at least two trumpets is shown playing from the balcony.[28]

The arias

Caldara's two dozen arias with obbligato trumpet(s) are listed in Table 4. His chief contributions lie in the variety of his scorings and the virtuosity demanded, rather than in innovations to a type of piece that had a long tradition in Italian dramatic writing, from Alessandro Scarlatti to Handel.

The settings range from one trumpet to eight trumpets with timpani in double choirs. Arias with solo *clarino* may be scored for voice and *basso continuo* only or for a full complement of strings. There are also settings for two *clarini* in both duet and antiphonal textures, while a number of works require the standard Imperial full choir. Two arias, both with texts by Zeno, call for the full double complement: 'Qual piacer, o Tebro invitto' from *Lucio Papirio dittatore*, and 'Abbiam vinto' from *Il Venceslao*.

Table 4. *Caldara's arias with trumpet(s)*

Operas

1709 *Il nome più glorioso* (Pariati)
    'Se mai rimbomba' — bass, 2 trombe, (oboes, bassoons), strings à 4, basso continuo

1718 *Ifigenia in Aulide* (Zeno) (for the nameday of the Emperor)
    'Asia tremi' — alto, 4 trombe, timpani, oboes, (bassoons), strings à 4, basso continuo
    'La vittor a segue, o Carlo' (*Licenza*) — soprano, tromba, basso continuo

1719 *Lucio Papirio dittatore* (Zeno) (for the nameday of the Emperor)
    Qual piacer, o Tebro invitto' — alto, 2 choirs of 2 clarini, 2 trombe, and timpani, basso continuo

1721 *Ormisda, re di Persia* (Zeno)
    'Chi a te rende omaggio' — alto, clarino, strings à 4, basso continuo

1722 *Scipione nelle Spagne* (Zeno) (for the nameday of the Emperor)
    'Di timpani, e trombe' — bass, 2 clarini, 2 trombe, timpani, strings à 4, basso continuo

1723 *La concordia de'pianeti* (Pariati)
    'Da mia tromba' — alto, tromba, strings à 4, basso continuo

1724 *Gianguir* (Zeno)
    'Date, o trombe' — alto, tromba, strings à 4, basso continuo

Table 4. (contd)

1725 *Il Venceslao* (Zeno)
'Abbiam vinto' — tenor, 2 choirs of 2 clarini, 2 trombe and timpani, strings à 3 (violins in unison), basso continuo

1726 *I due dittatori* (Zeno) (for the nameday of the Emperor)
'Nulla bada destrier generoso' — alto, tromba, strings à 4, basso continuo
'Il suon delle trombe' — tenor, 2 trombe, basso continuo

1736 *Il Temistocle* (Metastasio) (for the nameday of the Emperor)
'Ah! d'ascoltar già parmi' — alto, clarino, strings à 4, basso continuo

Feste, servizios, cantatas

1723 *La contesa de'numi* (Prescimonio) (for the birthday of the Emperor)
'Vivi, Regna' — alto, clarino, strings à 4, basso continuo

1726 *Ghirlanda di fiori* (?) (for the birthday of the Archduchess Marianna)
'Sono di quello de l'Aurora' — soprano, tromba, strings à 3, basso continuo

1727 *Melibeo e Tirsi* (?)
'Trombe care ditelo voi' — bass, 2 trombe, strings à 4, basso continuo

1729 *Il natale di Minerva Tritonia* (for the birthday of the Empress)
'Colla tromba degl'eroi tornerà' (Licenza) — alto, clarino, strings à 3 (violins in unison), basso continuo

Oratorios

1719 *La caduta di Gerico* (Gargieria)
'Col sol fiato di poche' — alto, 2 trombe, basso continuo
'Risvegliare metalli' — alto, 2 trombe, basso continuo

1720 *Assalonne* (Bergamori)
'A l'armi a battaglia' — alto, 2 clarini, 2 trombe, timpani, (oboes, bassoon?), strings à 4, basso continuo
'Al suono guerriero' — soprano, 2 clarini, 2 trombe, timpani, (oboes, bassoon?), strings à 4, basso continuo
'Fra l'armi, fra carmi di trombe guerriere' — tenor, 2 clarini, basso continuo
'Il suon de la tromba' — tenor, 2 trombe, basso continuo

1723 *Ester* (Fozio)
'Vuò che mora' — tenor, tromba, strings à 4, basso continuo

1725 *Il trionfo della religione, e dell'amore* (G.D.B.)
'Al formidabil suon di libera tromba' — soprano, tromba, strings à 4, basso continuo

1726 *S. Giovanni Nepomuceno* (?)
'Al l'invito di suono guerriero' — soprano, tromba, strings à 3 (violins in unison), basso continuo

1726 *Gioseffo* (Neri)
'Dolce suono di tromba' — alto, clarino, strings à 4, basso continuo

Operas for Salzburg

1721 *Il germanico Marte* (?)
'Del mio gracino camittori' — alto, 2 clarini, 2 trombe, timpani, basso continuo

1722 *Camaide, imperatore della China* (Lalli)
'Se non torno fra voi vincitori' — bass, 2 trombe, timpani, 2 oboes, bassoon, strings à 4, basso continuo

'Abbiam vinto', serving both as the finale of the overture and as the beginning of the first act, is an exceptional case and perhaps its 'finale' meter of 3/8 and extravagant scoring are explained by its unique position. As in virtually every aria by Caldara the shape is a full *da capo* structure. The initial ritornello, which accounts for nearly all the trumpet material, exploits antiphonal, hammerstroke and coloristic scoring. However, the dimension of exchange between the two choirs is too small for the antiphony always to be effective (Ex. 4). As in the overtures, the fanfare idiom again is combined with rushing scales in the strings, but here these two figures rhetorically underline the text of the first part:

> Abbiam vinto. Amico Regno,
> N'è tuo frutto, e gloria, e pace.

If the antiphonal element is not thoroughly realized in 'Abbiam vinto', this is certainly not the case in 'Qual piacer, o Tebro invitto'. Scored for just two full choirs and *basso continuo*, no listener can miss the

Example 4. *Il Venceslao* 'Abbiam vinto' bars 1-22

Ex. 4 (contd)

Ex. 4 (contd)

Ex. 4 (contd)

Ex. 4 (contd)

antiphonal effect as the initial exchange of material is made at phrase level (Ex. 5). In the second part the trumpets are more subdued: a lower *tessitura* centering on e¹ is used. (This use of the fourth overtone is similar to that found in the modulatory sections of the *Introduzione*.) In terms of sound alone, this piece is clearly the most spectacular example of Caldara's multiple-trumpet writing.

Example 5. *Lucio Papirio dittatore* 'Qual piacer, o Tebro invitto' bars 1–21

Ex. 5 (contd)

[repeat played by Choir 2]

Ex. 5 (contd)

Ex. 5 (contd)

Ex. 5 (contd)

Ex. 5 (contd)

As we might expect, the five arias scored for a single brass choir pale in comparison with 'Qual piacer'. However, only two of these occur in Caldara's operas written for Imperial celebrations: 'Di timpani, e trombe' in *Scipione nelle Spagne*, and 'Asia tremi' in *Ifigenia in Aulide*. (In this latter aria the trumpets appear only at the end of each part.) Two other arias appear in the oratorio *Assalone* (as noted above, a genre in which the presence of trumpets is unusual), and another in *Il germanico Marte*, an opera commissioned for Salzburg.

Also of interest is Caldara's eighteen-bar-long attempt at a single choir accompaniment to the aria 'Il suon delle trombe' in *I due dittatori* which appears on pp. 321–24 of the autograph manuscript. He subsequently abandoned this version, crossed out each page of the score (Plate 3), and on p. 325 began the setting for 'due trombe' and continuo now to be found in the extant copyist's score.[29] Whatever the reason for the rejection of this initial version it certainly was not the lack of available players, for in Act V, Scene 2, he was to score a *sinfonia* for double choirs of trumpets. Musically, the first version seems almost commonplace when compared with the antiphonal and virtuosic dialogue of the revision, a dialogue that could only have been performed by the most accomplished trumpeters at the Viennese court (Ex. 6). The continual exchanges suggest a competition between the two players in which their mastery of breath control, tonguing, range, and stamina were taxed to the utmost.[30]

Example 6. *I due dittatori*: trumpet obbligato parts in 'Il suon delle trombe' (*A*-section)

Ex. 6 (contd)

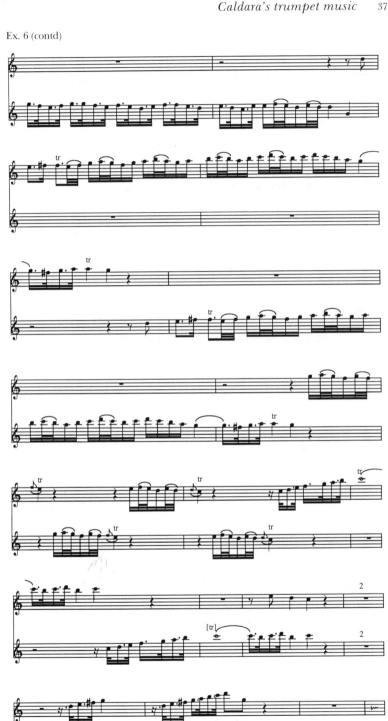

Ex. 6 (contd)

Ex. 6 (contd)

This aria notwithstanding, Caldara's most demanding trumpet parts are to be found in those arias that pit one trumpeter against a *prima donna* or *primo uomo*. The climax to this category comes, appropriately, in one of the composer's last arias: 'Ah! d'ascoltar già parmi' from *Il Temistocle* (1736) (Ex. 7). Already in the opening measures the trumpeter works his way up to e^{III} with successive trills on d^{III}, c^{III}, and b^{II}. The passage which follows again rises to e^{III} after four measures that make no allowance for breathing. Such demands are continued in the final ritornello where, following a device already used in *I due dittatori* (see Ex. 6), six cadenza-like measures of sustained trills ascend to the concluding cadence.

Example 7. *Il Temistocle*: *clarino* obbligato in 'Ah! d'ascoltar già parmi' (*A*-section)

Ex. 7 (contd)

This aria also illustrates one type of text and sentiment frequently associated with 'trumpet aria' repertoire:

> Ah! d'ascoltar già parmi
> Quella guerriera tromba,
> Che fra le stragi e l'armi
> M'inviterà per te.

Here the central topic is war, and the traditional sounding of the trumpet signals the beginning of battle. But the trumpet can also herald victory and, as the trumpet aria in *Gianguir* tells us, victory in battle creates heroes, glory and peace:

> Date, o trombe, il suon guerriero,
> Certo invito alla vittoria.

Such celebrations must be heard throughout the world and, as is made clear in *Scipione nelle Spagne*:

> Di timpani, e trombe
> Il cielo rimbombe

or in the oratorio *Assalonne*:

> Il suon delle trombe
> Si alto rimbombe

it is trumpets and timpani, the very combination of the Imperial brass choir, that can best make the universe resound.

The texts of the *licenze* to the festival operas will often be more direct with personal allusions to the Imperial couple, but as the trumpet aria in the *Licenza* to *Ormisda* shows, the sentiment is no less deserving of emphatic statement:

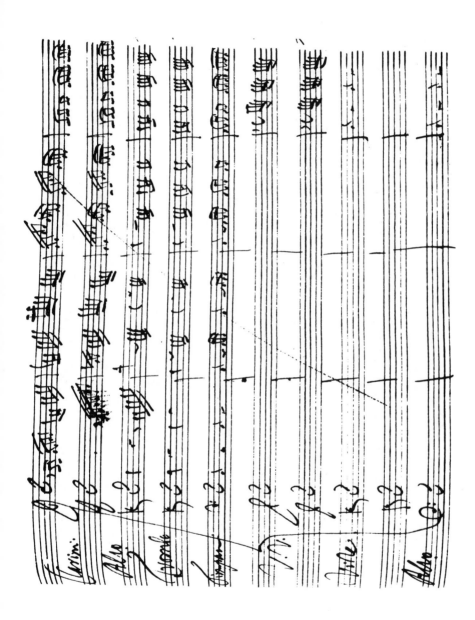

Plate 3. Caldara *I due dittatori*. The abandoned version of the aria 'Il suon delle trombe'. (A-Wgm: A382)
Reproduced by permission of the Gesellschaft der Musikfreunde, Vienna

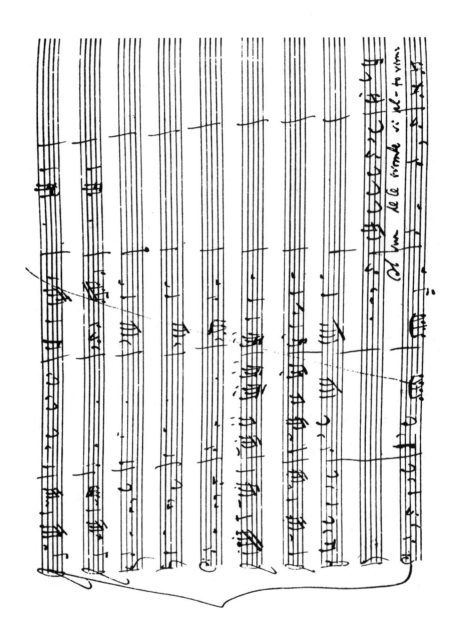

Plate 3. (contd)

Chi a te rende omaggio
Di applauso sincero,
Non pensa al tuo impero,
Ma parla al tuo cor.

E il cor, chi si sente
Dir giusto, clemente,
Magnanimo, e saggio,
Ne ha gioja, e ne ha pace.
Da lode verace
Non vien mai rossor.

*   *   *   *   *

One baffling aspect of the Imperial trumpet music written by Caldara and others during the reign of Charles VI is the total absence of scores which call for more than the full double-choirs of trumpets and timpani when, in fact, the resources of the *Hofkapelle* obviously were large enough to accommodate four to six full choirs of trumpets. This absence becomes all the more curious in the light of reports which document the appearance of more than two choirs of trumpets and timpani for non-Imperial celebrations. These were not even isolated instances. In addition to the procession of 1716 mentioned earlier, we can cite, *via* the *Wienerisches Diarium*, two further celebrations held in 1731. One in which four trumpet-choirs were involved was the *Hochamt* of the 'Mährische Landes-Genossenschaft alheir ihr jährlich gewöhnliches National-Fest zu Ehren ihrer Landes- und Schutz-Patronen denen heiligen *Cyrilli* und *Methudii*' which took place at the *Michaelerkirche* on 4 March. Three choirs participated in the 'Andachts-Eifer und offentlicher Verehrung des Heil. Martyrs und grossen Blut-Zeugen Joannis von Nepomuck' which provided in addition to 'vortrefflichen Vocal- und Instrumental-Music die Laurentanische Litaney und darauf erfolgten Te Deum, etc ... '[31] Surely, then, we might expect the Imperial *Gala-Tage* to have required, if only for prestige, a larger number of celebratory trumpet and timpani ensembles than the above-named festivities.

As an explanation of this seeming anomaly I would like to propose that the lack of expansion beyond the setting of double choirs is but one further symbolic/allegorical interpretation of the *Imperium* of Charles VI and Elisabeth Christine. It is well known that Charles VI's personal motto was *Fortitudine & Constantia*. As has been pointed out, his pretension to the throne of Spain was likened to Hercules's Spanish labour which Hercules commemorated by establishing the two great rocks or pillars today known as Mount Abyla on the coast of North Africa and Mount Calpe on the European side of the Strait of Gibraltar.[32] The Emperor's motto became explicitly associated with the Herculean rocks as early as 1723 in Heraeus's *Inscriptiones et Symbolia* published in Nuremburg and Vienna:

Exprimunt *Columnae Herculeae & Carolinae* postliminio restitutae, non modo ob Nominis, Generis, Imperiique; sed maxime ob Expeditionis Gaditanae in sexto & quinto Carolo paritatem. Illarum significatio haud quidem aliena est ab Inscriptione; Quoniam Fortitudo ferens Columnam, Constantia innixa Columnae pingitur: Non tamen efficit *Impresam* proprie dictam; Sed Emblema potius Morale. In eo, praeter Impresae Praecepta, sensum Moralem statim prodit Significatio Hieroglyphica, non Naturalis. Ita ut post hanc Explicationem Columnae Carolinae possint, etiam absque lemmate, CAESARIS FORTITUDINEM & CONSTANTIAM in Ornamentis Hieroglyphicis designare. Ut vero magis exprimatur Character Herois, (quod Symbolorum praecipuum est officium) Columnarum alteram *Laurus* adsignat Bello, alteram *Palma* *Paci [*Recentiori potius, quam antiqua significatione. Priscis (praeter palmam, quae est in pace Titi) Olivia pacis symbolum, sed illa cum Lauro facile confunditur.] quae in finiendis domi Herculeis laboribus non minori laude dignam Constantiam requirit. Sic *Diadema Imperatorium* primariis in utroque tempore fulcris sustinetur.[33]

Perhaps the most famous visual representation of the rocks/pillars is to be found in the two columns incorporated in the façade of Johann Bernhard Fischer von Erlach's *Karlskirche* (1716-1739), built by the Emperor as an offering after the plague of 1713. The most direct musical representation of Charles's motto is to be found in the antiphonal choirs of trumpets and timpani of the overture to the work which bears the motto itself as its title: Fux's festival opera *Costanza e Fortezza*. Less obvious, but no less significant is the reservation, almost without exception,[34] of the double-trumpet-choir scoring for the operas celebrating the Emperor's nameday — arguably the most important of all *Gala-Tage*. Constantly, at least throughout the 1720s, Caldara's double-choir *introduzioni* reinforced the twin aspects of the Imperial motto. Even the uninitiated must have perceived something of the splendour, majesty and might of the Habsburg empire embodied in the sheer sound of these compositions.

While Charles's motto may have died with him, the connection of the *Imperium* with double choirs of trumpets apparently continued. For the birth of the future Emperor, Joseph II, on 13 March, 1741, the architect, Franz Sebastian Rosenstingl (1702–85) created the so-called 'Temple of Joy' which featured antiphonal choirs of trumpets amongst a series of pillars.[35] The dual choirs of trumpets, not triple or quadruple ones, were used to celebrate an Imperial heir.

In addition to explicating the Emperor's motto and its representation, Heraeus points to the heroic character of the columns, indicating that they also represent the polarities of '*Laurus* adsignat Bello, alteram *Palma* Paci.' This, too, seems represented in Caldara's trumpet music. As we have already seen, Caldara's trumpet arias maintain the association of trumpets with war and the trumpet's traditional function of signalling troops to battle. On the other hand, the trumpet was also used to sound victory and peace after battle. One of the mainstays of such celebrations and their subsequent anniversaries was the performance of the *Te Deum*, and in concertato scorings trumpets were obligatory in the setting of this text of praise.

In retrospect, Caldara's trumpet writing in non-liturgical compositions can be seen as a response to a number of traditions in ceremony, symbolism, and allegory — as well as a response to the librettos themselves and to the availability of virtuoso trumpeters at the Imperial court. The writing is always brilliant and at times exceeds the usual demands made on the Imperial trumpeters in liturgical and gala functions. Yet overtures and arias alike still remain an unknown repertoire for modern performers. On the other hand, the trumpet's role, especially in the arias, emphasizes an aspect of Caldara's operas that is often criticized in light of today's operatic expectations. It has been argued that his settings of libretti by Zeno and Metastasio are inherently undramatic, hampered by excessively long recitatives and hindered by too many arias. But despite all the theoretical discussions and tracts, drama in the modern sense was not the goal of many of these operas.[36] Rather, their sole purpose was to celebrate the *Imperium* of the Habsburg dynasty. The trumpet music by Caldara, and by other composers at the court, was one way of accomplishing this, and aurally at least, it certainly was one of the most effective.

Notes

[1] On this term see Hans Sedlmayr 'Die politische Bedeutung des deutschen Barocks (Der "Reichsstil")' *Gesamtdeutsche Vergangenheit, Festgabe für Heinrich Ritter von Srbik zum 60. Geburtstag* (Munich, 1938) pp. 126–40, and Friedrich W. Riedel 'Der Reichsstil in der deutschen Musikgeschichte des 18. Jahrhunderts' *Bericht über den Internationalen Musikwissenschaftlichen Kongress Kassel 1962* Ed., Georg Reichert and Martin Just (Kassel, 1963) pp. 34–6.

[2] See the statistics given in Ludwig Ritter von Köchel *Die Kaiserliche Hof-Musik-kapelle in Wien von 1543 bis 1867* (Wien, 1869), and Eleanor Selfridge-Field 'The Viennese court orchestra in the time of Caldara' pp. 124–5 below.

[3] See Guido Adler 'Die Kaiser Ferdinand III., Leopold I., Joseph I. und Karl VI. als Tonsetzer und Förderer der Musik' *Vierteljahrsschrift für Musikwissenschaft* VIII (1892) pp. 252–74.

[4] Court calendars with the *Hof-Statt* can be found in the Österreichische Nationalbibliothek (1716, 1726, 1729, 1731), the Wiener Stadtbibliothek (1723, 1725, 1728), and the library of the Haus-, Hof- und Staatsarchiv in Vienna, which has the most complete run (1715–18, 1720–22, 1727, 1730–31, 1733–39).

⁵ A complete run of the *Wienerisches Diarium/Wiener-Zeitung* is located in the Wiener Stadtbibliothek. A sampling from the *WD* for 1731 is found in Andreas Liess *Ein Jahreskreis im Barocken Wien: Kultur und Leben* (Wien, 1965).

⁶ A-Wn: S.m. 2503. A summary of this document is found in Köchel *op.cit.,* pp. 135–44.

⁷ The number comes from a copy of the *Kaiserlicher Hof- und Ehren-Calender*, Österreichische Nationalbibliothek 544720-A.

⁸ During the summer the Imperial family held court at the summer palaces outside of Vienna at Laxenburg and the Neue Favoriten.

⁹ See Reinhardt's *Rubriche Generali*, Friedrich W. Riedel *Kirchenmusik am Hofe Karls VI. (1711–1740)* (München-Salzburg, 1977) pp. 231–309.

¹⁰ See Riedel (*Kirchenmusik ...* , pp. 113, 174–6, 204–5 and 207–17) for a discussion on these various occasions. Some of the *Intraden* appear to have been improvised, perhaps on traditional formulae. Those interpolated into performances of the *Te Deum* were played immediately before the 'Te ergo quaesumus'. No music appears to have survived; contemporary instrumental parts (such as those for Caldara's *Te Deum Laudamus* (1734) A-Wn: Mus.Hs. 16072) merely are inscribed 'Toccata di Trombe'. This practice evidently continued to the end of the century for it can be found in performance material dating from the 1790s of a C major setting of the *Te Deum* by Leopold Hofmann (A-Wn: H.K. 479).

¹¹ For the works performed on these occasions, see Franz Hadamowsky 'Barocktheater am Wiener Kaiserhof. Mit einem Spielplan (1625–1740)' *Jahrbuch der Gesellschaft für Wiener Theaterforschung 1951–52* (1955) pp. 69–117; Otto Erich Deutsch 'Das Repertoire der Höfischen Oper, der Hof- und der Staatsoper' *Österreichische Musikzeitschrift* XXIV/7 (1969) pp. 369–91; and Ludwig Ritter von Köchel *Johann Joseph Fux, Hofcompositor und Hofkapellmeister der Kaiser Leopold I., Josef I. und Karl VI. von 1698 bis 1740* (Wien, 1872) pp. 485–558.

¹² The *Hof-Statt* is contained in most of the *Kaiserlicher Hof- und Ehren-Calender*. See Note 4. Tables 1 and 2 were compiled from these lists.

¹³ The trumpeters were Rudolf Hien, Daniel Teplizka, Paul Zeillinger, Matthias Koch, Jo[hann] Mich[ae]l Rebhindl and Franz Bonn. Johann Gottfried Denck was the timpanist.

¹⁴ See Edward H. Tarr 'Trumpet' *The New Grove Dictionary of Music and Musicians* (London, 1980) 19, p. 217.

¹⁵ See Anton Ferdinand von Geusau *Geschichte der Stiftung. Erziehungs- und Unterrichtsanstalten in Wien* (Wien, 1803) pp. 310–11.

¹⁶ As quoted in Altman Kellner *Musikgeschichte des Stiftes Kremsmünster* (Kassel, 1956) p. 427.

¹⁷ See Alois Joseph Hammerle *Mozart und einige Zeitgenossen* (Salzburg, 1877) pp. 45–6. For further documents on these and other Viennese trumpeters see Köchel *Fux ...* , Documents nos. 34–39, 40, 46, 137, 138, 145 and 217.

¹⁸ For example, from the liturgical sphere we have for the birthday of the Emperor:

> Messa solⁿᵉ con Trombe, e Timpani,
> Introito Statuit ei Anus. Offertorio de
> Confessore, senza Vespro, se non cade in
> giorno d'una Festa.

¹⁹ Librettists included Zeno, Metastasio, Pariati, Fozio and Pasquini; the composers Fux, Caldara, Reinhardt, Conti, Porsile and Georg Reutter d.J.; and, as designers, Ferdinando, Alessandro, Francesco, Giuseppe and Antonio Galli Bibiena. To some extent the employment of these two quite different genres for the *Gala-Tage* must have arisen out of practical considerations. Even the resources of the Imperial court would have been overextended if four new festive operas were staged within a period of less than three months between 28 August and 19 November. The

most ambitious undertakings must have been the operas which began the annual *Gala-Tage* cycle — those celebrating the birthday of the Empress. Several of these, including Caldara's *Imeneo*, *Enone* and *Ciro riconosciuto*, were performed 'nel Giardino dell'Imperial Favorita' (the summer palace) to take advantage of the time of year. However, perhaps the most famous of these summer productions was not an obligatory birthday opera, but one which celebrated a specific event: Fux's *Angelica, vincitrice di Alcina* (1716) written for 'la Felicissima e Gloriosa Nascità di Leopoldo, Arciduca d'Austria' and performed 'sopra la grande Peschiera dell'Imperiale Favorita.' Lady Wortley Montagu comments on this performance in her letter of 14 September, 1716, in *Letters from the Right Honourable Lady Mary Wortley Montagu 1709 to 1762* (London, 1906) pp. 66–7.

[20] Ursula Kirkendale 'The War of the Spanish Succession Reflected in Works of Antonio Caldara' *Acta Musicologica* 36 (1964) pp. 230–231.

[21] *WD* Anhang to Nr. 94, 24 November, 1723. See also Paul Nettl 'Opernaufführung zu Znaim anno 1723' *Beiträge zur böhmischen und mährischen Musikgeschichte* (Brno, 1927) pp. 14–17.

[22] The overture to *Costanza e Fortezza* is scored for two choirs each of four trumpets and timpani. According to the Court documents quoted by Egon Wellesz, only four trumpeters and one timpanist were included in this *Hofreise*. However, the billeting list for the Imperial entourage during its sojourn in Prague includes ten trumpeters and two timpanists. Possibly some of these players returned direct to Vienna after the Coronation festivities, leaving only the five used by Caldara to accompany the Imperial couple. Alternatively, the scoring of *La concordia* may have been tailored to suit the presumably cramped conditions of the performance. See Egon Wellesz's 'Einleitung' to his edition of Fux *Costanza e Fortezza* in *Denkmäler der Tonkunst in Österreich* 34–35 (Wien, 1910) pp. x–xi, and Paul Nettl 'Das Prager Quartierbuch des Personals der Krönungsoper 1723' *Mitteilungen der Kommission für Musikforschung* 8 (Wien, 1957).

[23] Concerning Fux, see the speculations of Andreas Liess *Fuxiana* (Wien, 1958) pp. 17–18; Egon Wellesz *Fux* (London, 1965) pp.4–5; and Hellmut Federhofer 'Fux, Johann Joseph' *The New Grove Dictionary of Music and Musicians* (London, 1980) 7, p. 43. On Caldara in Venice, see Eleanor Selfridge-Field 'Addenda to Some Baroque Biographies' *Journal of the American Musicological Society* XXV (1972) pp. 239–40.

[24] Special note should be made of the more extensive style-change in *Achille in Sciro*, which was composed for the nuptials of the Archduchess (and future Empress) Maria Theresa with Franz Stephan von Lothringen. Although its first movement is indistinguishable in approach from its other counterparts, both the central movement and finale clearly belong to the new idiom of the concert symphony. Whether this heralded a permanent change in Caldara's style or an accommodation to the new generation of rulers cannot be ascertained since this was one of his last works. For further on Caldara's Viennese overtures see Hisako Serizawa 'The overtures to Caldara's secular dramatic compositions, 1716–1736' pp. 79–94 below.

[25] Ursula Kirkendale considers it not to be an oratorio as it was known variously as a 'Theatral-Festin', 'Serenata' and 'Festa sacra'. See her *Antonio Caldara: Sein Leben und seine venezianisch-römischen Oratorien* (Graz-Köln, 1966) pp. 142–3.

[26] Even if no reworkings of other 'trumpet' overtures are discovered, two reworkings in the reverse direction (that is, with trumpet parts added to overtures originally scored for strings) are extant:

Sinfonia (A-Kr: 32.282) is the overture to *Il Temistocle* (A-Wn: Mus. Hs. 17182). Here the Kremsmünster source adds *clarini* but with the indication 'absolute n'oblig.'

Sonata (A-Wn: S.m. 3616) is a pastiche made up from movements of the overtures to *Apollo in cielo* (1720) and *Euristeo* (1724). As in the case of the *Sinfonia* (A-Kr: 32.282), the brass (two *clarini*, one *tromba* and timpani) have been added to the original scoring. Twelve performance dates between 1746 and 1753 are recorded on the *Umschlag*.

Nothing is known to suggest Caldara was connected with these reworkings. The performance dates on the manuscripts in A-Wn may not indicate accurately when these arrangements entered the court's repertoire; the original folders may well have been replaced. However, the reduced scorings, as well as the limited brass additions, do suggest the economies introduced into the *Hofkapelle* by Maria Theresa after 1740.

27 Both A-Wn: S.m. 3616 and A-Wn: S.m. 3617 seem to have been used on this feast-day, 25 March. The performance date on S.m. 3616 has been partly trimmed away: '[2]5 Marzo [1]749'; the entry on S.m. 3617: '25 Marti [1752] Marialauret:' indicates the Loretto chapel in the Augustinerkirche in Vienna.

28 Reproduced in Riedel *Kirchenmusik* ... facing p. 17.

29 Autograph A-Wgm: A382; copy, A-Wn: Mus. Hs. 15903.

30 One could speculate that the players were Küffel and Holland.

31 Liess *op.cit.*, pp. 24, 45–6.

32 See Kirkendale *op.cit.*, p. 231.

33 Gustav Heraeus *Inscriptiones et Symbolia* (Wien, 1723) n.p. The page is reproduced in George Kunoth *Die Historische Architektur Fischers von Erlach* (Düsseldorf, 1956) p. 145.

34 The exceptions were *Ciro riconosciuto* (1728, 1736) (for the birthday of the Empress) and the wedding opera *Achille in Sciro*.

35 A view of the temple is provided in a Salomon Kleiner engraving which can be seen in Gerda Mraz *Maria Theresia* (Wien, 1979) p. 62, and in Christian M. Nebehay *Katalog 68* (Wien, 1980) p. 4.

36 For this criticism of Caldara's operas, see Robert S. Freeman *Opera without Drama: Currents of Change in Italian Opera, 1675–1725* (Ann Arbor, 1981) pp. 253–5.

Antonio Caldara's *Credo à 8 voci:* a composition for the Duke of Mantua?

Reinhard G. Pauly and Brian W. Pritchard

Zusammenfassung

Antonio Caldaras *Credo à 8 voci*: eine Komposition für den Herzog von Mantua?

Aus den Jahren, in denen Caldara als *maestro di capella* beim Herzog von Mantua, Ferdinando Carlo, diente, existieren fünf Originalmanuskripte liturgischer Kompositionen. Drei davon (ein *Kyrie à 8 voci* in A-Moll, ein *Gloria à 8 voci* in A-Moll und ein *Gloria* in B-Dur) stammen aus dem Jahre 1705 und die vierte (ein *Gloria* in D-Moll) aus dem Jahre 1706. Eine fünfte Kompositionen (ein *Gloria à 8 voci* in C-Dur), datiert Venedig, September 1707, wurde in den letzten Exilmonaten des dortigen Hofes (Mantua war in diesem Jahr durch österreichische Truppen belagert und eingenommen worden) geschrieben. Auf Grund der Ähnlichkeiten zwischen dem Manuskript dieses *Gloria* und dem des *Credo à 8 voci* in C-Dur kann das letztere aus Caldaras letzten Monaten im Dienste Ferdinando Carlos zugeordnet werden. Es ist jedoch nicht möglich, die Aufführung dieser Kompositionen mit einem bestimmten Ereignis in Verbindung zu bringen.

Von den drei Fassungen des Credo-Textes, die vor Caldaras Anstellung am kaiserlichen Hof in Wien abgefaßt wurden, ist das 'Mantua'-Credo das bedeutsamste. In der Ordnung der sieben Sätze zeigt sich, daß Caldara dem Stilelement des Kontrasts durch Vielfalt besondere Aufmerksamkeit widmet. Der gesamte Tonbogen gibt dem Werk seine Einheit. Die Behandlung der zwei Chorsätze reicht von kurzen homophonischen 'Blockwechseln' im ersten Satz zu einer groß angelegten Fuge (beide Chöre gemeinsam) im 7. Satz. Es gibt zwei Sätze für Solisten: 'Qui cum Patre' für Sopran und Alt, und 'Crucifixus' für Sopran. Das letztere scheint durch eine frühere Fassung ersetzt worden zu sein. Als *aria senza basso* weist sie moderne Stilelemente auf, einschließlich der einzigen virtuosen Solopassage in diesem Werk. Alle Chorsätze werden von einem fünfteiligen Streichorchester (Violine 1, 2, Alt- und Tenorviola, Baß) begleitet, das recht verschiedenartig eingesetzt wird. Das Duett ist lediglich für Continuo bestimmt, die Sopranarie für *violini unisoni* (mit Continuo in den Ritornelli).

Caldaras Kunst kommt in dieser ehrgeizigen, vielfältigen und engagierten Komposition hervorragend zum Ausdruck.

Antonio Caldara's *Credo à 8 voci:* a composition for the Duke of Mantua?

Reinhard G. Pauly* and Brian W. Pritchard

O F THE THREE periods when Antonio Caldara held musical positions at courts in Italy and Austria, it is the first — from *c*1700 to 1707, when he was *maestro di cappella* to Ferdinando Carlo, Duke of Mantua — that is least known to music historians and most poorly represented among his surviving compositions. For this, the political turmoil in which the Duke was embroiled during those years must very largely be blamed. A supporter of the Bourbons during the Spanish War of Succession, he was early forced to flee Mantua (in August, 1702) for the stronghold of Casale after Austrian troops had laid siege to the city for six months.[1] His return, late in 1705, was shortlived. Within fourteen months he was in exile, this time in Venice. Advancing Austrian troops took Mantua in April, 1707, ending the centuries-long rule of the house of Gonzaga and turning the city's cultural life into a mirror of Austrian taste and style. In the face of such upheavals, further complicated by the Duke's extensive sojourn in Paris during 1704, it is not surprising that musical activity at the court of Mantua, wherever it was located, was at best fitful and discontinuous. To be sure, the culture-loving and extravagant Duke took his retinue of musicians with him into his various retreats and exiles and supported his singers and instrumentalists in performances of compositions by his new *maestro*

---

* This *Credo* for eight voices and instruments came to my attention several years ago when I was primarily engaged in research into the music of the Salzburg musical establishment (see Reinhard G. Pauly, ed., 'Johann Ernst Eberlin: Te Deum, Dixit Dominus, Magnificat' *Recent Researches in Music of the Baroque Era* 12 (Madison, 1971) and the articles 'Adlgasser, Anton Cajetan', 'Eberlin, Johann Ernst' and 'Haydn, (Johann) Michael' in *The New Grove Dictionary of Music and Musicians* (London, 1980) 1, 5 and 8). Caldara had a close connection with the Salzburg Court especially during the 1720s but he had visited there as early as 1712. However, it is unlikely that this *Credo* was known at Salzburg. Nevertheless its musical attractiveness continued to interest me and I prepared a performing edition and a set of vocal and instrumental parts. This edition was used for two performances in 1976 and has been published by E. C. Schirmer (Boston, in 1986).

di cappella in these various places. But such an atmosphere of physical insecurity and political instability could hardly have stimulated the thirty-year-old Caldara to put down roots and systematically develop the promising talent which, doubtless, had secured him his position.[2]

Given this situation, the lack of a sustained succession of compositions that might well have emerged (and survived) under more favourable circumstances should not astonish us. In this respect, this period of Caldara's employment differs markedly from the two which followed. We have many, perhaps even all, of the compositions Caldara wrote as *maestro di cappella* to Prince Ruspoli in Rome from 1709 to 1716 and as *Vizekapellmeister* at the Imperial court in Vienna from 1716 until his death in 1736. For both of these periods, and especially for the former, a substantial number of documents that record details of performances, the payments made to singers, instrumentalists and copyists, and even the every-day occurrences in the musicians' lives also have survived.

Caldara and the Mantuan court

In general our points of orientation of time and place in Caldara's career during the first seven years of the eighteenth century come from performances of his operas. Yet even here we depend more on the evidence afforded by libretti than by the scores themselves. Indeed only one score, that of the *Opera pastorale* written 'nell'anno 1701 in Mantova', has survived — one work from Caldara's one year of peace. The subsequent performances of operas, Ferdinando Carlo's greatest passion, reveal the movements of the court: *Gli equivoci del sembiante* was produced at the Teatro nuovo in Casale, probably during the Carnival of 1703; *Farnace*, performed at the Teatro S. Angelo in Venice at the end of the same year by a cast which included some of the Duke's singers, suggests a temporary sojourn in the city that was eventually to be the court's last refuge. The ducal singers appeared in Caldara's *L'Arminio* at the Teatro nuovo presso S. Agostino in Genoa during the Carnival of 1705, the court having arrived there either from Casale or, more likely, from Tortona where the recently bereaved Duke had married Susanna Enrichetta di Lorena-Elbeuf in November, 1704. The last recorded appearance of the '*Virtuosi del Serenissimo di Mantova*' in an opera by their *maestro di cappella* took place in Venice during the Carnival of 1707. This may also have been Ferdinando Carlo's last act of patronage. He had already been in exile since January, and even while Caldara's *Il selvaggio eroe* and *La Partenope* were occupying the stage of the most celebrated opera house in Venice, the Teatro S. Giovanni Grisostomo, Austrian troops were occupying Mantua.

It is impossible to determine how many of the operas Caldara wrote for the Duke of Mantua have been lost. Those mentioned above are surely but a portion of his output.[3] Operas would have been required for the annual winter 'seasons' and the Carnivals, and it is likely that Caldara would have supplied 'occasional' operas to celebrate events in his patron's career — the Duke's safe arrival in Casale in 1702, his marriage in November, 1704, his return to Mantua in December, 1705, and the arrival there of the new Duchess in the following March.

If our knowledge about the composition and performances of Caldara's operas is incomplete, it is certainly no better with regard to his oratorios. Ursula Kirkendale suggests that at least five oratorios, *La frode della castità, Le gelosie d'un amore, Il trionfo dell'innocenza, Il ricco Epulone* and *La castità al cimento* may stem from these years but assigns no date of composition to any work, and only postulates performances at either Venice or Mantua.[4]

The situation becomes even more complex when we turn to the sacred music. While the operas date from throughout Caldara's time at the Mantuan court, the few surviving liturgical compositions come only from the last three years (Table 1):

Table 1. *Chronology of Caldara's compositions written during his Mantuan years*

Year	Place	Opera	Oratorio	Sacred Music
1699	Mantua	*L'oracolo in sogno* (collab.)		
1700	Venice	*L'oracolo in sogno* (revival)	*Il ricco Epulone* (earlier?)	
1701	Mantua	*Opera pastorale*		
	Mantua	*La Partenope?*		
	Venice or Mantua?		*La frode della castità Le gelosie d'un amore Il trionfo dell'innocenza* (all post-1700?)	
1703 'Carnival'	Casale	*Gli equivoci del sembiante*		
'Autumn'	Venice	*Farnace*		
1704 'Spring'	Mantua	*Paride sull'Ida* (collab.)		
1705 'Carnival'	Genoa	*L'Arminio*		
	Casale?			*Gloria à 8 voci* (Bb major)
	Rome?		*La castità al cimento* (1705? or 1709?)	
December	Mantua			*Kyrie à 8 voci* (a minor) *Gloria à 8 voci* (a minor)
1706	Mantua?			*Gloria à 4 voci* (d minor)
1707 'Carnival'	Venice	*Il selvaggio eroe*		*Credo à 8 voci* (C major)
'Carnival'	Venice	*La Partenope* (revival?)		
September	Venice			*Gloria à 8 voci* (C major)

It is in this area that Caldara must have been most affected by his unstable environment and our loss, if only of potential compositions, is greatest. Had the situation at Mantua been more settled, we could reasonably have expected a regular and long-continued production of church music even though Ferdinando Carlo was unlikely to have been the most ardent supporter of such music and the liturgy of the ducal chapel probably was far less demanding than that which Caldara was to encounter at Vienna.

As it stands, Caldara's surviving church music seems to have been written for specific occasions rather than for a liturgical cycle. Four of the six autograph manuscripts (the only body of holographs from these years) give precise dates of composition. Two also give a location. The fifth manuscript has a non-autograph date. The sixth, our *Credo à 8 voci*,[5] although lacking inscriptions of date and place, can be associated with the other compositions on grounds of internal and external evidence.

Three of the five dated autographs come from the one year, 1705: the 'Gloria a 8 Voci con Stro$^{[t_i]}$' in B-flat major; the 'Chirie à 8 Con Strom$^{[i]}$' in a minor; and the 'Gloria à 8 Voci con Strom$^{[i]}$' in a minor. The B-flat *Gloria* has the further inscription (partly cut away in a later trimming of the manuscript): 'di Ant^o Cald^a 1705 adi 3 Marzo' on the first page of the score. About the middle of the nineteenth century, when this manuscript was already in the Archiv of the Gesellschaft der Musikfreunde in Wien, the collector, Aloys Fuchs, added the title now on the front board: ' "Gloria in Excelsis Deo" / a 8 Voci — B$^{\underline{dur}}$ / con stromenti / comp: 3 Marzo 1705. a Roma / di / Antonio Caldara / M. d. Cap: Imp. e R. in Vieña / Partitura Autographa'. The autograph itself, however, offers no evidence to support the stated place of composition.[6] Indeed, as we shall see, Caldara seems to have stopped work on the piece for some considerable time. The scoring (4 violins, alto and tenor violas, basso, two SATB choirs and soloists) and the stature of the first three movements (almost certainly all that was composed in March, 1705), suggest that the *Gloria* was originally intended for an occasion of some magnificence.[7]

According to Caldara's inscriptions (on f.1a and f.16b of the manuscript[8]) the *Kyrie à 8 voci* was begun on '9 Xbre 1705' and completed within a week: 'Finis / a 14 Xbre 1705 M$^{\underline{a}}$'. What must surely be its companion piece, the *Gloria à 8 voci* in a minor, identical in its five-part string accompaniment, was started two days later: 'adi 16 Xbre [1]705'.[9] Unfortunately, Caldara added no date of completion, merely writing 'Finis' at the end of the score. These two compositions must be closely associated with Ferdinando Carlo's return to Mantua after three years of refuge at Casale. Again the scale of the settings, especially the elaborate solo movements of the *Gloria*,[10] can only suggest an event of considerable importance. Obviously the Duke's decision to return to his ancestral seat would not have been hurriedly made. Perhaps as early as November, Caldara, together with the ducal *cappella*, had been sent to Mantua, where the *maestro* was to organise the musical celebrations and prepare appropriate music. With the musicians resettled in what must have seemed a new environment and the celebrations planned, Caldara began composition. Perhaps the two extant church pieces were the last completed; other compositions, such as a *Te Deum* or an opera, might have occupied the preceding weeks. Even if the thirteen-movement *Gloria* took only as long to write as the *Kyrie*, time was indeed short. The ink on the instrumental and vocal parts could scarcely have been dry before rehearsals took place, and precious few of these could have been held before the Duke entered the city on 22 December.[11]

The fourth autograph provides less information. This *Gloria à 4 voci* in d minor carries no title or inscription of location. Caldara's 'Finis' appears on f.26b and a non-autograph and barely legible date 'Dre [?] 1706' on f.27a. The year has been incorporated by Fuchs into his title on the manuscript's cover: 'Gloria in D 4 Voci con / Stromenti. (1706) / Comp: di Antonio Caldara / Partitura Autograffa. [sic]'.[12] Only when the month has been clarified can we suggest a connection with the celebrations marking the arrival of the new Duchess in Mantua in March, 1706 — an event for which no other music (sacred or secular) by Caldara seems to have survived.[13]

The last of the dated autographs is connected with the final events in the saga of the Gonzaga dynasty — the exile in Venice. The C major *Gloria à 8 voci* is inscribed 'In Venezia 1707 nel Mese di 7bre'.[14] It is not certain when Caldara finally left the Duke's service. If we assume he departed at the very latest possible date, that is, following the Austrian Emperor's decree of November, 1707, which required all those still employed at the Court-in-exile to sever their connection forthwith,[15] the *Gloria* can be counted as part of the Mantuan repertoire. However, it is possible that it represents an independent attempt by Caldara to impress future would-be patrons — including the Procurati of the Basilica of S. Marco. To be sure, the few members of Ferdinando Carlo's *cappella* who remained with the Duke at this late date could not have performed such an enormous work. Nevertheless, it is possible that the Duke, in an act of generosity to a loyal retainer, may have sponsored its performance, perhaps in the Basilica itself — a building in which it would have been heard to great effect. Scored for two *trombe*, two oboes, violins 1 and 2, alto and tenor violas, two SATB choirs and twelve soloists, and with its fourteen movements ranging from an alto solo with oboe obbligato through strict *da cappella* writing to ten-part vocal counterpoint, it is by far the most impressive sacred composition Caldara had written up to that time.

In terms of tonality and vocal and instrumental scoring, the *Credo à 8 voci* in C major relates most closely to the a minor *Kyrie* and *Gloria* settings.[16] An examination of the structure of the first movement of the *Gloria* and the 'Et resurrexit' of the *Credo* produces further parallels. Both movements are built up on rapid changes between homophonic block choral writing and imitative lines involving identical voices in the two choirs. The homophonic writing in both works comprises brief, non-melodic but rhythmically vital bar-long phrases tossed back and forth between the choirs (Ex. 1). Caldara reduces the instrumental scoring at the imitative passages in both compositions. In neither does a homophonic or imitative passage extend over more than twelve bars. Because of the vaster scale of the whole piece, the opening movement of the *Gloria* is considerably longer than the 'Et resurrexit' and its contrasting passages (with the text repeated) more numerous. But, like the *Credo* movement, it also climaxes in a tutti statement with both choirs coalesced into real eight-part writing.

Example 1
(a) *Gloria à 8 voci* (a minor) 'Gloria in excelsis' bars 73–75
(b) *Credo à 8 voci* 'Et resurrexit' bars 6–8

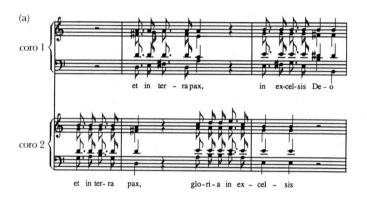

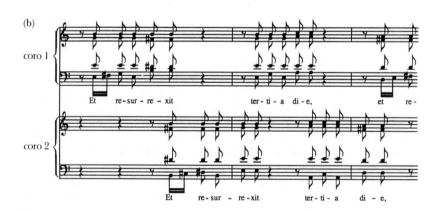

These similarities suggest that the *Credo* was a companion of the a minor *Kyrie* and *Gloria* settings, but a consideration of the manuscript paper points to another conclusion. Although all five eight-voice compositions were written on paper with sixteen staves per page, a consideration of watermarks and of differing scribal practices in the ruling of the staves allow us to distinguish two types of manuscript.[17] That used for the a minor *Kyrie* and *Gloria* has vertical guide lines (ruled from the top to bottom edges of each sheet) at which the scribe began and ended the stave rulings. The staves themselves have been ruled with an eight-stave rastrum. This same paper (devoid of any watermark), which we may label Type A, was also used for the first gathering of the B-flat major *Gloria*; thus it is common to all works dating from 1705. However, the paper used for the subsequent gatherings of the B-flat major *Gloria* has been ruled with a four-stave rastrum and lacks the vertical guide lines. There is also an obvious pattern at the end of each ruling (Diagram 1). Moreover it seems either this paper (Type B), containing both watermark and countermark (Diagram 2), has been inverted in the course of the ruling process, perhaps prior to the initial cutting of the full sheets, or the direction of ruling has been reversed for the lowest ruling of each sheet (Diagram 3). As a result of whichever occurred some leaves now show the commencements of three rulings and the conclusion of one ruling. The recurrence of this sequence together with the reappearance of the irregular pattern of stave endings within one ruling and the complete absence of vertical guide lines in the manuscripts of the C major *Gloria* and the *Credo à 8 voci*, seem to indicate that all the paper for these works was prepared at the one time and place.[18] Such a conclusion is bolstered by the presence of the watermark and countermark of the Type B paper in each gathering of the *Gloria* and *Credo* manuscripts.

Diagram 1. Characteristic pattern at the end of a single ruling by the four-stave rastrum used in preparation of Type B paper

On the basis of the date of the C major *Gloria*, it is possible to suggest not only that the *Credo* comes from the same year but that it, too, originates during the Court's months of exile in Venice. The similarity of the layout of the title pages of these two works, quite different from the brief headings jotted on the other scores, also presupposes a close connection.

We can try to account for the juxtaposition of Type A and B papers in the B-flat major *Gloria* in three ways: first, that the work was completed

(a)

(b)

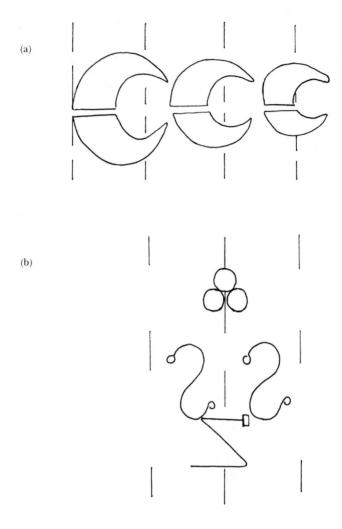

Diagram 2. Watermark and countermark of Type B paper

only to the end of the 'Gratias agimus tibi' in 1705 and finished in Venice two years later; second, that all the gatherings except the first were lost at some time during 1705 or 1706, forcing Caldara to supply new movements for a performance in Venice; third, that Caldara substantially revised the whole composition in Venice, retaining unaltered the first three movements contained in the first gathering but possibly incorporating some of the other movements of the original setting among those written later on Type B paper.[19]

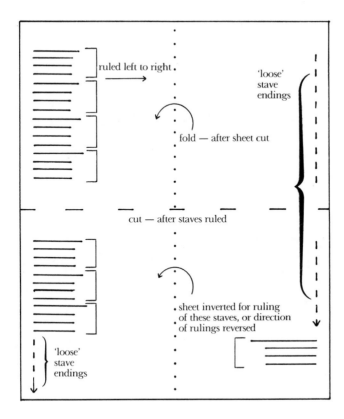

Diagram 3. Possible preparation of Type B paper

The manuscript of the *Credo à 8 voci* consists of one gathering of nine sheets (eight of Type B paper) giving a total of 18ff. In its present state, the leaf which may be regarded as f.1 is pasted to the inside of the front board, with the autograph title appearing on f.3a. In actual fact, the gathering initially was made up of seven sheets, the title being on the original f.1a. Apparently Caldara misjudged the amount of paper required, and rather than compile a new gathering, added two extra sheets for the 'Et vitam venturi' fugue. These, of course, were added outside the outermost sheet of the original gathering. This left two unused leaves in front of the original f.1, as the final fugue fitted onto the two extra leaves at the rear of the original gathering. Even so Caldara was pressed for space and the last bar of the 'Et vitam venturi' movement went over the centre fold of the last leaf and onto what had become the new f.1a. With this leaf now securely pasted to the front cover, the cadential bar has been lost. Even though its reconstruction requires little effort, this action of some past collector or curator also has deprived us of any autograph inscription of place and/or date which Caldara

may have added upon completing the composition (Diagram 4). Only
if this leaf is prised from the cover is the question of where and when
the *Credo* was written likely to be answered.

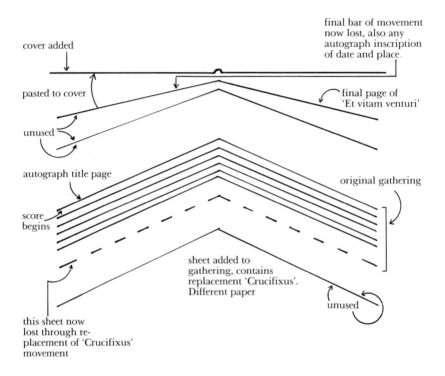

Diagram 4. Make-up of the manuscript of the *Credo à 8 voci*

These two added sheets are not the only alterations to the manuscript.
At some point Caldara appears to have discarded the original 'Crucifixus'
movement by removing the innermost sheet of the gathering. The
substitute setting also is written on one folded sheet but the *hoch-format*
paper is of slightly smaller dimensions (27.7cm x 21cm) and of a quite
different type. It has seventeen staves per page apparently drawn with
six-stave (two rulings) and five-stave rastra. The staves do not continue
across the fold. It is impossible to determine the setting that the present
movement (an aria for soprano solo, violin obbligato and continuo)
replaced or when the substitution occurred. However, as the only other
solo movement in the *Credo*, the 'Qui cum Patre', is scored for soprano,
alto and continuo,[20] the discarded 'Crucifixus' may have been a
complementary movement for tenor, bass and continuo. A variety of
reasons ranging from Caldara's own dissatisfaction with the movement
to a revival of the work in a quite different situation and with soloists
of different abilities, could account for the substitution.

At an even later date, perhaps after the manuscript had come into the possession of the Gesellschaft der Musikfreunde, pagination was added. The outside of the front cover became p.1, the reverse of the leaf pasted to the inside became p.2, and numbering continued to p.37, the inside of the rear board. As a result of this process the original title page is now p.5, the score itself begins on p.6, and the added sheet containing the 'Crucifixus' is numbered pp.17-20 although the movement occupies only pp.17-18; pp.19-20 are unused. Aloys Fuchs's label, pasted on the front cover, reads: 'Credo à 8 Voci con Strom / (C dur) / comp: di Antonio Caldara / Vice Maest: di Cap. I. e R / (Vienne) / Partitura Autographa'.

The fate of this manuscript throughout the eighteenth century is unknown. It may have remained in Caldara's possession and together with other compositions, including all the autographs which now survive from his Mantuan years, been brought to Vienna when he took up his appointment as *Vizekapellmeister* at the Imperial court in 1716. He may even have taken it to Vienna at the time of his first visit in 1712.[21] At the beginning of the nineteenth century this manuscript, along with the majority of Caldara's autographs extant today, was in the possession of the Archduke Rudolph, Archbishop of Olmütz and patron of Beethoven. Under the terms of his bequest (1831) the Gesellschaft der Musikfreunde was to receive his music collection and the manuscripts were transferred from Kremsier to Vienna in 1834.

The *Credo à 8 voci*

Nearly all of the seven movements of the *Credo à 8 voci* coincide with the divisions customarily found in settings of the Credo text. The exception is movement 5 'Qui cum Patre et Filio', a portion of text seldom set as a separate movement. Three substantial choruses (movements 1, 4 and 7), varied in style and treatment of the musical resources, provide the structural framework for the composition. The central 'Et resurrexit' is flanked on both sides by the only solo movements (3 and 5). Between these and the opening and closing choruses lie two expressive/descriptive choral movements, generally homophonic in texture and brief in duration. This mirror construction of the work (Figure 1) is emphasised by its tonal scheme. The move from the tonic tonality of the first movement, *via* the relative minor, to the dominant and its relative in the fourth movement, is reversed over the second half of the composition. The 'sharp' G major/e minor tonalities of the central movement mark the peak of the arch of the overall tonal scheme and, as 'higher' keys, seem to symbolise the movement's text: 'Et resurrexit'.

The three major choruses provide an interesting diversity of choral and orchestral textures and compositional devices. The two choirs are treated homophonically in the first, homophonically and imitatively in clearly separated passages in the second (movement 4), and in an entirely contrapuntal manner in the four-part fugue (both choirs combined) of the concluding movement. In this last Caldara has the instruments double the voices throughout[22] but in the two earlier movements the instrumental accompaniments lend considerable colour and strength to the music.

Figure 1. Construction of the *Credo à 8 voci*

Movement	Text	Type	Length	Tonality
1	Credo in unum Deum	chorus	65	C major–F major
2	Et incarnatus	chorus	14	C major–c minor
3	Crucifixus	solo	33	a minor
4	Et resurrexit	chorus	41	e minor–G major
5	Qui cum Patre	solo (à 2)	64	C major
6	Et exspecto	chorus	16	a minor
7	Et vitam venturi	chorus	92	C major

In the first chorus Caldara creates dramatic tension in his accompaniment by allocating two roles to the instruments and reinforcing these by rigid timbre distinctions. The movement is constructed on an *ostinato* figure (Ex. 2) which remains the property of the fundamental instruments. It is given one full statement before the choirs and upper strings enter.[23] The two violins, first heard at the entry of the chorus, have a reiterated quaver figure characterized by the drop of either a fifth or an octave on the first two notes (Ex. 3). This figure (which the violins never relinquish) is the basic source of momentum for the movement, imparting a sense of urgency and drive to the melodically-conceived crotchet *ostinato* figure. The force of the repeated quavers hurries the music towards the new tonal area reached at the end of nearly every statement of the *ostinato*. The chorus — in this movement we may regard the two choirs as functioning as one unit — by not siding with either component of the accompaniment, effectively brings them together. Its slow-moving minims act as a foil to both the *ostinato* and quaver motives while its homophonic texture clarifies the harmonies implied by the two accompanying lines. In many respects the chorus serves as a 'continuo realisation', linking the treble/bass polarity of the instrumental parts.

Example 2. *Credo à 8 voci* 'Credo in unum Deum' bars 1–7

org.

Example 3. *Credo à 8 voci* 'Credo in unum Deum'
(a) bars 8-10
(b) bars 32-34

(a)
vn 1
vn 2

(b)
vn 1
vn 2

We find this three-unit texture and the particular role of each component reinforced by Caldara's revision of the two viola parts. His alteration of the original instruction 'Le Viole si cavano dalle Parte' to 'Le Viole suonano il Basso'[24] confirms the total independence of choral and instrumental textures and reinforces the deep sonority of the *ostinato* motive.

Although treated as one unit in the overall textural plan of the movement, the two choirs do retain some individuality through brief points of imitation at the beginning of each phrase of the text. The motives themselves are simple and, seemingly inspired by the verbal accentuations of the text, have rhythmic rather than melodic interest (Ex. 4). In this way the choral writing is constantly enlivened despite its close adherence to a pattern of imitative entries moving to a homophonic full close at the end of each phrase of the text (Ex. 5).

Example 4. *Credo à 8 voci* 'Credo in unum Deum'
(a) bars 9-12
(b) bars 18-19
(c) bars 24-26
(d) bars 31-32

(a)
sop. 1

Cre – do   in   u – num De-um,   Pa – trem

(b)
sop. 1

fa – cto – rem   cae – li

(c)
sop. 1

vi – si – bi – li – um   o – mni-um

(d)
sop. 1

Et   in   u-num   Do – mi-num

Example 5. *Credo à 8 voci* 'Credo in unum Deum' bars 8-15

These closes, further reinforcing the new tonal centres reached by the *ostinato* bass line, produce the following internal structure:

Figure 2. Structure of the first movement: 'Credo in unum Deum'

text:		'Credo in unum Deum'		'factorem caeli ... '	
bars:	1	8		16	
key:	C	C	G	G	C
	(ostinato figure only)				
	'visibilium omnium ... '	'Et in unum ... '		'Et ex Patre ... '	
	24	31		39	
	C a	a	e	e	G
	'Genitum ... '	'Qui propter ... '			
	49	53			
	G C	C	F		

The final twelve bars of this movement (bars 53–65) are by way of a coda. The violins maintain their reiterated quaver motive but both choirs (at 'Qui propter') forsake their usual imitative start at a new phrase of the text for a straightforward homophonic statement which seems to underline 'nos homines' — mankind as one body without distinction or barrier. Allusion becomes illustration with 'descendit' set to an obvious figure. This, however, is actually a fragment of the *ostinato* motive, now integrated into the overall fabric for the first time (Ex. 6). Caldara uses tonality to stress further the concluding phrase 'descendit de caelis'. The move from C to F major which occurs in these last twelve bars has been completed at 'et propter nostram salutem' enabling the entire final phrase to be set in the subdominant tonality — a 'descent' from the tonic which Caldara makes no move to counter before the movement closes with a very truncated statement of the *ostinato* motive by the continuo line alone.

Example 6. *Credo à 8 voci* 'Credo in unum Deum' bars 58–61

In contrast to the three-unit texture of the first chorus, (perhaps an allusion to the Holy Trinity), that of the second major chorus (movement 4 'Et resurrexit') is more complex. We can distinguish three units in the accompaniment alone, but no longer are they set against one another. Rather they work together to produce an integrated and full string texture. These three units are distinguished both by timbre (violins 1 and 2; violas 1 and 2; and continuo) and by rhythmic motives:

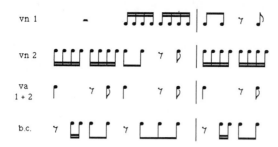

As in the accompaniment of the first movement, Caldara eschews melodic interest and again sets up a relentless rhythmic drive against which he can unfold the more leisurely-moving vocal lines. The violins are occupied with a rather basic arpeggio figure; the violas merely add to the harmonies. Only the bass line develops an overall sense of direction as the descending repetitions of its motive, coupled with a cadential figure, create a six-bar phrase (Ex. 7). This phrase underpins the first entry of the choirs but thereafter is less rigidly applied than the *ostinato* motive of the opening chorus (Plate 1).

Example 7. *Credo à 8 voci* 'Et resurrexit' bars 1–6

Although this rhythmically-oriented accompaniment imparts a remarkable unity to the 'Et resurrexit', the movement's internal structure is derived more from the alternation of passages of homophonic and imitative writing for the two choirs. Three homophonic 'block' exchange passages frame two linear passages. That these latter provide the most detailed musical representations of the text to be found in this movement is, perhaps, no accident. Caldara may well have planned the sequence of alternations to allow the imitative passages to coincide with the 'graphic' phrases of the text, perhaps feeling that musical pictorialisms could best be worked out (and easiest heard) in the freedom of these more extended vocal lines. 'Et ascendit in caelum' is set to a rising phrase which reaches its highest note at 'caelum'. This phrase is first heard in the two bass-voice parts and moves upwards through the two choirs in imitation. The setting of 'Et mortuos' for the basses only of each choir provides a 'low' sound, symbolic of death. The overall descent of the interweaving vocal lines is an expected 'madrigalism' but the abrupt halting of the violins' lively motive and the fall of a tenth in violin 1 and an octave in violin 2 to a pedal C, solemnly intoned in quavers in unison with the violas, is a much more ingenious move (Ex. 8).

The homophonic passages for the two choirs call for no particular comment. In each the writing is rhythmically buoyant and proceeds by bar-long motives tossed to and fro between the choirs. In this movement the vocal bass lines of the homophonic passages move with the continuo bass. The bustling, vigorous atmosphere that pervades the entire movement, excepting the contrived contrast at 'Et mortuos', is obviously in response to the movement's very first words 'Et resurrexit'.

By having the strings double the voices in the final movement. ('Et vitam venturi'), Caldara immediately focuses attention on his contrapuntal writing. Considerations of instrumental colour or accompaniment patterns are not to distract us from the main issue. Over ninety-two bars he unfolds a movement which not only is the longest in this composition but which is also longer than the concluding fugues

Plate 1. Caldara *Credo à 8 voci.* Entry of both choirs (bar 6) in the 'Et resurrexit'.
(A-Wgm: A330)
Reproduced by permission of the Gesellschaft der Musikfreunde in Wien

Example 8. *Credo à 8 voci* 'Et resurrexit' bars 28–33

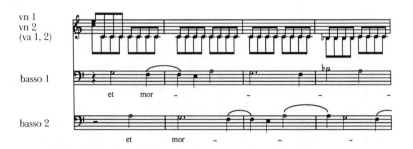

of the C major and a minor *Glorias*. To be sure, this 'Et vitam venturi' setting cannot compare with that contrapuntal *tour de force*, the eight-part double fugue at the end of the B-flat major *Gloria*. Nevertheless, the vigour of its striding subject (Ex. 9), enhanced by the triple metre, is well calculated to match the rhythmic dynamism characteristic of movements 1 and 4.

Example 9. *Credo à 8 voci* 'Et vitam venturi' bars 1–6

Caldara's 'Et incarnatus' settings, whether scored for solo voice and obbligato instrument or for chorus and orchestra, are always among the most sensitively written movements of his masses. The present example is no exception, suggesting that if this *Credo à 8 voci* does indeed represent Caldara's earliest involvement with this text, his special affinity for these particular lines has been there from the outset. The movement is only fourteen bars long, homophonic in texture and rhythmically uncomplicated in its note-per-syllable presentation of the text. Yet it radiates a profundity that belies its technical simplicity. Much of its strength derives from the powerful seventh and diminished chords which frequently move in unexpected chromatic shifts. Harmonically, it is by far the richest movement in the composition — as the carefully figured continuo line demonstrates. Caldara uses this resource to intensify the shift from major to minor tonality (which occurs at the beginning of the movement) into an atmosphere of reverence and awe at 'Et homo factus est' (Ex. 10).

Example 10. *Credo à 8 voci* 'Et incarnatus' bars 8–14

The other expressive movement ('Et exspecto') deals with a single phrase of the Credo text: 'Et exspecto resurrectionem mortuorum'. Caldara extracts all possible drama from this with such determination that the thirteen-bar movement falls into three sections; each word receives an individual setting. A strident, *forte*, 'Et exspecto', on a half close, is followed by a bar of silent anticipation which is itself intensified by a general fermata.[25] The three-bar *Allegro* at 'resurrectionem' sees the two choirs involved in jubilant half-bar affirmations, the violins surging upwards, 'alive' in semiquaver runs. In the seven-bar *Adagio* setting of 'mortuorum', seven[26] imitative entries grind downwards through the two choirs in anguished suspensions. Not only does each entry begin on a 'dead' area of a bar (the weak second and fourth beats) but the duration of the first note ensures that the second also falls on the following 'dead' beat. In painstaking detail Caldara has the *Adagio* commence on a 'dead' chord (the third is omitted) and in an almost extreme touch, has a 'lifeless' pedal bass on the tonic (itself the most static note possible) support six of the section's seven bars.

The use of an *ostinato* figure as a constructional/unifying device reappears in the 'Qui cum Patre' (movement 5) — possibly the one surviving original solo number of the *Credo*. As in the opening movement, the *ostinato* is given out unadorned by any upper parts. This makes its principal component, an untied suspension across the bar-line (Ex. 11), more easily recognizable as the basic motive of the free interludes which link the more or less exact repetitions of the figure at bars 18–24 and 44–49 and its final appearance at bars 58–64. These mid-way repetitions clinch modulations to the new tonal centres of G major and a minor. Above the continuo bass, the soprano and alto soloists[27] present the text phrase by phrase. With one exception each phrase is given a new melodic motive and each begins with a point of imitation between the voices. Although neither voice has the *ostinato* figure itself at any stage, each motive actually incorporates some element of the *ostinato* — the suspension or the characteristic rising fourth or falling second (Ex. 12). The reappearance of the motive used at the second entry of the voices ('simul adoratur') for the final phrase of the text ('in remissionem') increases the unity of a movement that already displays a remarkable economy of thematic material.

Example 11. *Credo à 8 voci* 'Qui cum Patre' bars 1–7

Example 12. *Credo à 8 voci* 'Qui cum Patre'
(a) bars 7–9
(b) bars 11–13
(c) bars 20–22
(d) bars 26–27

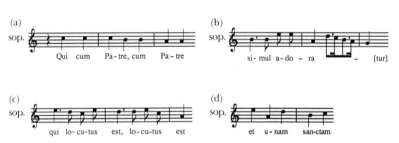

Only in the substituted 'Crucifixus' (movement 3), is Caldara's more familiar world of secular music apparent in this composition. Stylistically, this *aria senza basso* is the most modern of the seven movements and sits rather uneasily among its companions. It is the only movement in which melodic and even virtuosic elements predominate in both the vocal and instrumental parts (Plate 2). The idiomatic and carefully articulated writing for the unison violins as well as the soprano soloist's quite lengthy melismatic passages (which the violins support by using the head-motive of the opening ritornello as a bass), are marked departures from the

Plate 2. Caldara *Credo à 8 voci*. 'Crucifixus' for soprano solo, *violini unisoni* and continuo.
(A-Wgm: A330)
Reproduced by permission of the Gesellschaft der Musikfreunde in Wien

style and techniques of the other movements. We may even see Caldara's deflection of the closing ritornello into a coda of a more appropriate atmosphere as an attempt to remedy the situation. Chromatic harmonies, and especially the chromatic descent of the bass line in the penultimate bars, revive time-honoured musical expressions of pain and suffering (Ex. 13).

Example 13. *Credo à 8 voci* 'Crucifixus' bars 28–31

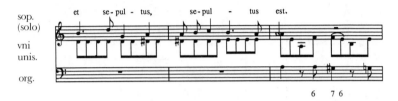

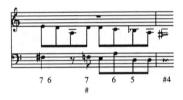

*   *   *   *   *

On the evidence of the manuscripts now extant, Caldara apparently had no occasion to return to the Credo text for a number of years after completing his *Credo à 8 voci*. In fact, we know of only two other settings which predate those he made in the course of providing more than one hundred masses for the *Hofkapelle* at Vienna between 1716 and 1736. One, another double-choir setting but with continuo accompaniment only, is inscribed 'Fine adi 18 Aprile 1712 in [?] Vienne' on the final page of the score.[28] The other, scored for four-part chorus and string orchestra, is undated but almost certainly was written before Caldara finally quitted Italy.[29]

Neither work shows such a diverse range of textures as the C major *Credo* although both consist of several distinct sections. Some of the pictorialisms found in the Mantuan work, such as rising motives at 'Et ascendit in caelum' and joyous semi-quaver figuration in the violin parts at the beginning of 'Et resurrexit', reappear in the seven-movement *à 4* setting. The most atmospheric moments are again the 'Et incarnatus' and 'Crucifixus' movements. The latter, set for four bass voices and continuo only, is the most unusual number in this work. Its scoring contrasts markedly with the rather virtuoso setting of this text in the *Credo à 8 voci*; the starkness of its imitative texture and its dark sonorities create a singularly appropriate atmosphere. However, a dramatic interpretation of 'Et exspecto resurrectionem mortuorum' is missing from this setting. This line of text is merely treated within the 'Et unam Sanctam' movement and leads without even a token pause into the 'Et vitam venturi' fugue.

The eight-voice *Credo* of 1712 is briefer than either of its companions. Its three movements are uninterrupted by solo numbers and its homophonic choral writing is unrelieved by contrapuntal textures. No changes of metre or tempo distinguish section from section. Even the customary fugue at 'Et vitam venturi' is foregone in this *brevis* setting whose frequent overlappings of the text preclude either choir from singing it in its entirety. The whole setting appears almost casual; even the most obvious dramatic/expressive phrases of the text are glossed over.

If these three compositions are, in fact, the only settings Caldara made of the Credo text prior to the last phase of his career, there can be little doubt that the Duke of Mantua was well served by his erstwhile *maestro di cappella*. Although the circumstances of its creation and performance must await further clarification, we cannot question the quality of this ambitious, varied and engaging setting that is the *Credo à 8 voci*.

Notes

1   Caldara's years at the court of Mantua are discussed in Ursula Kirkendale *Antonio Caldara: Sein Leben und seine venezianisch-römischen Oratorien* (Graz-Köln, 1966) pp. 29–39. She closely examines the connection between the libretti of Caldara's operas and the fortunes of the court in 'The War of the Spanish Succession Reflected in the Works of Antonio Caldara' *Acta Musicologica* 36 (1964) pp. 221-33.

2   It is impossible now to determine when Caldara first came to the attention of Ferdinando Carlo. As a devotee of opera, the Duke may have been aware of Caldara as early as 1689 when his *L'Argene* was performed at the Teatro alli Saloni in Venice. He can scarcely have been ignorant of Caldara's subsequent operatic efforts, *Il Tirsi* and *La promessa serbata*, produced in 1696 and 1697 respectively, as *L'oracolo in sogno*, in which Caldara collaborated with Antonio Quintavalle and Carlo Francesco Pollarolo, was performed at Mantua in 1699. But Caldara may also have been made known to the Duke *via* Marc'Antonio Ziani who in 1686 became *maestro di cappella* at the Basilica of S. Barbara in Mantua. Ziani, along with Caldara, was a founding member of the Guild of S. Cecilia in Venice in 1687, and perhaps it was at Ziani's own request that the Duke allowed (and paid) Ziani to instruct his younger fellow-Venetian. Possibly it was Ziani, too, who recommended Caldara for the position of *maestro di cappella* at the court on

the eve of his own departure to take up the post of *Vizekapellmeister* at the Imperial court in Vienna. (See Theophil Antonicek 'Ziani, Marc'Antonio' *The New Grove Dictionary of Music and Musicians* (London, 1980) 19, p. 673 and his 'Die *Damira*-Opern der beiden Ziani' *Analecta Musicologica* 14 (1974) p. 180.) Finally, we should note that in 1699 Caldara enhanced his reputation through the publication (both by Sala) of two compositions — a set of 12 trio sonatas (*Suonate da Camera* Op. 2) and a set of 12 cantatas for solo voice and continuo (*Cantate de camera a voce sola* Op. 3).

[3] Caldara may also have supplied at least some of the music for *La Partenope* performed at Mantua in 1701. Kirkendale (*Antonio Caldara ...* p. 37) speculates that the *La Partenope*, performed in Venice during the Carnival season of 1707, with some of the Duke's singers participating, may have been a slightly altered version of the 1701 score. In spring, 1704, *Paride sull'Ida ovvero gli amori di Paride con Enone* was performed at the ducal theatre in Mantua. This was a collaboration between Caldara and Quintavalle. The latter may have been responsible for the whole work, supplying new recitatives and some arias, but incorporating other arias from earlier works by Caldara (*ibid.*, pp. 33-4). For a discussion of a contemporary *rifacimento* see Olga Termini '*L'Irene* in Venice and Naples: tyrant and victim, or the *rifacimento* process examined' pp. 367-96 below.

[4] Kirkendale *Antonio Caldara ...* pp. 113-15. *Il trionfo dell'innocenza* may also have been performed in Florence in March, 1704; *La castità al cimento* may date from 1705, but probably from 1709.

[5] A-Wgm: A330. The autograph title-page reads: 'Credo à 8 Voci Con / Strom.ᵗⁱ / di Ant.º Caldara'. A setting of the Psalm *Dixit Dominus* by Caldara, and dated 1703 on the manuscript's title page, is at B-Bc: Ms.103. There is no evidence to confirm this date or directly connect the composition with the court of Mantua.

[6] A-Wgm: A326.

[7] If we take into account the fact that Mantuan *virtuosi* (and, no doubt, Caldara himself) were in Genoa for the performance of *L'Arminio* during the Carnival of 1705, and accept that the Duke and his retinue also were resident in the city, one possibility may have been a final display of extravagance (perhaps in the form of a votive mass) prior to the court's return to Casale. But whatever the event, if in fact it took place, this *Gloria* was not part of it — unless another composer supplied music to follow Caldara's first three movements.

[8] A-Wn: S.A67. B100. There is another copy, in the hand of Raphael Georg Kiesewetter (1773-1850), at the same call number. Kirkendale mistakenly describes the autograph as 'verschollen' (*Antonio Caldara ...* p. 36, note 59).

[9] A-Wgm: A327. There seems no reason to doubt that this is when composition was begun. In no surviving autograph has Caldara written the date of completion at the head of the score. However, after his move to Vienna, he apparently abandoned his practice of noting the date of commencement on his liturgical scores.

[10] Both the 'Laudamaus te' and 'Glorificamus te' contain obbligatos for *violoncelli soli*. Caldara may well have performed in these movements.

[11] If a celebratory Mass was delayed until Christmas more time would have been available for rehearsals.

[12] A-Wgm: A328. Fuchs's use of the upper-case 'D' should not be interpreted as D major. He adds a '#' to denote a major tonality.

[13] Perhaps it is more likely that this shorter setting (eleven movements) with its reduced vocal scoring (the customary five-part string accompaniment remains) was commissioned for some other, less spectacular, event.

[14] A-Wn: Mus.Hs. 18981.

[15] Kirkendale *Antonio Caldara ...* p. 38. A number of the Duke's singers had already departed during the preceding years. The majority either went to the court at Florence or were engaged at theatres in Venice.

[16] All three are scored for violins 1 and 2, alto and tenor violas and continuo. However the tutti movements in both the *Kyrie* and *Gloria* feature a 'violoncino' part usually independent of the fundamental bass line. This line also appears in the B-flat major *Gloria* which is scored for four violins, two violas and continuo, but not in the C major *Gloria*. The oboe is used only in an obbligato role in the a minor and B-flat major *Glorias*, not as a member of the orchestral tutti.

[17] There are, however, similarities between the two papers. In both, the staves have been ruled before the sheets (*c*60 cm x 46 cm) were folded and perhaps before they were cut. In all probability Caldara received the paper (already ruled and cut?) in *quer-format* sheets approx *c*44.0/46.0 cm x 29.5/30.5 cm. These he assembled in gatherings of between five and eight sheets each, folding each gathering to produce *hoch-format* booklets of 20 to 32 'sides', and with margins only at the outer edges. Subsequent trimming of the manuscripts allows only approximations of the original dimensions of the sheets.

[18] It cannot be determined whether the staves were ruled before the paper left the mill or whether the ruling was done by a scribe attached to the court or even by a local paper supplier. Dr Rosemary Moravec, Music Department, Austrian National Library, Vienna, and Dr Otto Biba, Curator, Gesellschaft der Musikfreunde, Vienna, kindly provided valuable information about the paper used in manuscripts S.A67.B100 and Mus.Hs. 18981, and A326, A327 and A330 respectively.

[19] The first hypothesis seems further indicated by the fact that the outer side of the last leaf of the first gathering originally was left blank. Caldara's setting of the 'Gratias' ended on the inner side of this leaf. (This movement has now been concealed through the last three leaves being stuck together with drops of wax.) If, at that time, Caldara had gone straight on with the next movement, 'Domine Deus, Rex caelestis', it surely would have been started on the very last side of the gathering. That it was not suggests that Caldara broke off composition at this point — perhaps the occasion for which it was intended (such as has been intimated in Note 7) was cancelled or the court moved (from Genoa?) before the next movement could be written. Thus it is unlikely that we have lost any gatherings of the manuscript. On resuming the work (later in Venice?) Caldara discarded the completed setting of the 'Gratias', sealed off the pages, and on the remaining blank side of the first gathering began a new version which he continued directly onto the new gathering prepared from Type B paper. Even assuming Caldara rewrote the 'Gratias' immediately, it seems strange that his supply of Type A paper also should have run out at this point. It is worth noting that he very seldom discarded an entire movement. It does not happen in any other Mantuan autograph; even small deletions are rare.

[20] Caldara heads this movement 'à due' meaning probably, but not necessarily, two soloists. In our performances, all sopranos and contraltos participated.

[21] It cannot be established whether Caldara's autographs remained in his possession or became the property of his employer. Considering the upheavals of the Mantuan court, especially during its last years, Ferdinando Carlo may not have been too concerned about the ownership of each music manuscript. We do know that the Duke's valuables, furniture, paintings and 'libri' followed him to Venice. Possibly the music library of the ducal *cappella* was included among these effects. The performance of *La Partenope* in Venice from the Mantuan score suggests this was the case. However, this does not necessarily mean that Caldara's autographs were among the *cappella*'s holdings. Caldara must have been sufficiently astute to see that Mantua was about to be lost and may well have deliberately retained his own manuscripts.

[22] Caldara heads this movement 'à 4 Tutti. Li Stromᵢ Si cavano dalle Parti'. The most appropriate doubling would be violins 1 and 2 unison with the soprano, alto viola unison with the alto, and tenor viola unison with the tenor vocal part.

[23] This initial statement raises some performance problems. Caldara's cue at the first bar 'Forte Org^ni soli' suggests the use of at least two organs (one to support each choir with perhaps a third for the orchestra) although only one bass line is written

in the score. Interestingly, the C major *Gloria* begins in a like manner with a four-bar motive for bass instruments alone. Caldara adds no performance cue to this manuscript but performance material now preserved at Cs-Pnm: xxxvi A97, includes parts for four organs, each of which has this opening motive. The multi-organ implications of the *Credo* score could readily have been met by the use of portable organs — a by-no-means unusual feature of Venetian performances at this time. The term 'soli' can be variously interpreted. As these opening bars are entirely instrumental, it may merely have warned the organist(s) to prepare an appropriate registration. It is also possible that 'Organi soli' literally meant 'organs alone', that is, without any other fundamental instruments (violoncelli, contrabassi or even fagotti). One further alternative would be to perform these opening bars unrealised.

[24] This cue is written in between the two viola staves at the point of the instruments' first entry; 'suonano' and 'Basso' are written over 'si cavano' and 'Parte', 'dalle' is crossed out and 'il ' written above.

[25] This bar, the third in the movement, originated in a revision. Initially Caldara placed the fermata over the last syllable of 'exspecto', sung to the second minim in bar 2. This indication was subsequently removed, almost without trace. A bar-line was then introduced into the score creating an 'extra' bar between the original second and third bars, and a breve rest with fermata inserted into this cramped space in all parts.

[26] Only the vocal bass of the second choir does not participate; doubled by the continuo bass it sets up a tonic pedal.

[27] See Note 20.

[28] D-ddr-Dlb: 2170-D-1. This autograph manuscript is part of a setting of the first three movements of the Ordinary of the Mass. The following *Sanctus* and *Agnus Dei* movements, written on manuscript paper of a similar type, may also belong to these movements, although the date added at the end of the *Credo* rather suggests that Caldara intended (at least at first) that the composition should end there. This would accord with the Venetian conception of a Mass setting.

[29] D-ddr-Bds: Mus.ms. Autogr. Caldara A5. This autograph is bound together with settings by Caldara of the Kyrie and Gloria texts. The paper of the *Credo* is quite different from that used for the *Kyrie* and *Gloria*, both of which are in d minor and seem to have been written as a pair.

The overtures to Caldara's secular dramatic compositions, 1716–1736: a survey and thematic index

Hisako Serizawa

Zusammenfassung

Die Ouvertüren zu Caldaras weltlichen Musikdramen, 1716–1736: ein Überblick mit thematischen Verzeichnis

Es ist Aufgabe der vorliegenden Studie, die instrumentalen Opern-Einleitungen von Caldara aus stilgeschichtlichem Standpunkte zu untersuchen.

Caldara, dessen Vaterstadt Venedig war, war seit Juli 1716 in Wien tätig, und wirkte dort als Vizekapellmeister Karls VI. Die meisten seiner Opern schrieb Caldara in Wien für die kaiserliche Hofkapelle.

Ein Vergleich seiner Ouvertüren mit denen des österreichischen Hofkapellmeisters Johann Josef Fuxens ist ferner für Erkenntnis des italienischen Vizekapellmeisters von Interesse.

Die Betrachtung der instrumentalen Opern-Einleitungen von Caldara zeight ihn in dieser Gattung als hochbefähigten Eklektiker verschiedener Stilrichtungen, wobei durch den Italiener Caldara natürlich die italienische Stilrichtung stärker vertreten wird.

Es konnten im wesentlichen drei Typen aufgewiesen werden: (i) der italienische Sinfonie-Typus; (ii) der französische Ouvertüren-Typus; (iii) der venezianische Fanfaren-Typus. Von diesen Typen steht der erste mit 40 Belegen weitaus an erster Stelle.

Dieser Aufsatz untersucht die Struktur von Caldaras Ouvertüren, besonders die verschiedenen Muster, die in den ersten Sätzen des italienischen Typus verwendet werden. Untersucht werden auch der hauptsächliche thematische Stoff dieser Sätze und die Art, auf die er vorgestellt wird, sowie die Orchestrierung Caldaras.

Die Ouvertüren zu Caldaras dramatischen Werken (Opern und *festa da camera*), die von 1716 bis seinem Tode im Jahre 1736 in Wien und Salzburg komponiert wurden, sind in thematischen Verzeichnis aufgezählt.

The overtures to Caldara's secular dramatic compositions, 1716–1736: a survey and thematic index

*Hisako Serizawa**

I T IS WELL-KNOWN that the two main types of opera overtures in the Baroque period were the French *ouverture* and the Italian *sinfonia*. It is equally well-known that both varieties spread far beyond their national boundaries and frequently were employed by composers who had no direct connection with either country. This study is concerned with the overtures written by an Italian working at a court which was receptive to both French and Italian musical influences, and which was staffed by musicians whose origins made it perhaps the most cosmopolitan court in Europe.

Antonio Caldara wrote some fifty dramatic works with overtures during the twenty years he spent as *Vizekapellmeister* at the Imperial court in Vienna.[1] An examination of the general characteristics of these overtures (it is not possible to consider each in detail) allows us to see not only the diversity of Caldara's instrumental writing but also the modifications and adjustments which he made to accommodate some of the particular traits of both the French and Italian styles with local musical preferences. Moreover, it draws attention to a repertoire largely ignored by performers for more than two centuries.[2]

* * * * *

In the light of his career up to 1716 it is not surprising to see the Italian-overture style influencing the majority of Caldara's Viennese overtures — whether they are cast in the well-established three-movement (fast-slow-fast) pattern or in a truncated two-movement plan. It is, however, more difficult to declare all the individual movements to be Italian. In

* This essay is an expanded and revised version of an article published in the *Journal of the Japanese Musicological Society* 16 (1970). The Thematic index of Caldara's overtures has been specially prepared to accompany the essay. The editor is indebted to Maureen Heffernan of the Japan Consular Office, Christchurch, New Zealand, for the translation from the Japanese original.

particular, some of the central slow movements are influenced by French traditions, most obvious in the dotted rhythms and strong up-beat patterns. Other movements with their contrapuntal presentation of the thematic material may be regarded as a response to local taste. In still others, thematic and structural designs seem related to the particular instrumental resources demanded by the specific occasions on which the operas were performed.

Design and structure

Caldara employs the French-overture pair of slow-fast movements in only two overtures.[3] He specifically designates the opening nineteen-bar *Andante* of *Amalasunta* as 'alla francese' — a term highlighted by the pervasive dotted rhythms but which also probably demanded a specific manner of performance. The *Largo e staccato* opening to *La verità nell'inganno* (1727) is much more brief but the fugal *Allegro* comes closer to its French counterparts than that of *Amalasunta*. It is also worth noting that the introduction to *Amalasunta* has the only 'Ouverture' designation in Caldara's output.

In his first opera overture for Vienna after his appointment in 1716 (that to *Cajo Marzio Coriolano*, 1717) Caldara retains a specific variety of the Italian overture. This single movement *Introduzione* (*Allegro*, with a six-bar *adagio* coda) stands in the Venetian *intrada* tradition.[4] Scored for brass, woodwind and string groups, each differentiated by distinctive thematic material, it shows a strong influence of Venetian colour contrasts. The 'fanfare' aspect of the *intrada* is obvious in the opening bars: four *trombe* (with timpani) present in stretto fashion a motive $\boxed{A}$ which is a rhythmic extension of the tonic (C major) chord (Ex. 1). In contrast, the material $\boxed{B}$ given to the woodwind group (two oboes and bassoon) is flowing and presented in a texture close to trio sonata scoring (Ex. 2). These two areas provide the pillars in the construction of the overture.

Example 1. *Cajo Marzio Coriolano*: material $\boxed{A}$ (*trombe*)

Ex. 1 (contd)

Example 2. *Cajo Marzio Coriolano*: material ⬚B⬚ (woodwind)

ob 1

ob 1

bn.

The strings underpin the sequential development passages (⬚a⬚ , ⬚b⬚ etc.) but do not dominate except to provide two central episodes Ⓒ . These are clearly distinguished by idiomatic figurations (Ex. 3).

Example 3. *Cajo Marzio Coriolano*: material Ⓒ (strings)

vni

basso

They also mark two important tonal areas (emphasized by pedal points in the bass) which establish the tripartite design of the overture:

			seq.	episode			seq.		
thematic areas:	[A]	[B]	[a]	Ⓒ	[B]	[A]	[b]	[B]
key:	C				G	C			a

	episode	seq.			seq.			
	Ⓒ	[c]	[B]	[d]	[A]	adagio coda
		e		C		

The six-bar coda which brings the instrumental groups together in ♩.♫♫ rhythms is, perhaps, a deliberate ploy to refocus the listeners' attention and direct it towards the opening scene of the opera on stage.

Although Caldara does not write another overture which parallels exactly the *Introduzione* to *Cajo Marzio Coriolano*, several of its traits continue in many of those overtures that may be labelled as 'Italian'. For example, it foreshadows the two-movement overtures whose opening *allegro* movements conclude with a few *adagio* bars by way of a coda; it also anticipates those overtures whose second or third movements lead directly into the first scene of the opera. More important is its influence on the 'festive' overtures (such as that to *Enone*) which form a distinctive group within Caldara's 'Italian' overtures. In their first movements the thematic diversity, colourful scoring and periodic structure of *Cajo Marzio Coriolano* are retained.

The forty-five-bar first movement of the *Introduzione* to *Enone* is constructed around two main thematic areas ([A] , [B]). Their repetitions are separated by passages of sequential development ([a] , [b] etc.).

		seq.			seq.		seq.
thematic areas:	[A]	[a]	[B]	[A]	[b]	[A]	[c]
	strings	strings	clarini	strings	tutti	strings	strings
key:	C				a		

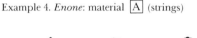

seq.		seq.				
A	d	A	e	B	A	f
strings	tutti	strings	tutti	clarini	strings	tutti

G   e   G   C

Thematic area A remains the property of the strings throughout.[5] It comprises an angular, rhythmically vital subject whose effect is dependent upon close imitation (Ex. 4).

Example 4. *Enone*: material A (strings)

Thematic area B is the property of the brass group. Here the traditional roles of *clarini* and *trombe* and timpani are immediately apparent; the *clarini*, unrestrained, carry the melody lines, the *trombe* and timpani supply harmonic filling and rhythmic emphasis. The parallel thirds of the *clarini* contrast with the imitative writing of the A area. In the ♩ 𝄾 ♩ 𝄾 and occasionally ♪ 𝄾 ♪ 𝄾 ♪ 𝄾 ♪ 𝄾 scoring of the *trombe* and timpani parts we find an accompaniment technique which frequently occurs in string writing when the emphasis is on vertical/homophonic, not contrapuntal textures[6] (Ex. 5). The a , b areas (usually scored for strings and brass) which follow the A passages, are constructed on sequential patterns and do not develop any of the principal material. On occasion, however, the melodic shape given to the syncopated rhythmic patterns on which these areas are based, may resemble the opening motive of A . This strong rhythmic drive is not reserved for the sequential areas: it permeates all of Caldara's writing and holds together the diverse areas of this *Introduzione*. Indeed, the very regular pulse of the overture stands in sharp contrast to the ebb and flow of tempi produced by the arias of opera itself.

Example 5. *Enone*: material B (brass choir)

In the first movements of the 'Italian' overtures scored for strings (with doubling woodwind)[7] Caldara tends to produce much more tightly-knit structures on a distinct tripartite plan. Perhaps it is too extreme to see in these a foreshadowing of sonata form, but the essentials of exposition, development and recapitulation areas definitely are present. The repetition of the exposition area (usually in its entirety) as the recapitulation probably stems from the *da capo* aria, but the central development area usually is more extensive and complex than the corresponding *B*-sections of Caldara's opera arias. The typical structure of these first movements is demonstrated in:

Figure 1. Structure of the first movements

| Overtures to: | *Allegro* first movement | | |
	Exposition bars	Development bars	Recapitulation bars
La clemenza di Tito	1-12	12-31	32-43
Don Chisciotte	1-20	20-32	33-52
I due dittatori	1-15	16-26	27-41
Il natale di Minerva Tritonia	1-12	13-36	36-48

Caldara's procedures within each of these three principal sections are more difficult to categorize, especially his handling of the development sections. Nevertheless we can note that the expositions begin and end in the tonic key and include two thematic areas (or a principal theme and a closing cadence area) separated by a bridge passage;[8] and that the developments are built on new as well as previously heard materials taken in sequential patterns through a wide range of keys. The developments close either in the tonic key itself or on a dominant cadence in preparation for the recapitulation. Consider the *Introduzione* to *Il natale di Minerva Tritonia*:

Figure 2. *Introduzione* to *Il natale di Minerva Tritonia*: structure of the first movement

	Exposition		
area:	first subject	modulatory passage	closing material
bars:	1-5	6-9	10-12
key:	D		D

		Development		
sequential passage (a)	first subject (curtailed)	sequential passage (b)	first subject	sequential passage (c)
13-16	16-19	19-24	25-29	30-36
	A		b	D/V
		Recapitulation = Exposition		
		37-48		

In *Don Chisciotte in corte della duchessa* the exposition is expanded with the first subject area including two distinct themes (further distinguished by instrumentation) (Ex. 6):

Example 6. *Don Chisciotte*: first subject area themes

a bridge passage which leads to the dominant for the second subject area, and a closing cadence area. The development is built on two statements of new material and concludes with return of the second subject in the tonic which then leads directly into the recapitulation (exposition unchanged).

Figure 3. *Introduzione* to *Don Chisciotte*: structure of the exposition

	Exposition			
area:	first subject area	bridge passage	second subject	closing cadence area
	a b			
bars:	1-4 5-7	7-10	11-14	14-20
keys:	G G	G-D	D	G

If the *Introduzione* to *Don Chisciotte* is more complex than that to *Il natale di Minerva Tritonia*, then the overture to *I disingannati* seems to further advance some of the developments of *Don Chisciotte*.[9] This overture to the Carnival opera of 1729 may well represent Caldara's most advanced construction of the first movement of an Italian *sinfonia*. The exposition (one of the few for which a repeat is specified) features a balanced four-bar (2 + 2) principal theme, a bridge passage to the dominant key, and a clearly defined cadence area (with its own motive) closing in the dominant. The development is built around three quite extensive passages for solo violin (accompanied by violins 1 and 2). These passages are separated by a statement of the first subject now linked directly to the cadence figure, in the relative minor (f-sharp), and a curtailed statement of the first subject only in the subdominant (D) — the two related key centres usually employed for statements of principal material in the development areas. The recapitulation is no perfunctory repeat of the exposition: Caldara dispenses with the double statement of the principal subject and drastically alters the bridge, leaving only the cadence area (now in the tonic) untouched.

Figure 4. *Introduzione* to *I disingannati*: structure of the first movement

		Exposition		
area:	principal subject		bridge passage	closing cadence area
bars:	1-4 (vn 1) 5-8 (vn 2)		8-13	14-20
key:	A-E E-A/^{V}		A-E/^{V}	E-E
		Development		
	sequential passage (solo violin)	principal subject (head motive)		closing cadence area (curtailed)
	21-39	40-41 42-43 44-45		46-49
	E-f#/^{V}	f# E A		f#
	sequential passage (solo violin)	principal subject (curtailed)		sequential passage (solo violin)
	49-56	57-58		59-65
	F#-D	D		D-A/^{V}
		Recapitulation		
	principal subject	bridge passage		closing cadence area
	66-69	70-75		76-82
	A	A		A

While most of these first movements of the Italian overtures include homophonic and imitative textures, some are contrapuntal throughout and may well be considered as freely constructed fugues set in a ternary framework. In the *Introduzione* to *Scipione Africano il maggiore*, Caldara presents the subject in a three-voice exposition (violas do not have the subject) which is followed by a lengthy closing cadence area. This ends on the dominant of the relative minor (g) and ushers in a second, identical exposition in that key. The closing cadence area now ends on the dominant of c minor and the ensuing episode (development) area comprises four statements of the subject in c minor, f minor, b-flat minor/B-flat major, and E-flat major. A three-bar bridge links into the final exposition (recapitulation). Here, the entries are reduced to two (violins 1 and 2 present the subject in thirds) and the cadence area is diverted from its original move to g minor, to close in B-flat major.

Figure 5. *Introduzione* to *Scipione Africano*: structure of the first movement

	Exposition I	
area:	subject	cadence area
bars:	1-2 (vn 1), 3-4 (vn 2), 5-6 (basso)	7-14
key:	B-flat	B-flat-g/^{V}
	Exposition II	
	subject	cadence area
	15-16 (vn 1), 17-18 (vn 2), 19-20 (basso)	21-27
	g	g-c/^{V}
	Episode (development)	
subject	subject	subject
28-29 (vn 1)	30-31 (vn 2)	32-33 (vn 1)
c	f	b-flat/B-flat
subject		bridge
34-35 (vn 2)		36-38
E-flat		E-flat-B-flat/^{V}
	Exposition (recapitulation)	
subject		cadence area
38-40 (vn 1 + 2), 40-42 (basso)		42-47
B-flat		B-flat

As we might expect, the second and third movements are less substantial.[10] Of the twelve 'Italian' overtures which can be classed as two-movement works, only a handful of the second movements are in a slow tempo. Invariably, these lead straight into the first act of the opera. Those second movements in a fast tempo almost always are preceded by a few *adagio* bars tagged on to the end of the *allegro* first movement. There seems no particular reason why Caldara should not have converted these codas into separate movements. Several are longer than the middle (slow) movements of the three-movement overtures: for example, both *Camaide* and *Nitocri* have eight-bar codas; the separate slow movements of *Mitridate* and *Il Temistocle* are each of six bars, that of *I disingannati* is merely three bars. It is noticeable, however, that from the mid-1720s most of Caldara's overtures are in three movements with the slow movements growing in melodic and harmonic interest, especially the former. The rather plain *Grave* of the overture to *Astarto* (Ex. 7) is far removed from the graceful lines of the slow movements in *Il Demetrio, Demofoonte,* or *Ciro riconosciuto* (Ex. 8).

The majority of the slow movements, whether belonging to two- or three-movement overtures, follow no set pattern, although in some the influence of dance forms is apparent. The slow (*largo*) movements of *Apollo in cielo* and *Euristeo*, for example, are based on the *sarabanda*; that of *L'amor non ha legge* (*Aria alla pastorale*) is a *siciliano*. French

Example 7. *Astarto*: second movement, *Grave*

Example 8. Ciro riconosciuto: second movement, *Andante*

influences also are not lacking; for example, the *Largo* of *Il Temistocle* (Ex. 9) and the *Largo e staccato* of *Enone*.

Example 9. *Il Temistocle*: second movement, *Largo*

Caldara tends to use the term *Aria* for the slow movements in his later overtures, allowing their affective harmonies, rhythmic complexity and texture, together to set an appropriate tempo.

Caldara obviously prefers the *minuet* as the *Allegro* finale for both two- and three-movement overtures. In doing so he adheres to the Italian tradition; the trills and syncopations of his melodic lines suggest he was thinking more specifically of the Neapolitan-style *minuet*.[11] The other type of finale which he favours is the march-styled ₵ metre *allegro*. In many overtures the tempo designation is again replaced by *Aria* — a practice which both here and in the slow movements may have been taken over from contemporary ballet music where time and again, dances obviously in the tradition of the *minuet, bourrée, gavotte*, etc., are headed *Aria*.[12] But whatever the designation of Caldara's light-weight overture finales, there is no doubting their particular characteristics: a strong, regular pulse, the obvious phrase structure of the melodic line, uncomplicated textures (melody — *violini unisoni*; harmony — viola and basso), and binary structure.

Differences between the *minuet* and *aria* finales can be seen in Ex. 10.

Example 10
(a) *Enone: Minuet* (third movement)
(b) *Imeneo: Aria* (third movement)

The melodies of the *minuet* movements are rarely extended through the sequences that produce the wide-ranging spans of the *aria* lines.

Thematic material

The large number of overtures notwithstanding, Caldara's principal themes of the first movements fall into two general categories: those which are built on a triadic motive; and those which revolve around one note, or which are dominated by the repetition of one note.

The triad-based themes may have their origins in Caldara's pre-Viennese years, especially in his experience of the Venetian *intrada*.[13] In Vienna, however, he found such motives particularly useful for the 'festive' *introduzioni*. The triadic/arpeggio outline produced effective thematic material for the brass groups. Moreover, it worked well in the imitative/antiphonal writing that was so much a feature of the brass scoring of these overtures,[14] and contrasted vividly with the scalic figures given to the strings (Ex. 11).

Example 11
(a) *Ormisda, re di Persia*: entry of *clarino* 1 (*coro* 1) and *clarino* 1 (*coro* 2)
(b) *Il Venceslao*: entry of *clarini, coro* 1 and *coro* 2
(c) *Adriano in Siria*: entry of strings
(d) *Achille in Sciro*: entry of strings

In the overtures scored for strings, free from the technical limitations of the brass instruments, Caldara converts the triadic motives into themes of remarkable diversity. Some are enlivened by vigorous syncopations; in others, scalic writing links the notes of the fundamental arpeggio (Ex. 12).

Example 12
(a) *Introduzione* to *L'olimpiade*: 'basic' triadic motive
(b) *Introduzione* to *Dialogo trà la vera disciplina ed il genio*: 'syncopated' triadic motive.
(c) *Introduzione* to *Andromaca*: notes of the triadic motive linked by scalic passages

Ex. 12 (contd)

A strong rhythmic drive lies behind the success of Caldara's repeated-note themes, seen in their most basic form in the overtures to *Scipione Africano il maggiore* (Ex. 13a) and *Semiramide in Ascalona* (Ex. 13b).

Example 13
(a) *Scipione Africano il maggiore*: first movement
(b) *Semiramide in Ascalona*: first movement

Elements of the triadic motive can be combined with the repeated-note theme, as in *Demofoonte* (Ex. 14):

Example 14. *Demofoonte*: first movement

and the repeated-note motive can also climax rapid scalic progressions, as in the overture to *Ifigenia in Aulide* (Ex. 15):

Example 15. *Ifigenia in Aulide*: first movement

The theme which revolves around one note may be seen in the overtures to *Lucio Papirio dittatore* (Ex. 16) and *La clemenza di Tito* and, in a slightly broader context, in *Imeneo* (Ex. 17) and *Don Chisciotte*.

Example 16. *Lucio Papirio dittatore*: first movement

Example 17. *Imeneo*: first movement

Caldara also favoured the thematic shape of Ex. 16 for closing cadence areas or for motives treated sequentially in the development sections, such as we find in *Don Chisciotte* (Ex. 18).

Example 18. *Don Chisciotte*: first movement (development)

Not unexpectedly, the more complex themes incorporating the triadic motive as well as the repeated-note and/or 'central' note motives are less common. Perhaps those with which the overtures to *Ormisda, re di Persia* (Ex. 11a) and *Astarto* (Ex. 19) begin, best represent Caldara's melodic resources for the *allegro* first movements of his Viennese overtures.

Example 19. *Astarto*: first movement

The presentation of the thematic material of the first movement ranges from an unaccompanied statement by a single instrument (*Il natale di Minerva Tritonia*) through two-part (melody/bass) homophony (*I*

disingannati), imitation (especially favoured in the 'festive' overtures), to fugal exposition (*Scipione Africano*). In *Don Chisciotte*, where a tonic pedal bass supports the first subject given by unison violins until the four string parts coalesce in a unison cadence figure, Caldara creates an opening that seems to foreshadow many of the dramatic gestures of the early classical symphonists.

Instrumentation

For all overtures the basic group is a string body comprising violins 1 and 2, viola and basso. The violins are independent of each other in most of the first movements; *unisoni* writing is encountered much more frequently in the second and third movements. Only in the *Introduzione* to *Amalasunta* are violins in unison in all three movements. The strings probably were doubled by oboes and bassoons on most occasions (oboe 1 = violin 1; oboe 2 = violin 2; bassoon = cello and double bass). Unfortunately, the eighteenth-century performance material extant today comprises only the string parts.[15] Thus, except for those scores which include specific cues for oboes and bassoons, it is difficult to provide Caldara's exact instrumentation for any particular overture.[16] Where oboes and bassoons are cued in a score, it is at solo passages, Caldara clearly intending them to be a tonal contrast to either full tutti (brass, strings and woodwind) or string scorings. The independent oboe parts throughout all three movements of the overture to *Don Chisciotte* are exceptional.

The inclusion of brass instruments in Caldara's overtures was determined by the occasions for which the operas were written.[17] Those operas which commemorated *Gala-Tage* at the court (usually the name- and birthdays of the Emperor and Empress) or celebrated special events, such as the marriage of an Archduchess, had their festive character reinforced by the inclusion of trumpets in the overture. The small-scale *festa da camera* which could also mark Imperial *Gala-Tage* were not so scored. No overture to any opera written by Caldara for the Carnival seasons (*Amalasunta, Don Chisciotte, I disingannati, La pazienza di Socrate*,[18] and *Sancio Panza*) is scored for trumpets. Trumpets and timpani were usually employed in choirs, each comprising two *clarini*, two *trombe* and timpani. Seven of the nine overtures scored for double trumpet-choir belong to operas associated with Emperor's *Gala-Tage*.[19] It is apparent from the scores of the operas themselves that the instrumentation of the overtures frequently was unrelated to that of the aria accompaniments. Rather, Caldara used the resources of the *Hofkapelle* to create in these preludes sounds that in their own way were to be as colourful and varied as the costuming and scenic designs about to be revealed on the stage.

Opportunities for solo display are not lacking in Caldara's overtures. In some, such as that to *I disingannati* in which a violin soloist is limited to arpeggiated passage work, the solo-tutti contrast itself seems the principal interest. In others, such as the *Introduzione* to *Adriano in Siria,* extensive bravura passages focus attention on the abilities of the soloist. Indeed, in *Adriano in Siria* passages for solo violin and solo cello are so extensive that they become an important constituent in the overall structure of the first movement:

Figure 6. *Introduzione* to *Adriano* in *Siria*: first movement, structure and scoring

area:	tutti (strings, brass choirs)	solo (violin)	tutti (strings)	solo (cello)	tutti (strings)	tutti (strings, brass choirs)
bars:	1-19	19-25	25-28	29-36	37-40	41-56

*   *   *   *   *

In the Baroque period, the overture to a dramatic work was usually less significant than the music which followed. Nevertheless, when a composer shows by thematic material and often by instrumentation as well, that the overture is independent of the body of the opera, and when, as in Caldara's case, we have a large number of overtures stretching over a considerable period, we are justified in assessing them in their own right. For us, his overtures represent the largest amount of instrumental writing to come from his years of maturity. While these works may not be particularly experimental in material or design, surely they depict the prevailing taste and style of the Viennese court — an amalgam of French and Italian traditions modified by local characteristics and partialities. It was on this foundation that the great age of Viennese symphonic writing was to stand.

Notes

[1] The overtures considered here are those to the operas and *festa di camera* which Caldara wrote after his appointment to the Habsburg court in 1716. Although the majority were written in honour of members of the Imperial family and were staged in the court theatre, Caldara's operas for Salzburg are also included. Not included are the overtures to the small-scale cantatas that Caldara also wrote during his Viennese years. For an example of such an overture see *Il giuoco di quadriglio*

in *Antonio Caldara, Kammermusik für Gesang, Denkmäler der Tonkunst in Österreich* 75 (1932)

2   Five of Caldara's overtures to secular dramatic works and one overture to an oratorio appear in facsimile, with an 'Introduction' by Bernard Toscani, in *The Symphony 1720–1840* Series B.II (New York, 1983).

3   The court's *Kapellmeister*, Johann Joseph Fux, also made only infrequent use of the traditional French overture. Two of his operas were headed by this type of prelude although elements of the French style appear in many others — perhaps to a greater extent than in Caldara's overtures. Both Caldara and Fux retained the slow-fast plan for the overtures to their oratorios, but here the influence is that of the first two movements of the *sonata da chiesa*.

4   Several of Fux's opera overtures also are in this tradition. That to *Angelica vincitrice di Alcina* (1716) may well have inspired Caldara's overture to *Cajo Marzio Coriolano* (1717).

5   In opening with the string group, *Enone* is the exception among Caldara's 'festive' overtures. All others begin with an extensive passage for the brass choir(s); see the structural plan for the *Introduzione* to Caldara's *Gianguir* in A. Peter Brown 'Caldara's trumpet music for the Imperial celebrations of Charles VI and Elisabeth Christine' p. 21.

6   This type of accompaniment is termed ' "dünnen" Akkordsäulen' by Ursula Kirkendale who notes its use in overtures to Caldara's Roman oratorios; *Antonio Caldara: Sein Leben und seine venezianisch-römischen Oratorien* (Graz-Köln, 1966), p. 291.

7   Caldara's scorings are discussed on pp. 93–4.

8   While Erich Schenk's terminology (*Vordersatz, Fortspinnung, Schlußgruppe*) may be applied to these areas, the strong element of continuity and gradual evolution in the thematic material implied by the *Fortspinnungs* technique is lacking in many of these movements. Rather, Caldara seems to create quite distinct areas. For example, compare the single-movement overture to *Dafne* in which the *Fortspinnungs* technique is apparent, with the overtures to *Don Chisciotte* and *I disingannati*.

9   Caldara's overtures should not be understood to form a chain of development, with each example representing an advance on its predecessors. There is nothing to suggest that Caldara was working toward some as yet unrealised concept of the overture.

10 Apart from the *Introduzione* to *Cajo Marzio Coriolano*, that to *Dafne* is Caldara's only other single-movement overture. It is extremely brief (8 :‖: 14), strongly French in its dotted-rhythm motives (imitated between violins 1 and 2), but Italian in its light-weight nature and lively *allegro* manner. The overture to *Lucio Papirio dittatore* is Caldara's only four-movement *Introduzione*. Although no tempi are given for the last two movements, their melodic style and texture suggests *Allegro — Grave*. The six-bar concluding movement which leads directly into the first act is, arguably, a coda to the third movement. The overtures to *L'inganno tradito dall'amore* and *La pazienza di Socrate*, each comprising three *allegro* movements are unique in Caldara's output.

11 Fux also favoured the *minuet* finale to his overtures. However, most of his *Minuets* are in the conservative 3/4 metre, of rather staid rhythmic patterns, less wide-ranging in melodic shape and, at least in the early works, scored for four-part orchestra. Only later does Fux turn to the lighter Italian texture (melody given unison violins, accompaniment to viola and basso) used by Caldara, Porpora, etc.

12 See the discussion in Andrew D. McCredie 'Nicola Matteis, the younger: Caldara's collaborator and ballet composer in the service of the Emperor, Charles VI' pp. 162 and 166 below.

13 Caldara was not alone in using such themes; they can be found in Fux's opera overtures. Caldara, however, uses them so consistently and extensively that they

may well be regarded a hall-mark of his instrumental style.

[14] The introduction to *Cajo Fabbricio* is the exception. This begins with a generous, flowing theme for *clarino* 1 of the 'primo coro'. It is not treated in imitation by the other trumpets in the choir, or answered antiphonally by the second choir.

[15] Now held in the music collection of the Austrian National Library, Vienna. Although performance material is available for the majority of Caldara's dramatic compositions, only one copy of each string part for each composition has been retained.

[16] Caldara, himself, is not always clear in his indications, especially where 'general' doublings rather than solo passages are involved. For example, the only indication that oboes and bassoons double the strings in the first movement of the overture to *Adriano in Siria* is his annotation 'Senza Trombe l'aria seguente, e senza Oboè' at the conclusion of the movement. This instruction was omitted by the copyist who prepared the full score for the *Hofkapelle* collection (A-Wn: Mus.Hs. 17162) from Caldara's autograph (A-Wgm: A388).

[17] With flow-on consequences for the thematic material and structural design of these overtures.

[18] Music for the second act was by Georg Reutter, the younger. There is no reason to doubt that Caldara did not write the overture. On the other hand, as Reutter composed the first act of *La forza dell amicizia* (1728) — with Caldara providing Acts 2 and 3 — we may assume the overture to be Reutter's.

[19] See A. Peter Brown 'Caldara's trumpet music for the Imperial celebrations of Charles VI and Elisabeth Christine' p. 5 and especially Table 3.

Thematic index

All sources are autograph unless otherwise indicated.

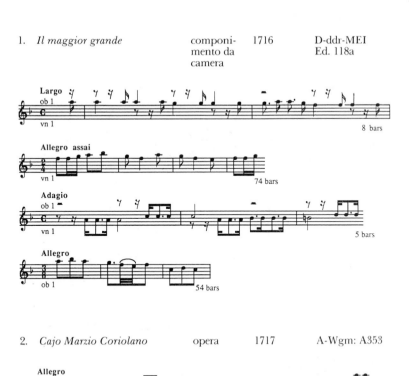

1. *Il maggior grande*   componi-   1716   D-ddr-MEI
           mento da   Ed. 118a
           camera

2. *Cajo Marzio Coriolano*   opera   1717   A-Wgm: A353

3. *Il Tiridate ossia La verità*
    nell'inganno   opera   1717   A-Wgm: A354

Largo

vn 1   10 bars

Presto

vn 1   104 bars   (adagio C b.74; presto 3/8 b.78)

4. *Ifigenia in Aulide*   opera   1718   A-Wgm: A355

Allegro

vn 1

                                                    14 :||: 18 bars

Aria

vni unis   14 :||: 18 bars

5. *Dafne*   dramma   1719   A-Wgm: A358
                                     pastorale

Allegro   tr

vn 1   8 :||: 14 bars

6. *Sirita*   opera   1719   A-Wgm: A357

Allegro assai

basso   16 :||: 36 bars

Andante

vn 1   6 bars

Allegro assai

vn 1   8 :||: 16 bars

7. *Lucio Papirio dittatore*   opera   1719   A-Wgm: A359

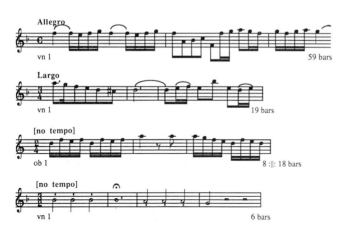

8. *L'inganno tradito dall'amore*   opera   1720   A-Wgm: A360

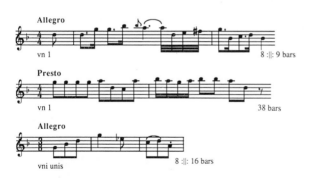

9. *Apollo in cielo*   servizio di   1720   A-Wn: Mus. Hs.
                                       camera   18241 (*Hof* copy)

10. *Il germanico Marte*   opera   1721   A-Wgm: A362

Allegro assai

vn 1

45 bars (adagio coda)

Aria Allegro

vni unis   12 :||: 11 bars

11. *Ormisda, re di Persia*   opera   1721   A-Wgm: A361

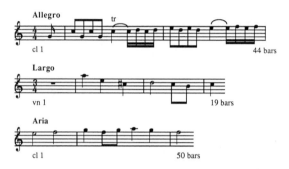

Allegro

cl 1   44 bars

Largo

vn 1   19 bars

Aria

cl 1   50 bars

12. *Camaide, imperatore della
     China*   opera   1722   A-Wgm: A365

Allegro assai e spiritoso

vn 1   42 bars (adagio coda)

Aria Allegro

vni unis   13 :||: 18 bars

13. *Nitocri*   opera   1722   A-Wgm: A363

Presto

vn 1

51 bars (adagio coda)

Aria

vni unis   12 :||: 20 bars

14. *Scipione nelle Spagne*   opera   1722   A-Wgm: A364

15. *La contesa de'numi*   servizio di 1723   A-Wgm: A395
                               camera

16. *La concordia de'pianeti*   festa teatrale 1723   A-Wgm: Q1229

17. *Euristeo*   opera   1724   A-Wn: Mus. Hs.
                                          17184 (*Hof* copy)

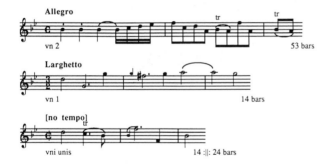

18. *Il finto Policare*   opera   1724   A-Wgm: A367

19. *Andromaca*   opera   1724   D-ddr-Bds:
                                                                       Mus.ms. Autogr.
                                                                       Caldara A2

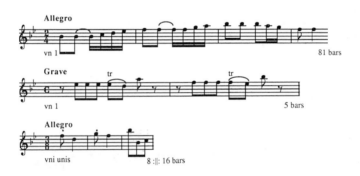

20. *Gianguir, imperatore de Mogol* opera   1724   A-Wgm: A366

21. *Astarto*   opera   1725   A-Wgm: A368

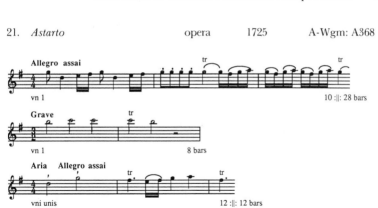

22. *Semiramide in Ascalona*   opera   1725   A-Wgm: A369

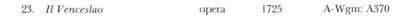

23. *Il Venceslao*   opera   1725   A-Wgm: A370

24. *Amalasunta*   opera   1726   A-Wgm: A371

25. *L'Etearco*   opera   1726   S-St: E.4

26. *I due dittatori*   opera   1726   A-Wgm: A382

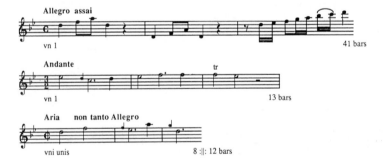

27. *Ghirlanda di fiori*   festa   1726   A-Wgm: A396 (i)

vni unis   8 :||: 12 bars

28. *Don Chisciotte in corte della   opera
    duchessa*   serioridicola 1727   A-Wgm: A372

vni unis   52 bars

Aria

ob 1   42 bars (repeat of last 20 bars
                                             Allegro assai follows)

29. *La verità nell'inganno ossia
    Arinsoe*   opera   1727   A-Wgm: A373

vn 1   5 bars

Allegro assai

vn 2   48 bars

30. *Imeneo*   opera   1727   A-Wgm: A374

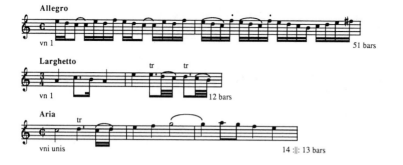

vn 1   51 bars

Larghetto

vn 1   12 bars

Aria

vni unis   14 :||: 13 bars

31. *Ornospade*   opera   1727   A-Wgm: A375

32. *Mitridate*   opera   1728   A-Wgm: A379

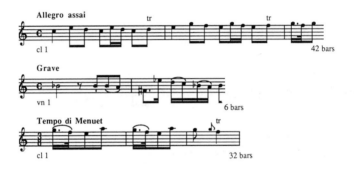

33. *Ciro riconosciuto*   opera   1728/1736   A-Wgm: A377

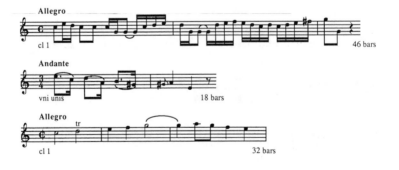

34. *L'amor non ha legge*   pastorale   1728   A-Wgm: A376

35. *I disingannati*   opera   1729   A-Wgm: A378

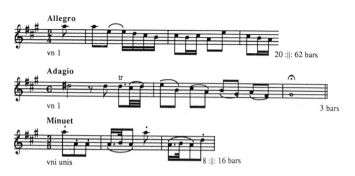

36. *Cajo Fabbricio*   opera   1729   A-Wgm: A382

37.   *Enone*   pastorale   1729/1734   A-Wgm: A383

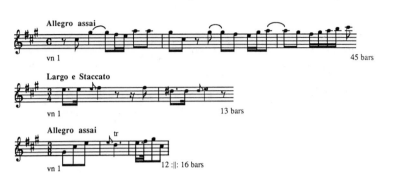

38.   *Dialogo trà la vera disciplina*   festa di
      ed il genio   camera   1730   A-Wgm: A398 (ii)

39.   *Sancio Panza, governatore dell'*
      isola Barattaria   opera   1730/1733   A-Wgm: A384

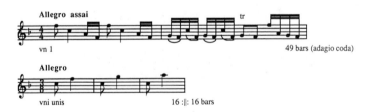

40.   *La pazienza di Socrate con due*   scherzo
      mogli   drammatico 1731   A-Wgm: A385

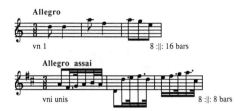

41. *Il Demetrio*   opera   1731   A-Wgm: A387

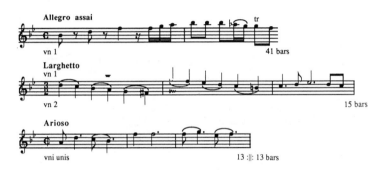

42. *Livia*   festa teatrale 1731   A-Wgm: Q1227
(copy)

43. *L'asilo d'amore*   festa teatrale 1732   A-Wgm: A386

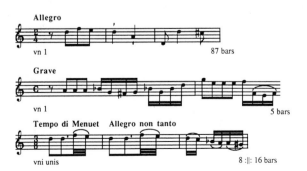

44. *Adriano in Siria*   opera   1732   A-Wgm: A388

45. *Demofoonte*   opera   1733   A-Wgm: A389

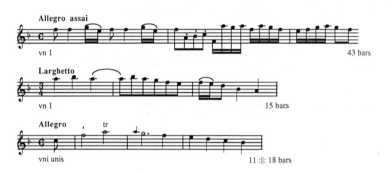

46. *L'olimpiade*   opera   1733   D-ddr-Bds:
                                                            Mus. ms. Autogr.
                                                            Caldara A3.

47. *Le lodi d'Augusto*   festa da   1734   A-Wgm: A399
                                   camera

48. *La clemenza di Tito*   opera   1734   A-Wgm: A390

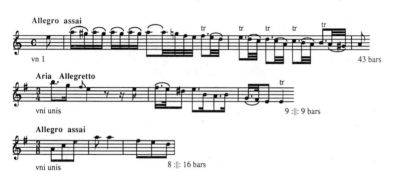

49. *Le Cinesi*   componi-   1735   A-Wgm: A392 (iii)
                                   mento
                                   drammatico

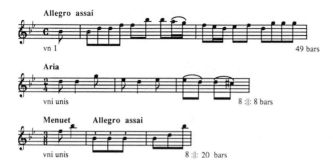

50. *Il natale di Minerva Tritonia*   festa per   1735   A-Wgm: A392 (i)
musica

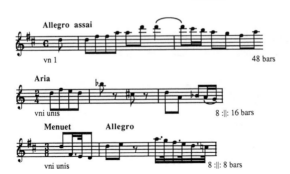

Allegro assai
vn 1   48 bars

Aria
vni unis   8 :||: 16 bars

Menuet   Allegro
vni unis   8 :||: 8 bars

51. *Scipione Africano il maggiore*   festa di   1735   A-Wgm: A391
camera

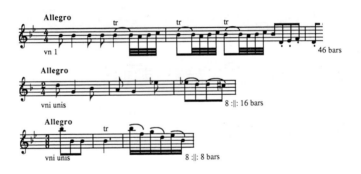

Allegro
vn 1   46 bars

Allegro
vni unis   8 :||: 16 bars

Allegro
vni unis   8 :||: 8 bars

52. *Le grazie vendicate*   festa teatrale 1735   A-Wgm: A392 (ii)

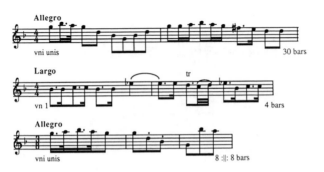

Allegro
vni unis   30 bars

Largo
vn 1   4 bars

Allegro
vni unis   8 :||: 8 bars

53.   *Achille in Sciro*   opera   1736   D-ddr-Bds:
                                                                         Mus. ms. Autogr.
                                                                         Caldara A1

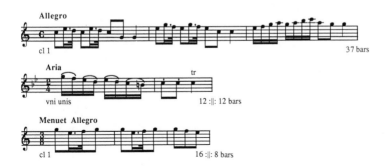

54.   *Il Temistocle*   opera   1736   A-Wgm: A393

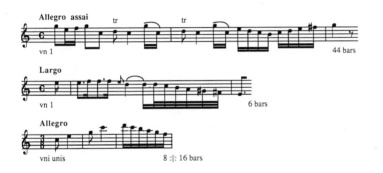

The Viennese court orchestra
in the time of Caldara

Eleanor Selfridge-Field

Zusammenfassung

Die Wiener Hofkapelle zur Zeit Caldaras

Die Amtszeit Antonio Caldaras als Vizekapellmeister am Habsburger Hof fiel mit einer Zeit zusammen, die von großer Bedeutung in der Entwicklung der europäischen Hofkapelle war. In den frühen Jahrzehnten des achtzehnten Jahrhunderts besaßen diese Kapellen keineswegs einen einheitlichen Charakter; in ihrer Zusammensetzung gab es große Unterschiede, sowohl von Ort zu Ort wie auch von Jahr zu Jahr. Obwohl es sich wohl nicht mit Sicherheit feststellen läßt, inwieweit die Sonderentwicklung der Hofkapelle in Wien der Anwesenheit Caldaras zuzuschreiben ist, bietet eine Untersuchung der Entwicklung der Kapelle in ihrer eigenen früheren (vor 1716) wie späteren (nach 1740) Phase einerseits, und andereseits der Ensembles, mit denen Caldara in Italien eine Verbindung gehabt hatte, einige interessante Vergleichspunkte und trägt zum besseren Verständnis der Veränderungen bei, dei während seines Aufenthalts von zwanzig Jahren an der Wiener Hofkapelle stattgefunden haben.

Die früheste Erfahrung Caldaras in mehrstimmigen Partituren stammte aus seiner Teilnahme an der Kapelle der Basilica von S. Marco, Venedig (bis 1699). Seine Zeit bei dieser Kapelle fiel mit einem Höhepunkt in deren Entwicklung zusammen (Tabelle 2). Neben einer erheblichen Menge von Kompositionen für vier- and fünfstimmige Streichgestalten sind einige der frühesten selbständigen Begleitstimmen Caldaras (für Oboe) in Kirchenkompositionen für Venedig und für den Hof zu Mantua zu finden, wo er 1700–1707 tätig war. Verfeinerung der Partiturentechnik und erhebliche Erfahrung im Komponieren für selbständige Streichbegleitstimme scheinen das bedeutendste Erbe seiner Römerzeit (1708–1715) zu sein — Jahre, in denen eine ungeheure Menge stimm- und instrumentalbegleiteter Kantaten enstanden ist.

Die Amtszeit Caldaras als Vizekapellmeister in Wien fiel auch mit dem Höhepunkt der Hofkapelle zusammen (Tabelle 3). Was die Gesamtzahl der Musiker und die Vielfalt der Instrumenten betrifft, stand Caldara einer der reichsten Kapellen Europas zur Verfügung. Er wußte diese Mittel voll auszunützen, besonders in seiner Kirchenmusik, wobei er ein Kaleidoskop des Klanges in ganz konzentrierton Kompositionen aufbaute. Zu den Grundstreichgestalten (häufig durch bis zu vier Trompeten und Pauken in tutti-Passagen gestärkt) kamen selbständige Begleitstimmen für Klarintrompete, Posaunen, Violini, Violoncelli und Fagotti hinzu. Holzblasinstrumente (Oboen und Chalumeaux) wurden in Oratorien und Opern in Soloistenrolle verwendet. In diesen größeren Werken figurierte die instrumentale Begleitstimme in selbständigen Ariensätzen, im krassen Gegensatz zur Vermischung der Soloinstrumente bei den häufig ganz komplizierten concentrante-Sätzen der Kirchencompositionen.

Der schnelle Verfall der Hofkapelle unter den von Maria Theresa durchgeführten Sparmaßnahmen machte effektiv dieser Blütezeit ein Ende und führte zweifellos teilweise dazu, daß während der vierziger-Jahre viele der reich partiturierten Kirchenstücke Caldaras dem Hofrepertoire entfernt wurden.

The Viennese court orchestra in the time of Caldara

Eleanor Selfridge-Field[*]

T HE TENURE OF Antonio Caldara as *Vizekapellmeister* at the
Habsburg court coincided with a period of considerable
importance in the general development of the European court
orchestra. In the early decades of the eighteenth century these bands were
certainly not characterized by uniformity. Their make-up varied greatly,
not only from place to place but sometimes also from year to year. While
it is almost impossible to gauge the extent to which the particular course
of development of the *Hofkapelle* orchestra in Vienna can be attributed
to Caldara's presence, an examination of its progress *vis-à-vis* its own
earlier (pre-1716) and later (post-1740) phases as well as the ensembles
with which Caldara had been associated in Italy offers some interesting
points of comparison and aids our understanding of the changes that
occurred in the Viennese orchestra during his sojourn of twenty years.

The Venetian Heritage

In his youth Caldara was trained both as a contralto and as a cellist.
His father, Giuseppe (*c*1650-*c*1710), was a violinist although it was as
a theorbo player that Caldara senior was temporarily engaged at the
Basilica of San Marco in Venice in 1693 and 1694.[1] It is not inconceivable
that Antonio's instrumental tuition, like that of so many of his peers,
occurred solely at home, for the evidence that the theorbo and the cello
were used interchangeably in Italy in the late seventeenth century grows
steadily.[2]

* The statistical information on Vienna included in this essay was assembled and examined
on the IBYCUS computer system at the Centre for Computer Assisted Research in
the Humanities in Menlo Park, California. I am especially grateful to Walter B. Hewlett
for providing access to this system, designed by David Woodley Packard, during its
developmental stage in 1984. I am also greatly indebted to Brian W. Pritchard for
providing many of the musical examples and recondite facts included in this article.

If the estimate that Caldara was born in c1670 is correct, then he made a favourable impression at an early age. He was named in the list of founding members of the *souvegno* Santa Cecilia in 1687,[3] was engaged as a supernumerary cellist at San Marco from 1688,[4] and saw his first stage work, *L'Argene*, produced at the small Teatro ai Saloni in Venice in 1689. From 1695 until 1700, when he left Venice for Mantua, he was hired on a regular basis as a contralto at San Marco.

Most of Caldara's time at Venice coincided with the peak years of the orchestra at San Marco, but he also witnessed the very beginning of its gradual decline, an ostensible consequence of the deaths of Giovanni Legrenzi (*maestro di cappella*) in 1690 and the Doge, Francesco Morosini, in 1694 (see Tables 1 and 2). In 1696 the position of *maestro di'concerti* — the office most directly related to the performance of instrumental music — was abolished. The reservoir of available instruments remained relatively large, but the focus shifted to solo and trio sonatas and, in the vocal repertoire, to motets. For example, Vivaldi's father, Giovanni Battista, was a violinist in the string trio that was formed at San Marco in 1689.[5] By 1708, when Caldara had completed his time in Mantua but had not yet taken up an appointment in Rome, the San Marco orchestra had been reduced to:

Table 1. *The orchestra at San Marco, Venice, in Caldara's time*

	1689 (Caldara engaged at San Marco)	1699 (Caldara leaves San Marco)	1708[6]
violins	16	12	12
violas (*violette*)	5	4	5
cellos (*viole*)	4	3	3
(*violoni*)	2	3	3
basses (*violone grosso*)	1	1	1
theorbos	4	4	4
harp	1	1	1
cornetti	5	2	2
trumpets (*trombe*)	1	2	2
trombones	5	5	3
oboe	—	1	1
bassoons	2	—	—

The brass instruments were holdovers from the ancient corpus of *piffari*, a band that was in the process of dissolution;[7] the first oboe had been substituted for a *cornetto* in 1698. The remaining *cornetti* were not required in any surviving repertoire of the time, and it is not inconceivable that trumpets were occasionally used in their place. When the first trumpeter was officially appointed to the orchestra in 1714, it was in response to a plea for 'a useable wind instrument'.[8] The last trombone player died in 1732 and the last theorbist in 1748.[9]

The growing interest in the use of solo wind instruments around 1700 was something to which Caldara apparently responded both in Venice and during his subsequent appointment at the ducal court in Mantua from 1700 to 1707.[10] His undated but undoubtedly early setting of Psalm 110/111, *Confitebor tibi Domine* for soprano solo, SATB chorus,

Table 2. *Venice: the orchestra at San Marco, 1679-1720*

Doge	2° Organo	Maestro di Cappella	Year	Vn	Va	Vc	Vne	Vgr	Ct	Trp	Trb	Ob	Bn	Hp	Thb	Total
Contarini	Spada	Monferrato	1679	5	2	1	3	1	3	-	3	-	2	1	4	25
			1680	5	2	1	3	1	3	-	4	-	2	1	4	26
			1681	5	2	1	3	1	3.	-	4	-	2	1	4	26
			1682	7	2	2	3	1	4	-	4	-	2	1	4	30
			1683	8	2	2	2	1	4	-	3	-	2	1	4	29
Giustiniani			1684	11	2	2	2	1	4	-	3	-	2	1	4	32
		Legrenzi	1685	12	3	3	2	1	5	-	4	-	2	1	5	38
			1686	13	3	4	2	1	5	-	4	-	2	1	5	40
			1687	13	3	4	2	1	5	-	4	-	2	1	4	39
Morosini			1688	13	3	4	2	1	5	-	4	-	2	1	4	39
	C.F.P.*	Volpe	1689	16	5	4	2	1	5	1	5	-	2	1	4	46
			1690	17	5	4	2	1	5	1	5	-	2	1	5	48
		Partenio	1691	15	5	4	2	1	4	2	5	-	2	1	5	46
			1692	15	5	4	2	1	4	2	5	-	2	1	5	46
			1693	14	5	4	3	1	4	2	5	-	2	1	5	46
Valier			1694	13	5	4	3	1	4	2	5	-	2	1	5	45
			1695	13	4	3	3	1	3	2	5	-	2	1	4	41
			1696	13	4	3	3	1	3	2	5	-	2	1	4	41
			1697	12	4	3	3	1	3	2	5	-	-	1	4	38
			1698	12	4	3	3	1	2	2	5	1	-	1	4	38
			1699	12	4	3	3	1	2	2	5	1	-	1	4	38
Mocenigo	Lotti		1700	12	4	3	4	1	2	2	5	1	-	1	4	39
			1701	12	5	3	3	1	2	2	4	1	-	1	4	38
			1702	12	5	3	3	1	2	2	4	1	-	1	4	38
			1703	12	5	3	3	1	2	2	4	1	-	1	4	38
			1704	12	5	3	3	1	2	2	4	1	-	1	4	38
	Vinaccesi		1705	12	5	3	3	1	2	2	4	1	-	1	4	38
			1706	12	5	3	3	1	2	2	4	1	-	1	4	38
			1707	12	5	3	3	1	2	2	3	1	-	1	4	37
			1708	12	5	3	3	1	2	2	3	1	-	1	4	37
		Biffi	1709	8	4	3	3	-	1	2	1	1	-	-	3	26
			1710	8	4	3	3	-	1	2	1	1	-	-	3	26
			1711	8	4	3	3	-	1	2	1	1	-	-	3	26
			1712	8	3	2	2	-	1	1	1	1	-	-	3	22
			1713	5	3	2	2	-	1	1	1	1	-	-	3	19
			1714	8	6	1	3	-	1	1	1	1	-	-	3	25
Corner			1715	8	6	1	3	-	-	1	1	1	-	-	2	23
			1716	9	4	1	3	-	-	1	1	1	-	-	1	21
	Tavelli		1717	9	4	1	3	-	-	1	1	1	-	-	1	21
			1718	9	4	1	2	-	-	1	1	1	-	-	1	20
			1719	9	4	1	2	-	-	1	1	1	-	-	1	20
			1720	11	4	3	3	-	-	1	1	1	-	-	1	25

* C.F. Pollarolo

obbligato oboe and strings,[11] would have suited the resources of San Marco in 1698 or 1699 extremely well. It may even have been written to welcome the Basilica's first oboist, Onofrio Penati. We also find large-scale arias with oboe obbligatos in his *Gloria* in B-flat ('Domine Fili unigenite') and the *Gloria* in a minor ('Domine Deus, Agnus Dei') both dating from 1705. However, his most extensive use of wind instruments comes in the C major *Gloria* written in Venice in September, 1707. Two obbligato oboes accompany the soprano soloist in the 'Laudamus te' aria and alternate with two *trombe* in the 'Quoniam tu solus'. These four instruments also indulge in brief solo exchanges in the monumental opening chorus. We should note, too, that in these same years Caldara (together with Albinoni and C. F. Pollarolo, both of whom also were closely associated with Mantua) contributed to a volume of cantatas which allowed for optional trumpet and recorder parts.[12] The foundations of the skilful and fluent obbligato writing demonstrated in so many of his Viennese works may well be traced back to the resources at his disposal during these formative years.

The Roman Heritage

The musical practices that Caldara encountered in Rome during the years in which he served Prince Ruspoli as *maestro di cappella* (1709–16) were different from those of Venice. In place of public opera, there was private oratorio. Instead of the great spectacles of public worship at San Marco, there were private and contemplative devotions. Refinement of the art of the solo (whether illustrated by Pasquini's harpsichord pieces or Corelli's violin sonatas) had been an important feature of musical life in the courts of the cardinals for the last two decades of the seventeenth century; in Venice it was only emerging as these figures were about to pass from view. String music was the preferred instrumental medium; brass and woodwind instruments were found only rarely. But string orchestras in Rome were often much larger than the string-and-wind ensembles of Venice and the doubling of string parts already was common practice in Rome in the late seventeenth century. For example, a concerto by Corelli was performed at the Palazzo Pamphili in 1689 by an orchestra of seventy-six stringed instruments and two trumpets.[13]

While Venice was dominated by a few institutions with fixed feasts, the musical focus of Rome was diffuse and the occasions for performance varied and unpredictable. Thus in an era in which the concept of norms did not exist, Rome was particularly flexible in its musical practices. Resident house-orchestras had as few as nine or ten members, while for special occasions their ranks could swell to seventy or more. These large orchestras seem to have played in the sinfonias, prologues and, perhaps, in the ritornellos of vocal works (such as serenatas) staged in Arcadian gardens and oratorios performed in adjacent *palazzi*.

The practice of employing *concerto grosso* instrumentation in diverse circumstances seems to have persisted well beyond the death of Stradella in 1682[14] — or so the fluctuations in the number of available instruments would seem to suggest. At the court of Pietro Cardinal Ottoboni, the nephew of the Venetian pope Alexander VIII (1689–91), a *pastorale* given in 1690 required three violins, two violas, a cello and a string bass, but sixteen violins, four violas, seven cellos and four string basses were added to these instruments for the sinfonia that preceded it. Two trumpets also played in the *pastorale* and a trombone in the sinfonia.[15] A similar relation between larger and smaller ensembles pertained to the Good Friday service in the Cancelleria in 1692, except that a lute was included and the brass excluded.[16] For Lulier's oratorio, *Betsabea provato*, given in the same year at the Casa Savelli, forty-seven instruments were employed:

> 23 violins
> 7 violas
> 8 cellos
> 5 string basses
> 2 lutes
> 2 harpsichords[17]

The fact that nearly a third of these were continuo instruments suggests diversification in the accompaniments of individual singers or of particular kinds of arias, rather than an integrated body overwhelmed by accompaniment instruments.

At the Palazzo Ruspoli an *alfresco* performance of a cantata given before an Arcadian gathering on 9 August, 1694, involved thirty-six violins, five violas, twenty-five cellos and double basses, and a lute.[18] Such large assemblies of instruments cannot be associated only with performances in palaces. A similarly-sized group with only minor differences in distribution performed in an oratorio at the Seminario Romano in 1695.[19] A composite list of the instrumentalists available in the Ruspoli household during Caldara's years included the names of twenty-five violinists, six violists, five cellists, three double bassists, and seven oboists.[20]

We know that in 1711 Caldara was involved in a performance in Novara that included among the 'primi virtuosi d'Itaglia' sixteen violinists, four violists, three cellists, four double bassists, four oboists, a theorbist, and two trumpeters.[21] In 1713 an even larger number of performers took part in a performance of one of his cantatas written 'Per la Notte de SS^mo Natale'. The forty-eight instrumentalists were divided into two ensembles: a *concertino* of two violins, cello, double bass, lute and harpischord, and a *concerto grosso* of forty-two players (12 first and 12 second violins, 6 violas, and 12 basses — *violoni* and *contrabassi*).[22] The 'tutti' and 'soli' markings in the violin parts in a contemporary score of Caldara's large-scale secular cantata, *La libertà contenta*, written at Rome,[23] may indicate a similar practice.

The Viennese *Hofkapelle*

The most extensive and comprehensive study of the staffing of the
Viennese court *Kapelle* is that recorded by Ludwig Ritter von Köchel
in two books: *Die Kaiserliche Hof-Musikkapelle in Wien von 1543 bis
1867* (Wien, 1869) — which includes a listing of every instrumentalist
hired between 1637 and 1792, although specific instruments are rarely
indicated before 1680 — and *Johann Josef Fux, Hofcompositor und
Hofkapellmeister der Kaiser Leopold I., Josef I. und Karl VI. von 1698
bis 1740* (Wien, 1872).

On a cursory reading of this material three clerical practices create
the impression that there were more instrumentalists than was in fact
the case. First, the appointments of many musicians were reported several
times. Frequently, existing staff members were 'rehired' at the start of
a new reign, so that several entries for the same person, usually with
a single uniform termination date, have been recorded. Second, the
problem of multiple listings for single individuals has been compounded
by variations in spelling that reflect the lack of standardization in the
original records. The family recorded here in the present Appendix as
Bayer was also cited in Köchel's data as Payer and Peyer. At times Köchel
confused baptismal names. In this way two entries, although agreeing
in surname and instrument, leave open the question of a single or double
identity whenever the first entry cites but one given-name and the
subsequent entry two given-names, one of which is that of the first entry.
Third, a few musicians, particularly wind players, performed on more
than one instrument, though not necessarily throughout the whole of
their tenure.

Köchel's invaluable data have now been systematized to facilitate the
tracing of the broad outlines of the court orchestra between 1680, when
data about instruments began to be recorded systematically, and 1770,
by which time details such as the rates of payment began to be ignored.
Using the IBYCUS computer system, Köchel's original records were
entered, edited to eliminate duplications, and then examined in a series
of arrays correlating chronology with the distribution of instruments
and the nationality of the players.[24] The edited and alphabetically arranged
list of musicians which emerged, and on which Table 3 of this essay
is based, appears as an Appendix. By using this, a reader with interests
not addressed here can revise the numbers to suit his own purposes.[25]

There are some additional caveats about Table 3. We should note
that for the 1680s and several decades following, it is unlikely that all
the instruments listed ever performed together as an 'orchestra'. The
widespread practice of the sixteenth and seventeenth centuries was for
courts to house a series of consorts, a handful of minstrels, and a group
of ceremonial brass instrumentalists. Thus the four trumpeters, cornettist,
and three trombonists resident in 1680 may well have functioned as an
independent group. The string players (violists are consistently subsumed
in the violin category of Köchel's data) would have accompanied sacred
vocal works. The theorbo presumably was used to accompany solo vocal

music and to supplement the continuo, but it was also given the occasional solo part.

We should note, too, that totals within specific categories are subject to various refinements. Numerous details in Köchel's *Fux* indicate that these figures were vulnerable to the same circumstances that affected similar computations made of the music personnel of other institutions — the tacit inclusion of unpaid (and thus usually unreported) apprentices in performances, the tacit absence of the ill and elderly (whose names were recorded because they continued to be paid), and the occasional use of supernumeraries on special occasions. In addition, some of the court's composers may have performed more regularly than this format of record-keeping shows.

In the third place, even though there is no evidence to show that the practice was ever used in Vienna, we should remember that in the larger courts and churches of Italy, France, and England two similarly-composed groups of performers often alternated from occasion to occasion. If such a system was employed in Vienna, its result would have been to halve the numbers given.

Finally, let us note that in Vienna at this time, numerical changes in the list are as likely to have reflected the taste of the Emperors as that of the musical directors. Joseph I and Charles VI were able musicians and composers as well as vigorous supporters of Italian culture. They may well have been involved more directly in the conduct of musical affairs at court than was generally the case elsewhere in Europe.

Irrespective of whether the Viennese orchestra was a federation of ensembles or an integrated body, it was among the largest and most continuous of the court-based instrumental groups of the era. By 1720 the apparently integrated court orchestra was a familiar phenomenon throughout Germany, although in Paris single-timbre ensembles were still identifiable. In Italy the church and its representatives were the chief sponsors of large orchestras. Over much of the rest of Europe opera houses provided the most consistent patronage and the most important initiatives for the incorporation of new timbres and the fusion of miscellaneous consorts into a single group.

Several of the German courts at which instrumental music was most ardently cultivated — Berlin, Hanover and Mannheim — were Protestant and thus not directly influenced by Italian church music. However, the love of varied timbres that was associated with the oratorio of northern Italy was soon evident in the opera of Protestant cultures. Hamburg, noted throughout the first half of the eighteenth century for its opera, boasted an especially diversified stable of instrumentalists. In 1738 it included two *chalumeaux*, two *cornetti*, two oboes d'amore, a viola d'amore, a gamba, a transverse flute, two piccolos, a recorder, and two tin whistles (*ziffoli*) — all in addition to fifteen conventional stringed instruments, the same number of conventional winds, ten brass, and one drum.

The Viennese court, favoured both by geography and by cultural orientation, was well-placed to absorb these diverse traditions and developments. Many of the best instrumentalists in Vienna in the seventeenth century were Italians and their numbers could only have been increased by the opening of an Italian theatre at court in 1686. Fux, who was hired in 1713, was the first non-Italian *Kapellmeister* at the Imperial court. Only after 1740 were the court composers predominantly German-speaking, although a broader range of national backgrounds had come into the rank and file of the *Kapelle* early in the eighteenth century, as Austria itself assumed a commanding position in international affairs.

Table 3. *Vienna: the* Hofkapelle *orchestra, 1680–1770*

Emperor	Vizekapellmeister	Kapellmeister		Strings				Wind							Acc./Perc.			Totals	
				Vn*	Vc	Vne	Gmb	Btn	Ct	Trp	Trb	Hn	Ob	Bn	Lt	Thb	Tmp		**
			1680	10	3	-	-	-	1	4	3	-	-	1	-	1	-	23	19
			1681	10	3	-	-	-	1	4	3	-	-	1	-	1	-	23	19
			1682	11	3	-	1	-	1	4	3	-	-	2	-	1	-	26	22
			1683	10	3	-	1	-	1	4	3	-	-	2	-	1	-	25	21
			1684	9	3	-	1	-	1	4	3	-	-	2	-	1	-	24	20
			1685	8	3	-	1	-	1	4	3	-	-	1	-	1	-	22	18
			1686	9	4	-	1	-	1	4	3	-	-	1	-	1	-	24	20
			1687	10	4	-	1	-	1	4	3	-	-	1	-	1	-	25	21
			1688	10	4	-	1	-	1	3	3	-	-	1	-	1	-	24	21
Leopold I		Draghi	1689	9	4	-	1	-	2	3	3	-	-	1	-	1	-	24	21
			1690	10	4	-	1	-	2	3	3	-	-	1	-	1	-	25	22
			1691	11	4	-	1	-	2	3	3	-	-	1	-	1	-	26	23
			1692	12	4	-	1	-	2	3	3	-	-	1	-	1	-	27	24
			1693	11	4	-	1	-	2	3	3	-	-	1	-	1	-	26	23
			1694	11	4	-	1	-	2	3	3	-	-	1	-	1	-	26	23
			1695	10	4	-	1	-	2	3	3	-	-	1	-	1	-	25	22
			1696	11	4	-	1	-	2	3	3	-	-	1	-	1	-	26	23
			1697	12	4	-	2	-	2	3	3	-	-	1	1	2	-	30	27
			1698	14	4	-	2	-	2	7	4	-	-	1	1	2	-	37	30
			1699	14	4	-	2	-	2	7	4	-	-	1	1	2	-	37	30
			1700	17	4	-	2	-	3	6	4	-	-	1	1	2	-	40	34
			1701	17	4	1	2	-	3	7	4	-	-	1	1	3	-	43	36
	M.A. Ziani		1702	19	5	1	2	-	3	6	5	-	2	1	1	3	-	48	42
		Pancotti	1703	18	5	1	2	-	3	6	5	-	2	1	1	3	-	47	41
			1704	18	5	1	2	-	3	6	5	-	2	2	1	1	-	46	40
			1705	19	6	2	2	-	3	5	5	-	6	3	1	1	-	53	48
Joseph I			1706	23	6	2	2	-	3	7	5	-	6	3	1	1	-	59	52
			1707	23	6	2	4	-	3	7	5	-	6	3	1	2	-	62	55
			1708	24	6	2	4	-	3	7	4	-	6	4	1	2	-	63	56
			1709	24	6	2	4	-	2	7	5	-	6	4	1	1	-	62	55
			1710	23	7	2	4	-	2	7	5	-	7	4	1	-	-	62	55
Charles VI	Fux	M.A. Ziani	1711	20	7	2	4	-	2	14	5	-	8	4	1	1	-	68	54
			1712	22	6	2	2	-	1	15	3	2	6	3	1	1	-	64	49
			1713	25	6	3	2	-	1	16	3	2	7	3	1	1	-	70	54
			1714	24	6	3	2	-	1	15	3	2	7	3	1	1	-	68	53
			1715	22	6	3	1	-	1	15	3	2	6	3	1	1	-	64	49

Table 3. (contd)

Emperor	Vizekapellmeister	Kapellmeister		Strings				Wind							Acc./Perc.			Totals	
				Vn	Vc	Vne	Gmb	Btn	Ct	Trp	Trb	Hn	Ob	Bn	Ct	Thb	Tmp		**
Charles VI	Caldara	Fux	1716	22	6	3	1	-	1	15	3	2	6	3	1	1	-	64	49
			1717	23	6	3	1	-	1	15	3	2	6	3	1	1	-	65	50
			1718	23	6	3	1	-	1	15	3	2	5	3	1	1	-	64	49
			1719	23	7	2	1	-	1	13	3	1	5	3	1	1	-	61	48
			1720	23	7	2	1	-	1	14	4	1	5	3	1	1	2	65	51
			1721	30	7	3	1	1	2	18	4	1	9	4	1	1	2	84	66
			1722	30	6	4	1	1	2	17	3	1	8	5	1	1	2	82	65
			1723	30	6	3	1	1	2	17	3	1	8	4	1	1	1	79	62
			1724	30	6	3	1	1	2	15	3	1	8	4	1	1	1	77	62
			1725	29	7	3	1	1	2	14	4	1	7	5	1	1	1	77	63
			1726	29	7	3	1	1	2	14	4	1	7	4	1	1	1	76	62
			1727	32	7	3	1	1	2	14	4	1	6	4	1	1	1	78	64
			1728	30	7	3	1	1	2	13	4	1	5	4	1	1	1	74	61
			1729	30	7	3	1	1	2	13	4	1	5	4	-	1	1	73	60
			1730	31	7	3	1	1	2	14	4	1	5	4	-	1	2	76	62
			1731	30	7	3	1	1	2	14	4	1	5	4	-	1	3	76	62
			1732	30	7	3	1	1	2	13	4	1	6	4	-	1	3	76	63
			1733	26	7	3	1	1	2	13	4	1	6	5	-	-	2	71	58
			1734	24	7	3	1	1	2	13	4	1	6	4	-	-	2	68	55
			1735	24	7	3	1	1	2	13	4	1	6	4	-	-	2	68	55
			1736	27	7	3	1	1	2	13	4	1	6	4	-	-	2	71	58
			1737	27	7	3	1	1	2	13	4	1	6	4	-	-	2	71	58
			1738	26	7	3	-	1	2	13	4	1	6	4	-	-	1	68	55
			1739	25	7	3	-	1	2	13	4	-	6	4	-	-	1	66	53
			1740	25	7	3	-	1	2	12	4	-	6	4	-	-	-	64	52
Maria Theresa	Predieri	Reutter	1741	17	4	3	-	-	1	6	5	-	3	3	-	1	-	43	37
			1742	17	4	3	-	-	1	6	5	-	3	3	-	1	-	43	37
			1743	17	4	3	-	-	1	6	5	-	3	3	-	1	-	43	37
			1744	16	4	3	-	-	1	6	5	-	3	3	-	1	-	42	36
			1745	16	4	3	-	-	1	7	5	-	3	3	-	1	-	43	36
			1746	16	3	3	-	-	1	7	5	-	3	3	-	1	2	44	37
			1747	15	3	3	-	-	-	7	5	-	3	3	-	1	2	42	35
			1748	15	3	3	-	-	-	6	5	-	3	3	-	1	2	41	35
			1749	13	2	3	-	-	-	6	5	-	3	3	-	1	2	38	32
			1750	13	2	3	-	-	-	6	5	-	3	3	-	1	2	38	32
			1751	13	2	3	-	-	-	4	5	-	3	3	-	1	2	36	32
			1752	13	2	3	-	-	-	4	5	-	3	3	-	1	2	36	32
			1753	12	2	3	-	-	-	4	5	-	3	2	-	1	2	34	30
			1754	11	2	3	-	-	-	4	5	-	3	2	-	1	2	33	29
			1755	9	2	3	-	-	-	3	5	-	3	2	-	1	2	30	27
			1756	9	2	3	-	-	-	4	5	-	3	1	-	-	2	29	25
			1757	9	2	2	-	-	-	4	5	-	3	1	-	-	2	28	24
			1758	9	2	2	-	-	-	4	5	-	3	1	-	-	2	28	24
			1759	9	2	2	-	-	-	3	5	-	3	1	-	-	2	27	24
			1760	9	2	2	-	-	-	3	5	-	2	1	-	-	2	26	23
			1761	7	2	1	-	-	-	3	4	-	1	1	-	-	1	20	17
			1762	6	2	1	-	-	-	3	4	-	1	1	-	-	1	19	16
			1763	4	1	1	-	-	-	-	3	-	1	1	-	-	1	12	12
			1764	3	1	1	-	-	-	-	2	-	1	1	-	-	-	9	9
			1765	3	-	1	-	-	-	-	2	-	1	1	-	-	-	8	8
			1766	3	-	1	-	-	-	-	2	-	1	1	-	-	-	8	8
			1767	7	-	1	-	-	-	-	3	-	1	1	-	-	-	13	13
			1768	6	-	1	-	-	-	-	2	-	-	1	-	-	-	10	10
			1769	6	-	-	-	-	-	-	2	-	-	1	-	-	-	9	9
			1770	6	-	-	-	-	-	-	2	-	-	1	-	-	-	9	9

Konzertmeister included in totals from 1698 to 1740
**Totals excluding trumpets

The specific phases in the development of the musical chapel can be examined in five segments: 1682–99; 1700–10; 1711–15; 1716–40, and 1741–70.

1682–1715: the *Hofkapelle* before Caldara

(i) 1682–99

The latter half of the reign of Leopold I (*d*1705) was dominated by the musical direction of Antonio Draghi, who served as *Kapellmeister* from 1682 to 1700. While Draghi's impact on the overall dimensions of the instrumental ensemble can be seen from Table 3 to have been slight, he undoubtedly had some influence on its balance. An immediate effort to strengthen the bass register seems evident from the introduction of a gamba and a second bassoon in 1682 — although from 1686 an additional cello apparently was preferred. The replacement of a deceased trumpeter (Wolfgang Khlepauer, *d*1687) by a second *cornetto*-player in 1689 highlights the longevity of that instrument in Vienna. In Italy by that time the *cornetto*'s importance was already waning, but at the Imperial court it was to continue for several decades as a ripieno instrument (and even to undertake an occasional obbligato) in liturgical compositions.

The appointment in 1697 of Antonio Pancotti as the first *Vizeka-pellmeister* after a long hiatus could have been prompted by Draghi's need for assistance in his declining years. It also could have signalled some recognition of the growing importance of instrumental music, for almost universally in Europe the direction and close supervision of instrumental music fell to a subordinate, whatever his title. This growth in the status of instrumental music at the court seems confirmed by the establishment in 1698 of the position of *Konzertmeister* to which Kilian Reinhardt was appointed. Here the *Hofkapelle* stands in striking contrast to San Marco in Venice where, as we have seen, that same position had been abolished in 1696. During these final years of the century the number of violins was increased to fourteen (including the concertmaster) and the gambas to two. A lutenist and a second theorbist were added in 1697 and there was a substantial increase in the brass section, especially of trumpets. Overall there was an increase from twenty-six instruments in 1696 to thirty-seven in 1699.

(ii) 1700–1710

In general terms, Pancotti's tenure as full *Kapellmeister* (1700–09) seems to have been uneventful, but the appointment of Marc'Antonio Ziani as his assistant in 1700 apparently provided for the continuation of a large *Kapelle*. The duration of the positions of *Vizekapellmeister* (1697–1747) and *Konzertmeister* (1698–1740) coincided with the period during which the number and variety of instrumentalists was greatest and when both the sacred and secular music-making of the *Hofkapelle* were at their height.

Among the striking features of the first decade of the new century (see Table 3) were the augmentation of the string section from twenty-three to thirty-six (including the concertmaster), the introduction of the double bass (*violone*), and the growing tendency to staff the various string positions in even numbers — a possible indication either of divided sections or of alternating responsibilities. While the lute remained a fixed member of the ensemble, the number of theorbos declined,[26] perhaps in response to the growing importance of the double bass and the abundant supply of gambas and cellos.

The oboe, which was introduced into the *Hofkapelle* in 1701, had been used sporadically in Venetian opera over the preceding decade, and its appearance at Vienna may well be attributed to Ziani.[27] The increase in bassoons from one to four may have represented an effort to support the oboes, which numbered seven by 1711. At no time throughout the eighteenth century was the flute ever a member of the *Hofkappelle* ensemble, a curious fact considering that it was called for in several of Caldara's secular cantatas and *feste di camera* and was prevalent in German courts by the third decade of the century.[28] The augmentation of the woodwinds (oboes and bassoons) greatly changed the relative balance among the sections of the orchestra over this decade:

Table 4. *Proportions of the court orchestra, 1700–1710*

Year	Strings	Brass	Woodwind
1700	23	13	1
1710	36	14	11

This broad distribution of timbres substantially mimicks the string-and-wind tradition long associated with Venetian sacred practice.

(iii) 1711–1715

In April 1711, Charles VI succeeded Joseph I as Emperor. Within two years Fux succeeded Ziani as *Vizekapellmeister* and in the winter of 1715 succeeded him as full *Kapellmeister*. Of the musical changes that accompanied these deaths and replacements,[29] the doubling of the trumpets to fourteen was the most striking. This increase must have been requested by the Emperor himself, for the numbers were halved after his passing. These trumpeters and timpanists formed a separate body, the *Musikalische Trompeter und Hör-Paucker*, which, at least for administrative purposes, seems to have been kept more or less distinct from the *Hofkapelle*.[30] As A. Peter Brown points out, so large a number of trumpets does not appear to have been combined with the other instruments — two choirs, each comprising four trumpets and timpani, are the maximum brass scorings found in liturgical or secular music written for the court.[31]

While the number of trombones was only a fraction of that of trumpets, their value, perhaps, was greater. Until the mid-century, trombone obbligatos frequently appeared in sacred vocal works, and for even longer, *ripieno* trombone parts (doubling the altos and tenors of the chorus) remained an essential element of their scorings.

1716–1740: Caldara's era

The remaining years of the reign of Charles VI (1716–40) represent the golden age of the court's *Kapelle* as far as orchestral resources are concerned. They also encompass Caldara's time as *Vizekapellmeister* (1716–36). To this extent the further evolution of the *Kapelle* (see Table 3) can be said to reflect Caldara's administrative influence (especially as Fux's health declined in the late 1720s) and the Emperor's wishes, although in what proportion it is impossible to say. During this period the contours of the court orchestra came to resemble those of the later classical orchestra even though the mid-century years were to bring retrenchment and neglect.[32] Such gentle instruments as the lute, theorbo, and gamba — once vital components but now more and more out of place in this period of modernisation — disappeared through natural attrition in 1728, 1732 and 1737 respectively.

This gradual growth rather than any radical change in direction or balance suggests that in general Caldara exercised his influence to maintain the overall *status quo* while keeping abreast of developments in other orchestral establishments. A closer inspection, however, does reveal some important internal changes which could well be related to Caldara's past experiences. The most significant is the almost fifty per cent increase in the size of the violin section (arguably a Roman trait) between 1716 and 1727. However, in the latter years of this period, this rise in numbers may not represent accurately the realities of the situation. In 1729 ten violinists were excused from customary service because of old age or ill health,[33] but their names remained on the books until their deaths. The impetus for excusing them may well have been to improve the quality of the playing.[34] The discrepancy between the number of violinists who appeared on the official lists and the number most likely to have performed became most acute between 1730 and 1740:

Table 5. *Violinists in the court orchestra*

Year	Number of violinists on official roster	Number of violinists performing
1730	31	21
1731	30	21
1732	30	21
1733	26	20
1734	24	19
1735	24	19
1736	27	22
1737	27	22
1738	26	22
1739	25	22
1740	25	22

The year 1721, in which the spectacular increase in violins from twenty-three to thirty boosted the orchestra to its maximum size, seems to have been especially remarkable. The *cornetti*, for example, were increased permanently to two. This may only indicate that it was now considered appropriate to use them in pairs, as was generally the case with oboes and clarinets elsewhere. But it may also be seen as a move to reinforce more strongly the *ripieno* soprano line in liturgical music against the weightier violin tone. Bassoons, too, seem to have been increased in 1721 to at least four — perhaps to provide better support for the oboes which were themselves increased to peak figures between 1721 and 1726. The number of trumpet players also reached an all time high, with eighteen being listed in 1721, although their numbers were to fluctuate between twelve and fourteen over the next fifteen years.

If we exclude the baryton, lute and theorbo, the proportions of the court orchestra during this period show, on the one hand, an increasing ratio of strings to brass instruments, and on the other, an almost static relationship between woodwind and strings:

Table 6. *Proportions of the court orchestra, 1716–1740*

Year	Strings	Brass	Percussion	Woodwind
1716	32	21	0	9
1721	41	25	2	13
1736	38	20	2	10
1740	35	18	0	10

The mingling of different nationalities among court musicians was also at its most extreme during the 1720s. Excluding Fux, the Italians Badia (1712–38), Conti (1713–32), Porsile (1720–40) and Palotta (1733–41/58) dominated the roster of court composers until 1740. Even after that date the responsibility for composition was transferred only gradually to Austrians and Germans. However, the majority of instrumental performers hired around 1720 were of German and Austrian extraction. Some sixty-eight of the instrumentalists on the roster for 1721 had German or Austrian surnames. Between 1713 and 1740 there was an average of thirteen instrumentalists with Italian surnames at any given time; their numbers peaked at fifteen in 1732 but dropped dramatically to six in 1741, when Maria Theresa made her first moves to reduce the *Hofkapelle's* personnel. It is perhaps natural to imagine that the Italians were engaged chiefly as violinists but, in fact, this was not at all the case. Italians appeared in every section of the orchestra and lacked association only with the gamba, lute and horn. The sole baryton player was an Italian as were four of the six theorbists. Over the entire ninety-year span from 1680 to 1770, Italians accounted for about fifteen per cent of all players. German and Austrian violinists were greatly valued, to judge from their numbers, in the reign of Charles VI, despite the Emperor's well-known respect for Italian virtuosi such as Antonio Vivaldi. When Ferdinand Grossauer was hired as a violinist in 1732, it was noted that he was 'a very good virtuoso with a good bow, good intonation, perfect tempo, and a musical ear.'[35]

Polish and Slavic surnames are found sparingly in the roster between 1706 and 1740, and French surnames appear from 1697 to 1755. With one exception the Polish and Slavic musicians were trumpeters: the French members included three bassoonists, two trumpeters, and the sole lutenist of the orchestra.[36]

The actual deployment of the available instruments is perhaps best illustrated in the sacred music of this period. For the most part it displays the greatest diversity of scorings (more so even than the court operas) and it represents the most substantial surviving repertoire that can be dirctly linked with the *Hofkapelle* over the first half of the century.

In large measure its diverse scorings stem from the many *concertante* and cantata settings of the liturgical texts produced by Fux and Caldara. In both composers' output the SATB chorus areas were reinforced by *cornetto*, alto and tenor trombones, and bassoon respectively; violins, usually independent, were occupied with figuration patterns although in substantial fugal movements they joined the *cornetto* in doubling the soprano line. The *concertante* passages for the vocal soloists within the chorus movements usually were accompanied by obbligatos for the violins, occasionally joined by the viola. In the independent aria movements, violins, trombones, bassoons and trumpets (*clarini*) were all possible obbligato instruments. In general, the obbligato was limited to one melodic instrument but pairs of trombones (alto and tenor) and trumpets were not uncommon. Two solo violins were especially favoured in smaller liturgical works such as antiphons and offertories. Here, in the often extensive ritornellos framing the solo voice lines, the influence of the trio sonata seems quite apparent.[37] The appearance of brass and timpani was governed more by the liturgical status of the day than by considerations of the text. The *solenne* settings (of which there appear to be more by Caldara than by Fux), distinguished by the addition of two or four trumpets and timpani, were reserved for high feast-days and special commemorations.[38]

With more than one hundred settings of the Ordinary of the mass and, perhaps, twice as many settings of Psalm and miscellaneous liturgical texts to his credit, Caldara provided the bulk of the *Hofkapelle's* repertoire. It is not too much to say that in the obbligato parts which abound in this immense output, his fluent and stylistic writing for solo instruments found its greatest expression.[39]

The ubiquitous obbligatos for violin (or violins) could accompany any of the three upper voices. Cello or bassoon obbligatos, far fewer in number, usually were reserved for the solo bass voice, while trombone obbligatos accompanied either an alto or tenor soloist. The alto trombone was particularly favoured and Caldara's obbligatos for that instrument ranged from the remarkably mobile and extensive writing which accompanies the alto and tenor soloists at 'Jesu spes paenitentibus' in the Hymn *Jesu dulcis memoria* (*c*1721) to the restrained and introspective phrases of the 'Et incarnatus' (for alto solo) in the *Missa Commemorationis* (1729) (Ex. 1).

Bravura display was reserved for the trumpet obbligatos which usually accompanied soprano or bass solos. In these the influence of the text

Example 1
(a) Caldara *Jesu dulcis memoria* bars 75–93
(b) Caldara *Missa Commemorationis* 'Et incarnatus'

Ex. 1 (contd)

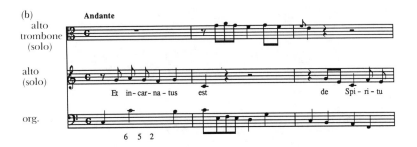

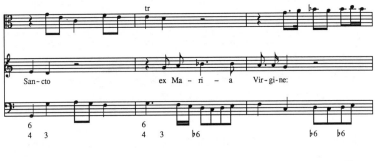

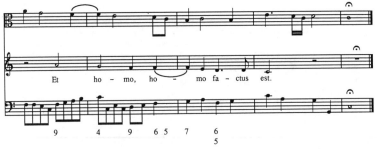

became more obvious with Caldara using the *clarino* to reinforce sentiments of rejoicing, victory or majestic power. Doubtless, the famed abilities of several of the court trumpeters inspired many of his obbligatos, just as they stimulated Fux and, later, Georg Reutter d.J. The dazzling range and exhausting phrases of the obbligato in the 'Quoniam tu solus' (for soprano solo) of Caldara's *Missa in spei resurrectionis* (1736) show this type of writing to perfection (Ex. 2). But we can only speculate about its performer — Franz Josef Holland, Johann Hainisch or the *Ober-Trompeter*, Franz Küffel, himself.

Example 2. Caldara *Missa in spei resurrectionis* 'Quoniam tu solus' bars 1–25

Ex. 2 (contd)

Noteworthy in their own way are the composite obbligato movements. These involve several instruments and singers in succession, a new instrument being introduced at each change of the vocal soloist. One of the most complex examples occurs in Caldara's 1736 setting of Psalm 111/112, *Beatus vir qui timet Dominum*. Four soloists — soprano, alto, tenor, and bass, accompanied by obbligato trumpet, alto trombone, violins *unisoni*, and bassoon respectively — appear in the course of a single movement which encompasses verses 5 to 8 of the text. These instruments are shown off with idiomatic passages which are, except for the trumpet's opening phrases, thematically independent of the vocal material (Ex. 3).

Caldara also readily accommodated the available resources of the court orchestra in his operas and oratorios, but the kaleidoscope of instrumental colour seen in the compact liturgical scores is far less noticeable in these more extensive compositions. For Vienna alone Caldara composed some

Example 3. Caldara *Beatus vir qui timet* 'Jucundus homo' bars 1–15, 45–54, 65–75, and 92–99.

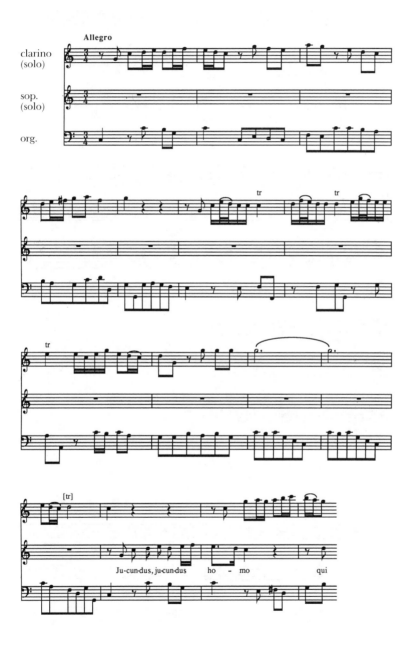

Ex. 3 (contd)

Ex. 3 (contd)

Ex. 3 (contd)

thirty-four operas and twenty-five oratorios during the last twenty years of his life, and he wrote several other works in both categories for performance in the nearer reaches of Austria. The string orchestra, with its upper instruments combined in various ways (two violins and viola, two violins without viola, violins *unisoni* with viola, and violins *unisoni* without viola) provided the bulk of the accompaniments in both genres. Indeed, in some operas, *buffa* and *seria* alike, such as *I disingannati* (1729) and *Adriano in Siria* (1732), the concerted string tone was entirely unrelieved outside of the overture. Nevertheless, we can observe a steady, though not lavish, employment of obbligato instruments in the operas and oratorios of Caldara's Viennese years. Among such works we may note[40]:

Table 7. *Obbligato instruments used by Caldara*

Year	Work		Obbligato Instrument(s)
1717	*Il Tiridate ossia La verità nell'inganno*	(opera)	cello
1719	*Lucio Papirio dittatore*	(opera)	*chalumeau*; violin
1720	*Assalonne*	(oratorio)	*clarini*; violins
1721	*Ormisda, re di Persia*	(opera)	oboe and bassoon; cello; *chalumeau*; *clarino*
1722	*Il Re del dolore*	(oratorio)	trombone
1722	*Scipione nelle Spagne*	(opera)	mandolin
1723	*Ester*	(oratorio)	*tromba*
1723	*La contesa de'numi*	(opera)	*clarino*
1724	*Gianguir*	(opera)	*tromba*
1724	*Euristeo*	(opera)	*chalumeau*; flute; bassoon; violin (this opera was performed by members of the nobility)
1726	*I due dittatori*	(opera)	*trombe*; bassoons
1727	*Imeneo*	(opera)	*chalumeaux*
1729	*Naboth*	(oratorio)	trombone and bassoon
1730	*La passione di Gesù Cristo*	(oratorio)	trombone
1732	*Sedecia*	(oratorio)	*salterio*; viola da gamba
1733	*Gerusalemme convertita*	(oratorio)	*chalumeau*; trombones; bassoon
1734	*San Pietro in Cesarea*	(oratorio)	*chalumeau*: trombone
1736	*Il Temistocle*	(opera)	*clarino*

In contrast to his liturgical scoring (both the oboe and *chalumeau* are absent), Caldara especially favoured woodwind instruments in obbligato roles in his operas and oratorios. As we have seen, the *chalumeau* does not even figure in the official list of the *Hofkapelle* members at this time. Yet its florid obbligatos in *Gerusalemme convertita* and *San Pietro in Cesarea* certainly presuppose the availability of a player (possibly an oboist) of some distinction (Ex. 4). The absence of oboe and *chalumeau* from Caldara's liturgical scores was matched, in reverse fashion, by the exclusion of trombones from his opera scores.

Example 4. Caldara *San Pietro in Cesarea* 'O croce! o morte!' bars 1–8

The apparent emphasis on woodwind instruments in the secular field should not be permitted to obscure the fact that the string trio sonata continued to thrive at the Imperial court. Friedrich W. Riedel calls attention to nineteen such works by Fux in the Austrian National Library, as well as to the fact that some of Caldara's trio sonatas (which in general were composed before his departure from Venice in 1700) continued to be recopied for performance in Vienna into the reign of Maria Theresa.[41] Certain members of the *Hofkapelle* orchestra, notably the violinists Johann Georg Hintereder (employed from 1721 to 1762) and Filippo Salviati (employed from 1727 to 1762), are themselves survived by trio sonatas ascribed to the 1730s.[42] Such works appear to have been used mainly in the Mass, particularly (as they were in Venice) at the Gradual. This general nostalgia for Venetian-inspired practices is evident, too, from the long list of works by Caldara and Ziani that continued to be performed well into the 1740s and from the striking fact that as late as 1740, a *Messa à 5* by Legrenzi (1626–90), who had no direct connection with Vienna, was offered during Lent.[43]

1741–1770: the *Hofkapelle* after the Golden Age

Nothing throws the character of the *Kapelle* of the era of Fux, Caldara and Charles VI into sharper relief than an overview of the *Kapelle* that followed the death of the Emperor in 1740. No sooner was Charles VI in his grave than dramatic changes took place. Almost immediately his daughter, the new Empress, Maria Theresa, instituted a policy of retrenchment of such magnitude that little other than music of chamber proportions could have been possible on all but the most important of state occasions. In variety of instruments and in numbers of performers the *Hofkapelle*'s ensemble was severely reduced (see Table 3) as baroque exuberance and ostentation were quickly shed by a court preoccupied with wars of succession. Not only were the violins immediately cut by one-third and the violoncellos and trumpets by one-half, but their numbers continued to decline in succeeding years. The position of *Konzertmeister* was eliminated and with it went the special attention that had been lavished on the orchestral side of the *Hofkapelle*. The baryton was discontinued, although the theorbo was reinstated in its place. The cornettist who died in 1740 was not replaced, and on the death of the remaining player (J. A. Christ) in 1746, this long-established *ripieno* instrument vanished forever from the court orchestra. Timpanists reappear[44] in Köchel's list in 1746 just when the number of trumpet players was momentarily boosted. But both timpanists had departed again by 1764, a year after the last three trumpeters, a pitiful remnant of Charles VI's glorious group, had been pensioned off.

There were fewest changes in the trombone, oboe and bassoon sections, where maintenance of pre–1740 staffing levels gave them a proportionally larger role in musical affairs throughout the 1750s. But even these areas fell away during the next decade, with the trombones, the mainstay of the *Hofkapelle*'s wind section for nearly a century, being the last to succumb.

The most conspicuous figure in the musical direction of the *Kapelle* at this time was the Italian-born Luca Antonio Predieri (1688-1767) who was named *Vizekapellmeister* in 1739 and *Kapellmeister* in 1746. He shared the overall direction of the *Kapelle* with the younger Georg Reutter, until Reutter assumed full direction from 1769 until his own death three years later. The Italian composers who still remained (Matteo Palotta to 1758, and Giuseppe Bonno to 1774) were completely undistinguished. Only Georg Christian Wagenseil, Court Composer from 1739, brought a spark of inspiration to the output.

It is especially odd that Vienna's instrumentalists kept dwindling at a time when, in the German *Hofkapellen*, the trend was entirely in the other direction. The total number of stringed instruments at various courts provides ready comparison with Vienna: in many northern courts their numbers greatly increased; in Vienna they dropped by half:[45]

Table 8. *Totals of stringed instruments in use at Vienna, Berlin, Mannheim*

Place	Number of Strings			
	1712	1720	1754	1756
Vienna	32	33	16	14
Berlin	18	n.a.	22	n.a.
Mannheim	n.a.	19	n.a.	30

In Dresden, a very significant increase in the number of strings preceded the arrival of Johann Pisendel as director of the orchestra (1730-1755):

Table 9. *Totals of stringed instruments in use at Dresden and Vienna*

Place	Number of Strings			
	1709	1719	1734	1736
Dresden	11	22	23	27
Vienna	36	33	35	38

The continued absence of the flute from the Viennese court is a further element of contrast with the German *Hofkapellen*, where it was in almost universal use. It had been incorporated into the Dresden orchestra as early as 1709.

The proportion of oboes to bassoons was roughly equal in all the German-speaking courts by the 1750s, although their combined strength relative to the total resources varied considerably from place to place. However, the absence of the horn in Vienna after 1738 was not matched elsewhere. Two was the norm for most court orchestras from the middle of the century; the Mannheim court had four in 1756. Statistics for the trumpets are somewhat elusive, since nearly everywhere trumpeters were engaged separately from ensemble instrumentalists. The largest body reported outside Vienna in the first half of the century was thirteen, recorded at Dresden in 1734.

From his studies of the orchestra in the classical period, Neal Zaslaw has deduced that 'no systematic pattern of growth in the size of orchestras' can be discerned for the period 1774 to 1796. But he does point out that on the basis of employing institutions, some norms emerge for the numbers of players of particular categories of instruments: thus, while private orchestras averaged seven violinists, church orchestras averaged eleven, court orchestras twelve, opera and theatre orchestras fourteen, and concert orchestras nineteen.[46] This puts the slow but continual decline of the Viennese court orchestra in a somewhat odd light. Nevertheless, this same decline may have allowed for the final consolidation of the diverse consorts of the Viennese orchestra into the sections of a single integrated body.

*   *   *   *   *

The particular course of Caldara's life is unique in relation to the history of the Baroque orchestra. His years of residence in Venice and Vienna coincided with the peak decades of the ensembles attached to the institutions by whom he was employed. (The plural traditions of Rome do not permit such generalizations but even there an element of the phenomenon pertained.) In both places, the underlying reason for these periods of instrumental *largesse* seems to have been primarily political.

From Table 2 we can see how dramatically the numbers of the orchestra at San Marco increased in the 1680s when the Holy League was formed and when Venice's last great naval commander, Francesco Morosini, brought fresh glory to its waning image. This cultural pride was reflected in the strength of the Basilica's orchestra throughout Morosini's dogeship (1688-1694) — the very years of Caldara's employment. The decline, political and cultural, was equally dramatic. By 1720 the instrumental force had dwindled to pre-1680 figures. About a quarter of a century later, a corresponding curve can be deduced from the statistics for the *Hofkapelle* in Table 3. Like its Venetian counterpart, this curve is also contained within a forty-year period (1701 to 1741) and its climax, in the reign of Charles VI, coincides with a similar period of cultural pride based on international stature.

Caldara was fortunate enough to have participated in both these peak phases. Prepared through his experience of the first, he was able to take full advantage of and make his own particular contribution to the second.

Notes

¹ Eleanor Selfridge-Field *Venetian Instrumental Music from Gabrieli to Vivaldi* (Oxford, 1975) p. 183.

² Ursula Kirkendale (*Antonio Caldara: Sein Leben und seine venezianisch-römischen Oratorien* (Graz-Köln, 1966) p. 25) suggests the possibility of a link between Caldara and Domenico Gabrielli, the Bolognese cellist and opera composer. It is a tantalizing one, for the warmth, ingenuity, and poetic sensibility of Caldara's music are in a general sense prefigured more in Gabrielli's works, which were terminated by his untimely death in 1690, than they are in the methodical works of Giovanni Legrenzi, who is alleged without foundation to have been Caldara's teacher.

³ Kirkendale *op.cit.*, p. 25.

⁴ Selfridge-Field *op.cit.*, p. 182.

⁵ The other members were Lorenzo Novelloni and Bernardo Cortella (Selfridge-Field *op.cit.*, pp. 302–3). Caldara's only sets of trio sonatas come from these years: *Suonate a tre* [da chiesa] ... *Opera Prima* (Venezia, 1693) and *Suonate da camera* ... *Opera seconda* (Venezia, 1699).

⁶ These numbers are based on data extracted in recent years from the records of the Procuratori de Supra in the Venetian State Archives.

All lists of figures of this type may vary with (a) the particular records consulted and (b) the way in which they are interpreted. Records were kept prolifically but inconsistently. In particular, the following factors must be arbitrarily resolved in order to form composite lists.

First, records invariably give names and dates on which service was initiated. They are less consistent in identifying the instruments played (these may be omitted or may be transcribed differently from one year to the next) and the date at which service was terminated. Dates of termination can sometimes be deduced from later hiring records, but obviously such deductions are not as reliable in assembling a composite picture as hard facts.

Second, some players, especially eighteenth-century performers, played two instruments but obviously not at the same time (which a literal interpretation of such a statistic might ludicrously suggest). Some positions in early orchestras were rather generic. There were continuo players who alternatively performed trombone or cello obbligatos and *violone* parts. The Viennese did not distinguish between violinists and violists in their records.

Third, the identification of instruments is not always clear. Scribes were not musicians; thus one scribe's *violone* and another's *violone grosso* might indicate the same instrument. The situation is compounded by the many ephemeral string instruments, such as the viola d'amore, that appeared briefly during the period considered here.

Fourth, records were compiled for officialdom, not for historians. Changes in practice often preceded official written acknowledgement by years, if not by decades. According to Austrian documents, instrumentalists played until they died or became incapacitated, whereas in actual practice younger apprentices, who in an era of change may have played more modern instruments, took their place.

Fifth, in many places including Venice, it was common practice for the total instrumental force to represent double the number of persons who performed on a given occasion: usually the *cappella* was served by alternating platoons and on only a few days in the year by all of the music staff.

[7] A list of all the *piffari* is given in the Italian translation of my *Venetian Instrumental Music (La musica strumentale a Venezia da Gabrieli a Vivaldi* Rome, 1980), pp. 288–9. A clear indication of the growing importance of strings is that some of the last official *piffari* were better known as cellists and violinists.

[8] Selfridge-Field *op.cit.,* p. 21.

[9] Over these years the orchestra came to admit a progressively greater number of string instruments, so that by 1766 its composition was:
12 violins
6 violas
4 cellos
3 double basses
4 oboes or flutes
4 trumpets or horns
Numbers derived from ASV, Procuratori de Supra, Term., Reg. 156, ff.93^V–98.

[10] In Mantua, Caldara was in no way cut off from Venetian musical life. He continued to have his operas produced in Venice and his compatriot, Marc'Antonio Ziani (who was to be his predecessor at the Viennese court) had taken up a post at the ducal theatre and the allied church of Santa Barbara as early as 1686. See also Reinhard G. Pauly and Brian W. Pritchard 'Antonio Caldara's *Credo à 8 Voci*: a composition for the Duke of Mantua?' pp. 51–3.

[11] GB-Lbm: Add. MS 31550, and US-Wc: M2021 C25C6 Case. The first modern edition, edited by Brian W. Pritchard, was published by Harmonia Uitgave, Hilversum, in 1975.

[12] A-Wgm: A326, *Gloria* in B-flat; A-Wgm: A327, *Gloria* in a minor; A-Wn: Cod. 18981, *Gloria* in C; and 'Cantate a 1. e ll. Voci Con Tromba e Flauti, e sensa. Del Illustr. Sig. Caldara, Polaroli, Albinoni, Marini e altri Autorye ... A Amsterdam, Aux dépens d'Estienne Roger ... [n.d.]'

[13] Adriano Cavicchi 'Una sinfonia inedita di Arcangelo Corelli nello stile del concerto grosso venticinque anni prima dell opera VI' *Chigiana XX* (1963) p. 45.

[14] See Owen Jander 'Concerto Grosso Instrumentation in Rome in the 1660s and 1670s' *Journal of the American Musicological Society* XXI (1968). The various uses of the *concerto grosso* and *concertino* are discussed on pp. 178f.

[15] Hans Joachim Marx 'Die Musik am Hofe Pietro Kardinal Ottobonis unter Arcangelo Corelli' *Analecta Musicologica* V (1968) p. 126.

[16] *Op.cit.,* p. 129.

[17] *Op.cit.,* p. 130.

[18] *Op.cit.,* p. 143.

[19] *Op.cit.,* p. 145. There were seven trumpets and three lutes, with a corresponding reduction in the number of bowed string instruments.

[20] Kirkendale *op.cit.,* pp. 353-55. They did not all perform on the same dates.

[21] *Ibid.,* pp. 61f.

[22] GB-Lam: Ms.46. The 'Numero de'Stromenti e Voci' have been added on f1^V of the full score which is in the hand of Francesco Lanciani, one of Ruspoli's principal copyists. Brian W. Pritchard kindly called my attention to this source.

[23] D-brd-MÜS: Hs. 770. This score is also in Francesco Lanciani's hand.

[24] The data on pay were not investigated statistically because of the apparent discontinuities in the Austrian currency system during this period and the likelihood that pay increases were not recorded consistently in the data given by Köchel.

[25] Recent readings of the documents consulted by Köchel, and of numerous additional archival series by both Hermine Williams and A. Peter Brown, have produced numbers slightly at variance with Köchel's. The task of reconciling these variations definitively cannot be appropriately attempted here; Table 2 is of value for the overview it gives of a century of orchestral development at Vienna. Its compilation has required decisions that occasionally exceed the limits of the information available (e.g. uncertainties of tenure or responsibility, of multiple responsibilities, and of variant spellings and thus identity). Also, as the figures given are summaries by year, they occasionally yield for a year in which a position is turned over, an artificially high reading, since two names pertain to that year but only one name to specific months within it. Where the succession is obvious from Köchel's records, an appropriate adjustment has been made in the Table. Those interested in the careers of particular musicians, however, should refer directly to Köchel's writings and the original materials on which they are based.

[26] However, the standard of playing certainly did not decline, thanks to the skill of the remaining theorbist, Francesco Bartolomeo Conti, whom J. J. Quantz regarded as one of the greatest players of all times. Conti was appointed theorbist in 1701, and on being made a *Hofcompositor* in 1713, combined both duties. His prowess as a player may have shifted the theorbo from its fundamental role into the domain of the obbligato instruments.

[27] Ziani also scores for the *chalumeau* in his opera *Caio Pompilio*, performed at the court in 1704.

[28] Its absence from the *Hofkapelle* may, perhaps, be attributable to religious conservatism: papal Rome consistently frowned on recorders and flutes on account of the association with lasciviousness alleged by ancient writers.

[29] The figures given by Hermine Williams in the 'Introduction' to her edition of *Nine Sinfonie* by Francesco Bartolomeo Conti in *The Symphony 1720–1840* Series B,II (New York, 1983), are based on a fresh reading of archival documents of the *Hofkapelle*. In particular, she calls attention to a court decree of September, 1711, which sought to reduce the instrumental staff. According to her figures, its principal results were to reduce the number of oboes from nine in April, 1712, to four in December, 1712, and bassoons from four to three.

[30] This may account for the absence of timpanists from Köchel's list until 1720. According to the *Hof-Calender* both J. G. Denk (Denck) and M. Hellmann (Köchel's earliest timpanists) had already given years of service in this capacity prior to 1720.

[31] See A. Peter Brown 'Caldara's trumpet music for the Imperial celebrations of Charles VI and Elisabeth Christine', p. 43. Brown takes his figures from the series of *Hof-Calender*.

[32] The horns departed in 1738; the oboes had vanished by 1768. The timpani which made their debut in Köchel's list in 1720 disappear from it between 1740 and 1746. However, performance dates show that a number of liturgical compositions which required timpani were performed during these years. A younger Maximilian Hellmann (son or nephew of the Hellmann mentioned in Note 30) who was appointed timpanist in 1746, had been 'Cimbalist' from 1740 to 1746 and presumably combined both roles. This seems confirmed by Köchel's list for the period 1756–1771, which names Hellmann in both categories.

[33] They are named in J. J. Fux's petition for their release (31 December, 1729) which is reproduced in Köchel *Fux ...* p.424; see also the Appendix.

[34] Although as *Hofkapellmeister* Fux petitioned for the retirement of these players from active service, he may not have instigated the move. Andreas Amiller, who was appointed *Konzertmeister* in April, 1729, after the death of Reinhardt, may

have begun an overhaul of the *Hofkapelle*'s proficiency and suggested possible retirements to Fux.

[35] Köchel *Fux . . .* p. 249.

[36] Many instrumentalists are named among the musical staff who accompanied Charles VI to Prague for his coronation in 1723 in Paul Nettl 'Das Prager Quartierbuch des Personals der Krönungsoper 1723' *Mitteilungen der Kommission für Musikforschung* 8 (Wien, 1957). I should like to thank Neal Zaslaw for calling my attention to this source.

[37] Only a small portion of Fux's liturgical music and even less of Caldara's have been published. The reader is especially referred to the volumes that have appeared in *Johann Joseph Fux: Sämtliche Werke* (Kassel-Graz, 1959–   ).

[38] See Friedrich W. Riedel *Kirchenmusik am Hofe Karls VI (1711–40)* (München-Salzburg, 1977) for a comprehensive survey of the liturgical protocol at the Imperial court.

[39] Throughout his life Caldara cultivated the virtue of the solo instrument. His Viennese *oeuvre* includes a large number of pedagogical works for cello, a handful of sonatas for violin and cello, and at the very end of his life a set of sonatas for violoncello and continuo. For a bibliography of Caldara's instrumental works, see Selfridge-Field *op.cit.*, pp.183f.

[40] This inventory is based in part on Robert S. Freeman *Opera Without Drama: Currents of Change in Italian Opera, 1675–1725* (Ann Arbor, 1981) pp. 331–38.

[41] Riedel *op.cit.*, pp. 216–20.

[42] *Ibid.*, p. 218. However, wind instruments were also occasionally employed in the trio sonata. In some of Fux's sonatas a trombone or a bassoon is substituted for the fundamental string instrument.

[43] *Ibid.*, p. 247.

[44] But see Note 32.

[45] These figures are based on the tables given by Heinz Becker 'Orchester, B. Das neuere Orchester' *Die Musik in Geschichte und Gegenwart* 10 (Kassel 1962), following col. 192.

[46] Neal Zaslaw 'Toward the Revival of the Classical Orchestra' *Proceedings of the Royal Musical Association* 103 (1976–7) p. 179.

Appendix

Instrumentalists at the *Hofkapelle* in Vienna, 1680–1770

Abendt (Abend)[1]	Andr.	1686	1729	violin
Adam	Jos.	1767	1771*	violin
Adò	Pietro	1720	1762	cello
Alber	Joh.	1706	1740	violin
Alber	Paul	1701	1732**	violin
Alborea	Franz	1721	1739	cello
Amiller	Andr.	1729	1740	cello (*Konzertmeister*)
Angermayr	Joh. Ign.	1721	1732	violin
Angropoli	Nicolo	1713	1732**	violin
Apuzzo	Domen.	1713	1740	violone
Baufils	Joh.	1705	1711	bassoon
Bayer (Peyer)	Ferd. Barth.	1691	1714	violin
Bayer (Peyer)	Joh Ernst.	1733	1762	trumpet
Berti	Marc. Ant.	1721	1740	baryton
Bon	Thom.	1698	1717	trumpet
Bonn	Joh. Franz	1720	1720	trumpet
Boog	Andr.	1720	1763	trombone
Boor (Pohr)	Andre	1697	1728	lute
Cammermayer	Franz	1741	1760	violone
Castro	Giusto a	1680	1682	violin
Christ	Joh. Ad.	1738	1746	cornetto
Christian	Christian	1698	1712	trombone
Christian	Hanns Georg	1702	1721	trombone
Christian	Leopold	1679	1730	trombone
Christian	Leop. (jr.)	1712	1760	trombone
Christian ⎫[2]	Leop. Ferd.	1736	1771*	trombone
Christian ⎭	Ferd.	1756	1771*	trombone
Clementi	Orazio	1663	1708	theorbo
Conti [3]	Franc. B.	⎧1701	1703	theorbo
		⎩1711	1732	theorbo

Crammer	Joh.	1705	1740	cello
Crammer	Mich. Jac.	1708	1713	violin
Czizek	Joh.	1711	1714	trumpet
Denk	Joh. Gottfr.	1720	1732	timpani
Denk (Denckh) (Denck)	Jos. Karl	1713	1761	violin
Denk	Karl Jos.	1737	1770	violin
Denk	Leop.	1746	1760	timpani
Drenger	Karl Fr.	1725	1745	cello
Engl	Joh. Reinh.	1698	1724	trumpet
Fasching	Jos.	1712	1732**	violin
Fasser	Franz	1713	1714	oboe
Fichtel (Fichtl)	Ferd. Friedr.	1705	1722	violone
Fontana	Joh. Friedr.	1670	1707	trombone
Fontana	Silv. Ang.	1709	1711	trombone
Franck	Jos.	1702	1713	violin
Franckh)[4]	Jac. Alb.	1712	1733**	violin
Frankh)	Joh. Alb.	1690	1733**	violin
Freitig	Andreas	1701	1718	violone
Friedrich	Joh. Jac.	1725	1741	bassoon
Friedrich	Franz Phil.	1740	1771*	bassoon
Gabrieli	Joh.	1705	1740	oboe
Gazzaroli (Gazzaroll)	Zach.	1732	1759	oboe
Giegl	Karl	1741	1767	violin
Gigl	Sebast.	1712	1740	violin
Glaetzl	Franz	1701	1717	oboe
Glaetzl	Roman	1701	1727	oboe
Glaetzl	Xav.	1705	1726	oboe
Gortschek)[5]	Georg	1706	1712	trumpet
Gortschek)	Joh.	1712	1718	trumpet
Griesbacher	Joh. Georg	1721	1740	cornetto
Grossauer	Ferd	1732	1763	violin
Grünauer	Christ.	1721	1721	trumpet
Grünauer	Joh.	1698	1704	trumpet
Hain	Joh. Albr.	1706	1727	violin
Halber (Hälber)	And.	1750	1762	trumpet
Ham	Leop. Ign. von	1706	1710	violin
Hammer	Georg Sigm.	1670	1700	trumpet
Hammer	Joh. Paul	1732	1748	violin
Hammer	Matth. Jos.	1679	1711	trombone
Hanisch (Hainisch)	Joh.	1730	1740	trumpet
Hartmann	Dan. Franz	1721	1760	oboe
Hartmann	Karl	1708	1730**	violin
Hellmann	Jac. Leop.	1730	1740	timpani
Hellmann	Max	1720	1722	timpani
Hellmann	Max	1746	1763	timpani
Hermann	Dav.	1721	1721	oboe
Hien (Hein)	Georg. Rud.	1713	1740	trumpet
Hintereder	Franz	1712	1724	violin
Hintereder	Joh. Georg	1721	1762	violin
Hölzl	Ferd.	1738	1740	trumpet
Hoffer	Joh. Jac.	1698	1737**	violin
Hoffer)[6]	Joh. Jos.	1687	1706	violin
Hoffer)	Jos.	1695	1705	violin
Holland)[7]	Jos.	1741	1747	trumpet
Hollandt)	Franz Jos.	1711	1740	trumpet
Huefnagel	Franz	1707	1714	gamba
Huefnagel	Jos.	1697	1711	gamba
Jesorcka (Jesorka)	Nic.	1706	1737	trumpet
Kammermayr	Franz Karl	1736	1740	violin
Keller	Georg Ign.	1767	1771	violin
Khämpfl	Marx	1680	1699	trumpet

Khlepauer	Wolf	1670	1687	trumpet
Khugler	Burkart	1640	1683	violin
Khugler	Ign. Leop.	1674	1686	violin
Koberer	Rud.	1721	1721	trumpet
Koch	Math.	1713	1740	trumpet
Kreybich	Franz	1738	1762	trumpet
Küefel (Kueffel)	Franz	1711	1754	trumpet
Kündler	Jac.	1700	1708	violin
Laboussier	Peter	1701	1713	trumpet
Lemberger	Ferd.	1698	1740**	violin
Leuttner	Wenzel	1705	1711	oboe
Libano	Leop.	1721	1754**	violin
Lindt	Ferd.	1709	1710	violin
Lorber	Jos.	1705	1724	oboe
Maillard	Ant.	1733	1755	bassoon
Maillard (Mailliard)	Karl	1704	1733	bassoon
Malagodi (Malagotti)	Jos.	1702	1719	cello
Mangiarotti	Siro	1662	1684	bassoon
Marcheselli	Pelegr.	1689	1711	cornetto
Matteis	Nicol.	1700	1737**8	violin
Müller	Franz	1687	1701	violin
Muffat	Gottfr.	1701	1709	violin
Muffat	Joh. Ernst	1730	1746	violin
Nanini	Domen.	1705	1708	violin
Nassoto	Seb.	1701	1733	trumpet
Otto	Friedr.	1712	1718	horn
Pernember	Franz Karl	1727	1754	violin
Pernember	Tob. Andr.	1698	1727	trumpet
Perroni	Giov.	1721	1748	cello
Piani)9	Giov. Ant.	1721	1740	violin
Piani	Jos. Ant.	1741	1760	violin
Piani	Tomaso	1717	1760	violin
Pramayer (Bromayer)	Leop.	1700	1737	cornetto
Pückl	Ferd. Leop.	1686	1711	cello
Pückl (Bickl)	Paul	1650	1688	violin
Ragazzi	Angelo	1713	1740	violin
Rajola	Ant.	1721	1740	cello
Rauch (Ruch) (Ruech)	Mich.	1664	1711	violin
Rebhendl	Joh. Mich.	1713	1723	trumpet
Reinhard	Joh. Franz	1730	1761	violin
Reinhard	Kilian	1698	1729	violin (*Konzertmeister*)
Reinhart (Reinhard)	Franz	1706	1727	violin
Reittenberger	Bened.	1678	1708	cornetto
Ressler (Rössler)	Leop.	1659	1692	violin
Reutter	Georg	1697	1703	theorbo
Riotta (Riotti)	Joh. B.	1667	1683	violin
Römer	Franz	1696	1700	violin
Röttig	Christian	1740	1764	cello
Rosetter)10	Joh. Ant.	1709	1740	violin
Rosetter	Joh. Otto	1712	1740	violin
Rosetter	Otto Joh.	1741	1752	violin
Rossi	Wenzel	1712	1738	horn
Sackh	Joh. G.	1684	1694	violin
Salchi	Joh. Ant.	1682	1711	violin
Salviati	Filippo	1727	1762	violin
Sarao	Joachim	1741	1755	theorbo
Sauli	Fil.	1707	1709	theorbo
Schilling	Joh. Ferd.	1675	1684	violin
Schindler	Joh. G.	1722	1725	bassoon
Schmelzer	Andr. Ant.	1671	1700	violin
Schmelzer	Pet. Clem.	1692	1740**	violin

Schmidbauer	Franz Ant.	1707	1737	gamba
Schmidbauer	Karl	1682	1711	gamba
Schmidt (Schmid)	Math.	1711	1750	trumpet
Schnautz	Ant.	1710	1721	cello
		1721	1756	violone
Schnautz	Franz Peter	1719	1722	cello
		1722	1755	violone
Schnautz	Johann	1752	1768	violone
Schön	Franz	1721	1731	trumpet
Schön	Ludw.	1711	1740	oboe
Schulz	Ludw.	1721	1740	oboe
Schweinberger	Gottfr.	1727	1740	violin
Sesler	Jac. Ernst	1721	1739	trumpet
Stadlmann	Ign.	1736	1753	violin
Steinbruckner	Andr.	1721	1724	trombone
Steinbruckner	Ign.	1725	1762	trombone
Strael	Franz	1702	1710	violin
Strael	Joh. Bon.	1670	1702	violin
Sturmb	Franz Mart.	1708	1739	bassoon
Sturmb	Joh. Fr.	1682	1722	bassoon
Täuber	Matth.	1767	1771*	violin
Tepser	Steph.	1730	1767	trombone
Thomas	Wenzel	1767	1771*	trombone
Timmer	Franz Jos.	1721	1731	violin
Trani	Jos.	1767	1771*	violin
Tuma	Jac.	1767	1771*	violin
Turnovsky (Turnowsky)	Franz	1711	1738	trumpet
Vogl	Leop. Phil.	1731	1737	timpani
Wagenhuber	Andr.	1670	1701	trumpet
Weidlich[11]	Ferd.	1745	1749	trumpet
Weidlich	Ferd.	1756	1758	trumpet
Wenger	Kasp.	1702	1711	violin
Widmann (Widtmann)	Andr.	1721	1767	oboe
Wlach	Thom.	1711	1740	trumpet
Woller	Ferd.	1707	1736	violin
Woller	Franz	1721	1731	violin
Woller	Jac. Jos.	1736	1748	violin
Woschitzka (Woschitka)	Tob.	1721	1752	bassoon
Zächer	Andr.	1700	1707	violin
Zechart	Andr.	1711	1730	trumpet
Zechner	Joh. G.	1710	1711	oboe
Ziller	Bernard	1721	1743	violin

[1] The spelling of names (and variants) and the abbreviations of first names are those given by Köchel in *Die Kaiserliche Hof-Musikkapelle in Wien von 1543 bis 1867*.

[2] Single identity? See Köchel *ibid.*, listings 994, 1106, 1172 and 1249.

[3] Köchel provides different years of appointment in *Fux* ... : 1701–1705, and 1708–32 (the year of death). Hermine Williams (*op.cit.*, p. XV) notes that Conti was principal theorbist 'until 1727, when illness forced him to resign. Conti also held a position as *Hof-Compositor* from 1713. His son, Ignazio, also served as theorbist, but as a *Hof-Scholar* is not included in Köchel's list.

[4] Single identity? See Köchel *ibid.*, listings 724 and 903.

5 Single identity? See Köchel *ibid.*, listings 804 and 1001.

6 Single identity? See Köchel *ibid.*, listings 634 and 723.

7 Single identity? See Köchel *ibid.*, listings 806, 1012 and 1109.

8 Köchel *ibid.*, listing 731 gives 1738.

9 Single identity? See Köchel *ibid.*, listings 925 and 1068; but also note 1145 (a superfluous reference?).

10 Single identity? See Köchel *ibid.*, listings 749, 917 and 1069.

11 Single identity? See Köchel *ibid.*, listings 1113 and 1176.

* Continued in service after 1771. The year given for each other instrumentalist is either the year in which he received a pension or the year of death, with service continuing until then. These discrepancies in Köchel's list should be noted: Franz Cammermayer, pens. 1756 (listing 1090), in service until death, 1760 (listing 1161); Leop. Ferd. Christian, pens. 1771 (1106), in service until death, 1783 (1249); Karl Giegl, pens. 1760 (1153), pens 1767 (1083); And. Halber, pens. 1760 (1114), pens. 1762 (1177); Joh. Georg Hintereder, pens. 1757 (1071), pens. 1762 (1147).

** Inactive after 1729; named in Fux's petition of 31 December, 1729, for release from service. Köchel apparently did not take this into consideration when compiling his list. By supplying the date of death he implied that each instrumentalist continued in service into the year given in the Appendix.

Nicola Matteis, the younger: Caldara's collaborator and ballet composer in the service of the Emperor, Charles VI

Andrew D. McCredie

Zusammenfassung

Nicola Matteis der Jüngere: Caldaras Mitarbeiter und Ballettkomponist im Dienste Kaisers Karl VI.

Dieser Aufsatz behandelt das Leben und Wirken des in England geborenen Violinisten-Komponisten Nicholas Matteis, der von 1700 bis zu seinem Tode am 18. Oktober, 1737 im Dienste der kaiserlichen Habsburgischen Hofkapelle zu Wien tätig war. Nach seiner Ausbildung, die er zum Teil von seinem Vater, dem italienischen Violinisten und Komponisten Nicola Matteis d.Ä. erhielt, genoß Matteis hohes Ansehen als Virtuose innerhalb der Londoner Konzertwelt am Ende des 17. Jahrhunderts. Um 1700 verließ er London, und wanderte nach Wien, wo er zuerst eine Stellung als Mitglied der dortigen Hofkapelle erwarb. Nach dem Rücktritt 1712 des damaligen *Direttore della Musica Instrumentale*, J. J. Hoffers, wurde Matteis als Nachfolger Hoffers berufen. Als *Direttore della Musica Instrumentale* Komponierte Matteis die Musik zu den Balletaufführungen, die regelmäßig in den Zwischenakten sowie am Abschluß der Opern stattfanden. Als Caldara die Stellung des Vizekapellmeisters neben J. J. Fux antrat, entwickelte sich rasch eine Zusammenarbeit mit Matteis, der die Aufgabe erfüllte, die Balletmusik zu den Wiener Opern Caldaras zu liefern. Von seiner Feder entstanden insgesamt 33 Partituren im Dienste der ebensovielen Opern Caldaras. Insofern als die meisten dieser Aufführungen zum Anlaß der kaiserlichen Namensfeiern, Geburtstage oder Hochzeiten stattfanden, hatte Matteis die Möglichkeit Aufmerksamkeit sowie Anerkennung auf seine Leistungen zu lenken. Die 33 Ballettpartituren die in Suiten eingeteilt sind, und die sich in den Opern Caldaras eingegliedert befinden, bestehen aus 426 Sätzen, von denen etwa die Hälfte nun die einfache Bezeichnung Arie tragen. Doch vertreten diese Tänze beinahe alle Genres, die damals Mode waren. Zahlreiche Beispiele sind außerdem als programmatische bzw. Charaktertänze zu betrachten. Mit einer reichhaltigen Orchesterbesetzung zur Verfügung hatte Matteis die Möglichkeit eine manchmals fantasievolle Instrumentationskunst zu entwickeln.

Nicola Matteis, the younger: Caldara's collaborator and ballet composer in the service of the Emperor, Charles VI

Andrew D. McCredie

For vienna, the reign of the Emperor, Charles VI (1711–1740), despite the initial limitations it had imposed upon the development of the *Hofkapelle*, proved to be one of the richest epochs of collective creativity the city and empire had known. Composers, instrumentalists and singers were attracted from centres as far afield as Naples, Barcelona and London. This collective creativity between composers of such geographically disparate origins is perhaps no better demonstrated than in the collaboration between Antonio Caldara and Nicola Matteis, the younger. The latter, an English-born composer of Italian patrimony, furnished ballet music for at least thirty-three operas composed either entirely or in part by the Italian master — an output which, according to the extant sources, amounts to some 426 danced instrumental movements (see Table 1).

* * * * *

Matteis was the son of the Italian violinist-composer, Nicola Matteis, who appears to have settled in London in 1672, eventually becoming anglicised. Unfortunately, no material survives to establish the birth dates of either father or son, although the latter may have been born in or just before 1677. There is, however, ample documentation of the activities of the pair. Roger North's descriptions are particularly striking. Of the father he wrote:

> His profession was the violin and guittar, but withall an accomplisht musitian, and I know no master fitt to be named with Corelli but him; all his compositions are full of the most artfull harmony, and his fire exquisite. His manner of using his violin was much out of the comon

road of handling, but out of it he made the utmost of sound, double, single, swift, and all manners of touch, which made such impressions that his audience was not onely pleased but full of wonder at him, and his way of performing.[1]

According to North, Matteis senior not only introduced many new bowing techniques to England, but also various Italian harmonic innovations:

As a gratefull legacy to the English nation, [he] left them with a generall favour for the Italian manner of harmony, and after him the French was wholly layd aside, and nothing in towne had a relish without a spice of Italy. And the masters here began to imitate them, witness Mr H. Purcell in his noble set of sonatas, which however clog'd with somewhat of an English vein, for which they are unworthily despised, are very artificiall and good music.[2]

Again, according to North, the senior Matteis's last years were ill-starred:

He took a large hous and had a thing called a wife, and pretended to entertein, which by the Nicety of his Wine shewed he was no detter to his Genius. Excess of pleasure threw him into a dropsie, and he became very poor; he made his condition knowne to his freinds, but would take no bounty, but upon his obligation, such was his pride, to repay it. He came at last to loos both his Invention, and hand and in a miserable state of body purs and mind, dyed.[3]

The exact date of his death still eludes us. Schmidl offered no more than 1704 in his description of him as 'profundo contrappuntista, uno dei più ammirati violinist del tempo, in bell'attivita fino al 1704,'[4] and Michael Tilmouth commented 'for it seems that Thomas Brown supposed that he was dead by 1702.'[5]

Details of the early education of the young Matteis are exceedingly sparse. Wasielewski suggests that the elder Matteis had early trained his son 'as one of the finest violinists of the day, who was able to play Corelli's solos with an inimitable simplicity and grace'.[6] Roger North, however, reveals differences in the techniques of father and son:

The former had an absolute power of his trill, and used it always in time; and so slow, as permitted the ingredients in his shakes to be distinctly heard sounding; which made some, that understood no better, say that he had not a good shake. But the other had a spring so active, that during his trill the sound was stopt, because the notes had not time to sound.[7]

and guardedly evaluates their respective merits:

On which to pick, however convinc't, I will not stay to dispute, but alledge onely their different manners. The father's was virile and the son's effeminate.[8]

Of the younger Matteis's subsequent departure from England, employment and recognition in Europe, North comments only fleetingly.

Hee being invited went over into Germany and hath ever since bin there
and now resides at Vienna, in full payment for all the masters wee have
received out of those countrys.[9]

The details of his removal from London to Vienna have been a source
of conjecture in later biography and historiography, with varying
assertions being made by Viotta 'Hij studeerde in Duitsland';[10] Gerber
' ... und brachte es auf diesem Instrumente so weit, daß, als er in der
Folge einem Rufe nach Wien folgte, er in der dasigen Kaiserl. Kapelle
unter 23 Violinisten die oberste Stelle erhielt. Diese bekleidete er in den
Jahren 1721, und noch 1727, ... ';[11] Bernsdorf 'um 1717 eine Anstellung
in der kaiserlichen Kapelle in Wien erhielt';[12] and Dlabač who placed
his arrival in Vienna as 'vor das Jahr 1717'.[13] Wasielewski follows
Bernsdorf in citing 1717, ignoring Köchel's then recent research among
the Imperial records in Vienna which established 1 July, 1700, as the
date Matteis initially was engaged as a violinist in the *Hofkapelle*.[14]
In fact, several documents in the Court Archives (*Hofparteiprotokollen*)
confirm this date. No fewer than three of these originate from 1701,
the earliest being the petition of 22 March, 1701:

Allergenädigster Kaiser und Herr. Nicola Matteis bittet aller unterthänigst
mit Besoldungsordnanz ans Hofzahlambt angewiesen zu werden und die
Grade erhalten zu dürfen, in Eure Kayserliche Music in Dienst
aufgenommen zu werden[15]

Appended to this application is a favourable report by the *Kapellmeister*,
Antonio Pancotti, testifying to the probationer's exceptional talent and
pre-eminence as a violinist. Matteis was to receive a salary of 250 thalers[16]
upon completion of the ordinance of 1 July, 1700.

Further details of Matteis's salary for his first eighteen months of service
are given in the *Hofzahlamtsrechnungsbuch* (court accounts book) for
the year 1701:

Ferner hat Herrn Nicola Matteis an seiner Besoldung jährlich 900 Gld.
die Gebuhr vom 1. juli, 1700 (als Zeit des Anfangs) bis letzten September
1701 auf beikommende Hofordnanz und dessen Quittung hierbei also 1125
Gld in bar.[17]

The third source is the petition of 10 October, 1701, in the
Hofparteiprotokollen:

Der engelländische Geiger Nicola Matteis verlangt, seine Kinder aus
England abzuholen und hierher bringen, damit sie aus die uncatholischen
Länd kommen und weil die Hin- und Herfahrt und Kost ... [18]

From this application Matteis received 200 ducats towards the alleviation
of expenses incurred through travel to London in order to bring his
children to Vienna.

The *Hofparteiprotokollen* continue to afford details on Matteis's
incumbency, including his salary adjustments of 12 August, 1706, and

the new annual salary of 1440 florins he received on his appointment as *Direttore della musica instrumentale* in 1712.[19] He was emerited (*jubilato*) as violinist in the *Hofkapelle* on grounds of age on 31 December, 1729.[20] But he continued to draw his full salary in the specialized appointment as ballet-composer, producing ballet scores until his death in October, 1737.

The exact date of Matteis's death also has been a matter of contention owing to the wide discrepancy between that given by Köchel (23 October, 1737)[21] and 'about the year 1749' alleged by Charles Burney.[22] Confusion has been compounded by Burney's claim that Matteis returned to England[23] and that he himself 'learned French and the violin of this master' some time after 1737. Paul Nettl's championing of Köchel has now been vindicated by documents which Peter Keuschnig unearthed during research undertaken in Vienna in the 1960s. These include the *Totenprotokoll* (Register of Burials) of the parish of Sankt Jakob, Penzing, for 1737, which provides the evidence Nettl fruitlessly sought among the records of the Stephansdom (the burial place of many court musicians) in Vienna:[24]

> Anno 1737, Nicolaus de Matteis, die Octb. 23 sepultus e at St. Jacobum primus in Chribdam, nobilis dominus Nicolaus de Matteis Cesareus supremus Musica et Componista seu Compositor natione anglus in Baumgarten habitans p[ro]p'[rae]-terito, aetatis suae circiter 60 annorum, vir magna sapientia in omni scibili, non minoris pietatis[25]

Matteis's own last will and testament, signed and dated 18 October, 1737 (now in the Gerichtsarchiv der Stadt Wien[26]), as well as the testament of his widow, Susanna, and other papers concerning the administration of his estate (also in the Gerichtsarchiv), all provide further confirmation. Matteis's will and testament reads:

Mein letzter Willen
Uneracht ich nicht in stant bin ein Testament aufzurichten, indeme mein Vermegen sich nicht dahin erstrecket, das ich mit solchen meiner dermahligen Ehefrau mir wirklich zue gebrachtes, und gegebenes Hayrathgueth sambt der Widerlag abfu-'hre, wie ich schuldig bin. Nichts destoweniger, weilen mir meine Ehefrau selbst willig erlaubet hat ein Testament zu machen, und versprochen solches zu vollziegen, so habe ich gegenwertiges aufsetzen lassen, und zwar also.

Meine Universal Erbin ist meine dermahlige Ehefrau Susanna, und zwar aller meiner immer habenten sachen.

Meiner Tochter Maria aus erster Ehe Vermache ich pro Legitima

My last will and testament
Although I am hardly in the position to make a testament in that my means are not substantial, I reimburse my present wife with all the dowry brought by her into the marriage, as I feel obliged. Nevertheless since my wife has given consent for me to make a will and has promised to be its executrix, I therefore set out the following:

my principal heiress is my present wife Susanna, and she should inherit all my possessions

to my daughter Maria from my first marriage, I bequeath Pro Legitima paterna drey Hundert gulden mit der Bedingung, das wan sie mit solcher Legitima nicht wolle Content sein, und wider meine Universal Erbin wolle gerichtlich agiern, so solle meine universal Erbin auch dise dreyhundert gulden nicht schuldig sein zu geben, sondern kan solche selbst behalten.

Meinen Sohn Joanni, kan ich nichts Vermachen, weilen er mich allzu viel gecost.

Fur arme Leuth Vermache ich Zwölff gulden.

Wo, und wie ich sollte begraben werden, überlasse ich meiner Ehefrau, jedoch ganz gemein. Letzlich übergibe ich meine Seel in die gnadenreiche Hent Gottes, und befihle meinen gemachten Letzten Willen zur gnaden meiner Hochen Instanz und Obrigkeit.

Baumgarten den 18 Octb: 1737.

Nicola Matteis
Derectore della Musica
Instrumentalle de Sua Maista
C. et Catolica.

Susanna Matteis

[Vermerk:] Anheunt ist gegenwärttiges Testament in Beyseyn des Doctoris Renz und Andre Huber Richter von Paumgarten bey dem keysl. Obrist Hof Marschall-amt eröfnet und publiciert worden welches bey der Canzley aufzubehalten, und denen Interessirten hirvon Abschriften zuertheillen, Wien den 8 9bris 1737.

[Gezeichnet:] Graf Auersperg

Paterna 300 guilders under condition that if in the event of her being dissatisfied with such a Legitima, and takes legal proceedings against my principal heiress, the last named under such circumstances should also receive the 300 guilders

to my son Joannes I have nothing to bequeath, as he has already cost me too much

I give 12 guilders to the poor

the location and method of my burial I assign to my wife in an altogether humble way. Finally I commit my soul to the merciful hands of God, and commend this last will and testament to the attention of the requisite highest authority.

Baumgarten, 18 October, 1737

Nicolas Matteis
Direttore della Musica
Instrumentale de Sua Maesta
C. et Catolica

Susanna Matteis

[Comment:] This will was read and gazetted to-day in the presence of Dr Renz and Andre Huber, Magistrate of Paumgarten in official court chancellory in order to be retained there, and to issue copies to the interested parties. Vienna, 8 November, 1737

[Signed:] Graf Auersberg

The ballet at the Imperial court

Matteis's appointment as ballet-composer continued a succession of such musicians at the Habsburg court — a lineage which dated back for nearly a century and included Wolfgang Ebner (1612–1665), Johann Heinrich

Schmelzer (1623–1680), Andreas Anton Schmelzer (1653–1701) and Johann Joseph Hoffer (1666–1729). At the commencement of the reign of Charles VI, restrictive economic circumstances necessitated a rationalisation and reduction in the size of the *Hofkapelle*. The composers (the *Kapellmeister*, Marc' Antonio Ziani, and the *Vizekapellmeister*, Johann Joseph Fux), together with the *Konzertmeister* (Kilian Reinhardt) were responsible for preparing a new list of personnel and responsibilities. As originally drawn up in April, 1712, this list appears to have omitted the name of the current ballet-composer, J. J. Hoffer. However, according to a revision dating from December of the same year, he was reinstated at a salary of 1440 florins, but subsequently his name was ruled out in ink. In the baptismal register for 1708 at the Stephansdom we find Hoffer referred to as *R.K.H. Musicus Instrumentalis und reservierten Kais. Hofkassa Direktor*.[27] Subsequently in the process of the rationalisation of 1712, he appears to have redirected his career from ballet-composer to a middle-ranking court *Beamte*, thereby creating a vacancy into which Matteis could be promoted while still continuing to serve as a first violinist. Matteis's first ballet scores for the Imperial court operas appear to date from 1714 — for *Alba Cornelia* and *I satiri in Arcadia* by Francesco Conti, and for *L'Atenaide* for which Ziani, Antonio Negri and Caldara each furnished one act, with Conti supplying the *Intermezzi* and the *Licenza*. No ballet music for any of these productions appears to have survived.

When Caldara was appointed *Vizekapellmeister* to the Habsburg court in succession to Fux, who in turn had replaced the recently deceased Ziani, the terms of his contract were demanding. In addition to providing a substantial quantity of liturgical compositions, he was also required to furnish important dramatic works for Imperial name- and birthdays,[28] as well as for other special occasions, such as the nuptials between the Archduchess Maria Josepha and Friedrich August of Saxony (1719). Moreover, from 1726, due to the ill-health of Francesco Conti, Caldara was usually responsible for the annual Carnival opera. To these can be added the special theatrical performances which marked Imperial visits to centres beyond Vienna. For example, that to Graz in 1728, was celebrated by the production of *La forza dell'amicizia overo Pilade ed Oreste*.

All of these events represented major collaborations between Caldara and Matteis[29] and resulted in thirty-three of the fifty-eight ballets Matteis wrote between 1714 and 1737.[30] The remaining ballets were composed for operas by Bononcini, Conti, Fux,[31] Lotti, Porsile and Predieri, as well as for Matteis's own dramatic work *Lo Sciocco deluso* (1729), written for and performed by the children of the court nobility, but for which no musical sources have survived.

In providing ballets for the operas of Caldara and other composers, Matteis enjoyed the collaboration of some of the best choreographers and dancing masters of the day; among them Alessandro Phillebois, Pietro Scimoni Levassori della Motta, and later, Franz Hilverding van Wewen, sometimes regarded as one of the precursors of Noverre's dramatic ballet. In addition to these figures, the Viennese court also employed various lesser-known dancing masters such as Claudio Appelshofer (1698), Pietro Rigler and Tobias Gumpenheuber (1708).[32]

Matteis also had the advantage of composing in a period awakening to the expressive possibilities of the dance. Treatises on the dance (such as those by Ménéstrier), often published in response to the influence of rhetorical ideas, had been well known in France since 1670. The influence of these treatises found a ready response in German-speaking countries. Centres as different as Vienna, Hamburg, and later Mannheim, engaged the services of French dancing-masters and choreographers, while the first German-language treatises, Gregorio Lambranzi's *Neue und curieuse theatralische Tantz-Schul* (Nürnberg) and Gottfried Taubert's *Rechtschaffener Tantzmeister* (Leipzig), appeared in 1716 and 1717 respectively. It was Taubert who outlined quite specifically the theatrical role of the ballet composer in such statements as:

> Componist principaliter auf die Materie, davon der Actus oder Theil desselbigen Schauspiels handelt, bey welchem das Ballett getanzt werden soll, reflectieret werde ... Handelt die Materie von Schäffern und die Scenen presentieren Schäffereyen, so kann ein Schäfferballett aufgeführt werden. Begreift der Actus ein Feldschlacht in sich, so kann die Entrée de Combattant employret werden.[33]

Although according to this view, the Furies, Amourettes and other figures could be incorporated into ballets, the use of such figures was to correspond to a division of ballets into serious, historical, fantastic, poetic, allegorical, moralistic or satirico-comic genres.

In the ballets devised for Caldara's operas, the implications of such a division appear to have exercised a greater scenographic than musical immediacy. Thus while Matteis's selection of dance movement and genres conforms with the make-up of the prevailing German *Suite*, the scenography detailed in his ballets which terminate or, occasionally, open the acts of the Viennese operas[34] (Plate 1), falls into a wide range of categories, many of which can be traced back to the representational stage musics in favour since the Renaissance. They include the supernatural ('Ballo di Semidei' in Lotti's *Constantino* (Act V), 1716); the martial ('Ballo di Guerreri' in Caldara's *Il Tiridate ossia La verità nell'inganno* (Acts I and II), 1717); the Arcadian ('Ballo di Ninfe e Pastori seguaci di Cere terrenti in mano altri ghirlande' in Caldara's *Imeneo* (Act I), 1727); the pastoral ('Ballo di Esopo e di Paesani di Lidia' in Conti's *Creso* (Act I), 1723); the maritime ('Ballo di Marinari orientale, che barcano dalle navi' in Caldara's *Mitridate* (Act III), 1728); and the hunt ('Ballo di Cacciatori e Cacciatrice' in Caldara's *Sirita* (Act II), 1719). Other scenographic categories frequently encountered in Matteis's ballets are representations of the four seasons (in Caldara's *Gianguir* (Act V), 1724) and of popular mythological or allegorical topoi ('Ballo di Custodi del Tempi d'Apollo' in Caldara's *Andromaca* (Act I), 1724). Occasionally, the emerging taste for embellishment and *chinoiserie* that was soon to be identified with the Rococo and *stil galant*, appeared in scenographic superscriptions for ballets. The first-act ballet for Conti's *Astarto* (1718) was entitled 'Ballo di Pagodi e ridicoli Cinesi'.

Within these broad categories we can frequently encounter quite specifically defined subspecies, themselves determined by the general settings of the parent operas. The martial category is a particularly fruitful area. A sample from Caldara's operas alone includes: 'Ballo di Giovanni Nobili Romani in Exerzizio militare' *Lucio Papirio dittatore* (Act II), 1719; 'Ballo di Cavallieri Egiziani' *Nitocri* (Act III), 1722; 'Ballo di Cavalieri Polacchi e Lituani' *Il Venceslao* (Act V), 1725; and 'Ballo di Cavalieri, che doppo d'essere, viati da Chisciotte, gli formano un trofeo e lo corano' *Don Chisciotte in corte della duchessa* (Act V), 1727.

Special titles affixed to individual dances within an end-of-act ballet are less common. We may note three, the 'Aria per li Bacchanali', the 'Aria per un Satiro' and the 'Aria per li Satiri', all to be found within the second-act ballet for *Cajo Fabbricio* (1729). However, from about 1730 Matteis increasingly dispenses with scenographic or programmatic superscriptions and lists nothing more than a loose sequence of dance genres.

In performance, Matteis's ballets must have benefited immensely as part of a world of scenic architecture, stage design and costuming, presided over by the renowned Galli Bibiena family. Indeed, some of the scenographic titles of the ballets for Caldara's operas hint at riotously-coloured stagings: 'Balli di Nazioni diversi' *Sirita* (Act III); 'Ballo di Maschere di vario genere bizzaramente abbligliate' *Cajo Fabbricio* (beginning of second act); 'Ballo di Pagodi e di Indiani artifici della Porcellana', 'Ballo in cui si rappresentano uno sposalizio di paesani Indiani' *Gianguir* (Acts II and III); and 'Ballo di Contadini con istromenti rusticali in memoria e lode di Cerere [sic] inventrice dell'agricoltura' *Imeneo* (Act II).

While the score (or libretto) of any particular opera rarely mentions the dancers, the *maîtres de ballet* responsible for the choreography of the various end-of-act ballets usually are named. Phillebois and Levassori della Motta nearly always were associated with Caldara's operas. For example, in his *I due dittatori* (1726):

> Il primo, e Terzo Ballo, furono vagamente concertati da Alessandro Philebois, M̄stro di Ballo di S: M: Ces: e Catt̄?
>
> Il Secondo Ballo fù altresi vagamente concertato da Simone Pietro Levassori della Mota M̄stro di Ballo di S: M: C: e C:

In *Cajo Fabbricio* their duties were reversed (see Plate 1).

The ballet music

(i) the dances

From the Table 1 it can be seen that 204 movements, or nearly half of the total number of dance movements supplied by Matteis for Caldara's Viennese operas, are of the genre loosely designated *Aria* (Plate 2). However, according to their rhythmic and metric character or tonal and

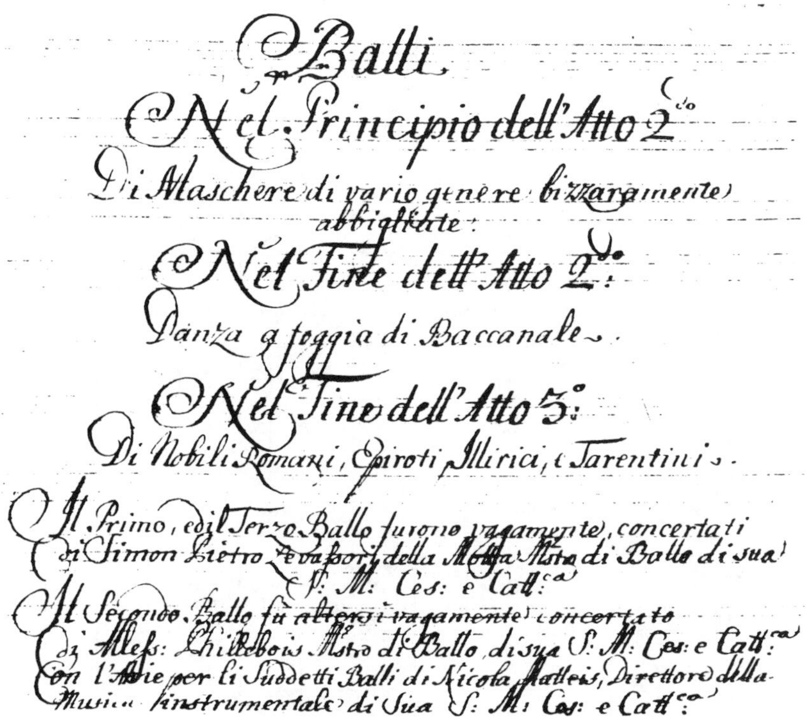

Balli.

Nel Principio dell'Atto 2do

Di Maschere di vario genere bizzaramente abbigliate:

Nel Fine dell'Atto 2do:

Danza a foggia di Baccanale.

Nel Fine dell'Atto 3o:

Di Nobili Romani, Epiroti, Illirici, e Tarentini.

Il Primo, ed il Terzo Ballo furono vagamente concertati di Simon Pietro Levassori della Motta Mstro di Ballo di sua S: M: Ces: e Catt:ca

Il Secondo Ballo fu altresi vagamente concertato di Aless: Phillebois Mstro di Ballo di sua S: M: Ces: e Catt:ca

Con l'Arie per li Suddetti Balli di Nicola Matteis, Direttore della Musica instrumentale di Sua S: M: Ces: e Catt:ca

Plate 1. Caldara *Cajo Fabbricio*. Description of the 'Balli' in the full score prepared by a court copyist. (A-Wn: Mus.Hs. 17148)
Reproduced by permission of the Österreichische Nationalbibliothek, Musiksammlung, Vienna

Table 1. Matteis's ballet music for Caldara's operas for Vienna, 1717–1736

OPERA	Intrada	Entrée	Marche	Aria	Sarabanda	Gigue	Minuet	Rigaudon	Passepied	Gavotte	Bourrée	Grotesca	Loure	Chaconne	Passacaille	Retirada	Other
Cajo Marzio Coriolano (5) (only third-act ballet music extant)	-	1	-	1	-	1	-	-	-	-	-	-	-	1	-	-	1 (Preludio)
Il Tiridate ossia La verità nell' inganno (21)	-	1	1	10	-	-	4	-	-	1	-	1	-	3	-	-	-
Ifigenia in Aulide (16)	-	1	-	4	1	1	2	1	3	1	1	-	-	1	-	-	1 (Rondo)
Sirita (13)	-	2	1	2	-	-	2	-	2	1	-	-	1	-	1	-	-
Lucio Papirio dittatore (18)	-	-	2	8	-	-	-	-	-	-	2	-	1	2	-	-	3 (1 Rondo, 2 undesignated)
Ormisda (12)	-	-	2	6	1	-	-	-	-	-	-	-	1	1	-	-	1 (Moresca)
Nitocri (15)	-	-	-	7	1	3	-	-	-	-	-	-	1	-	2	-	1 (Furlana)
Scipione nelle Spagne (16)	-	2	3	6	1	1	-	-	-	-	-	-	1	1	-	-	1 (Furlana)
Euristeo (19)	-	2	-	5	2	-	6	-	2	1	1	-	-	-	-	-	-
Andromaca (11)	1	1	-	6	-	-	-	-	-	1	-	-	-	2	-	-	-
Gianguir (14)	-	-	1	11	-	1	-	-	-	-	-	-	-	1	-	-	-
Semiramide (11)	-	-	-	7	-	-	1	-	-	-	-	1	-	1	-	-	1 (undesignated)
Il Venceslao (14)	-	-	-	14	-	-	-	-	-	-	-	-	-	-	-	-	-
I due dittatori (18)	1	1	1	9	1	-	-	-	-	-	-	1	-	1	-	-	2 (1 Rondo, 1 undesignated)
Don Chisciotte in corte della duchessa (17)	-	1	-	8	1	1	1	-	-	-	-	1	-	-	-	-	3 (1 Allegro, 2 coro)

Table 1. (contd)

OPERA	Intrada	Entrée	Marche	Aria	Sarabanda	Gigue	Minuet	Rigaudon	Passepied	Gavotte	Bourrée	Grotesca	Loure	Chaconne	Passacaille	Retirada	Other
Imeneo (8)	-	-	1	3	-	-	-	1	-	-	-	-	1	1	-	-	1 (Sinfonia)
Ornospade (15)	1	1	1	6	1	1	-	-	1	-	-	2	-	1	-	-	1 (undesignated)
La forza dell' amicizia (4)	-	-	-	3	-	1	-	-	-	-	-	-	-	-	-	-	-
Mitridate (15)	-	1	1	5	-	-	-	-	1	2	-	2	2	-	-	1	-
I disingannati (15)	1	1	-	8	1	-	1	1	-	-	1	-	1	-	-	1	-
Ciro riconosciuto (10)	-	-	-	4	1	-	-	-	-	-	-	2	-	2	-	-	1 ("La Favorita")
Cajo Fabbricio (14)	-	1	1	7	-	1	-	-	1	-	-	2	-	1	-	-	-
La pazienza di Socrate (15)	1	-	-	7	-	1	1	-	-	-	-	1	1	1	1	-	1
Il Demetrio (13)	-	1	-	5	-	-	-	1	-	-	-	3	-	-	2	-	-
L'asilo d'amore (5)	-	1	-	2	-	-	-	-	1	-	-	-	-	-	-	-	-
Adriano in Siria (12)	-	1	2	3	-	-	1	-	-	1	1	-	1	-	-	-	1 (undesignated) (Presto)
Sancio Panza (9)	-	-	-	6	-	-	-	-	-	-	-	1	-	1	-	-	1 (undesignated)
L'olimpiade (13)	-	-	-	10	-	1	-	-	-	-	-	-	-	-	-	-	2 (1 Hornpipe) (1 undesignated)
Demofoonte (7)	-	-	1	3	-	-	-	-	-	-	-	2	-	1	-	-	-
Enone (9)	-	1	1	5	1	-	-	-	-	-	-	-	-	1	-	-	-
La clemenza di Tito (15)	-	1	2	10	-	-	-	-	-	-	-	-	-	1	-	-	2 (1 Largo) (1 Allegro)
Achille in Sciro (19)	-	1	-	11	1	-	-	1	-	-	-	2	-	2	-	-	-
Il Temistocle (8)	1	-	-	2	-	-	-	1	-	-	-	1	-	1	-	-	-
TOTAL 426	6	22	21	204	13	18	18	6	12	8	8	20	13	25	6	2	24

cadential organisation, many of these are not radically different from recognised dance categories. In general, Matteis's *aria* movements adhere to the binary-based dance form, and to the symmetrical antecedent/consequent quadratic structures and periodicity favoured in the properly designated dance movements. Neither is their appearance a novel development in the Viennese opera ballet. J. H. Schmelzer had frequently used this nomenclature for many of his dances written for earlier Viennese operas. Successions of such movements found in older codices frequently bore collective titles such as *Arie per li Balletti*, a practice still retained on many of the title pages of the scores and libretti for Caldara's operas: 'Con l'Arie per li ... Balli di Nicola Matteis Direttore della Musica Instrumentale di S: M: Ces: e Catt?'

Between the movements simply termed *Aria* and the specifically labelled dances, comes an intermediate classification — movements which, having been initially designated *Aria* are then subtitled: 'Tempo di Sarabanda', 'Tempo di Bourrée', 'Tempo di Minuet', and so on. In the absence of fixed rhythms identifiable with one or other of these dance forms, yet where an overall structure conforms with a binary or ternary *Liedform*, such movements seem to have been intended for rustic, folkloristic burlesque scenes.

A separate category comprises the twenty movements labelled *Aria grotesca*. This dance, possibly Matteis's own innovation,[35] was described some forty years after his death in J. G. Sulzer's *Allgemeine Theorie der schönen Künste*:

> Ihr Charakter ist Ausgelassenheit oder etwas abentheuerliches. Diese Tänze stellen im Grund nichts als ungewöhnliche Sprünge und seltsame närrische Gebehrden, Lustbarkeiten und Abendtheuer der niedrigsten Classe der Menschen vor. Der gute Geschmack kommt dabei wenig in Betrachtung, und es wird auch so genau nicht genommen, ob die Cadenzen der Tänzer mit denen, die die Musik macht, so genau übereinstimmen oder nicht.[36]

As a rule, the *Aria grotesca* movements can be identified through their use of such predominantly syncopated patterns as:

2/4   ♪ ♩ ♪

3/4   ♪ ♩ ♪ ♩

6/8   ♪ ♩ ♫♩

Usually these movements are in an animated duple time. The most common formal arrangement is a bi- or tripartite structure with two reprises; otherwise a *da capo* design appears to have been favoured. The repetition of entire bars and sequences is a device frequently encountered in these movements.

Perhaps impelled by a search for possible musical or dramatic unity, Matteis occasionally arranges his movements into groups based upon a design requiring the ordered recurrence of, usually, the first *Aria* of

Plate 2. Matteis's first-act ballet music for Caldara's *Demofoonte. Violino primo* part-book. (A-Wn: Mus.Hs. 17169)
Reproduced by permission of the Österreichische Nationalbibliothek, Musiksammlung, Vienna

such a group. Thus in the 'Ballo di Soldati Polacchi' which concludes the first act of *Il Venceslao* he uses the sequence: *Aria* I, *Aria* II, *Aria* II *(da capo), Aria, Aria* II *(da capo), Aria* I *(da capo)* with a D, G, G, G, G, D key scheme. The dances in the 'Ballo di Cavalieri Polacchi e Lituani', concluding the fifth act of the same opera, are in a binary arrangement: *Aria* I, *Aria* II, *Aria* II *(da capo), Aria* I *(da capo)* with a C, a, a C key scheme.

The *aria* group aside, the *intrada* and *entrée* movements on the one hand, and the *chaconne* and *passecaille* movements on the other, represent the genres most favoured in Matteis's ballets for Caldara's operas. Six movements are labelled *Intrada* and twenty-two are designated *Entrée* in the Viennese manuscripts. As a rule, the *intrada* movements introduce their respective suites of dances. Matteis casts them in duple metre and usually favours a deliberate march-styled texture and emphatic dotted rhythms — a ceremonial character underlined in some movements by the festive solemnity of their instrumentation: four *clarini* and timpani are combined with strings in the *Intrada* of the third-act ballet for Caldara's *Ornospade* (1727). By way of contrast, *entrées* are among those movements that reveal an unmistakable French influence, best identified through the short quaver anacrusis with which they commence, the preference for a duple metre punctuated by dotted rhythms and a bipartite reprise form. Another concommitant feature of such movements is their dependence upon various stereotyped rhythmic formulae.

Closely allied to the *intrada* and *entrée* movements are the various movements in the Italian *marcia* and French *marche* styles. We can find twenty-one of these in Matteis's ballets for Caldara's operas. As they, too, usually head the end-of-act ballets, their function is almost identical with that of the *intrade* and *entrées*. In the 'Ballo di Giovanni' which concludes the second act of Caldara's *Lucio Papirio dittatore*, the *Marche* reappears *da capo* at the end of the ballet, thus also serving as a *retirada*. However, movements specifically designated *Retirada* will be found in only two ballets for Caldara's operas: that for the fifth act of *Mitridate* and that for the third act of *Cajo Fabbricio*. In the latter instance, the festive, fanfare-like character of the movement is heightened by the *trombe* and timpani instrumentation which is also used for the *Entrée* of the same ballet.

The *chaconnes* and *passecailles* form the next most numerous categories in Matteis's production. He uses the *chaconne* on no less than thirty-five occasions in his entire output and on twenty-five occasions (together with six *passecailles*) in his ballets for Caldara's operas. Whereas the *Chaconne* in *Ormisda, re di Persia* (Act I), 1721, employs an extended eight-bar *basso ostinato* theme, those for other operas feature four-bar themes. The essentially three-bar themes found in the *chaconnes* for Caldara's *Ciro riconosciuto* (Act III), 1728, *Sancio Panza* (Act II), 1730/33 and *Lucio Papirio dittatore* (Act II), are the only deviants from this principle.

On occasion, Matteis will interpolate alien structures into an extended *chaconne* to create a through-composed ballet score of considerable complexity. A *Gigue* and *Bourrée* appear in the second-act *Chaconne* for *Lucio Papirio dittatore* and a *Trio* in the *Chaconne* for *Ormisda*. Perhaps the most notable example is the *Chaconne* which with its interpolated *Entrée, Loure* and *Aria (Largo)* comprises the entire third-act ballet for Caldara's *Demofoonte* (1733). Here Matteis creates a seven-station sequence of 240 bars, headed by an eighty-seven-bar section, designated *Chaconne*. This begins with a series of fugal entries for the three parts (violin 1, violin 2 and basso), in which the *ostinato* theme is first heard in the uppermost part. However, there is no consequent development of the *ostinato*, the caesuras being signified through cadences. The second station, a sixteen-bar *Entrée* in *alla breve* time, is based on two halves, each of eight bars, which are themselves subdivided into two quadratic structures. The third station (bars 104–128) continues the original *Chaconne* material, but without any specific bass formula, while the fourth station, a *Loure* (bars 129–147), consists of a bipartite reprise with the respective segments comprising |: 6+1:||:11+1:| bars. The undesignated[37] fifth station (bars 148–175) is a further extension of the *Chaconne*. The sixth station is a simple *Largo* in duple rhythm, its symmetrical bipartite reprise form of sixteen bars mirroring the internal structure of the *Entrée*. At the seventh station the *Chaconne* material reappears in the fugato style of its original presentation, all voices now enjoying almost equal roles. In the solemn unfolding of this d minor movement, arguably one of his most powerful creations, Matteis seems to transcend the utilitarian function of operatic ballet-music.

The *Passecaille* which concludes the ballet-music to Caldara's *Il Demetrio* (1731) is an even more extensive structure. In this instance the movement comprises three principal parts: (i) a g minor section, 127 bars in length, subdividing into the *Passecaille* itself, (bars 1–80) and a *Trio* 'di Flauti Soli' (bars 81–127), (ii) an *Entrée* of thirty-three bars in a bipartite reprise leading into (iii) a *Passecaille* in G major of 146 bars. In each of the two *Passecaille* sections there is a four-bar *basso ostinato*. The *ostinato* of the second section subsequently is extended through sequential processes to as many as thirteen bars, while above it the first violin is treated as a concertising soloist.

Putting aside the many movements classified as *aria* but which are cast in one or other of the main dance forms, the remaining movements in Matteis's ballet music can be summarized: first, the *sarabanda* (13) and *gigue* (18) inherited from the traditional four-movement (*allemande-courante-sarabanda-gigue*) suite; second, the other, usually binary, dance movements of later origin commonly encountered in instrumental suites or theatrical ballets of the period (these include the *minuet* (18), *loure* (13), *passepied* (12), *gavotte* (8), *bourrée* (8) and *rigaudon* (6)); third, a small number of other movements carrying either abstract (*rondo, sinfonia*) or affective/programmatic titles, such a 'La Plaisanterie' or 'La Favorita'.

In considering the first of these three classifications, we should also note the almost complete absence of several of the longest-established dance genres, such as the *allemande* and *courante*, from Matteis's ballets.

As a composer who usually favoured simple homophonic textures for many of his dance movements, he may have found the more polyphonic predispositions of the *allemande* or *courante* unsuited to the obvious scenographic intentions of the court ballets.

One of the most regularized dances of the seventeenth and eighteenth centuries, the *sarabanda* traditionally was given a symmetrical binary structure of two four- or eight-bar periods. However, in most instances Matteis judiciously expands this into a three-part structure, but with two reprises: |:8 :||: 16 (8 + 8):| Generally Matteis's *sarabanda* movements commence upon the downbeat; only three begin with a crotchet anacrusis. But if there is any one characteristic which distinguishes these from those of earlier Viennese ballet-composers, it is the enlivened rhythmic figures upon the upbeats which see erstwhile standardized patterns such as:

3/4   ♩ ♩. ♪ | ♩. ♪♩

3/4   ♩ ♩. ♪ | ♩ ♩.

3/4   ♩ ♩ ♩ | ♩. ♪♩

being replaced by:

3/4   ♩ ♩ ♩♪ | ♩. ♪♩♪

3/4   ♩ ♩ ♩♪ | ♩ ♩. ♪

3/4   ♩ ♩ ♩♪ | ♩ ♩ ♩♪

Not only is the rhythmic character of Matteis's *sarabandas* emphasized by his penchant for dotted rhythms, but it is also reinforced through his generous use of syncopations and cross-rhythms. His preference for thematic head-motives characterized by initial upward or downward leaps of a fourth or fifth is obvious in the melodic lines of many of these movements (Ex. 1).

Example 1
(a) *Sarabanda*, first-act ballet to Caldara's *Enone*
(b) *Sarabanda*, first-act ballet to Caldara's *Nitocri*

(a)

Ex. 1 (contd)

(b)

As a rule Matteis's *gigues* are homophonic in texture. Such polyphony as does occur is of minimal duration, and is confined to short-winded imitative entries in the middle voices. Certainly, the fugal devices characteristic of the second part of many German binary fugues are not to be found in Matteis's *gigues*. Moreover, whereas earlier composers (J. H. Schmelzer, for example) favoured a bipartite *gigue* with two reprises, Matteis prefers a tripartite movement. The structures of these dances, far from being built up on periods of monotonous quadratic symmetry, frequently are enlivened by a co-existence of five- or seven-bar units with those of four bars. Motivic continuity is maintained through the inclusion of head-motive materials from the main themes into the mobile lower strands of the textures. Although many of Matteis's *gigue* movements are in 6/8, a number use other compound metres 9/8, 12/8, and even 3/2. Usually they commence with a quaver upbeat but a few begin with: ♪♫ .

Matteis's eighteen *minuet* movements are all in triple time and commence strongly on a downbeat. By favouring patterns such as:

3/4 ♩ ♩ | ♩ ♩ | ♩ ♩ ♩ | ♩ ♫♫

he shows a predilection for Lombard-style rhythms in the opening bars. As if following Lully's example, there are four instances where Matteis orders two *minuets* in sequence, so that the second assumes the relationship of an *alternativ* movement to the first, but retains its own identity through variant tonality and instrumentation — usually a trio texture. These paired sequences of minuets appear in such patterns as: *Minuet* I — *Minuet* II — *Minuet* II — *Minuet* I or: *Minuet* I — *Minuet* II — *Minuet* I — *Minuet* II.

Matteis's *passepieds* usually commence on crotchet upbeats and tend to be cast in a tripartite form with two reprises. The *Lied*-like character of these movements, already a feature in J. J. Hoffer's *passepieds*, is consolidated by Matteis. He avoids dotted rhythms and instead shows a strong preference for fluent quaver movement (Ex. 2).

Example 2. *Passepied*, first-act ballet to Caldara's *Mitridate*

The *loures* in Matteis's ballets usually are in a commodious triple metre and most are introduced by characteristically pointed upbeat figures:

$$\quad \quad \flat \! \downarrow \; \; \text{or} \; \; \text{JI}$$

which frequently reappear at the beginning of the second part of the binary form. Matteis's most common structures are bi- or tripartite forms with two reprises. The third part is usually no more than a cadential reinforcement of the tonic and occupies only a few bars. A commanding feature of these dances is the composer's frequent reliance upon dotted rhythms, in particular the 3/4 $\text{JI} | \! \downarrow$ anacrusal upbeats. These are particularly obvious in the bass lines and often are developed in sequential patterns throughout the movements. A number of model rhythms tend to emerge as musical topoi for the melodic phrases:

$$3/4 \quad \flat\!\downarrow \; | \; \downarrow \; \downarrow \; \downarrow \; | \; \downarrow. \; \flat\!\downarrow \; |$$

The melodic shapes of the head motives fall into four relatively standard patterns: first, an ascent of three consecutive steps followed by a downward leap; second, its inversion, a stepwise descent of three or four notes, followed by an upward leap; third, a *nota cambiata* followed by a downward leap; and, fourth, varying patterns based upon the $\text{JI} | \! \downarrow$ anacrusal motive (Ex. 3).

Example 3
(a) *Loure*, third-act ballet to Caldara's *Scipione nelle Spagne*
(b) *Loure (Aria)*, second-act ballet to Caldara's *Gianguir*
(c) *Loure*, third-act ballet to Caldara's *Imeneo*
(d) *Loure*, fifth-act ballet to Caldara's *Mitridate*

Keuschnig finds twenty-nine *gavottes* within Matteis's total production of ballet music,[38] eight occurring in the scores for Caldara's operas. As a rule, Matteis's *gavottes* are commodious in pace – twenty in C metre, eight in 4/4, and one in 2/2. All can be identified by a two-crotchet upbeat formula, a device more variably used by earlier Austrian ballet composers. Most are in a two- or three-part form with two reprises, the second of which usually is longer than the first. Matteis's tonal structure adheres closely to the tonic-dominant :‖: dominant-tonic plan, but there are occasional deviations to major or minor parallels.

As noted earlier, a considerable portion of Matteis's so-called *aria* movements accord with the principal characteristics of the named dances. Thus it is not surprising that the total number of *gavottes* in his scores proves to be much higher than those so named. Likewise the twenty movements that can be classified as *bourrées* in the ballet music for Caldara's operas far exceeds not only the eight movements actually designated by Matteis himself in these scores but even the total number of dances termed *bourrées* in his complete output of ballets.

Matteis's approach to the *bourrée* was less innovatory than that adopted for some of the other dances. Indeed, he seems to owe much to the formal, periodic structure already cultivated by earlier generations of Viennese ballet composers (that is, successions of four-bar units which could be extended by the addition of sequences), emphasising the two- or three-part form with two reprises.[39] All these characteristics are made clear by one of the non-designated *bourrée* movements: the programmatically titled 'Aria per li Bacchanali', the third dance in the second-act ballet for *Cajo Fabbricio*, is simply a short movement of twenty-four bars, of binary structure with two reprises, and in a strictly quadratic structure: ‖:4+4:‖:4+4+4+4:‖.

The *rigaudon*, with its Provençal origins, does not appear to have entered the repertoire of the Habsburg theatrical ballet until the closing years of the seventeenth century, when it found favour in the works of Matteis's predecessor, J. J. Hoffer, who preferred a distinctive metrical pattern: ♩ | ♩ ♩ ♩. ♪ | for this movement. In general, the seventeen *rigaudons* scattered throughout Matteis's total production can be readily identified through head-motives such as:

¢ ♩ | ♩ ♩ | ♩ 𝄾 𝄾 ♩ | ♩   and: ¢ ♩ | ♩ ♩ ♩ ♩ | ♩

and variants. In the six found in the ballet music for Caldara's operas – *Sirita* (Act II), *Imeneo* (Act III), *I disingannati* (Act II), 1729, *Achille in Sciro* (Act III), 1736, *Il Temistocle* (Act II), 1736 and *Il Demetrio* (Act II) – these rhythms are combined with melodic lines which, whether ascending or descending, are of a decidedly triadic character (Ex. 4).

As a rule Matteis preferred a bipartite structure for his *rigaudons*, although that in the ballet music for *Il Demetrio* is in four sections (with three reprises), a formal disposition which Mattheson described in his *Das neu-eröffnete Orchestre*:

> ein bestiger auch in gerader Mensur bestehender Tantz, bey Rejouissancen und grotesquen Ballets gebräuchlich. Ihr Takt ist 4/4. Hat aber insgemein drei bis vier Reprisen, wovon die dritte gantz kurz und badine zu seyn pflegen.[40]

Example 4
(a) *Rigaudon*, third-act ballet to Caldara's *Achille in Sciro*
(b) *Rigaudon*, second-act ballet to Caldara's *I disingannati*

All of the dances discussed so far belong to that cosmopolitan repertoire of French, Italian and German genres which Matteis shared with other composers of instrumental suites whatever their national origins. To this basic reservoir Matteis added other, rather more exotic dances, such as the English *hornpipe*. He had long been familiar with this dance through his father's compositions and the theatre music of Purcell and other Restoration composers, genres in which he had exercised his own performing skills before leaving England.[41] The masculine syncopations of the *hornpipe* (as seen in the first-act ballet music for Caldara's *L'olimpiade*, 1733) may well have stimulated a lively response in the frequent syncopations found in other dance types, especially in the *Aria grotesca*. It was the *Aria grotesca* which also enabled Matteis to incorporate other musical idioms from the British Isles into his theatrical ballets. The ballet concluding the first act of Caldara's *Sirita* included, for example, an *Aria Burlesca Scozzese*. However, it remains to be established whether these Anglo-Celtic syncopated styles galvanized the enthusiasm for Lombard rhythms so apparent in numerous later ballet movements.

This early response to English and Scottish musical folklore typifies Matteis's ready acceptance of whatever influences were on hand. In his later response to the musical folklore of Upper and Lower Austria, he continued a trend that had already become manifest in dances of J. H. Schmelzer, whose music demonstrated a synthesis of courtly and popular elements. Schmelzer's own immediate successors had failed to maintain this fusion, and it seems to have been Matteis, the foreigner, who resumed the incorporation of local Viennese dances such as the *Dreher* and *Stampfer* into the court ballets.[42] Notated in 3/4 or 6/4 metres, and cast as bi- or tripartite aria forms with two reprises, they can also be found as one of the many varieties of the so-called *Aria* movements. Noteworthy examples occur in the ballets to Act I of Caldara's *Il Tiridate*, Act III of *Ormisda* and Act II of *Gianguir*. A particular feature of the melodic shapes of these movements is a dependence upon the *Naturtöner* of the

Alphorn and other wind instruments, yielding frequent sequences based on octaves, sixths, fifths, fourths and major thirds.

Other unusual dances which appear in Matteis's ballets for Caldara's operas include an *Aria moresca* (*Ormisda*, Act II) and the *furlana* (*Nitocri*, Act I, and *Scipione nelle Spagne*, Act I). The *moresca* had been one of the most common dances of the seventeenth-century ballet pantomime. It introduced a special exoticism by requiring the dancers to wear black masks.

A comparison of Matteis's ballets with those by other composers as well as with the *Ouverture*-suite repertoire of the period, suggests that his unity of tonality was often tempered through the introduction of related or even more alien tonal centres. Whereas the movements in each of Matteis's violin sonatas appear to adhere to a common tonality, the ballet suites show a marked flexibility among their individual movements. In *Il Tiridate*, the first-act ballet music moves from C major *via* a minor to end in A major. The second-act ballet proceeds from G major to g minor. In the third-act ballet the prevailing C major tonality is relieved by an 'Aria per li Sultani' in G major, the second of two *minuets* of an *alternativ* coupling, in c minor and one *Aria* in a minor. The sequences of dances in the three end-of-act ballets for Caldara's next opera, *Ifigenia in Aulide* (1718), show a marked preference for minor keys, one appropriate to the opera's subject. The first-act ballet, for example, has a sequence of five dances in g minor before concluding with a *Chaconne* in d minor. The second-act dances resume in g minor before ascending the quintal cycle to d and a minor. For the third-act ballet the prevailing tonal centre of a minor is relieved through the incorporation of two dances (both 'Aria da villanos Hollandes') in C major. In *Gianguir*, the first-act dances move from F major to its dominant and back, the three third-act dances from C major to a minor, while the fifth-act dances, the first four of which represent the four seasons, yield a sequence of tonalities G major–g minor–G major–e minor, the last being 'Winter'. The remaining two dances, a *Gigue* and *Ciacona comica* see the return from e minor to G major. In the ballets to the second and third acts of *Cajo Fabbricio*, the movement is from the tonic (C major) to the double dominant (D major), and from G major *via* g minor to C major respectively.

Turning to the ballets for the operas of Caldara's last year, we find the dances for the first-act ballet for *Il Temistocle* move g minor–G major–g minor; those for the second act progress from g minor to C major; and those in the third act return to G major. In *Achille in Sciro* the tonal progressions — A major to D major (Act I), g minor to G major (Act II) and C major–c minor–G major–g minor (Act III) — again reveal mobility between the steps of a quintal cycle.

It is clear from this that Matteis's choice of tonalities represents a degree of flexibility and deviance within a rather hidebound system of norms. The persistence of such a system can be seen not only in J. S. Bach's four orchestral suites but also in the eighty-six orchestral suites and *Musice di Tavola* Christoph Graupner (1683–1760) wrote for the Duke of Hessen-Darmstadt. An investigation of the movement sequences of Graupner's *oeuvre* reveals only a rare divergence from a strict adherence to a basic tonality.[43] Moreover, this conservative scheme was to outlast Matteis's own lifetime by another two generations. Its hardy durability is still observable in the late eighteenth century in the extensive repertoire of *Feldparthien, Divertimenti, Cassations, Notturni* and *Serenaden*, whether in the Salzburg works of Michael Haydn or in the outputs of the *Kleinmeister* working at courts throughout central Europe.[44]

(ii) instrumentation and scoring

Notwithstanding the ordinances rationalising the strength and dimensions of the Imperial *Hofkapelle* on the accession of Charles VI in 1711, the subsequent expansion of the court orchestra allowed Matteis an abundance, quality and variety of orchestral personnel and instruments equalled in few other centres. Some court orchestras, such as those at Darmstadt and Karlsruhe, and for a time, the orchestra at the commercially-managed Oper am Gänsemarkt in Hamburg, could pride themselves on extensive permanent or readily-available personnel resources as well as on large *instrumenteria* which quickly came to include the most recent developments in the manufacture and technology of instruments.[45] Other institutions, such as the orchestra presided over by Hasse at the Dresden court, were distinguished by the presence of individual virtuosi and an especially high standard of string playing.

The picture of orchestral resources and standards conjured up by Matteis's ballet music suggests a generous supply of woodwind and brass personnel, an availability of both the older and newer woodwind instruments, and a high professional profile among the string players. This last is reflected in a number of dances bearing superscriptions requiring specific methods of attack and technical execution. These include an *Aria* 'spiccata e forte' for Caldara's *La pazienza di Socrate* (Act II) 1731, a *Rigaudon* 'forte e spicato' for *I disingannati* (Act II), and the *Aria* movements 'Largo e spiccato' for *Enone* (Act III) 1728/ 34 and 'staccato' for *I due dittatori* (Act I). In the ballet music for the fifth act of *Gianguir*, the movement 'Aria per l'Inverno' is characterised by tremolando techniques, already familiar to Matteis from the 'Frost' scene of Purcell's *King Arthur*.

Blessed with such ample resources, it is hardly surprising that Matteis should have been tempted into some enterprising selections of orchestral colour. The early enrichment of the *Hofkapelle* through two Bohemian horn-players, Wenzel Rossi and Friedrich Otto, whose names appear in personnel lists from 1712, provided Matteis with the opportunity to furnish several ballet scores with parts for these instruments.[46] Their inclusion in the ballet music for *Sirita* seems to be their earliest connection with Caldara's operas. In this instance the traditional association of horns with the hunt must have dictated their appearance in the second-act 'Ballo di Cacciatori e Cacciatrice'. The layout of this score is unusual, the staves being headed: 'Violini e Oboe unisoni'; 'Corno I'; 'Corno II'; 'Viola'; and 'Basso'.[47]

From time to time Matteis would also call for wind instruments that were almost obsolete or recently invented. The former is represented by the *cornetto* which he specifies for the *Marcia burlesca* in the first-act ballet music for Caldara's *Sirita* — a movement set out in *particello* with the upper stave designated 'Violini unisoni con il Cornetto'.[48] The latter is represented by the *chalumeau*, the newcomer to the woodwind family which was used in Viennese opera scores as early as Giovanni Bonocini's *Endimione* (1706), Antonio Bononcini's *La conquista delle Spagne* (1707) Attilio Ariosti's *Marte placato* (1707) and Fux's *Julo Ascanio* and *Pulcheria* (both 1708). It first appears in Matteis's scores for Caldara's operas in 1721 in the *Chaconne* of the first-act ballet music for *Ormisda*. This movement contains a section (bars 60–106) for a wind trio of two flutes and *chalumeau*, designated 'Flauti soli e Schalimo Basso' in the score. By that time the instrument was in demand among many German composers including Keiser,[49] Hasse, Telemann,[50] and Molter.[51] Graupner wrote for various types of *chalumeaux* and explored their different registers in his chamber sonatas and overture suites. In the latter he made considerable demands upon the instrument's abilities in a solo role.[52]

In the scores for the ballets Matteis supplied for Caldara's Viennese operas, six types of orchestral disposition are employed.[53] The first of these is the *particello* layout comprising a two-clef (G2F4) *violini unisoni/ basso continuo* system. Some ballets, for example, those for *Nitocri, Euristeo* (1724), *Andromaca, Il Venceslao, La forza dell'amicizia, I disingannati* and *Ciro riconosciuto*, use this arrangement exclusively. The second most common system (found in the ballet scores for *Cajo Fabbricio, Enone, Demofoonte* and *Il Temistocle*), is the trio sonata (G2G2F4) arrangement, occasionally varied by the use of the string trio (G2C3F4) scoring. Numerous other ballet scores appear to alternate between the *particello* and trio sonata systems. Those for *Sancio Panza, L'olimpiade, Achille in Sciro* and *La clemenza di Tito* (1734) reveal an approximately even distribution between the two systems. The third most frequent score arrangement is the standard four-part layout (G2G2C3F4), used almost without exception in the ballet music to *Ifigenia in Aulide* and, apart from only a few movements, in *Lucio Papirio dittatore*.

In the remaining ballet scores Matteis employs a mixture of *particello* and trio sonata systems which are variously augmented to accommodate the larger forces (usually additional woodwind and brass) employed in specific movements. The first of the three most common additional scorings involves oboes and bassoons; the others involve brass and timpani.

Oboes and bassoons can appear in either a *particello* or a trio sonata arrangement and can be combined with *particello*, trio sonata or quartet arrangements of the strings and continuo. Combinations of this sort are required in the *Passepied* of the second-act ballet music for *Lucio*

Papirio dittatore, in the *Aria* for Act I of *Scipione nelle Spagne*, in the
Sinfonia for Act I of *Imeneo*, in an *Aria* for Act I of *Ornospade*, and
in the 'Aria per li Satiri' and 'Aria per un Satiro' in the ballet music
for Act II of *Cajo Fabbricio*. In his ballet music for Caldara's later operas,
such as *La clemenza di Tito* and *Il Demetrio*, Matteis views the wind
trio as a group able to both reinforce and contrast with the string ensemble.
In many of these later ballet scores we also find the bassoon incorporated
into the fundamental bass group whether or not oboes reinforce the
violin parts. Occasionally, the bass group is subdivided with the bassoon
and cello performing a decorative version of the bass (*violone*) part (for
example, the third-act ballet music for *Adriano in Siria* (1732), in which
the *particello* disposition becomes a G2F4F4 scoring).

Matteis handles the brass and timpani in two ways: first, in three
parts (*tromba* 1, *tromba* 2 and timpani) — as in the *Minuet* of the ballet
music to Act III of Caldara's *Sirita* — or in various expansions of this
group, depending on whether it was enlarged through the addition of
a third trumpet (as in the *Marche* of the music for Act III of *Lucio
Papirio dittatore*) or through a pair of *clarini* (as in the *Entrée* of the
ballet for Act III of *Scipione nelle Spagne*); second, in choirs of brass
and timpani as in the ballet music for Fux's *Enea negli Elisi* (1731).
Except for isolated *aria* and *minuet* movements, Matteis confines the
brass and timpani to movements of martial festivity such as *marches,
entrées* and *retiradas*. These various combinations of *clarini, trombe* and
timpani usually are located in the uppermost systems of any score. Other
instruments associated with them can be set out in any of the arrangements
described earlier.

The layout of Matteis's scores and his instrumentation are typical of
a composer whose activities traversed a period of relatively rapid change
from one style to another. His twenty-three years as *Direttore della musica
instrumentale* at the Habsburg court also coincided with the burgeoning
publication of dance manuals[54] and the evolving literary and aesthetic
debate. This involved recognition of other emerging forms of dance,
and in particular the increasing importance attached to the role of
rhetorical gesture and pantomimic dance. These latter were soon to prove
seminal for the innovative creativity of Hilverding van Wewen, whose
reforms were to incorporate what Taubert had promulgated as *tanzende
Schauspiele* in which grimace, gesture and movement would replace
verbalisation. This was the concept championed in the literary polemics
of both Gottsched[55] and the *Encyclopédistes*.[56] Hilverding, whose ballet
productions and choreography were later acclaimed by Gottsched as the
realisation of the new aesthetic ideals, entered Habsburg service as a
court dancer late in 1737, at the very end of Matteis's long incumbency
as resident composer of ballets.[57]

*   *   *   *   *

Throughout his incumbency Matteis enjoyed the same encouragement
and patronage that Charles VI and Elisabeth Christine accorded the
compositori Fux, Caldara and Conti, and the *literati* Metastasio, Zeno

and Pariati. Charles VI, as musically gifted as his predecessors, displayed great interest in the progress of the court operas and would follow the performances from carefully prepared full scores. On occasion he even assumed direction of the orchestra, leading the performance from the harpsichord, as in Caldara's *Euristeo* and Fux's *Elisa,* for both of which Matteis provided the ballet music.[58] Such active and committed royal patronage, which had already characterised Charles VI's predecessors was, with the possible exception of Joseph II, to remain unsurpassed from within the House of Habsburg.

Notes

[1] John Wilson (ed.) *Roger North on Music* (London, 1959) p. 309. For the most extended investigation into the life and work of Matteis senior, see Michael Tilmouth 'Nicola Matteis' *The Musical Quarterly* XLVI (1960) pp. 22–40.

[2] Andrew D. McCredie 'Nicholas Matteis – English Composer at the Habsburg Court', *Music and Letters* 48 (1967) p. 128.

[3] Roger North quoted in Tilmouth *op.cit.,* p. 32.

[4] Carlo Schmidl *Dizionario universale dei musicisti* (Milano, 1887) p. 63.

[5] Tilmouth *op.cit.,* pp. 32–33

[6] Wilhelm Josef Wasielewski *Die Violine und ihre Meister* 8th ed., (Leipzig, 1927) p. 189.

[7] Wilson *op.cit.,* p. 167.

[8] *Ibid.,* p. 358, n128.

[9] *Ibid.*

[10] Henry Viotta *Lexikon der Toonkunst* (Amsterdam, 1883) II, p. 560.

[11] Ernst Ludwig Gerber *Neues historisch-biographisches Lexikon der Tonkünstler* (Leipzig, 1813) III, p. 359f.

[12] Eduard Bernsdorf *Neues Universallexikon der Tonkunst* (Dresden, 1859) II, p. 914.

[13] [Bohumír] Gottfried [Jan] Johann Dlabač *Allgemeines historisches Künstler-Lexikon für Böhmen und zum Theil auch für Mähren und Schlesien* (Prague, 1815) p. 274f.

[14] Ludwig Ritter von Köchel *Die Kaiserliche Hof-Musikkapelle in Wien von 1543 bis 1867* (Wien, 1869) p. 69.

[15] Peter Keuschnig 'Nicola Matteis junior als Ballettkomponist' (D.Phil., diss. Universität Wien, 1966) p. 4.

[16] Köchel gives his salary as 75fl., a sum considerably above the remuneration of other court violinists, (*op.cit.*, p. 69).

[17] Keuschnig *op.cit.*, p. 4.

[18] *Ibid.*, p. 5.

[19] His salary appears to have remained at this figure up to his death. The salary of Gottfried Schweinberger (appointed to the court orchestra in 1727), whom Köchel lists as *Ballet-geiger*, was only 360fl. (Köchel *op.cit.*, p. 77).

[20] Ludwig Ritter von Köchel *Johann Josef Fux, Hofcompositor und Hofkapellmeister der Kaiser Leopold I., Josef I. und Karl VI. von 1698 bis 1740* (Wien, 1872) p. 424. Paul Nettl suggests Matteis was already ailing 'as early as 1723' (see 'An English Musician at the Court of Charles VI in Vienna' *The Musical Quarterly* XXVIII (1942) p. 319). Perhaps Schweinberger was appointed to relieve Matteis of all performance duties.

[21] Köchel *Die Kaiserliche Hof-Musikkapelle* ... p. 76; erroneously given as '23. Oct. 1738' on p. 69. Nettl (*op.cit.*, pp. 319-20) argues convincingly the correctness of Köchel's findings.

[22] Charles Burney *A General History of Music* (London, 1789) 3, p. 516. Burney's date is repeated by several later writers and is still retained by Michael Tilmouth 'Matteis [Mattheis], Nicola (ii)' *The New Grove Dictionary of Music and Musicians* (London, 1980) 11, p. 829.

[23] 'The younger Matteis must have returned to England soon after Mr North's *Memoirs of Music* were written; as I remember to have seen him at Shrewsbury, where he was settled as a language master as well as performer on the violin, in 1737' Burney *op.cit.*, p. 516. North wrote his *Memoirs* in 1728. Nettl dismisses Burney's claims, and even Percy A. Scholes, Burney's principal biographer, is hard-pressed to reconcile his subject's recollections with Nettl's arguments (see Scholes *The Great Dr. Burney* (London, 1958) I, pp. 17-18). Burney (b. 1726) could never have seen either the elder or younger Nicola Matteis — unless the latter made a hitherto undocumented visit to England early in the 1730s and, for some particular reason, stayed in Shrewsbury! His pronouncement that the younger Nicola 'played Corelli's solos with more simplicity and elegance than any performer I ever heard' (surely the source of Wasielewski's comment) can only be second-hand opinion. Most likely he was recounting an assessment made by Roger North. Burney, was one of the first to study North's *Memoirs* (see Wilson *op.cit.*, [p. xv]).

[24] Nettl *op.cit.*, p. 319.

[25] Keuschnig *op.cit.*, p. 4.

[26] Testamente: Bd. 1790-59, f. 253, Nr. 7252 Matheis Nikolaus, k. Instrumental-musikdirektor, Test. de publ. 8. November 1737.

[27] Keuschnig *op.cit.*, p. 4.

[28] See A. Peter Brown 'Caldara's trumpet music for the Imperial celebrations of Charles VI and Elisabeth Christine' p. 10.

[29] Corroboration of evidence was assisted through the co-ordination and comparison of results of a search of the manuscript sources with data supplied in Paul Nettl *op.cit.*, pp. 323-4; Anton Bauer 'Opern und Operetten in Wien' *Wiener musikwissenschaftliche Beiträge* II (1955); A. von Weilen *Zur Wiener Theaterge-schichte. Die vom Jahre 1629 bis zum 1740 am Wiener Hofe zur Aufführung gelangten Werke theatralischen Charakters und Oratorien* (Wien, 1910), and Franz Hadamowsky 'Barocktheater am Wiener Kaiserhof. Mit einem Spielplan 1625-1740' *Jahrbuch der Gesellschaft für Wiener Theater-Forschung 1951-52* (1955) pp. 7-

117. Further information provided by Dr Rosemary Moravec, Musikabteilung, Österreichische Nationalbibliothek, Vienna, is gratefully acknowledged.

[30] Keuschnig *op.cit.*, pp. 54–55. The fifty-eight ballets included 508 individual movements. The production, on 28 August, 1740, of Predieri's opera *Zenobia*, included a series of ballets with dance music supplied by Matteis, suggesting that the opera may have been planned and composed several years in advance. This is not impossible since Predieri, resident in Vienna from 1737, had already been appointed (in 1739, on Fux's recommendation) second *Kapellmeister* in succession to Caldara. The other possibility is that Matteis may have composed series of dances in the various genres and selected from these to meet the demands of each ballet. From such a resource it would have been possible to supply dance music for ballets first produced after his death.

[31] J. H. van der Meer 'Johann Josef Fux als Opernkomponist' *Utrechtse Bijdragen tot de Muziekwetenschap* 3 (1961) p. 157f.

[32] Keuschnig *op.cit.*, p. 38.

[33] Gottfried Taubert *Der rechtschaffener Tantzmeister* (Leipzig, 1717). Taubert was thoroughly familiar with French choreography having produced a German translation of Feuillet's *Chorégraphie*. His discussion of ballet, found in the second *Hauptteil* of his second book, recognized the divisions between 'Le Ballet sérieux' and 'Le Ballet comique ou grotesque', which encompassed theatrical as well as serious and comic dance. Cf. Andrew D. McCredie 'The Debate on the *Ballet d'Action* and its classical origins in Eighteenth-century German Poetics' *Music and Dance* Fourth National Symposium of the Musicological Society of Australia. (University of Western Australia, 1980) p. 73.

[34] Ballet music usually was supplied for each act of the three-act operas, and for the first, third and final acts of the five-act operas.

[35] Another interesting view of the *Aria* and *Ballet grotesque* appears in Joseph Gregor's *Kulturgeschichte des Ballets* (Vienna, 1944), p. 228. Gregor attributes some types of *aria grotesca* to the influence of the *commedia dell'arte*. Such dances might be done on stilts or presented in such a way as to make the performers appear crippled and for their movements to be sharp, angular and asymmetrical. The choice of masks for such performances emphasised figurines, usually the heads of various fauna, a development which Gregor saw, at least in part, as regressive.

[36] Johann Georg Sulzer *Allgemeine Theorie der schönen Künste* (1771–1774) IV, p. 506.

[37] Designations differ between the full-score (A-Wn: Mus.Hs. 17168) and the surviving instrumental parts (A-Wn: Mus.Hs. 17169). The *Loure* section is untitled in the 'Violino Primo' part; the fifth station is labelled 'Chiacona' in the 'Violin Primo' and 'Basso' parts, while the *Largo* is headed 'Aria' in the 'Basso' part-book.

[38] Keuschnig *op.cit.*, p. 226.

[39] Paul Nettl summarized Mattheson's description of the *bourrée* in his tract *Das neu-eröffnete Orchestre*, stating that 'the bourrées have dactylic measure in such a way that two eighths follow upon a quarter: the beginning is made with the last quarter of the upbeat, which thus becomes the last quarter of the first repetition.' Paul Nettl *The Story of Dance Music* (New York, 1947) p. 172.

[40] *Ibid.*, p. 173. Nettl's translation reads: 'It is a gay dance in even beat performed at festivities and in grotesque ballets. Its beat is 4/4, but it usually has three to four repetitions, of which the third is customarily short and humorous.'

[41] Keuschnig *op.cit.*, p. 234.

[42] *Ibid.*, pp. 235–6. Paul Nettl ascribes a seminal influence to Matteis's adoption of the minuet and trio, as well as Austrian dances, as providing a model which could have stimulated Viennese composers of the Monn-Wagenseil generation: 'and since Matteis wrote numerous minuets with trios for Viennese ballets, there is no doubt as to the sources of Monn's trio-minuets.' Nettl *op.cit.*, p. 207. In

the suite of six dances (compiled from Matteis's ballet-music for Caldara's *Il Tiridate* and *Il Venceslao*) which Nettl appends to his 'An English Musician ...' (*op.cit.*, pp. 324–8) he subtitles the last *Aria* as 'Ländler'.

[43] Andrew D. McCredie 'Christoph Graupner – the suites and sonatas for instrumental ensemble at Darmstadt' *Studies in Music* 17 (1983) pp. 96ff.

[44] The striking exceptions to these prevailing norms were composers of other than mainstream origins, such as Jan Dismas Zelenka, who evolved enterprising tonal structures and harmonic textures in his purely instrumental works.

[45] The most obvious example is the rapid incorporation of the *chalumeau* into these orchestras.

[46] It is most likely that Matteis first employed horns in the ballet music for Conti's *I satiri in Arcadia* (1714). See McCredie 'Nicholas Matteis – English Composer ...' *op.cit.*, p. 135.

[47] Klaus Haller 'Partituranordnung und musikalischer Satz' *Münchener Veröffentlichungen zur Musikgeschichte* 18 (1970) pp. 49, 173, 179 and 202.

[48] The *cornetto* had a more independent part in an *Aria* in the first-act ballet to Conti's *Archelao, re di Cappadocia* (1722). This, however, appears to have been the last work for the Viennese theatre in which the *cornetto* was required (see McCredie 'Nicholas Matteis – English Composer ... ' *op.cit.*, pp. 135–6). Caldara himself wrote no obbligatos for this instrument in his Viennese music, although he retained it in its usual *ripieno* role throughout his liturgical compositions. See: Eleanor Selfridge-Field 'The Viennese court orchestra in the time of Caldara' pp. 129 and 130.

[49] Andrew D. McCredie 'Instrumentarium and Instrumentation in the North German Baroque Opera,' (D.Phil., diss. Universität Hamburg, 1964) pp. 186–90.

[50] A. Hoffmann *Die Orchestersuiten Georg Philipp Telemanns* (Wolfenbüttel and Zürich, 1969).

[51] Heinz Becker (ed.) 'Klarinetten-Konzert des 18. Jahrhunderts' *Das Erbe Deutscher Musik* 41 (1957) pp. vii–viii.

[52] McCredie 'Christoph Graupner ... ' *op.cit.*, p. 99 and 103.

[53] The varieties of layout employed in Matteis's scores correspond to those used in other German states; see McCredie 'Instrumentarium ... ' p. 102f.

[54] French aesthetics of dance embodied in treatises such as those by Ménéstrier and Feuillet were translated into English (J. Weaver *Orchésography, or the Art of Dancing by characters and demonstrative figures* (London 1706) — being an exact translation from the French of Feuillet) and German (by Taubert, see Note 33). Later, they were adopted by the *Encyclopédistes*, who in turn influenced J. G. Sulzer as well as German lexicography and literary theory.

[55] Johann Christoph Gottsched *Versuch einer critischen Dichtkunst* J. and B. Birke (eds) *Gottsched Ausgewählte Werke* (Berlin and New York, 1973) VI/2, pp. 387, 555 and 571.

[56] Charles Batteux *Les beaux Arts réduits à une même Principe* (Paris, 1747) pp. 259f and 299f.

[57] Robert Haas 'Der Wiener Bühnentanz von 1740 bis 1767' *Jahrbuch Musikverlag Peters* (Leipzig, 1937) p. 77f.

[58] See Egon Wellesz's, 'Einleitung' to his edition of J. J. Fux *Costanza e Fortezza*, *Denkmäler der Tonkunst in Österreich* 34–35 (1910) p. xx. See also Haller *op.cit.*, p. 215 and Köchel *Fux* ... Beilage X, pp. 137–8.

The Italian cantata
in Vienna, 1700–1711:
an overview of stylistic traits

Lawrence E. Bennett

Zusammenfassung

Die italienische Kantate in Wien, 1700–1711: ein Stilüberblick

Nachdem sie fast 40 Jahre lang vernachläßigt wurde, hat die italienische weltliche Kantate um 1700 am Habsburger Hof in Wien wieder zu blühen begonnen. Das neue Interesse für gesungene Kammermusik ist z.T. dem Aufstieg des liberal gebildeten Joseph I. (1705–1711) zuzurechnen und z.T. dem Ende der langen Amtszeit des konservativen Kapellmeisters Antonio Draghi (1700 gest.). Zu der neuen Welle der Italiener, die Draghi ablösten, gehörten auch Carlo Agostino Badia, Giovanni Bononcini, Antonio Maria Bononcini, Marc'Antonio Ziani und Attilio Ariosti. Wir haben mindestens 98 noch erhaltene Kantaten von diesen fünf Komponisten identifiziert, sowie zwei anonymen Stücke. Im allgemeinen weisen ihre Kantaten keine ausschließlich Wienerischen Stilmerkmale auf. Die einzige, wohl bedeutendste Eigenschaft, die sie von anderen der Zeit unterscheidet, ist der Gebrauch von vielseitigeren Instrumentalbegleitungen. Dieser Überblick faßt neun Elemente des Kantatenstils zusammen: allgemeine Aufbausysteme, die Auswahl der Stimmen, die Instrumentation, Dynamik, Rezitativ und Arioso, Arientonarten, das Tempo und das Metrum, den Gebrauch von Devisen, und Arienaufbau. Der Überblick liefert auch den Hintergrund für weitere Studien über die Kantaten von Antonio Caldara, Francesco Bartolomeo Conti und Giuseppe Porsile, die während der Regierungszeit Karls VI. komponiert wurden.

The Italian cantata
in Vienna, 1700–1711:
an overview of stylistic traits

Lawrence E. Bennett

AMONG THE MANY Italian cantata composers active in the late seventeenth and early eighteenth centuries, very few appear to have been as prolific as Antonio Caldara. While a detailed index of the extant Caldara cantatas awaits publication, current research indicates that Robert Freeman's estimate of '*c*300 solo cantatas' plus 'numerous cantatas, 2vv' is probably accurate.[1] The total that eventually emerges may reveal Caldara to be the second-most productive cantata composer of all, and thus refute Burney's contention that Giovanni Bononcini 'was perhaps the most voluminous composer of cantatas, next to Ales. Scarlatti, which Italy can boast.'[2] In any event, advances in bibliographic research make the time now ripe for a full-scale stylistic study of the Caldara cantatas. The present study concentrates on the cantatas written for Vienna during the years 1700–1711 (the decade prior to Caldara's selection as *Vizekapellmeister*) by five composers who were actually his contemporaries. Knowledge of their works will deepen our understanding of the cantatas written by Caldara for the Habsburg court in the ensuing years.

During the Baroque era, Italian musical innovations spread rapidly throughout Habsburg lands. At the Imperial court in Vienna, opera, oratorio and cantata found complete acceptance by the middle of the seventeenth century. The Italian *Kapellmeister*, Giovanni Priuli (*c*1575–1629), Giovanni Valentini (1582/83–1649), Antonio Bertali (1605–1669) and Giovanni Felice Sances (*c*1600–1679), all contributed richly to the repertoire of vocal chamber music during the period 1620–1660. With the accession of Leopold I (*r*1658–1705), however, interest seems to have focused almost exclusively on large sacred and secular dramatic works. On the basis of extant sources, composers engaged by Leopold appear to have written fewer than fifty cantatas between 1660 and 1700.[3]

After some forty years of near neglect, the Italian secular cantata began to flourish again at Vienna around 1700. This fresh interest in vocal chamber music can be attributed partly to the rise of the liberally educated Joseph I (r1705–1711), and partly to the end of the long tenure of the conservative *Kapellmeister*, Antonio Draghi (1636?–1700).

The new wave of composers who served the ageing Leopold and his heir received their training in north-Italian centres. Together they brought the late-Baroque style to Vienna from cities such as Bologna, Venice and Florence, forming not so much a 'Viennese School' as a circle of north Italians active in Vienna. From Bologna came Giovanni and Antonio Maria Bononcini, Pier [Pietro] Francesco Tosi and Attilio Ariosti. From Venice the Habsburgs imported Carlo Agostino Badia and Marc'Antonio Ziani, and from Florence they attracted the theorbist, Francesco Bartolomeo Conti. Among the many important new composers who resided in Vienna during the years 1700–1711, at least five (Badia, the Bononcini brothers, Ziani and Ariosti) made significant contributions to the cantata literature.

The composers

Badia (1672–1738), the first of the new group of north Italians to receive an appointment, began his service in 1694.[4] Over the next forty-four years (in which time he served three Emperors, Leopold I, Joseph I and Charles VI) he supplied at least thirty-four oratorios and twenty-six secular dramatic works. He also composed at least fifty-three chamber cantatas and duets, virtually all of which date from between 1699 and 1712. Badia was not the most important composer of his generation at Vienna, but he holds the distinction of being the first to introduce the musical innovations of the late Baroque to the Habsburg court. Moreover, he led the re-establishment of the cantata as a popular genre.

Giovanni Bononcini (1670–1747) was one of the most popular and widely-performed composers of the early eighteenth century.[5] By the end of 1697 he had received an appointment at the prestigious Imperial court. On 7 January, 1700, he became only the third musician (after Badia and Fux) to be given the special designation of Court Composer (*Hofcompositor*). Almost from the outset of his service, Bononcini maintained a special relationship with the future Joseph I and his wife, Wilhelmine Amalie, a relationship that strengthened after Joseph's accession. But circumstances following the Emperor's death (17 April, 1711) brought a complete reversal of Bononcini's most-favoured position. Uncertainty about the precise membership of Charles VI's *Kapelle* persisted until a list was finally established on 31 December, 1712.[6] While musicians such as Ziani, Conti and Badia received fresh appointments, Bononcini did not, partly because Charles VI refused to assume responsibility for financial promises made by Joseph. Only in 1736, after a twenty-four-year absence, which saw him in service in Rome, London, Paris, Madrid and Lisbon, was Bononcini readmitted to the court at Vienna.[7]

During a remarkable period of nearly sixty prolific years, Bononcini composed approximately sixty-eight sacred and secular dramatic works, four masses, soloistic motets, occasional choral works, at least nine collections of instrumental music, and some 317 known chamber cantatas and duets.[8] Yet of the cantatas inventoried by the author, only five can be identified as works that were definitely composed during Bononcini's first residency in Vienna. It seems paradoxical that such a prolific and influential cantata composer should have written so few cantatas for Vienna just when the court was giving fresh attention to the genre. Perhaps this neglect was due to the steady stream of commissions he received for large dramatic works that paid homage to members of the ruling family, especially to Joseph and Wilhelmine.

Until late in life, Antonio Maria Bononcini (1677–1726) closely patterned his career after that of his older and more celebrated brother.[9] He followed Giovanni to Vienna after his appointment at the court but the exact date of his arrival at the Habsburg capital and the extent of his activities there before 1705 remain unknown. In any event, Giovanni's great influence with Joseph undoubtedly was the key which opened up his brother's successful career as a composer of dramatic music, beginning with *La Maddalena* in 1705. Antonio must have received an appointment as Court Composer early in 1710. He is so titled in the libretto for *Tigrane, re d'Armenia*, the second of two dramatic works dating from that year, and in that for *L'interciso*, written in the following year. But his career at the court was short-lived. Like his brother, Antonio was not retained by Charles VI after 1712. In contrast to Giovanni, Antonio was neither an extremely prolific nor influential composer, although his works show a great skill and attention to detail. His extant compositions comprise some fifteen operas, three oratorios, twelve sonatas for viola da gamba, a handful of sacred works and approximately thirty-eight cantatas. At least thirteen chamber cantatas and one 'grand cantata'[10] were composed for Vienna.

Marc'Antonio Ziani (c1653–1715) was one of the most acclaimed and influential composers to serve at Vienna in the early eighteenth century.[11] Following the death of Draghi, Antonio Pancotti was selected by Leopold as *Kapellmeister*. At the same time Ziani was called to Vienna to succeed Pancotti as *Vizekapellmeister*, receiving an official appointment on 1 April, 1700. His entrance into Viennese musical life was another milestone in the revitalization of the Habsburg chapel. After the death of Pancotti in 1709, Joseph did not appoint a new *Kapellmeister*, but temporarily left the post vacant. Following the death of Joseph, Ziani assumed leadership of the chapel, but only on 1 January, 1712, did he finally receive the official appointment as *Kapellmeister*. Unfortunately, he was to hold the honoured position for little more than three years before his death on 22 January, 1715. These years saw major changes both in the *Hofkapelle*'s personnel and in musical style at Vienna, but Ziani did not live to witness the full blossoming of music during the Fux-Caldara generation. Ziani was a prolific composer of operas, oratorios and sacred music, but he appears to have devoted little attention to the cantata; only about seven cantatas are extant. At least four of these were composed for Vienna, two of which are the *accademie* of 1706.[12] Perhaps the demands of his administrative duties limited his cantata output but, no doubt, the constant pressure of supplying large-scale works for church and theatre is more to blame.

One of the more shadowy figures of Baroque music history, Attilio Malachia Ariosti (1666–1729) may have studied along with the Bononcini brothers in the *scuola* of the Bolognese *maestro* G. P. Colonna. In any event, he was to become an early advocate of the viola d'amore and the instrument's leading virtuoso in the first half of the eighteenth century.[13] During the weeks from 20 June to 25 July, 1688, Ariosti was admitted to the Servite order at Bologna, but by spring, 1696, he had obtained release and was residing at Mantua. A settlement between the Gonzaga Duke, Ferdinando Carlo, and Sophie Charlotte, wife of Friedrich III, the Elector of Brandenburg, abruptly ended Ariosti's service at the Mantuan court. The composer journeyed to Berlin *via* Vienna, and by September or October, 1697, had officially entered the service of the Brandenburgs. Ariosti's religious vows ultimately prevented him from acquiring a permanent post at Berlin, and perhaps the influential Giovanni Bononcini (who had sojourned in Berlin from spring 1701, to March, 1703) lay behind his subsequent recognition at the Viennese court in the last years of Leopold's reign. Ariosti probably arrived there in late October or early November, 1703, and quickly received commissions for secular dramatic works. There is no evidence that he ever became a member of the Imperial chapel, but we have confirmation of his favoured position. On 15 April, 1707, Ariosti wrote to the Elector Palatine, Johann Wilhelm, that Joseph I was dispatching him to Italy as an agent-general, empowered to represent the Emperor to 'presso tutte le Corti e Principi d'Italia,' and that he had been granted a pension.[14] It seems likely that Joseph's considerable appetite for fresh compositions from Italy must have been satisfied in part by Ariosti who returned to Vienna from time to time. The composer retained his post as agent-general until the end of Joseph's reign. After the young Emperor's death, Ariosti was released by the Dowager Empress, Eleonora Magdalena, who served as Regent of the empire during the interregnum. Besides approximately twenty-one operas, five oratorios and a few sacred works, Ariosti composed some seventy-five instrumental pieces and a similar number of cantatas. Probably the best known cantatas are the six included in the *Cantates and a Collection of Lessons*, published during Ariosti's London sojourn in the 1720s. In addition, approximately seventy cantatas are preserved in some twenty-five manuscripts now in ten European libraries. Twenty-three cantatas are found in two manuscripts of Viennese origins.

In addition to the cantatas by Badia, the Bononcini brothers, Ziani and Ariosti, at least two anonymous cantatas belong to the period 1700–1711. The anonymous cantata, *Cetre amiche*, was written for the celebration of one of the Austrian victories at Landau during the war of the Spanish Succession. The victory was led by Joseph, identified in the text as the 'gran figlio d'Augusto'. Since Joseph's presence during the fighting at Landau inspired victories in both 1702 and 1704, the composition could have been a tribute to his heroism after either battle. Another anonymous cantata, *Alli giusti miei lamenti*, served a twofold purpose: it paid homage to Leopold shortly after his death on 5 May, 1705, while honouring Joseph as the empire's heroic new leader.[15]

The cantata repertoire — stylistic traits

The approximately 100 extant cantatas from the period 1700–1711 confirm a vigorous upsurge of cantata writing at Vienna in the early eighteenth century. The dates 1700 and 1711 should be understood as guidelines and not as absolute boundaries. Thus, for example, at least four cantatas by Badia date from 1699, but stylistically and historically these compositions obviously belong to the period under consideration. Likewise, a small number of cantatas were composed shortly after 1711. These include three by Giovanni Bononcini that probably date from the year 1712.

This body of cantatas is to be found in twenty-three primary sources: manuscripts and prints that are clearly of Viennese origins and dated or assignable to the period 1700–1711 on the basis of internal evidence. Five of these sources are copies of the one cantata publication, Badia's *Tributi armonici*, a set of twelve cantatas for solo voice, dedicated to Leopold and published by Weigel at Nuremburg between 1699 and 1704.[16] Holographs of two Ziani cantatas survive, as well as a possible holograph of a cantata by Badia. Eighty-five works are preserved in archival copies from the collections of Leopold I and Joseph I, now in the *Musiksammlung* of the Austrian National Library, Vienna.[17]

On the whole, these cantatas do not exhibit style characteristics unique to Vienna. Thus references to the 'Viennese composers' or the 'Viennese cantata' should not be taken as meaning a circle of composers who developed a style peculiar to Vienna. Perhaps the single characteristic that distinguishes cantatas in Vienna from cantatas written elsewhere in Europe is the tendency to include obbligato instruments more frequently and to use larger groups of instruments in general — features that may be attributed in part to the unusually large number of players available to Habsburg court composers. In addition, several 'grand cantatas' exceed the normal scope of the Baroque chamber cantata.

If few indigenous Viennese traits can be isolated in the cantatas written between 1700 and 1711, their general characteristics can nevertheless be summarized. The following overview considers a variety of basic features including the broad structural plans, the selection of voices and instruments, the recitative style, and aria designs.

Broad structural plans

While the cantatas of the Draghi generation consisted of a free intermingling of recitative, *arioso* and aria, the structure of the cantata evolved into a fixed pattern of alternating recitatives and arias[18] in the first decade of the eighteenth century. The first movement of a cantata may be either a recitative or an aria. Of the 100 cantatas analysed here, fifty-four begin with an aria, while the remaining forty-six open with a recitative. No cantata concludes with a recitative. The number of arias usually varies from two to four, although three exceptionally long cantatas contain between six and eleven arias. The patterns of clearly alternating recitative (R) and aria (A) found in ninety-seven of the early eighteenth-century Viennese cantatas are summarized in Table 1:

Table 1. *Patterns of recitative and aria*

Pattern	Badia	Ziani	Ariosti	G. Bononcini	A. M. Bononcini	Anon.	Total
A-R-A	17	0	16	1	3	0	37
R-A-R-A	14	0	6	3	3	0	26
A-R-A-R-A	8	1	0	1	1	1	12
R-A-R-A-R-A	9	1	1	0	4	0	15
A-R-A-R-A-R-A	1	0	0	0	0	0	1
R-A-R-A-R-A-R-A	3	0	0	0	1	0	4
A-R-A-R-A-R-A-R-A-R-A	0	1	0	0	0	0	1
R-A-R-A-R-A-R-A-R-A-R-A	0	1	0	0	0	0	1

The placement of two arias in succession can be found in only three cantatas. Of these the anonymous *Alli giusti miei lamenti*, written for the coronation of Joseph I, is a special case not only because of the juxtaposition of arias, but also because of its unusual length.

Table 2. *Unusual patterns of recitative and aria*

Pattern	Title	Composer
A-A-R-A	*Vorrei, pupille belle*	A. M. Bononcini
A-R-A-A-R-A	*S'una volta io potrò*	Badia
A-R-A-A-R-A-R-A-R-A-A-R-A-R-A-R-A-A	*Alli giusti miei lamenti*	Anon.

For the opening movement of *Vorrei, pupille belle*, Antonio Bononcini constructs a highly unusual design. It unfolds in the manner of a *da capo* aria, but the central section consists entirely of *recitativo semplice*,[19] contrasting with the outer sections which, scored for two violins and continuo, proceed in a strict metre (3/4) and tempo (*Largo*). The skilful use of recitative within this piece softens the effect of juxtaposing two arias. The two successive arias at the centre of Badia's *S'una volta io potrò* lack this touch but nevertheless contrast sharply in tempo and metre. However, the most unconventional overall scheme occurs in *Alli giusti miei lamenti*. Here the first aria (*da capo*) is repeated in its entirety after a recitative. Only a ritornello separates this repetition from the next new aria (also *da capo*), which also returns after an intervening recitative. (These two arias thus account for the first four arias in the plan given in Table 2.) The composer inserts only an instrumental ritornello between arias six and seven; likewise arias ten and eleven are divided by a brief instrumental passage, not by a recitative. Another special feature of this cantata is the thirty-six-bar-long concluding chorus, the only example to be found in any of the Viennese cantatas.

Independent instrumental movements also contribute to the broad outlines of seventeen cantatas. (The patterns of recitative and aria shown above do not take these into account.) Of the five composers, only Ariosti never includes separate instrumental music in his cantatas. Not surprisingly, the instrumental movements by other composers always occur in cantatas with obbligato or concertizing parts. They consist of introductions (brief or fairly extended), and ritornellos inserted between vocal movements.

Seven cantatas begin with instrumental introductions, variously termed *Sinfonia* (the anonymous *Cetre amiche* and Ziani's *Ahimè, ch'io son piagato*), *Preludio* (Giovanni Bononcini's *Clori, svenar mi sento* and Antonio Bononcini's *Ecco amor*), and *Entré* (Badia's *Qui fra l'ombre*). The manuscripts for two cantatas (Badia's *Scesa dal ciel* and Ziani's *Cieco fanciul*) do not provide genre designations for the instrumental openings.

The designs of the introductions vary considerably. Single-movement instrumental pieces head two cantatas by Badia and one by Antonio Bononcini. The opening of Badia's *Qui fra l'ombre* uses a homophonic texture and a binary structure, while his introduction to *Scesa dal ciel* and A. Bononcini's *Preludio* for *Ecco amor* are imitative and through-composed. The instrumental openings of three other cantatas fall into two movements, probably showing the influence of the French overture. *Cetre amiche* begins with a movement in ₵ time that has many phrase repetitions but no conventional design; it continues with an imitative section in 3/4 that is then repeated. Ziani's *Ahimè, ch'io son piagato* starts with a binary *Andante* in 4/4 and concludes with an imitative *Allegro* in the same metre. The introduction to Giovanni Bononcini's *Clori, svenar mi sento* consists of two binary movements — a stately *Largo* with frequent dotted notes and a dance-like *Presto* in 3/8. The three-movement introduction to Ziani's *Cieco fanciul* opens with a binary *Allegro* in 4/4, proceeds with a *Larghetto cantabile* (also in 4/4), and closes with a ternary (ABA^1) *Allegro* in 3/8.

Brief instrumental ritornellos, separated from surrounding vocal movements by double bars, occur in fifteen cantatas by Badia, Ziani, Antonio Bononcini, and the two anonymous composers. These ritornellos make use of the full instrumental ensembles. In ten cantatas (six by Antonio Bononcini, three by Badia and one by an anonymous composer) instrumental ritornellos appear only once. Bononcini prefers to position his tutti ritornello just before the final recitative and aria. Badia, on the other hand, favours it either at the centre or at the end of a long cantata. In two other works he introduces two independent ritornellos, employing a different plan in each cantata: A-R-A-Rit-R-A-Rit; and Rit-R-A-R-A-R-A-Rit. The two *accademie* by Ziani and the anonymous *Alli giusti miei lamenti* include from four to nine ritornellos inserted throughout the cantatas. The thematic material of a separate ritornello is usually derived from the preceding aria but its fuller instrumentation often contrasts with the aria's simpler continuo accompaniment. If the aria itself contains a recurring continuo ritornello, this may be omitted at the conclusion and replaced by the tutti ritornello.

Selection of voices

Ninety-three of the 100 cantatas relevant to this study are written for solo voice; six works require two singers, and one composition calls for three. The cantata for three voices also concludes with a five-part chorus. As in Italy, the selection of voices at Vienna reveals a very strong preference for the higher vocal ranges, a preference made clear in Table 3. The complete dominance of the soprano voice is not unexpected, but a total absence of cantatas for solo bass from this early eighteenth-century Viennese repertoire must be considered more unusual.

Table 3. *Vocal ranges of the cantatas*

Range(s)	No. of cantatas	Badia	Ziani	Ariosti	G. Bononcini	A. M. Bononcini	Anon.
S	68	43	2	12	4	7	0
A	23	5	0	11	1	6	0
T	2	1	0	0	0	0	1
SS	5	4	1	0	0	0	0
TB	1	0	1	0	0	0	0
SST	1	0	0	0	0	0	1

Instrumentation

The accompaniments for sixty-seven of the 100 cantatas consist of continuo only. Thus, a third of the cantatas include parts for one or more obbligato instruments. Not all of the composers consistently require additional instruments. Antonio Bononcini, for example, always writes obbligato parts, while Ariosti requests an additional instrumental line for only two arias in two different cantatas. Table 4 reviews the number of cantatas by each composer and indicates the percentage with obbligato instruments.

Table 4. *Cantatas with obbligato instruments*

Composer	No. of cantatas	No. with obbligatos	% with obbligatos
Badia	53	13	25
Ariosti	23	2	9
A. M. Bononcini	13	13	100
G. Bononcini	5	1	20
Ziani	4	2	50
Anonymous	2	2	100

Making use of the broad assortment of players at the Habsburg court, the composers score the cantatas for a colourful variety of instruments. The combinations of obbligato instruments, the number of cantatas in which each combination appears and the composers using each combination are set out in Table 5.

Table 5. *Obbligato instruments used in the cantatas*

Obbligato instruments	No. of cantatas	Badia	Ziani	Ariosti	G. Bononcini	A. M. Bononcini	Anon.
fls. 1–2	12	5	0	0	1	6	0
vns. 1–2	6	1	0	0	0	5	0
fls. 1–2, vns. 1–2	2	2	0	0	0	0	0
instr. in sop. clef (va. d'amore?)	2	0	0	2	0	0	0
vns. 1–2, va.	2	0	0	0	0	1	1
instr. in treble clef (fl.?)	1	1	0	0	0	0	0
vc.?	1	1	0	0	0	0	0
unison vns.	1	0	0	0	0	0	1
unison lutes	1	1	0	0	0	0	0
2 treble insts.	1	1	0	0	0	0	0
vns. 1–2, vc.	1	0	0	0	0	1	0
2 instrs. in sop. clef, 1 in alto clef	1	1	0	0	0	0	0
vns. 1–2, va. bns.	1	0	1	0	0	0	0
vns. 1–2, va. obs., bn.	1	0	1	0	0	0	0

This table also highlights the difficulties in determining precisely the obbligato instruments intended by the composers in undesignated scores. For example, in the first movement of *Un guardo solo, o bella*, Badia divides the bass line between a simple fundamental part and a more elaborate one. This latter is evidently intended as a cello obbligato and is so indicated in Table 5. The unspecified treble parts in Badia's *Scesa dal ciel* may be either for two flutes or for two violins, the paired obbligatos favoured by the composer elsewhere — the absence of clearly idiomatic figurations for flute or violin makes it difficult to determine the exact instrumentation. Badia also fails to stipulate instruments for the treble line in the *Entré* of *Qui fra l'ombre* and for the three upper parts (two in treble clef, one in alto) in *I sospiri dell'aure*, two of seven cantatas by the composer in A-Wn: Mus.Hs. 17721. The emphasis on flutes in other cantatas of this manuscript suggests their further participation in *Qui fra l'ombre* and *I sospiri dell'aure*. However, strings alone (violins 1 and 2, and violas), producing a homogeneous sonority, may have been intended for the latter cantata, although string and woodwind doublings were not uncommon.

Ariosti also does not specify the instrument for the single obbligato line in *Furie che ne gl'abbissi* and *Che mi giova esser regina*. Curiously, in each cantata he notates the obbligato in the soprano clef and places it *below* the vocal line, adding the rubric 'si suona' for the second aria of *Furie che ne gl'abbissi*. These procedures are unique in the Viennese cantata repertoire and suggest that the obbligatos were not intended for one of the standard treble instruments — violin, flute or oboe. The composer may well have written these parts for the viola d'amore, an instrument on which he himself excelled. Certainly, it was for this instrument that he wrote the obbligato line in *Pur alfin gentil viola*, although this cantata was not composed for Vienna. Unfortunately, the obbligato lines in the two Viennese cantatas for the most part lack idiomatic figurations that would help to identify the instruments, although string crossings are suggested by the many melodic sixths in the writing in *Furie che ne gl'abbissi*. The obbligato extends from f-sharp^I to g^{II} in *Che mi giova* and from a^I to g^{II} in *Furie che ne gl'abbissi*. Thus the lower limits remain well within the normal compass of the viola d'amore, whose lower strings were seldom used by eighteenth-century composers. Especially unusual, however, is the use of the soprano clef; composers customarily notated viola d'amore parts in the alto clef. Nevertheless, the composer's long association with the instrument and the inclusion of viola d'amore obbligatos in at least two contemporary Viennese operas (Fux's *Gli ossequi della notte*, 1709, and Ariosti's own *Marte placato*, 1707), support the conclusion that here, too, the viola d'amore was intended.

The manuscript of Giovanni Bononcini's *Clori, svenar mi sento* likewise leaves open the question of specific instrumentation. No instruments are designated for the two treble lines of the *Preludio*. However, the composer specifies 'flauto solo' for the obbligato of the first aria. Like the *Preludio*, the second aria requires two upper parts, but again these are left undesignated. At two points during this aria, the lower obbligato line drops out while the upper line (marked 'solo') continues; when the second line resumes, the parts are labelled 'tutti'. By 'tutti' Bononcini may simply have wished to draw attention to the resumption of both lines. But it is also plausible that if violins doubled flutes, the 'solo' passages were to be performed by the flute soloist of the first aria.

In cantatas beginning with an instrumental introduction, the non-continuo instruments almost always reappear in an obbligato role in arias, and sometimes also in tutti ritornellos. The exception to this practice is Badia's *Qui fra l'ombre*. Here the instrumental opening calls for one treble instrument and continuo, but throughout the remainder of the cantata no obbligato line occurs. Perhaps the instrumentalist of the introduction improvised obbligatos above the bass-line ritornellos of the arias. The exceptionally rudimentary character of these lines makes the addition of such obbligatos seem plausible. Only a few years earlier, during the last years of Draghi's tenure, scribes frequently wrote out only the bass lines of ritornellos, indicating that obbligato parts should be filled in by the performers. Moreover, the preceding cantata in Mus. Hs. 17721 (*I sospiri dell'aure*, with its three unspecified melodic instrumental lines) concludes with just such a bass ritornello, entirely separated from the final aria and inviting obbligato as well as continuo realization.

The most lavish orchestral accompaniments occur in works by Ziani and Antonio Bononcini. For the *prima accademia* of 1706 (*Cieco fanciul*), Ziani uses violins 1 and 2, viola, oboes, bassoon and continuo. In the first and third movements of the introduction, he assigns the bassoon a separate part, slightly more elaborate than the bass line; elsewhere the bassoonist probably doubled the bass line. The oboes play an independent line only in the fifth aria. The 'senza hautbois' marking for the obbligato of the first aria implies that they doubled the violins in most other places — a typical late-Baroque scoring. For the *seconda accademia* Ziani calls for a slightly smaller ensemble: violins 1 and 2, viola, bassoons and continuo. Again, he provides a separate line for the bassoons (once more a slightly modified version of the continuo line) only in the *Sinfonia*. The possibility that here, too, oboes doubled the violins cannot be excluded.

Antonio Bononcini's most elaborate orchestrations can be seen in *Mentre al novo apparir* which he scores for first and second violins, cello and continuo. This last is designated 'contrabasso e cembalo' in the opening aria which also features a cello obbligato. Bononcini's specific reference to the double bass (an isolated example in the Viennese cantata repertoire) gives fascinating evidence of Baroque continuo practices and also suggests that it may have been used in other cantatas scored for fairly large instrumental ensembles.

Solo-tutti contrasts in five cantatas confirm the orchestral nature of the instrumentation. For example, the title page of Antonio Bononcini's *Ecco amor* includes the description 'In Soprano Concertata con Violini e concerto grosso', and throughout the composition solo and tutti groupings are opposed. The composer exploits similar contrasts in the first and third arias of *Troppo rigore, Clori*, and in the third and fourth arias of *Mentre al novo apparir* he gives even more specific directions, drawing upon 'soli quattro violini' at times during the vocal sections and 'tutti' elsewhere. Ziani also specifies the precise number of violins in the middle movement of the introduction to *Cieco fanciul*, requiring two first and two second violins for this passage, and reserving the full complement for the outer movements. However, he does not supply such specific instruction for the aria accompaniments. The anonymous composer of *Cetre amiche* (a cantata scored for first and second violins, viola and continuo) contrasts 'tutti' with 'concertino' throughout the work.

It can readily be appreciated that cantatas scored for medium or large ensembles offered most opportunities for instrumental colour. The solo-tutti contrasts and the movement-by-movement changes of instruments in Badia's *Là nell'arabe selve*, Antonio Bononcini's *Mentre al novo apparir* and Ziani's *Cieco fanciul* exemplify this type of broad, but effective instrumental variety (Table 6).

Table 6. *Broad instrumental contrasts in three cantatas*

Là nell'arabe selve Badia

Aria 1:	fls. 1-2, vns. 1-2, bc.
Aria 2:	solo fl., bc.
Aria 3:	solo vn., bc.
Aria 4:	fls. 1-2, vns. 1-2, bc.

Mentre al novo apparir A. M. Bononcini

Aria 1:	vns. 1-2 (solo-tutti), vc. obbl., bc (cb., harps.)
Aria 2:	bc.
Rit.:	tutti
Aria 3:	vns. 1-2 (4 solo vns.-tutti), bc.
Aria 4:	unison vns. (4 solo vns.-tutti); vc. obbl., bc.

Cieco fanciul Ziani

Introduction:	
Allegro:	vns. 1-2 (doubled by obs. 1-2), va., bn., bc.
Larghetto cantabile	vn. 1 (2 soloists), vn. 2 (2 soloists), va., bc.
Allegro:	vns. 1-2 (obs. 1-2), va., bn., bc.
Aria 1:	unison vns. (without oboes), va., bc.
Rit.:	vns. 1-2 (obs. 1-2), va., bc.
Aria 2:	bc.
Rit.:	vns. 1-2 (obs. 1-2), va., bc.
Aria 3:	bc.
Rits.:	vns. 1-2 (obs. 1-2), va., bc.
Aria 4:	bc.
Rit.:	vns. 1-2 (obs. 1-2), va., bc.
Aria 5:	unison vns., unison obs., va., bc.
Aria 6:	bc.
Rit.:	vns. 1-2 (obs. 1-2), va., bc..

Note: Recitatives, always accompanied by continuo only, have been excluded.

Idiomatic instrumental writing is typical only of the cantatas by Antonio Bononcini. In string obbligatos, such as the solo violin part of *Sul margine adorato* (Aria 2), or the cello solos of *Mentre al novo apparir* (Arias 1 and 4), he demands rapid string crossings, large leaps and double stops. Trills and passages involving rapid figuration idiomatic to the flute appear in cantatas such as *Tutta fiamme e tutta ardore* (Aria 2). Characteristic flute trills and scales occur, though less often, in works by Badia (*Rusignol che tempri il canto*, Aria 1) and Giovanni Bononcini (*Clori, svenar mi sento*, Aria 2). Ariosti includes oscillating patterns indicative of string crossings in the unspecified obbligato part of *Furie che ne gl'abbissi* (Aria 2).

Antonio Bononcini also supplies markings for phrasing and articulation more frequently than his contemporaries, combining terms such as *staccato*, *battuto* and *cantabile* with tempo indications. The rare designation *battuto* (strictly measured) appears twice — at the beginning of the *Preludio* for *Ecco amor* and again for the second aria of *Sul margine adorato*.

Dynamics

With few exceptions, the composers reserve dynamics for arias and vocal ensembles, but the frequency and choice of markings depends upon the individual composer. Giovanni Bononcini, for example, uses no dynamics in his five Viennese cantatas, while Ariosti introduces only one *forte-piano* echo in a single cantata (*Ne spatiosi campi*, Aria 2). Ziani draws upon dynamic contrasts only slightly more often, and he, too, relies primarily upon simple echo effects. These also appear in the *Sinfonia* of the anonymous *Cetre amiche* which contains several *pianissimo-forte* contrasts. Badia especially favours the *piano* repetition of a phrase or group of phrases at the end of the *A*-section of a *da capo* aria, incorporating this device in at least twenty-five arias — so often, in fact, that it may be considered a hallmark of the composer's style. Occasionally he repeats the effect in the closing ritornello of an aria. Outside of echo phrases, however, dynamic shadings seldom appear in Badia's scores. Thus the first aria of *Scesa dal ciel*, in which the obbligato instruments are marked 'piano' for fragments of the ritornello and for the first entry of the tenor soloist, is exceptional.

Virtually every cantata by Antonio Bononcini displays some dynamic colouring. The composer only rarely employs the straightforward echo devices found in the scores of Badia and Ziani, preferring instead, dynamic markings for structural reasons or for expressive word-painting. He often sets apart the final phrase of a large vocal section by marking it 'piano'. Frequently the *A*- and *B*-sections of a *da capo* aria conclude with similar thematic material, and the use of a *piano* dynamic at both places subtly underscores the symmetry. Sometimes he varies this technique by applying it to the penultimate phrases of the *A*- and *B*-sections. Cantatas with solo-tutti passages are apt to include numerous *forte-piano* markings, but the instrumental and dynamic contrasts are not necessarily coordinated. The composer often selects ritornello fragments or entire ritornellos for dynamic shadings; thus, for example, in the middle of the *B*-section of the aria 'Quanto più cara, quanto più bella' (*Mentre al novo apparir*, Aria 3) he inserts a sudden *forte*, tutti ritornello. Occasionally he will prescribe the more extreme *pianissimo* in response to a simple *forte*. But he achieves perhaps the most refined effect of the Viennese cantata repertoire in the initial aria of *Vorrei, pupille belle*. As in many other arias, he concludes the *A*-section with a *piano* phrase. However, he marks the beginning of the written-out *da capo* 'piano', reserving *pianissimo* for the final phrase.

Recitative and *arioso*

The recitatives of the Viennese cantatas exhibit the familiar traits of late-Baroque *recitativo semplice*. Accompanied by continuo only, the vocal lines unfold in short, speech-like phrases, in note-per-syllable settings over largely static bass lines. A group of phrases concludes with a typical V-l or l^6_4-V-l formula in a new key, the continuo part cadencing immediately after the vocal line. The final group of phrases ends in a key related to the tonality of the ensuing aria, although usually not its tonic or dominant. Recitatives rarely exceed twenty bars in length. Fragments or entire sections of *arioso* may be interpolated or appended, according to the taste of the individual composer.

Harmonically, the *recitativo semplice* features unstable chords that produce a continuous sense of forward motion toward a new cadential formula. Thus, $^6_3$ chords outnumber triads in root position, and dominant sevenths in first and (more especially) third inversion are common. A typical recitative will open with a long tonic pedal over which the dominant seventh, its inversions, and the leading-note triad are sounded, the composer delighting in the dissonant effect of leading-note against tonic. Melodically, the vocal line will proceed mostly by steps and small skips, with occasional affective leaps such as the diminished fourth and the diminished seventh.

To these general observations some specific remarks about the recitatives of each composer can be added. Ariosti's rarely depart from the conventional style. He consistently begins an initial recitative with a V7/1 clash and often introduces an interior recitative with a $^6_3$ chord. Modulations by means of V^4_2 chords occur so frequently that they become clichés; rather fewer examples of the V^6_5 can be found. Ariosti's vocal lines include expressive melodic diminished fourths, but he seldom exploits melodic sevenths. Chromatic bass lines are equally rare.

Badia elicits all of the stock harmonic techniques, especially favouring V^4_2 and diminished-seventh chords. He writes very slow-moving bass lines that frequently settle on a single note for four or five bars. Even his modulations tend to proceed slowly. Against such foundations his vocal lines seem vigorous and include some daring melodic leaps, especially ascending minor ninths and major sevenths, that create emphatic dissonances with the bass line.

Ziani prefers more stable harmonies than his contemporaries, choosing plain, root-position triads and fewer V^4_2 chords. When used, the dominant seventh is placed in root position or first inversion. Ziani also reveals a more conservative melodic style. Affective intervals are few, although a descending diminished seventh occurs in at least one recitative.

Giovanni Bononcini frequently opens his recitatives with a stable, root-position triad, but thereafter favours quick harmonic and tonal changes. He writes long, directional bass lines and seems particularly fond of ascending patterns. Very often he achieves forward motion by having modulations rise by step — from c minor to d minor, or from D major to E major. Giovanni also draws upon colouristic chords, the Neapolitan sixth and the diminished seventh, for example, and his affective leaps encompass not only the customary diminished fourth and diminished seventh, but also more unusual intervals such as the diminished third.

Antonio Bononcini's recitatives contain many of the conventional formulas although he uses fewer dominant sevenths over tonic pedals than the other composers. Progressions in which a dominant seventh is followed immediately by the dominant seventh (or its inversion) of the relative key, and descending modulations using a series of V^4_2-I^6_3 chords, often lead rapidly from one tonality to another. The composer also explores more adventurous harmonic routes. In the *recitativo semplice* that forms the B-section of the opening aria of *Vorrei, pupille belle*, he shifts abruptly from f minor to e minor, and in the final six bars of the second recitative of *Sopra l'orme d'Irene* moves rapidly through a succession of seven keys: D major, G major, A major, D major, f-sharp minor, b minor and C major. Antonio's harmonic vocabulary also embraces unexpected resolutions of the diminished-seventh chord.

To varying degrees the composers insert *arioso* passages within their recitatives. Giovanni Bononcini includes no *arioso*, and his brother largely, though not entirely, avoids this style. Ziani appends an *arioso* in strict tempo to only one recitative. Badia composes *arioso* more often than Ziani or Antonio Bononcini, but Ariosti is the only composer who uses it regularly. His *ariosi* also tend to be more elaborate and florid than those of his contemporaries.

The dimensions and complexity of the *ariosi* vary considerably. They range from entire, separate movements to brief cadential flourishes. In general, the *ariosi* in the Viennese cantatas can be classified under five headings:

(i) complete, self-contained movements

These are distinguished from arias by their brevity and complete absence of *da capo*, binary, strophic, or other conventional designs. They are not necessarily distinguished by nomenclature. This is made clear by the fifteen-bar passage that occurs just before the final (second) aria of Ariosti's *E pur dolce a un cor legato*. He actually designates this passage an 'aria', but it consists only of a brief sequential statement in two segments. A similar, nineteen-bar *arioso*, in 3/2, follows the first recitative of his *L'idol mio de pianti miei*, although here the composer does not use the term 'aria'. *Un guardo solo, o bella*, the seventh cantata in Badia's printed collection, begins with an eleven-bar *arioso* marked *affettuoso*, and an exact duplicate follows an intervening, brief *recitativo semplice*. The entire movement resembles the opening of Antonio Bononcini's *Vorrei, pupille belle* — in both, *ariosi* passages in strict tempo frame *recitativi semplici*, creating *da-capo*-like designs. However, Badia's *ariosi* and recitatives are much shorter than the corresponding sections by Bononcini. One of Badia's chamber duets, *Chi brama d'amar*, includes a movement for two sopranos which begins in *semplice* style, but gradually becomes stricter in tempo, with florid vocal patterns and a melodic bass line.

(ii) long *ariosi* appended to *recitativi semplici*

The change from *semplice* style to *arioso* may be made clear by a specific tempo marking, a change of metre, the use of the term *a rigore*, or simply by an obvious shift to more melodic writing in both vocal and bass lines. The initial recitative of Antonio Bononcini's *Occhi, voi che mirate*, for instance, concludes with an expressive twenty-four-bar *Largo* in 3/4. Here (as elsewhere) we see the composer's mastery of chromatic harmony and melody as he employs both to paint the word *piangete* (Ex. 1).

Example 1. A. Bononcini *Occhi, voi che mirate*: first recitative, bars 14–37

The first recitative of *Se avessi in mezzo al petto* also ends with a *Largo arioso,* but in 4/4. Again Bononcini uses affective harmony and imitation between the vocal and bass lines, but he avoids ostentatious vocal flourishes. Badia adds a nineteen-bar *arioso* in 3/8 at the conclusion of the first recitative (in 4/4) of *A Clori, che fra l'erbe.* To clarify the change from *semplice* style to *arioso* at the end of the third recitative of *Ahimè, ch'io son piagato,* Ziani instructs the performers to execute the final fifteen bars *a rigore.* The passage opens with a two-bar, bass-line ritornello; it also includes imitation involving two motives but is not especially florid. Applying a similar technique at the conclusions of recitatives in *Ne spatiosi campi* and *Mi convien soffrir,* Ariosti uses the term *a tempo* to signal the beginnings of *ariosi.*[20]

(iii) brief cadential passages in strict tempo at the ends of *semplice* sections
These conclude many recitatives by Ariosti and Badia, especially those in cantatas included in A-Wn: Mus.Hs. 17574, 17591 and 17721. Less frequently they occur in the closing bars of recitatives by Antonio Bononcini. These final *ariosi* are seldom longer than four or five bars, but the composers invest them with surprisingly chromatic harmony, bits of imitation, expressive leaps and (especially Ariosti) exceedingly florid vocal patterns (Ex. 2).

Example 2. Ariosti *Che si può far?* first recitative, *arioso* close, bars 13–23

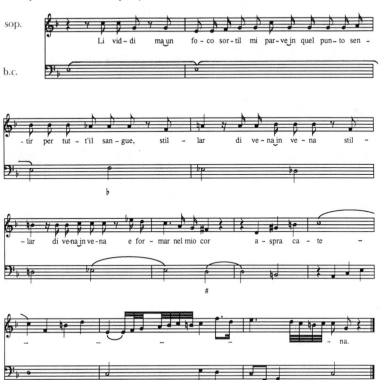

(iv) brief *ariosi* interpolated throughout *semplice* recitatives, particularly at cadences

The tendency to vacillate between *semplice* and *arioso* styles can be seen in cantatas such as Ariosti's *Tante e tante del ciel* and Badia's *D'amica selva*. Arosti again tends to incorporate more elaborate coloratura figures (Ex. 3).

Example 3. Ariosti *Tante e tante del ciel*: first recitative, bars 1–11

(v) melodic flourishes used primarily for word painting

Not restricted to cadences, these ornamental figures add colour and variety to the recitatives of Badia, Ariosti and Antonio Bononcini. The long melisma on the third syllable of 'gorgheggiani' in the first recitative of Badia's *Uno spirito galante* illustrates the exploitation of an obvious effect suggested by the text (Ex. 4).

Example 4. Badia *Uno spirito galante*: first recitative, bars 7–11

Aria keys

Not surprisingly, the composers neglect key signatures with large numbers of sharps or flats. In fact, only one aria in the entire *corpus* (the E major 'Quanto felice sei' in Badia's *Sovra carro di luce*) is set in a major key with more than three sharps; arias in flat-major keys are confined to either F or B-flat major (Table 7).

Table 7. *Major keys used in cantata arias*

Composer	Total arias	No. in major	B♭	F	C	G	D	A	E
Badia	134	83	14	14	9	17	11	17	1
Ariosti	48	23	3	9	1	2	4	4	0
A. M. Bononcini	34	14	5	5	0	2	0	2	0
Ziani	18	11	2	1	2	2	3	1	0
G. Bononcini	11	4	2	0	0	0	0	2	0
Anonymous	12	8	2	0	2	1	1	2	0
Totals	257	143	28	29	14	24	19	28	1

Minor keys with signatures of up to three flats are common, but those with sharp signatures are remarkably infrequent (Table 8). Antonio Bononcini's f-sharp minor aria ('Da primi nodi suoi' in *Tanto avezzo ho il core*) is quite exceptional.

Table 8. *Minor keys used in cantata arias*

Composer	Total arias	No. in minor	c	g	d	a	e	b	f♯
Badia	134	51	10	12	16	12	1	0	0
Ariosti	48	25	4	7	7	3	2	2	0
A. M. Bononcini	34	20	2	7	4	5	1	0	1
Ziani	18	7	0	1	1	1	0	4	0
G. Bononcini	11	7	0	5	2	0	0	0	0
Anonymous	12	4	0	1	0	2	1	0	0
Totals	257	114	16	33	30	23	5	6	1

The keys without sharps or flats (C major and a minor) are used less than keys such as g minor, d minor, F major, A major and B-flat major.

Table 9. *Incidence of aria keys*

| Key | Incidence | % of total arias | % of individual composers' outputs | | | | | |
			Ariosti	Badia	Ziani	G. Bononcini	A. M. Bononcini	Anon.
g	33	12.8	15	9	6	45	21	8
d	30	11.7	15	12	6	18	12	0
F	29	11.3	19	10	6	0	15	0
Bb	28	10.9	6	10	11	18	15	17
A	28	10.9	8	13	6	18	6	17
G	24	9.3	4	13	11	0	6	8
a	23	8.9	6	9	6	0	15	17
D	19	.7.4	8	8	17	0	0	8
c	16	6.2	8	7	0	0	6	0
C	14	5.4	2	7	11	0	0	17
b	6	2.3	4	0	22	0	0	0
e	5	1.9	4	.7	0	0	3	8
f#	1	.4	0	0	0	0	3	0
E	1	.4	0	.7	0	0	0	0

Table 9, which provides a complete analysis of the frequency with which keys are employed in the arias of the Viennese cantatas, also shows the overall preference for major keys — 143 arias (56%) to 114 arias (44%) in minor keys. Nevertheless, the composers draw upon two minor keys (g and d) more often than other keys. The Bononcini brothers seem especially fond of minor tonalities and of g minor in particular. Perhaps it is this partiality that endeared the pair to Pier [Pietro] Francesco Tosi, composer and author of *Opinioni de'cantori antichi, e moderni* (1723).[21] Their music, which Tosi undoubtedly came to know well between 1705 and 1711 when he, too, worked at the Habsburg court, must have seemed an antidote to the deplorable trends he discerned among 'the moderns' — an avoidance of arias in slow tempos, in 'pathetick' style, and in minor keys (those 'that have not the *Sharp* third').[22]

Continuum (tempo/metre)[23]

The cantata composers use a rich variety of tempos and metres. Table 10 inventories the tempo markings given for arias, but includes neither those for *ariosi* and instrumental movements nor all slight modifications of basic tempo markings. The latter have been included in the totals for the standard terms. A tempo marking made up of two common designations (e.g., *Andante e allegro; Affettuoso e adagio*), has been recorded under the first.

Antonio Bononcini tends to combine a tempo indication with an instruction for articulation, using pairings such as *Affettuoso e staccato, Andante e staccato* and *Spiritoso e battuto*. Ariosti sometimes writes a particular tempo marking twice at the beginning of an aria to strengthen its effect — *Largo Largo* or *Adagio Adagio*, for example, meaning very broad or very slow, respectively. For a similar purpose, both Badia and the anonymous composer of *Cetre amiche* add *assai* after *Allegro* in four of their arias. Composers occasionally qualify a familiar tempo with a negative — *non molto Allegro* (Ziani), *Allegro ma non presto* (Badia), *Andante e non presto* (Badia), and *non troppo Presto* (Badia). Antonio Bononcini is the only composer to invoke the terms *cantabile* and *tempo giusto*. Badia's isolated use of *alla francese*, unique in the cantata repertoire, presents an interesting conundrum. He employs it for the second aria of his cantata *Non so se più mi piace*, perhaps to indicate a particular aspect of performance practice, for the aria does not differ structurally or stylistically from any of his other *da capo* arias. For the present, the composer's precise intention must remain unclear, but the appearance of the term[24] further highlights French influence in Vienna, best seen in the ballet music, the penchant for the French overture, and the occasional use of choruses in large dramatic works.

Table 10. *Tempo markings used for arias*

Tempo	Ariosti	Badia	Ziani	G. Bononcini	A. M. Bononcini	Anon.	Total	% of 257 arias
[None]	28	75	3	3	2	11	122	47.5
Allegro	2	26	8	0	2	1	39	15.2
Adagio	3	11	0	2	0	0	16	6.2
Andante	1	6	2	0	7	0	16	6.2
Largo/Larghetto	10	4	1	0	1	0	16	6.2
Affettuoso	0	5	0	1	5	0	11	4.3
Vivace	3	0	1	2	4	0	10	3.9
Spiritoso/ con spirito	0	0	1	2	6	0	9	3.5
Presto	1	2	2	1	0	0	6	2.3
Cantabile	0	0	0	0	5	0	5	1.9
Non presto/ non troppo presto	0	4	0	0	0	0	4	1.6
Tempo giusto	0	0	0	0	2	0	2	.8
Alla francese	0	1	0	0	0	0	1	.4

A survey of the metres used in the cantata arias is given in Table 11.

Table 11. *Metres used for arias*

Metre	Ariosti	Badia	Ziani	G. Bononcini	A. M. Bononcini	Anon.	Total	% of 257 arias
4/4 (C)	24	67	10	6	18	6	131	51.0
3/4	9	32	3	3	8	2	57	22.2
3/8	5	16	5	2	2	1	31	12.1
6/8	2	8	0	0	1	2	13	5.1
12/8	3	7	0	0	3	0	13	5.1
2/2 (₵)	3	1	0	0	1	0	5	1.9
2/4	0	3	0	0	1	0	4	1.6
3/2	2	0	0	0	0	1	3	1.2

The trend toward choosing the crotchet rather than the minim as the basic value for the beat, already apparent in the cantatas of the late seventeenth century, becomes even more pronounced after 1700. Old-fashioned by the turn of the century, such metres as 3/2 appear in only a tiny portion of the arias. Nearly three-fourths of all of the arias involve standard modern metres such as 4/4 and 3/4, although composers seldom select 2/4. Increasingly popular are quick arias with the quaver representing one beat.

Only six of the 257 arias include sudden changes of tempo and/or metre. Giovanni Bononcini constrasts the 4/4 A-section of the second aria of *Or nel bosco* with a B-section in 3/8. In the first aria of *Sento dentro del petto* he uses the same two metres, co-ordinating them with the tempo markings *adagio* and *vivace*. Ariosti contrasts an opening *Vivace* in 3/4 with a central *Adagio* in 3/2 in the first aria of *Quando Nice era fida solo*. The second aria of his *Ne spatiosi campi* (not of the *da capo* variety) contains a central two-bar *adagio* phrase which features thematic material of the longer, surrounding *presto* sections. In the final aria of *Per te sola, Filli mia sentirò*, Badia applies a similar procedure, but to a standard *da capo* design. Here, an A-section marked no[n] *presto* leads to an *adagio* B-section constructed on the thematic ideas set forth in *A*. Badia varies both metres and themes between the sections of the third aria of *Scesa dal ciel* in which a 4/4 A-section is followed by a B-section in 3/8.

The use of mottos

Although mottos had become standard in arias by Italian composers in the late seventeenth century, none of the Viennese composers consistently includes a motto at the beginning of the first vocal area of the A-section of a *da capo* aria (Table 12). Only Ariosti seems to have taken up the device, using it in nearly two-thirds of his arias.

Table 12. *Use of the motto in the cantata arias*

Composer	Total arias	No. with mottos	% with mottos
Ariosti	48	31	65
Badia	134	23	17
A. M. Bononcini	34	2	6
G. Bononcini	11	0	0
Ziani	18	0	0
Anonymous	12	7	58

Aria designs

The *da capo* aria, together with its three variants (the modified, expanded and miniature *da capo*), completely overshadows all other types.[25] In the strict *da capo* the return of the A-section simply duplicates the opening except for the expected improvised ornaments; the *da capo* may or may not be written out in the manuscript. The modified *da capo* retains the essential *ABA* structure, but includes either some small written-in alterations in the *da capo* (the omission or abbreviation of a ritornello, or the condensation of a vocal section) or the replacement of an entire *B*-section with *recitativo semplice*. Still another modification can be seen in the final aria of Giovanni Bononcini's *Or nel bosco*, which adheres to the fundamental *da capo* design but involves repetition of each large section, resulting in an *AABBAA* scheme. The miniature *da capo* also displays the familiar three-part plan, but the dimensions of each section are limited to only a few bars. The expanded *da capo*, created by the addition of more components to the usual three sections, occurs most often in the works of Ziani. This composer creates such varied plans as *ABA¹ coda*, *ABA¹ C*, *ABCA¹ coda*, and *ABCA¹ A² coda*.

Strict binary arias (*AB*) with both sections repeated, appear only six times, all in cantatas by Badia. Two-part arias (*AA¹* or *AB*) without repeats are only slightly more common, appearing in cantatas by Ariosti, Badia and one of the anonymous composers. Tripartite arias (*AABBCC¹* or *ABCC*), not specifically related to the *da capo* structure, can be seen in two cantatas by Badia. The strophic aria, the most popular type during the Draghi generation, nearly disappears in the first decade of the eighteenth century. Ariosti uses it, but only twice. In addition, Badia experiments once with combining the strophic principle and a binary structure; each of the two strophes unfolds in a clear two-part pattern with repeats.

Table 13. *Aria designs*

Design	Ariosti	Badia	Ziani	G. Bononcini	A. M. Bononcini	Anon.	Total	% of 257 arias
Da capo	41	121	12	10	31	8	223	86.8
Modified *da capo*	2	2	0	1	1	1	7	2.7
2-part (*AB* or *AA¹*), no repeats	3	2	0	0	0	2	7	2.7
2-part (*AB*), with repeats	0	6	0	0	0	0	6	2.3
Expanded *da capo*	0	0	5	0	0	0	5	1.9
Miniature *da capo*	0	0	1	0	2	0	3	1.1
Strophic/modified strophic	2	0	0	0	0	0	2	.8
Strophic; each strophe 2-part, with repeats	0	1	0	0	0	0	1	.4
ABCC	0	1	0	0	0	0	1	.4
AABBCC¹	0	1	0	0	0	0	1	.4
Through-composed	0	0	0	0	0	1	1	.4

*   *   *   *   *

This overview of the stylistic traits of cantatas written for the Viennese court during the first decade of the eighteenth century provides a backdrop for a study of the cantatas written during the reign of Charles VI by Caldara, Conti and Giuseppe Porsile — the next set of favoured composers. With the appointment of Fux as *Kapellmeister* in 1715 and Caldara as *Vizekapellmeister* in 1716, Viennese musical life entered a new phase.

From the transitional years (*c*1711-1716) we have a few cantatas by Caldara and some of the other ambitious composers who arrived in Vienna, attracted by the possibilities of the changed circumstances, together with several by the earlier generation of established musicians. In this regard the volume of twelve cantatas (A-Wn: Mus.Hs. 17567) is of special interest:

Table 14. *Cantatas in A-Wn: Mus.Hs. 17567*

Composer	Title	Folios	Scoring
1. Giovanni Bononcini	*Non ardisco pregarti, amata bella*	1- 8v	S & bc.
2. Antonio Caldara	*Io soffrirò tacendo questo incendio*	9-17v	S & bc.
3. Francesco Conti	*Lasciami Amor, nemico del riposo*	18-25v	S & bc.
4. G. Bononcini	*Sento dentro del petto un lusinghiero ardor*	26-32v	S & bc.
5. Caldara	*Arda il mio petto amante olocausto fedel*	33-39v	S & bc.
6. Conti	*Dimmi, o sorte nemica, la nascasta cagion*	40-46v	S & bc.
7. G. Bononcini	*Rompi l'arco, rompi i lacci, rompi l'armi*	47-53v	S & bc.
8. Caldara	*Senti Filli incostante, non già i teneri affetti*	54-61v	S & bc.
9. Conti	*Tento scutore dal seno crudo stral*	62-69v	S & bc.
10. Emanuele d'Astorga	*Che ti giova, amor crudele, che il mio cor*	70-80v	S & bc.
11. d'Astorga	*Quando penso a quell'ore, ore felici*	81-88v	S & bc.
12. Andrea Stefano Fiorè	*Di quel sguardo fatal la dura piaga*	89-97v	S & bc.

Judged on its contents it seems most likely that the manuscript was copied in 1712, during the interregnum. For example, we know from the autographs that *Io soffrirò tacendo*, and *Senti Filli incostante*, the first and third of Caldara's cantatas in the volume, are dated 'Fine a 7 Marzo 1712 in Vienna' and 'Fine a 6 Marzo 1712 in Vienna' — products of the half year he spent in Vienna between February and June, 1712, seeking a major appointment in the *Kapelle* that was to serve the new Emperor.[26]

Astorga sojourned at Vienna from at least early 1712 until May, 1714. On 9 May, 1712, he participated in baptismal ceremonies for Caldara's daughter, Sophia Jacobina Maria.[27] Although a stay at Vienna by Fiorè has not been documented, this *maestro di cappella* at Turin apparently maintained ties with the Imperial court, for his operas were performed at Vienna during the period 1709-1713. One of these, *Ercole in cielo*, was written for the nameday of Charles III of Spain (the future Charles VI) in 1710.[28] That Giovanni Bononcini and Conti would have composed cantatas during the interregnum is not surprising, for in this period commissions for large-scale dramatic works were particularly sparse. As Bononcini had already departed for Italy by early 1713, it is most likely, therefore, that his cantatas and many of their companions in Mus.Hs. 17567 immediately predate the posting of the new list of chapel members at the very beginning of 1713.

In its mixture of composers familiar and unfamiliar at the Imperial court, this volume epitomizes the state of flux in matters musical. A closer study of its contents, seen against the well-established traits outlined here, may yield important clues about the direction of changes in cantata and aria style that were to occur at Vienna during the next decade.

Notes

[1] Robert Freeman 'Caldara, Antonio' *The New Grove Dictionary of Music and Musicians* (London, 1980) 3, p. 616.

[2] Charles Burney *A General History of Music* (London, 1776–1779), ed. Frank Mercer (New York, 1935) II, pp. 635–6.

[3] Sixteen cantatas by Antonio Draghi and three of his contemporaries, Filippo Vismarri, Carlo Capellini and Giovanni Battista Pederzuoli, as well as two early cantatas by Carlo Agostino Badia, are published in facsimile in *The Italian Cantata in the Seventeenth Century* XVI, selected and introduced by Lawrence Bennett (New York, 1985). For further information about the cantatas written for Vienna during the period 1660–1700, see Bennett 'The Italian Cantata in Vienna, c. 1700–1711' (Ph.D., diss. New York University, 1980) I, pp. 17–56.

[4] For biographical details, see Carl Nemeth 'Zur Lebensgeschichte von Carlo Agostino Badia (1672–1738)' *Anzeiger der phil.-hist. Klasse der Österreichischen Akademie der Wissenschaften* XCII (1955) pp. 224–36. See also Bennett 'Badia, Carlo Agostino' *The New Grove Dictionary of Music and Musicians* (London, 1980) 2, pp. 8–10.

[5] For general biographical studies, see especially Lowell Lindgren 'A Bibliographic scrutiny of Dramatic Works set by Giovanni Bononcini and his brother Antonio Maria Bononcini' (Ph.D., diss. Harvard University, 1972) I; also Anthony Ford 'Giovanni Bononcini, 1670–1747' *The Musical Times* 111 (July, 1970) pp. 695–9. See also Lindgren '(2) Giovanni Bononcini' *The New Grove Dictionary of Music and Musicians* (London, 1980) 3, pp. 30–4.

[6] The interregnum following the death of Joseph affected all Imperial court musicians. Clinging to his claim as the rightful heir to the Spanish throne, Joseph's brother Charles was still in Spain. While he returned to Austria, Leopold's widow, the Dowager Empress, Eleonora Magdalena, served as Regent of the empire. Austerity measures were announced, including a reduction of expenses for musical activities and personnel. Notices about the reductions were circulated on 3 and 11 September (see Ludwig Ritter von Köchel *Johann Josef Fux, Hofcompositor und Hofkapellmeister der Kaiser Leopold I., Josef I. und Karl VI. von 1698 bis 1740* (Wien, 1872) pp. 315–22). All musicians were to be paid through September (i.e., the end of the third quarter) but after September only church musicians

were to be retained. Most musicians remained in Vienna throughout 1711, expecting to be reinstated. Travelling from Spain through Italy to Frankfurt-am-Main, where he was crowned, Charles VI arrived in Vienna on 26 January 1712. Even then, nearly a year elapsed before the membership of the *Hofkapelle* was listed. About Bononcini's attempts to be reinstated, see Lindgren 'A Bibliographic Scrutiny ...' I, pp. 123–8.

[7] For details about Bononcini's final years in Vienna, see Kurt Hueber 'Gli ultimi anni di Giovanni Bononcini: notizie e documenti inediti' *Atti e memorie dell' Accademia di Scienze Lettere e Arti di Modena* Ser. 5, XII (1954) pp. 153–71.

[8] For a list of Bononcini's works, including text incipits for the cantatas, see Lindgren '(2) Giovanni Bononcini' *op.cit.,* pp. 32–4.

[9] Concerning Antonio Maria Bononcini, see Lindgren 'A Bibliographic Scrutiny ... ' especially I, pp. 56, 117–20 and 133–43. See also Lindgren '(3) Antonio Maria Bononcini' *The New Grove Dictionary of Music and Musicians* (London, 1980) 3, pp. 34–5.

[10] The term 'grand cantata' has been suggested by Efrim and Caroline Fruchtman 'Instrumental Scoring in the Chamber Cantatas of Francesco Conti' *Studies in Musicology* ed. James W. Pruett (Chapel Hill, 1969), p. 246; see also Bennett 'The Italian Cantata in Vienna ... ' I, pp. 59–60.

[11] For biographical information about M. A. Ziani, see especially Theophil Antonicek 'Die *Damira*-Opern der beiden Ziani' *Analecta Musicologica* 14 (1974) pp. 176–81, and his 'Ziani, Marc 'Antonio' *The New Grove Dictionary of Music and Musicians* (London, 1980) 20, pp. 673–5.

[12] The music for two additional *accademie,* both dating from 1707, appears to be lost. In Vienna, the term *accademia* first appeared in the title of Giovanni Battista Pederzuoli's set of six cantatas: *Accademie: cantate per l'anno 1685.* From this title and from the four undated *cantate per l'accademia* by the same composer, it is obvious that the concepts of cantata and *accademia* were intimately bound together in his mind. Pederzuoli's *accademie* follow an Italian practice of presenting in music philosophical debates about love and general questions of life. Academic cantatas written later for Vienna by Draghi and M. A. Ziani tend to be ensemble works accompanied by slightly larger groups of instruments, but even these *accademie* are basically chamber compositions, not theatrical works, and their texts are philosophical, not dramatic. About an academy founded in Vienna in 1657, see Marcus Landau, *Die italienische Literatur am Österreichischen Hofe* (Wien, 1879).

[13] For general biographical information and documents concerning the life of Ariosti, see Alfred Ebert *Attilio Ariosti in Berlin (1697–1703)* (Leipzig, 1905); Lodovico Frati 'Attilio Ottavio Ariosti' *Rivista Musicale Italiana* XXXIII (1926) pp. 551–7. See also James L. Jackman and Dennis Libby 'Ariosti, Attilio (Malachia)' *The New Grove Dictionary of Music and Musicians* (London, 1980) 1, pp. 582–5.

[14] For Ariosti's letter, see Alfred Einstein 'Italienische Musiker am Hofe der Neuburger Wittelsbacher (1614–1716)' *Sammelbände der internationalen Musikgesellschaft* IX (1907–8) pp. 416–17.

[15] Further about the anonymous cantatas, see Bennett 'The Italian Cantata in Vienna ... ' I, p. 101.

[16] Among the many cantata composers active at Vienna in the years 1690–1740, only Badia appears to have had a collection engraved while in the service of the Emperor. Concerning this print, see *ibid.,* pp. 232–7.

[17] For details about the cantata sources from the period *c*1700–*c*1711, see *ibid.,* I, pp. 229–47, and II, pp. 545–92; a thematic catalog of the pertinent cantatas is given in II, pp. 593–627.

[18] Fixed patterns of alternating recitatives and arias became the norm in cantatas by composers active throughout Italy during the early years of the eighteenth century.

[19] Concerning the use of this term in preference to the pejorative nineteenth-century term *recitativo secco*, see Daniel Heartz's 'Vorwort' to his edition of Mozart *Idomeneo, Neue Ausgabe sämtlicher Werke* Ser. II, 11, (Kassel, 1972) p. xxvi.

[20] *A tempo* sections at the ends of recitatives were especially common at Naples in cantatas by composers such as Nicola Fago and Francesco Mancini; see Josephine Wright 'The Secular Cantatas of Francesco Mancini (1672–1736)' (Ph.D., diss. New York University, 1975) p. 54 and p. 112.

[21] Certainly J. E. Galliard in his 1743 translation of Tosi's treatise, cited 'Bononcini' (together with Scarlatti, Gasparini and Mancini) as one of the composers intended by Tosi when he spoke of 'the best that are now living'. Pie[t]r[o] Francesco Tosi *Observations on the Florid Song ... Translated into English by Mr. Galliard* 2nd ed., (London, 1743) pp. 113–14.

[22] *Ibid.*, pp. 111–12.

[23] Concerning the term 'continuum', see Jan LaRue *Guidelines for Style Analysis* (New York, 1970) p. 90.

[24] One other French term, *air en rondeau*, also appears, if only rarely, in operas written for Vienna – in Ariosti's *Marte placato* (1707), for example.

[25] One of the seminal figures of the late Baroque era, Alessandro Scarlatti, did not adopt the *da capo* plan consistently for his opera and cantata arias until after about 1697 (curiously, at exactly the time *da capo* arias were becoming popular in Vienna), although three-part schemes had become common already in the Stradella generation. See Malcolm Boyd 'Form and Style in Scarlatti's chamber Cantatas' *The Music Review* 25 (1964) pp. 20–24.

[26] D-ddr-Bds: Mus. ms. autogr. Caldara A.10. and I-Bc: DD 326(6). A further 15 autograph cantatas dating from the first half of 1712 are contained in the Bologna manuscript.

[27] See Hans Volkmann *Emanuel d'Astorga* (Leipzig, 1911) I, p. 57, and Ursula Kirkendale *Antonio Caldara: Sein Leben und seine venezianisch-römischen Oratorien* (Graz-Köln, 1966) p. 67. Concerning cantatas written by Astorga during his stay at Vienna, see Volkmann II (1919) p. 142.

[28] Concerning Fiorè, see Sven Hansell 'Fiorè, Andrea Stefano' *The New Grove Dictionary of Music and Musicians* (London, 1980) 6, pp. 599–600.

The Caldara manuscripts
at Melk Abbey

Robert N. Freeman

Zusammenfassung

Die Caldara-handschriften von Kloster Melk

Die dreiunddreißig Caldara-Handschriften, die in der achtzig Kilometer westlich von Wien gelegenen Benediktiner-Abtei Melk aufbewahrt werden, sind aus einer ganzen Reihe von Gründen interessant. Zum einen lag das Kloster im unmittelbaren Einflussbereich des Komponisten; zum anderen war der Prälat von Melk, Berthold Dietmayr, dessen Amtszeit (1701–39) in etwa mit der Caldaras an der Wiener Hofkapelle zusammenfiel, ein enger Freund und Berater von Kaiser Karl VI. Caldaras hauptsächlichem Förderer. Trotzdem ist diese Sammlung, die auschließlich aus Kirchenmusik besteht, nicht weiter bekannt geworden.

Die vorliegende Arbeit untersucht die Melker Handschriften unter dem Gesichtspunkt der Schönschrift und der Gesichertheit des Textes. Einige werden mit den entsprechenden Wiener Quellen verglichen, die aus der kaiserlichen Hofkapelle stammen; als Ergebnis erhält man bemerkenswert wenige Diskrepanzen, selbst in Fällen, die fast ein dreiviertel Jahrhundert auseinanderliegen. Beispiele der Handschriften von sechs Abschreibern der Caldara-Manuskripte werden herangezogen, und indem man die Handschrift des ältesten und produktivsten von ihnen, des Organisten Joseph Weiss (1729–59), identifiziert, wird es zum ersten Mal möglich, das Melker musikalische Repertoire, so wie es im zweiten Viertel des 18. Jahrhunderts aussah, zu rekonstruieren. Ein thematisches Verzeichnis der Werke, die in der Melker Sammlung Caldara zugeschrieben werden, befindet sich im Anhang des Beitrags.

The Caldara manuscripts at Melk Abbey

Robert N. Freeman

L ONG BEFORE Antonio Caldara's formal appointment as *Vizekapell-meister* to the Imperial court chapel in Vienna in January, 1717, strong ties had been established between the Hofburg and the abbeys of Lower Austria that lay close to the periphery of the capital. Visible signs of these old historical connections could be seen in Caldara's time in the frequent visits to the abbeys by members of the Imperial family and in the expansive guest apartments maintained for such visits at the cloisters. The endowed abbeys, or *Stifte*, made up important administrative and economic entities within the empire, and several of them maintained their own 'courts' in Vienna in order to pursue direct lines of communication with the government, to market their various economic products, and to purchase required materials and supplies. Since important segments of the monastic community would reside there, most notably the novices studying at the Viennese university and the prelates themselves, the courts also served the abbeys as social and cultural outposts.

Not surprisingly, musical ties between the capital and the abbeys developed, corresponding to the political and economic connections. Works by Viennese court composers, such as those by Caldara, occupied an important place in the monastic music libraries. For example, an extraordinarily rich collection of Caldara's sacred music (126 compositions, including thirty-six Masses and forty-three offertories) was assembled for the Augustinians at Herzogenburg Abbey, according to a two-volume thematic catalogue begun in 1751.[1] The strength of this particular repertoire, of which, unfortunately, only remnants survive, was no doubt due to the fact that one of Caldara's few identifiable pupils, Georg Joseph Donberger (1709–68), served as music director there after his ordination in 1733.

At the Benedictine Abbey of Göttweig, where at least two music directors had received their training from Imperial court organists J. K. Kerll (*d*1693) and A. Poglietti (*d*1683), compositions by Viennese composers were equally well represented in the music archive. Some measure of how one of these collections could be built up is provided by the well-known 'Wondratsch' catalogue belonging to the abbey and recently published in facsimile.[2] According to this source, Caldara's music, for example, began to be acquired in 1724, that is a few years after he came to Vienna, and by 1795 some ninety-six compositions had been collected, of which seventy-six still survive. Of these, sixty-five bear dates which reveal that twenty-one works were acquired during Caldara's lifetime, thirty-two over the next seventeen years, but only a dozen more after 1755. These figures could well reflect the demand for the composer's church music at the abbeys in general during the eighteenth century.

Compared to Herzogenburg and Göttweig, much less is known about the Caldara holdings at the Benedictine Abbey of Melk, located on the Danube only eighty kilometres west of Vienna. Unlike the situation in Göttweig, there is hardly any evidence at Melk concerning the Caldara sources, when they were acquired and by whom they were copied. In his checklist Greenwood tabulated thirty-seven works here, but was unable to assign even an approximate date for them.[3] This is all the more disappointing because at no time were the contacts between this great abbey and Vienna stronger than they were under Abbot Berthold Dietmayr, whose rule (1701–39) roughly paralleled Caldara's tenure at the court chapel.

This relationship had been established from the very beginning of Dietmayr's administration when the Emperor, Leopold I (1640–1705), dispatched his theatrical personnel, including costumes, to Melk in order to participate in a performance of a Latin school opera, *Neo-Exoriens phosphorus*, written by the court composer Johann Joseph Fux to celebrate the abbot's investiture in 1701.[4] The close friendship between Dietmayr and Leopold's son, Charles VI, is well-known. Charles referred to him affectionately in his correspondence as his 'dear Abbot,' offered him the ambassadorship to Poland in 1719 (which Dietmayr refused on account of his unfamiliarity with the Polish language and customs), and by appointing him to the office of High Privy Councillor to the Emperor in June, 1728, brought the prelate into the exclusive inner circle of the Emperor's trusted advisors.[5]

Viennese court music of the baroque was held in the highest esteem at Melk as late as the first quarter of the nineteenth century. When Father Adam Krieg set about compiling the massive four-volume thematic catalogue of the abbey's music archive in 1821,[6] he began the very first page of the first volume with incipits of Caldara's Masses. Although far fewer in number than those at Herzogenburg and Göttweig, the Caldara manuscripts in the Melk collection seem to have remained more intact, at least since Krieg's time, and all of the nine Masses, sixteen offertories and graduals, seven Psalms and one Marian antiphon originally catalogued by him still survive. These thirty-three compositions are listed thematically in the Appendix.[7] It is the purpose here to scrutinize these works more closely, first by studying the various scribes involved in their preparation, and then by comparing selected manuscripts with older, Viennese sources. Although the aim of this study is to add to our knowledge of the dissemination of Caldara's church music in general and of the composer's relationship to Melk in particular, some light also will be shed on the make-up of the Melk repertoire itself as it stood in the second quarter of the eighteenth century.

An analysis of the manuscripts from the standpoint of calligraphy revealed no fewer than seventeen different eighteenth- and nineteenth-century copyists of which six could be eventually identified by name or date of activity at Melk. In chronological order, these are (see Plates 1-5 for examples):

> Joseph Weiss (1729-59)
> Melk copyist 2 (*c*1761-77)
> Franz Schneider (1766-1811)
> Rupert Helm (1768-91)
> Melk copyist 1 (Franz Horack [?] *c*1780-87)
> Amand Polster (1825-40)

In order to test the textual reliability of these copyists, a random selection of manuscripts (B.3, 10, 14 and D.1-2) was compared with concording Viennese sources known to be closely connected with the composer — those formerly belonging to the Imperial court chapel.

In general, the comparison revealed remarkably few discrepancies. The overall dimensions of the copies are identical, except for those sections in 4/2 metric notation, which at Melk are modernized into *alla breve* (¢). Variants in pitch are rare and occur with about the same degree of infrequency between both sets of copies. The Viennese sources are somewhat more complete and consistent as far as the notation of tempos, fermatas, dynamics and phrase markings are concerned, and interestingly, they also contain more ornaments, mostly trills concentrated in the solo sections, both vocal and instrumental. Perhaps at Melk ornamentation was governed by a stronger tradition of improvisation.

The comparative scorings reflect the smaller performing forces available at the abbey. Nevertheless, a noticeable tendency to imitate the basic sound concept of the court chapel is still evident. This is most clearly demonstrated in the *a cappella* or contrapuntally conceived sections of Caldara's music. Here the five Viennese sources show a set pattern of choral-orchestral doubling, a typically baroque *ripieno* orchestral treatment in which the outer voices are emphasized.

Table 1. *Comparative scorings*

Viennese Sources		Melk Sources	
S	= violins 1 & 2, *cornetto*	S	= violins 1 & 2
A	= alto trombone	A	= trombone 1
T	= tenor trombone	T	= trombone 2
B	= bassoon, cello, *violone*, organ,	B	= *violone*, organ

Text underlay is also remarkably consistent between the two sets of sources. The Melk manuscript of the offertory *Benedicite gentes* (B.3),

Plate 1. Title-page and first page of score for Caldara's *Messa â 4!ro Voci* (A.8), copied
Joseph Weiss. (A-M: I 1)
Reproduced by permission

Plate 2. Canto part for Caldara's *Missa* in D major (A.3), copied Melk copyist 2.
(A-M: I 5)
Reproduced by permission

Plate 3. Canto part for Caldara's offertory, *Super flumina Babylonis* (B.14), copied Franz Schneider. (A-M: II 33)
Reproduced by permission

Plate 4. Canto part for Caldara's *Salve Regina* in F major (E.1), copied Rupert Helm. (A-M: III 60)
Reproduced by permission

Plate 5. Canto part for Caldara's *Missa* in D major (A. 3), copied Melk copyist 1.
(A-M: I 5)
Reproduced by permission

for example, contains only one passage with a significant variation in this respect. In the older (1718) Viennese copy (Ex. 1a), as the imitative paired voices coalesce and drive toward the cadence, additional tension is created in bb. 24f. through the 'e' syllable of the bass conflicting with the 'au' of the upper voices, to be resolved only at the point of cadence on 'jus'. In the Melk source (Ex. 1b), the text is arranged in such a way that this tension is reduced, if not altogether eliminated. Rhythm and perhaps even pitch (tenor, b. 24) have been modified[8] in order to accommodate the new underlay.

Example 1. Caldara *Benedicite gentes* (B.3) bars 18–28
   (a) A-Wn: Mus.Hs. 16097
   (b) A-M: II 32

(a)

(b)

Some of the performance parts for this offertory were prepared by Franz Schneider, Melk organist from 1766 and music director after 1787 until 1811, who also copied at least two other Caldara offertories in 1788 (B.13–14). Although perhaps not taken directly from Viennese manuscripts, these later copies are remarkably faithful to the sources that were first performed by the court chapel seventy years earlier. It was precisely during the 1780s, when the abbey had to close its cloister school and disband the boys' choir, that Schneider was more apt to make radical abridgements and re-orchestrations of his own older compositions and those of other composers in order to adjust to changes of style and the realities presented by smaller performance forces.[9]

The only noticeable adjustment in the three offertories, apart from the absence of the *cornetto*, violoncello and bassoon (instruments that we have seen were not normally part of the regular church orchestra at Melk in the eighteenth century), is the apparent elimination of the violin parts, which in the *Hofkapelle* copies were *unisoni* with the soprano *ripieno*. It should be noted that in general all of the Caldara compositions that can be dated to Schneider's era, and more particularly post-1780 (A.2–3, 5, B.3, 13–14 and E.1), are without parts for violins 1 and 2. In contrast, most of the abbey's compositions by Caldara that can be assigned to earlier decades (and especially to Joseph Weiss's period as organist) are more generously scored (A.4, 6–8, B.5, 8, C.1–4, and D.1). Their performance material includes both violin parts and, very often, trombone parts as well, betokening a larger performance force supported by the abbey's greater prosperity.

That the 1780s was indeed a decade of considerable change at Melk seems confirmed by a comparison of the two versions of Caldara's Mass in D (A.3). The earlier version, in the hand of Melk copyist 2, contains parts for violin 1 and 2 that cannot be found in any other known manuscript source. No copy of this Mass can be located in the *Hofkapelle* repertoire, but other early-eighteenth-century sources agree on the instrumental doublings of the *ripieno* vocal parts (violini *unisoni* = S; alto trombone = A; tenor trombone = T; bassoon and *violone* = B),[10] and have the passages for the vocal soloists accompanied only by a continuo line (*violone* and organ). The first Melk version, however, provides independent lines for violins 1 and 2 at most of the chorus passages, excepting the *da cappella* areas such as the 'Christe eleison' and 'Et resurrexit', which retain the traditional doublings. In addition, the vocal soloists are accompanied by violin obbligatos that radically modify the effective soli-tutti contrasts of the 'authentic' scoring (Ex. 2). Even more substantial modifications are made to the 'Sanctus', 'Benedictus' and 'Dona nobis' movements. Besides the new accompanying violin parts provided for soloists and chorus, instrumental passages based on the vocal lines are added, extending these movements from twenty to thirty-three, eleven to twenty-two, and twenty-five to thirty-two bars respectively. Perhaps the 'Benedictus' (originally a duet for soprano and tenor with continuo) is changed the most by these additions and extensions (Ex. 3).

Example 2. Caldara *Missa* in D (A.3) 'Patrem omnipotentem' bars 1–14 (A-M: I 5, first version, *c*1778)

Ex. 2 (contd)

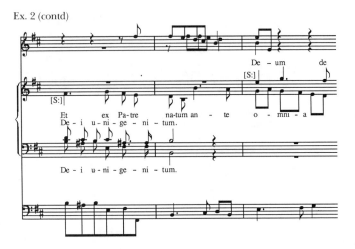

Example 3. Caldara *Missa* in D (A.3) 'Benedictus'
    (a) A-M: I 5, first version, *c*1778
    (b) A-M: I 5, second version, *c*1787

(a)

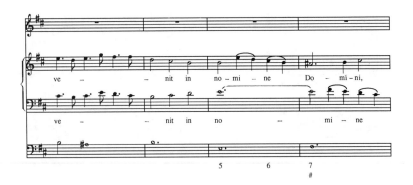

Ex. 3 (contd)

Ex. 3 (contd)

In the second, later version (in the hand of Melk copyist 1), all additional material — the violin accompanying lines as well as the instrumental preludes, interludes and postludes — has been removed. As a result, this copy with the customary *ripieno* trombone parts restored matches very closely those sources regarded as the most authoritative. In fact, the only substantial difference is the deletion of the seventeen-bar 'Osanna' from the Melk manuscript; instead, the text is accommodated in the last five bars of the 'Sanctus'. The date 'den 13 Aprill 1787' appended to the 'Alto Conc:' part strongly suggests that Schneider or his superior, Rupert Helm, music director from 1778 to 1787, had authorised this new version, while the date '1778' which appears on the modern wrapper containing both sets of performance material probably refers to the first arrangement.[11] It may be that this elaborate version with its extensions and additional parts was intended for a specific occasion and never became part of the abbey's regular repertoire. It is more certain that the 'reformed' version,[12] predating Schneider's copies of the two offertories by Caldara (B.13-14, and probably B.3) by at least one year, pointed toward the wide-ranging readjustment of the abbey's collection and the selection of works that would form a new repertoire suited to the institution's straightened circumstances. Indeed, this uncomplicated *Missa brevis*, in its 'original' setting, would have been particularly appropriate, and its dimensions closely resemble those of Caldara's Mass in F major (A.5), which on the evidence of the copyists involved was still being performed at the abbey during the 1780s.

That Caldara's compositions were little affected by the changing performance conditions at Melk (and, in the case of A.3, actually benefited from them) suggests that they continued to be highly regarded at Melk — an admiration that continued into the next century, as demonstrated by the further copies prepared by Amand Polster in the 1830s.

Of all the identifiable Caldara copyists at Melk, the earliest and most prolific was Joseph Weiss, organist at the abbey from 1729 until 1759, who produced at least twelve of the thirty-three surviving manuscripts, including all of the seven extant scores (A.7-8, C.1-5).[13] The identification of his script immediately opens at least two previously locked doors of musicological research at Melk. On the one hand, it is now possible to evaluate the Caldara manuscripts at the abbey more intelligently, and since Weiss came to Melk while Caldara was still active as *Vizekapell-meister* in Vienna, his copies are clearly of the greatest importance. On the other hand, it is possible to reconstruct at least in part, and for the first time, the musical repertoire at Melk as it stood in the second quarter of the eighteenth century. Such a reconstruction, however incomplete, is aided by the identification of thirteen additional copies made by Weiss of works by other composers. They are:

Georg Joseph Donberger (1709-68): Requiem in c minor (I 226)

Johann Joseph Fux (1660-1741): Sonata [da chiesa, KV 53] (V 1059)

Firmino Hörger (fl. second half of the eighteenth century): *Jesus auctor*, offertory in g minor (II 56)

Benedikt Klima (1701-48): *Missa Pastorella* in A major (I 51a)

Johann Georg Reutter (1708-72): Mass in B-flat major (I 85); *Rosa ridete*, offertory in D major (II 119)

Johann Georg Scheibl (1710-73): Mass in b minor (I 33)

Ferdinand Schmid (c1694-1756): two Requiems in c minor (I 228b-29); Miserere in c minor (III 53)

Johann Georg Zechner (1716-78): three Masses in a minor, A major and c minor (I 44-46)

Added together with the dozen Caldara examples copied by Weiss, these twenty-five compositions fall into two categories as far as the sphere of activity of their respective composers is concerned: a Viennese group consisting of Caldara (12), Fux (1), Reutter (2) and F. Schmid (3); and a Lower Austrian group consisting of G. J. Donberger of Herzogenburg (1), F. Hörger of Klosterneuburg (1), B. Klima of Wiener Neustadt (1), J. G. Scheibl of St. Pölten (1) and J. G. Zechner, active at Göttweig and later at Krems and Stein (3). Viewed in this manner, Weiss's efforts as a copyist were clearly directed towards Viennese church music (eighteen copies compared to seven by Lower Austrian composers), but cutting across both groups is the common thread of Caldara and his pupils, Donberger and Reutter.

It is evident, therefore, that through his activity as copyist, Weiss was a primary musical figure linking Melk to the Viennese court chapel in the first half of the eighteenth century. Yet he is an individual about whom little has previously been known, his name having eluded musical lexicographers past and present.[14]

Weiss was appointed Melk organist by Abbot Dietmayr on 15 December, 1729, only a month after the accidental death of his predecessor, Georg Honorius Freitag (organist 1721–29), from drowning in the Danube. Such a brief time interval would indicate either that Weiss had already been employed in Melk in some kind of assistant capacity, or that he had come there highly recommended. He received the regular organist's salary of 120 florins plus thirty more 'because of other music and services [Tafeldiensten].' That his roots were Viennese is suggested by the records certifying his marriage to Freitag's widow, Maria Anna, in July of the following year. From these we discover that both of his parents, Eva Rosina and Joseph père, were residents of Vienna. After the death of Maria Anna, a second, more propitious union followed on 7 February, 1741, with Polixena Bachschmidt, a member of an old and powerful family of Melk Thurnermeister.

Weiss's fortunes at Melk increased even further under the patronage of Abbot Thomas Pauer (reigned 1746–63). A month after the composer provided an applausus musicus, or a one-act Latin operetta, upon the occasion of Pauer's investment (26 June, 1746), the organist's salary was increased to an unprecedented two hundred florins. On 31 March, 1748, Weiss successfully applied for the position of schoolmaster/parish-organist in the Melk market town, and in April he was assigned two cantors to assist him in his dual role as organist at the abbey and at the parish church.

This long and successful career ended in less auspicious circumstances, however. Weiss came under heavy attack from the Melk citizenry who complained that he was 'negligent and lazy in his duties' as schoolmaster; he was forced to resign this post on 30 June, 1757. There then followed a long legal suit between himself as plaintiff and his successor, the abbey's bass, Johann Leuthner, regarding the schoolmaster's Deputation or pay-in-kind. This heated dispute was finally settled in November, 1757, partially in Weiss's favour, but it was a bitter victory; the composer suffered a stroke only fifteen months later and died on 13 February, 1759.

Weiss's activity as a composer can be gauged partly through documentary evidence and partly through surviving musical manuscripts attributed to him. It is known that he composed a *Requiem* upon the death of his first patron, Berthold Dietmayr, in 1739, the same year in which he produced a festive Mass for the investiture of Abbot Adrian Pliemel, Dietmayr's successor. Three Masses in C major, dated 1738, 1740 and 1754, are extant at Seitenstetten (E VIII 3 g–i), and at Melk a number of smaller church compositions survive: sets of six *Alma Redemptoris Mater* (III 137–42), *Ave Regina* (III 114–19), *Regina coeli* (III 178–83), *Salve Regina* (III 87–92) and a *Veni Sancte Spiritus* of questionable authenticity (III 184). But, as has already been seen, Weiss's energies were not confined to church music alone. He collaborated with Franz Tuma (1704–74), Fux's pupil in counterpoint, in composing music for an important one-act operetta, *Martis und Irene Verbindung*, the performance of which opened the new Dietmayr theatre at Melk in 1736. Although the music is lost, the surviving text[15] proves that this work was of particular historical significance. It was the earliest known specimen of independently performed German opera at Melk, predating similar productions at other locations such as Seitenstetten (*c*1750), Kremsmünster (1758) and Linz (1763). The collaboration with Tuma, who was at this time presumably in the employ of Count Franz Ferdinand Kinsky, is one more indication of Weiss's contacts with Viennese-oriented musicians.

Of the twelve Caldara compositions copied by Weiss at Melk, seven exist in score: the *Messa à 4^{tro} Voci* in a minor (A.8), the *Messa à 5. Voci* in A major (A.7) and the four Psalms and Canticle making up the *Vesperae de Dominicà* (C.1–5). Since no corresponding performance materials for these works survive at Melk, it is very likely that the copies may have been intended more for study than for performance. Precisely these kinds of scores were acquired by the abbey for the benefit of selected choirboys, and it is known, for example, that while a choirboy at Melk (1749–54), Johann Georg Albrechtsberger 'read the most profound theorists, studied the works of Fux, Caldara, Mann [sic], Pergolesi, Riepel, the Bachs, Graun, Handel, Benda, etc. which were available in the monastery, and which the choirmaster Kimmerling generously made available to him . . . '[16] These works, at least the ones by Caldara, however, were not given to Albrechtsberger by Robert Kimmerling (1737–99), who was at the time himself a fellow choirboy of Albrechtsberger. It was more likely Joseph Weiss who performed this task, because as Melk organist he was obliged by contract 'to faithfully teach one or more clerics or choirboys . . . as much as he knows of his art.' If Weiss was, in fact, one of Albrechtsberger's principal teachers in composition at Melk, he should be figured into the complex lines of Viennese teacher-pupil relationships that extended from Fux and Caldara and continued through Beethoven.

At the least, since Weiss's copies entered into and remained part of the Melk repertoire, he was in his way largely responsible for perpetuating the Imperial court church style at the abbey beyond the deaths of the Emperor Charles VI and the Abbot Berthold Dietmayr. The continuation of this tradition at Melk was assured when, in 1759, Albrechtsberger succeeded Weiss as organist. Albrechtsberger's training and experience at the abbey provided him with the appropriate credentials for his future in Vienna as Imperial court organist (1772), *Kapellmeister* at St. Stephen's cathedral (1791), and as a formidable source of conservatism within the Viennese Classical School.

Notes

[1] Barry S. Brook *Thematic Catalogues in Music* (New York, 1979) nos. 582-83, pp. 117-18.

[2] *Ibid.*, no. 471, pp. 98-9; the facsimile has been edited by Friedrich W. Riedel *Der Göttweiger thematische Katalog von 1830* (München-Salzburg, 1979) 2v.

[3] Barrie L. Greenwood 'Antonio Caldara — A Checklist of his Manuscripts in Europe, Great Britain and the United States of America' *Studies in Music* 7 (1973) p. 34.

[4] Friedrich W. Riedel 'Abt Berthold Dietmayr von Melk und der kaiserliche Hofkapellmeister Johann Joseph Fux' *Unsere Heimat* XXXVI (1965) pp. 58-64; see also his '*Neo-Exoriens Phosphorus*, ein unbekanntes musik-dramatisches Werk von Johann Joseph Fux' *Die Musikforschung* XVIII (1965) pp. 291-3.

[5] Documents concerning the two appointments are described in Rupert Feuchtmüller (ed.) *Jakob Prandtauer und sein Kunstkreis* (Wien, 1960) pp. 118-19; further on Berthold Dietmayr, see Friedrich Holly 'Abt Berthold Dietmayr von Melk' (D. Phil., diss. Universität Wien, 1949); and Ignaz Franz Keiblinger *Geschichte des Benediktinerstiftes Melk in Niederösterreich, seiner Bestizungen und Umgebungen* (Wien, 1851) I, pp. 940ff.

[6] *CATALOG, aller auf dem Stifts=Chore von Melk vorhandenen Musikalien. Verfasst im Jahr 1821*, A-M, 5 parts in 4 vols.; unlisted in Brook *op.cit.*

[7] Two graduals, 'Hodie scietis' and 'Prope est Dominus' share the same music. Caldara's works at Melk hereafter will be identified according to letters and numbers of this thematic listing; I was unable to locate four offertories/graduals tabulated by Greenwood *op.cit.*, p. 34.

8   The dissonance in b. 24 may be due to a scribal error.

9   Further, see Robert N. Freeman *Franz Schneider (1737–1812), A Thematic Catalogue of His Works* (New York, 1979) p. xxvii.

10 This Mass evidently was extremely popular throughout the Austro-Hungarian Empire. Copies prepared before 1750 are to be found in the collections of Stift Kremsmünster, Stift Lambach, Chorherrenstift Herzogenburg, the Moravské Muzeum, Brno (Stift Rajhrad, and the church of St Jakob, Brno), and the Schwarzenberg Archive, Česky-Krumlov, ČSSR. Occasionally the violin doubling of the voices varies; violin 2 doubles the soprano *ripieno*; violin 1 doubles the alto *ripieno* an octave higher.

11 Almost all original folders containing performance material were destroyed early this century. The titles and dates on the present covers may or may not have been accurately transcribed from the original wrappers; certainly, the titles cannot have been reproduced in full.

12 At present it is impossible to determine the source that may have been used for either version. Perhaps a set of parts had been in the abbey's collection for several decades, or the Melk copyists may even have worked from a full score owned by Weiss. The Mass could not have been 'restored' faithfully without reference to another source. I am grateful to Brian W. Pritchard for his generosity in making available to me extensive information regarding the two versions of A. 3.

13 The characteristics of Weiss's handwriting were established by matching the uniform hand of all known MSS attributed to the composer at Melk (III 87–92, 114–19, 137–42, 178–83) with that of the anonymous incomplete parts (violetta, organ and bass) catalogued under A-M: VI 1727, the original title page of which contained the composer's initials: 'Tantum ergo Sacramentum. Pro Benedictione consuetâ. â Quator Vocibus, in Contra puncto. Partes. 7. Ex Musicalibus I [oseph]: F[ranz?]: W[eiss]: Ao: $\overline{748}$.'

14 Unless otherwise indicated, the following bio-bibliographical information is based upon documents contained in my forthcoming study *The Practice of Music at Melk Abbey based upon the Documents, 1681–1826.*

15 Melk, Stifts-Archiv, 15. Gymnasium, Karton 2.

16 'Bericht über den Musikzustand des löbl. Stiftes Mölk in alter und neuer Zeit' *Allgemeinen musikalischen Zeitung mit besonderer Rücksicht auf den österreichischen Kaiserstaat* Jg. 1818, p. 359; republished in Rudolph Flotzinger (ed.) 'Biographische und topographische Beiträge aus der *Allgemeinen musikalischen Zeitung mit besonderer Rücksicht auf den österreichischen Kaiserstaat* (Wien 1817–1824)' (Quellen zur österreichischen Musikgeschichte, I) *Musicologica Austriaca* 3 (1982) pp. 31–36.

Appendix

Thematic listing of the compositions attributed to Caldara at Melk Abbey

All of the works listed below are MSS. Abbreviated tempos are spelled out, and original clefs are modernized. While reference is made to concording sources and catalogues ('other sources'), no attempt is made for completeness. Works cited in the principal thematic catalogue belonging to Göttweig Abbey are given according to the numbering system devised by Friedrich W. Riedel *Der Göttweiger thematische Katalog von 1830* (München-Salzburg, 1979) 2v. Besides RISM library sigla the following bibliographical abbreviations are used: FreemanS = Robert N. Freeman *Franz Schneider (1737–1812), A Thematic Catalogue of His Works* (New York, 1979); Kraus = Felix von Kraus *Biographie des k.k. Vice-Hof-Kapellmeisters Antonio Caldara* (D.Phil., diss. Universität Wien, 1894) 2v.; Melk doc. n. = documents to be published in Robert N. Freeman *The Practice of Music at Melk Abbey based upon the Documents, 1681–1826*, Appendix C (forthcoming).

A. Masses

1.

A-M: I 366.

    parts: 'Soprano', 'Alto', 'Tenore', 'Basso', 'Violino Primo', 'Violino II^{do}', 'Clarino I^{mo} in C', 'Clarino II^{do}', 'Timpani in C et G', 'Trombone Primo', 'Trombone Secundo', 'Organo'
    copyist: unidentified, second quarter 19th century

Other sources: A-GÖ: [category:] *Missae et de Requiem* 58 'Stor Angelor Custodum 1733.'; A-H: cat. 1751, [category:] *Missae solemnes* no. 6 'Missa Scotensis'; Kraus, v. 2, p. 95

2.

A-M: I 4.

          parts: 'Canto' (2 copies), 'Alto', 'Tenore', 'Basso', 'Alto Trombone',
                'Tenor Trombone' (with text), 'Organo', Violone' (with text)
      copyists: (i) Melk copyist 1
              (ii) unidentified, 18th century
              (iii) R. Helm, some captions and tempo markings.

Other sources: A-H: cat. 1751, [category:] *Missae sine clarinis & tymp.* no.
               70 'Missa Rorate' (attributed to Fux); Kraus, v. 2, p. 55

3.

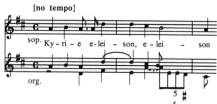

A-M: I 5.

          (Two sets of parts at same call number)
          (i) 'Canto', 'Alto' (1787), 'Tenore', 'Basso', 'Trombone Primo',
          'Trombone Secondo', 'Organo', 'Violone'
     copyist: Melk copyist 1

          (ii) with alterations, additions and variant text underlay 'Canto
          Conc:', 'Alto Conc:', 'Tenore Conc:', 'Passo Conc', 'Violino
          Primo', 'Violino Secondo', 'Organo', 'Violone'
     copyist: Melk copyist 2

Other sources: A-H: cat. 1751, [category:] *Missae sine clarinis & tymp.* no.
               6 'Missa Desponsatae virginis'; Kraus, v. 2, p. 97

4.

A-M: I 7.

          parts: 'Soprano Conc.^to', 'Alto Conc.^to', 'Tenore Conc.^to', 'Basso Conc.^to',
                'Violino P.^mo', 'Violin 2.do', 'Trombone P.^mo Conc.^to', 'Trombone
                2do Ripieno', 'Organo', 'Violone'
     copyist: J. Weiss

Other sources: A-GÖ: [category:] *Missae et de Requiem* 71 'Missa. Veni ad
               liberandum nos 1744.'; A-H: cat. 1751, [category:] *Missae sine*
               clarinis & tymp. no. 10 'Missa S. Patritii'; A-Wn: H.K.195 'Missa
               tolerabilis' (performed 1730); FreemanS s82; Kraus, v. 2, p. 67

5.

A-M: I 3.

      parts: 'Canto Concerto', 'Alto Conc:', 'Tenore Concerto', 'Basso Concerto', 'Alto Trombone', 'Tenore Trombone', 'Organo', 'Violone'
   copyists: (i) Melk copyists 1 and 2
           (ii) three unidentified 18th-century copyists

Other sources: A-H: cat. 1751, [category:] *Missae sine clarinis & tymp.* no. 82 'Missa Brevissima'; Kraus, v. 2, p. 107

6.

A-M: I 6.

      parts: 'Canto', 'Alto', 'Tenore', 'Basso', 'Violino P.mo Rip.no', 'Violino 2.do Rip.no', 'Trombone P.mo Rip.no', 'Trombone 2.do', 'Organo', 'Violone'
   copyist: J. Weiss

Other sources: A-GÖ: [category:] *Missae et de Requiem* 78 'Missa in A'; Kraus, v. 2, p. 57

7.

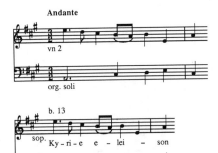

A-M: I 2.

      score: 'Messa / â 5. Voci. / 2 Violini. / 2 Tromboni. / è Violoncello / in Concertato. / Col / Organo. / Di Antonio Caldara. / vice Maestro di Capella / Di S.a M.a Ces.a è Catto.ca'
   copyist: J. Weiss

Other sources: Kraus, v. 2, p. 47

8.

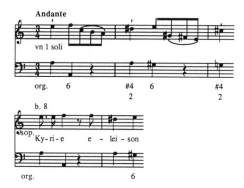

A-M: I 1.

score: 'Messa / â 4!^{tro} Voci. / 2 Violini. / i Trombone. / Alto Viola / in Concertato. / Col / Organo. / Di Antonio Caldara./ vice Maestro di Capella, / Di S^{a} Mª Ces^{a} è Catt^{oca}'

copyist: J. Weiss

Other sources: A-GÖ: [category:] *Missae et de Requiem* 66 'Missa Sti Leandri 1740.'; A-H: cat. 1751, [category:] *Missae sine clarinis & tymp.* no. 2 'Missa S Firmini'; Kraus, v. 2, p. 85

9.

A-M: I 343.

parts: 'Canto Conc^{to}', 'Alto Conc^{to}', 'Tenore Conc^{to}', 'Basso Conc^{to}', 'Violino 1mo' (two copies), 'Violino 2$^{\text{do}}_{\text{w}}$'. 'Trombone Alto', 'Trombone Tenore', 'Violoncello', 'Organo', 'Violone.' Organ headed: 'Missa in B / a / 4 Voci / 2 Violini / 2 Tromboni / Organo e Violone. / Del Sign. Antonio Caldara. / Maestro della capella imp. reale. / Ch. Mell./ 1836.'

copyist: A. Polster (most parts)

Other sources: A-GÖ: [category:] *Missae et de Requiem* 68 'Missa Sti Josephi 1743.'; A-H: cat. 1751, [category:] *Missae sine clarinis & tymp.* no. 9; A-Wn: H.K.194 'Missa Sancti Francisci' (performed 1753); Kraus, v. 2, p. 33

B. Graduals and Offertories

1.

(A) A-M: II 593 (2).

             parts: 'Canto', 'Alto', 'Tenore', 'Passo', 'Violetta', 'Alto Trombo:',
                  'Tenore Tromb:', 'Organo' (headed 'Offertorium')
          copyist: unidentified, mid-18th century

(B) A-M: II 594.

             parts: set of 14 (including multiple copies)
          copyist: A. Polster (most parts, *c*1838)

2.

(A) A-M: II 593 (8).

             parts: as for II 593 (2). Organ headed: 'Offertorium'
         copyist: as for II 593 (2)

(B) A-M: II 600.

             parts: set of 16 (including multiple copies)
         copyist: A. Polster (most parts, *c*1838)

3.

A-M: II 32.

            parts: 'Soprano Con.to', 'Alto Conc.to', 'Tenore Conc.to', 'Basso Conc.to',
                 'Trombone 1.mo,' 'Trombone 2.do', 'Organo', 'Violone'
       copyists: (i) Melk copyist 2
                 (ii) F. Schneider
                 (iii) two unidentified 18th-century copyists

   Other sources: A-GÖ: [category:] *Offertoria* 1074 'Offertorium de Vigilia
                Ascens. D: N. J. Xti'; A-H: cat. 1751, [category:] *Mottettae*
                miscellanae no. 30 'Motteta de Tempore Dnca 5 post pascha';
                A-Wn: Mus.Hs. 16097 'Offertorium à 4. Pro Dominica 5.a post
                Pascha.' (performed 1718); Kraus, v. 2, p. 179

4.

(A) A-M: II 593 (6).
>>> parts: as for II 593 (2). Organ headed: 'Offertorium'
>>> copyist: as for II 593 (2)

(B) A-M: II 598.
>>> parts: set of 16 (including multiple copies)
>>> copyist: A. Polster (most parts, *c*1838)

5.

A-M: II 37.
>>> parts: 'Canto Conc!º', 'Alto Conc!º', 'Tenore Conc!º', 'Basso Conc!º',
>>> 'Violino Primo', 'Violino 2!ᵈº', 'Organo'
>>> copyist: J. Weiss
>>> note: reworking of *Deus, Deus meus* (see below)

>> Other sources (with text 'Deus, Deus meus'): A-GÖ: [category:] *Offertoria* 1061
>> 'Offertorium de Dominica 2ª post Pascha 1724.'; A-H: cat. 1751,
>> [category:] *Mottettae miscellanae* no. 28 'Motteta de Tempore
>> Dnca post pascha'; A-Wn: Mus.Hs. 16092 'Offertorium à 4.
>> Pro Dominica 2ᵈª Post Pascha.' (performed 1719)

6.

(A) A-M: II 593 (4).
>>> parts: as for II 593 (2). Organ headed: 'Offertorium'
>>> copyist: as for II 593 (2)

(B) A-M: II 596.
>>> parts: incomplete set of 5
>>> copyist: A. Polster (most parts, *c*1838)

7.

(A) A-M: II 593 (3).
> parts: as for II 593 (2). Organ headed: 'Graduale Pro Domin: 2ᵈᵃ'
> copyist: as for II 593 (2)

(B) A-M: II 595.
> parts: set of 16 (including multiple copies).
> copyist: A. Polster (most parts, c1838)

8.

A-M: II 36.
> parts: 'Canto Concᵗᵒ', 'Alto Concᵗᵒ', 'Tenore Concᵗᵒ', 'Basso Concᵗᵒ',
> 'Violino Pᵐᵒ', 'Violino 2ᵈᵒ', 'Organo'
> copyist: J. Weiss

9.

(A) A-M: II 593 (9).
> parts: as for II 593 (2). Organ headed: 'Graduale. In Vigil: Nativit.
> D:'
> copyist: as for II 593 (2)
> note: reworking of *Prope est Dominus.* II 593 (7)

(B) A-M: II 601.
> parts: incomplete set of 3
> copyist: A. Polster (most parts, c1838)

10.

A-M: II 35.

   parts: 'Canto Conc.to', 'Alto Conc.to', 'Tenore Conc.to', 'Basso Conc.to',
      'Violino 1mo Conc.to', 'Violino 2do.', 'Organo', 'Violone'
  copyist: unidentified, 18th century

 Other sources: A-H: cat. 1751, [category:] *Mottettae miscellanae* no. 35 'Motteta
      de Tempore 6 post Pent.'; A-Wn: Mus.Hs. 16111 'Offertorium
      à 4. Pro Dominica 6ª post Pentecosten.' (performed 1729); Kraus,
      v. 2, p. 191

11.

(A) A-M: II 593 (7).

   parts: as for II 593 (2). Organ headed: 'In Dominica 4ta Adventus
      Graduale.'
  copyist: as for II 593 (2)
   note: reworked as *Hodie scietis.* II 593 (9)

(B) A-M: II 599.

   parts: set of 8
  copyist: A. Polster (c1838)

12.

(A) A-M: II 593 (5).

   parts: as for II 593 (2). Organ headed: 'Graduale Dominica 3tia'
  copyist: as for II 593 (2)

(B) A-M: II 597.

   parts: set of 7
  copyist: A. Polster (c1838)

13.

A-M: II 34.

> parts: 'Canto Conc.^{to}', 'Alto Conc.^{to}', 'Tenore Conc.^{to}', 'Basso.', 'Alto Trombone', 'Tenore Trombone.', 'Organo', 'Violone'
> copyist: F. Schneider
> note: Melk doc. n. 7882 (April-June, 1788): 'Ein Offertorium von Caldara, Si ambulavero in medio, neu abgeschrieben, 5 Bogen — 20 kr.'

Other sources: A-GÖ: [category:] *Offertoria* 1068 'Offertorium de Dom 20 p. Pentec: 1730'; A-H: cat. 1751, [category:] *Mottettae miscellanae* no. 45 'Offertorium 19 post Pent.'; A-Wn: Mus.Hs. 16124 'Offertorium à 4. Pro Dominica XIX post Pentecosten.' (performed 1718); Kraus, v. 2, p. 192

14.

A-M: II 33.

> parts: 'Canto Conc.^{to}', 'Alto Conc.^{to}', 'Tenore Conc.^{to}', 'Basso Conc.^{to}', 'Alto Trombone', 'Tenore Trombone', 'Organo', 'Violone'
> copyist: F. Schneider
> note: Melk doc. n. 7882 (April-June, 1788): 'Eben ein Offertorium von Caldara, Super flumina, 5 Bogen — 20 kr.'

Other sources: A-GÖ: [category:] *Offertoria* 1067 'Offertorium de 19 Dom. p. Pentec. 1730.'; A-H: cat. 1751, [category:] *Mottettae miscellanae* no. 46 'Offertorium 20 post Pent.'; A-Wn: Mus.Hs. 16127 'Offertorium à 4. Pro Dominica XX post Pentecosten.' (performed 1718); Kraus, v. 2, p. 196

15.

(A) A-M: II 593 (10).

> parts: as for II 593 (2). Organ headed: 'Offertorium'. Canto and alto contain performance dates, 1784, 1789
> copyist: as for II 593 (2)

(B) A-M: II 602.

> parts: set of 8
> copyist: A. Polster (most parts, c1838)

16.

(A) A-M: II 593 (1).

> parts: as for II 593 (2). Organ headed: 'Pro Dominica 1ª Adventus Graduale.'
> copyist: as for II 593 (2)

(B) A-M: II 593.

> parts: set of 14 (including multiple copies)
> copyist: A. Polster (most parts, c1838)

C. Vesper Psalms and Magnificat

1.

2.

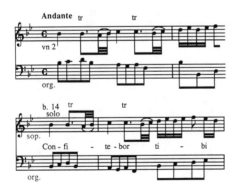

3.

4.

5.

A-M: III 9.

score: 'Vesperae de Dominica. / Dixit Dominus, / A Canto, / Alto,
2 Ten: 2 Bassis. 2 Violinis, Con Org? / Confitebor, / A Canto
et Alto Solo. 2 Violinis Con Org? / Beatus Vir / A Canto
et Alto Solo. 2 Violinis Conc.^tis è 4 Rip.^nis Con Org? / Laudate
Pueri, / A Canto Solo. 2 Violinis Con.^tis è 4 Rip.^nis Necess:
Con Org? / Magnificat, / A Canto, Alto, Tenore, Basso, Con
Org? / Del Sig.^re Antonio Caldara. / Vice Maestro di Cap.^la
Di S.^a M.ª Ces.^a'

copyist: J. Weiss

Other sources: A-GÖ: [category:] *Vesperae et Psalmi singulares.* 1942 'Psalmus.
Beatus vir 1735', 1945 'Psalmus: Confitebor', 1953 'Psalmus:
Laudate pueri 1729.' [= nos. 2-4]; A-H: cat. 1751, [category:]
Psalmus Dixit Dominus sine clarinis no. 2, [category:] *Psalmus
Confitebor* no. 4, [category:] *Beatus vir cum & sine clarinis*
no. 9 [anonymous attribution], [category:] *Laudate pueri* no.
7, [category:] *Magnificat* no. 6; Kraus, v. 2, pp. 140, 207 [=
nos. 1, 5]

D. Miserere (Psalm 50)

1.

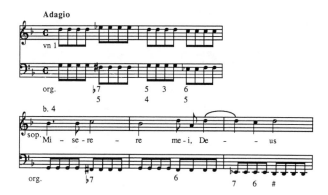

A-M: III 37.

      parts: 'Canto Conc.ᵗᵒ', 'Alto Conc.ᵗᵒ', 'Tenore Conc.ᵗᵒ', 'Basso Conc.ᵗᵒ', 'Violino Pᵐᵒ Conc.ᵗᵒ', 'Violino 2ᵈᵒ Conc.ᵗᵒ', 'Trombone Pᵐᵒ Conc.ᵗᵒ', 'Trombone 2ᵈᵒ Conc.ᵗᵒ', 'Organo', 'Violone'
   copyist: J. Weiss

Other sources: A-H: cat. 1751, [category:] *Psalmus Miserere* no. 2; A-Wn: H.K. 209 'Miserere a 4' (performed 1720); Kraus, v. 2, p. 174
     note: alternative attribution: A-GÖ: [category:] *Psalmus: Miserere mei Deus*: 2596 'Miserere 1733.' (attributed to Rathgeber)

2.

A-M: III 38.

      parts: 'Soprano Conc.ᵗᵒ', 'Alto Conc.ᵗᵒ', 'Tenore Conc.ᵗᵒ', 'Basso Conc.ᵗᵒ', 'Violino Primo Conc.ᵗᵒ', 'Violino 2do Conc.ᵗᵒ', 'Trombone Primo Conc.ᵗᵒ', 'Trombone 2do Conc.ᵗᵒ', 'Organo', 'Violone'
   copyist: unidentified, 18th century

Other sources: A-GÖ: [category:] *Psalmus: Miserere mei Deus*: 2542 'Miserere 1753'; A-H: cat. 1751, [category:] *Psalmus Miserere* no. 3; A-Wn: H.K. 210 'Miserere a 4 Voci' (performed 1744)

E. Marian Antiphon

1.

A-M: III 60.

parts: 'Canto', 'Alto', 'Tenore', 'Basso', 'Alto Trompon.', 'Tenor
Trompon.', 'Organo', 'Violone'
copyist: R. Helm (most parts)

Das mährische Musikleben
in der Zeit Antonio Caldaras

Jiří Sehnal

Abstract

Musical life in Moravia
at the time of Antonio Caldara

The historic musical collections of Moravia are very rich in works by A. Caldara, J. J. Fux and other composers of the Viennese court circle. This was partly due to the high standard of Moravian music centres, and partly to the close contact between Moravia and Vienna. The aim of this essay is to survey the most important music institutions in Moravia in the age of Charles VI and to provide information on their musical repertoire and/ or the collection of musical compositions in their possession.

Special attention is devoted to the social position of individual categories of musician. The typical baroque musical genre, the opera, was performed in Moravia by the three aristocratic orchestras (at Jaroměřice, Kroměříž, and Holešov) and by an Italian opera troupe (at Brno). The only other musical activity of these aristocratic orchestras was instrumental music. The most widespread genre, and that accessible to all social levels, was church music, practised in all municipal parish churches, and sometimes also in village parish churches, on Sundays and the holidays of the church year. A high standard of church music was achieved in the churches of the religious orders, especially among the Piarists and Jesuits, whose musicians were among the best, but also in the cathedrals of the Benedictines, Cistercians, Premonstratensians, Minoritens, and Augustinians. More modest forms of church music were practised in the churches of the Mendicants (Dominicans, Franciscans and Capuchins). The repertoire of individual musical institutions is given either according to the information in documents and old inventories, or to the surviving material.

It is clear that in the time of Caldara, the margravate of Moravia possessed a dense network of music centres, many of which lay far outside the political and economic centres. This was particularly beneficial for the cultural development of the country. For every 2000 inhabitants there were approximately eight to ten qualified musicians, well-trained in singing and playing instruments. The map included here shows Moravia in its old borders and contains all places mentioned in the essay with their size (according to the number of houses) shortly before 1750.

Das mährische Musikleben
in der Zeit Antonio Caldaras

Jiří Sehnal

MANCHE MUSIKALIENSAMMLUNGEN Mährens enthalten wertvolle Quellen zum Kirchenmusikschaffen A. Caldaras, J. J. Fuxens und anderer Komponisten des Wiener Hofs. Das Vorkommen dieser Werke im Repertoire mährischer Kirchen war einerseits auf das hohe Niveau der dort gepflegten Musik, andererseits auf die engen Kontakte mit Wien zurückzuführen. Unser Beitrag will eine Übersicht der Musikinstitutionen Mährens im ersten Drittel des 18. Jahrunderts bieten und deren Beitrag im Rahmen der Musikgeschichte werten.

Unter Karl VI. bot Mähren ein widerspruchsvolles Bild. Abgesehen vom Ostteil, der in den Jahren 1705-1709 von den Soldaten Rákóczys verwüstet wurde, war das Land von den Greueln des Kriegs verschont geblieben, dessen Bürde es allerdings zu tragen hatte. Bis in das Jahr 1715 zahlte Mähren fast eine Million Gulden jährlich an Kriegskosten und tausende junger Männer wurden zum Kriegsdienst einberufen. Das Jahr 1709 war von einer katastrophalen Mißernte begleitet, im Jahr 1710 brach die Pest aus, die im Jahr 1713 wiederkam und bis in das Jahr 1716 dauerte. Obwohl man erwarten könnte, daß in diesem so hart getroffenen, von Kriegssteuern ausgesogenen Land niemand Sinn für die Errichtung großer Bauten aufbringen werde, kulminierte gerade in dieser Zeit die barocke Baukunst. Wie aus einer anderen Welt gekommen wuchsen in ganz Mähren prachtvolle Architekturen, die wir noch heute bewundern. Die meisten wurden zum Schauplatz hervorragender Musikproduktionen. Nennen wir wenigstens einige von ihnen:

1687-1787	Schloß der Grafen Althan zu Vranov n.Dyjí (J. B. Fischer von Erlach)
1691-1737	Schloß der Familie Petřivalský in Buchlovice (D. Martinelli)
1700-1735	barocker Umbau des Zisterzienserklosters und der Zisterzienserkirche auf dem Velehrad.
1700-1737	Schloß und Kirche des Grafen Questenberg in Jaroměřice nad Rok. (J. Prandtauer)
1701-1740	Bau des Schloßes der Grafen Kaunitz in Slavkov (Austerlitz), (D. Martinelli)

1706–1723	Umbau des Zisterzienserklosters und der Zisterzienserkirche in Žďár n.Sázavou (G. Santini)
1712–1743	Bau der Jesuitenkirche Maria-Schnee in Olmütz
1717–1731	Landhaus (Neues Rathaus) in Brünn (M. Grimm)
1718–1722	Beendung des Jesuitenkollegs in Olmütz
1719–1722	Bau der St. -Nepomuk-Kirche bei Žďár n.Sázavou — eines Spitzenwerks der Barock-Gotik (G. Santini)
1719–1723	Umbau des Schloßes der Grafen Dietrichstein in Nikolsburg (Chr. A. Oedtl)
1721–1739	Klosterkirche der Benedictiner in Rajhrad (G. Santini)
1726–1730	Beendung des großartigen Klosterkomplexes der Prämonstratenser Hradisko bei Olmütz (G. Santini)
1727–1750	Bau der Prämonstratenserkirche in Křtiny (G. Santini)

Aus diesen Beispielen geht hervor, daß die Hauptinvestoren der Monumentalbauten geistliche Orden und hohe Adelige gewesen sind, während das Bürgertum nur in geringem Ausmaß teilnahm. Das entsprach der Machtstellung von Adel und Kirche in den böhmischen Ländern. Der Adel umfaßte zwar nur einen Bruchteil der Gesamtbevölkerung des Landes, besaß jedoch einschließlich der Kirche den Großteil von Grund und Boden. Dagegen war der Bürgerstand politisch und ökonomisch relativ schwach, zumal er im Jahr 1627 um die meisten seiner bisherigen Rechte gekommen war. 88% der Bevölkerung entfielen auf die Bauern, meist Untertanen des Adels oder der Kirche. Aus ihrer Arbeit floß der Reichtum des Adels und auf ihren Schultern ruhte die Last der Steuern, die Mähren dem Kaiser abzuführen hatte. Es bestanden aber manche Unterschiede zwischen den Ländern der Habsburger Monarchie, zu denen Mähren gehörte, und den Ländern Westeuropas. Während beispielsweise der König Frankreichs alle Macht und Herrlichkeit in die Hauptstadt und seinen kolossalen Sitz zu Versailles konzentrierte, bot Mähren das Bild eines nicht allzugroßen Landes mit einer Menge voneinander relativ unabhängiger kleiner Residenzen. Diese Dezentralisierung der Adelssitze, die größtenteils außerhalb umfangreicher Städte lagen, war für die böhmischen Länder typisch und verlieh ihnen den Charakter einer reich gegliederten, mit Kunstdenkmälern überfüllten natürlichen Parklandschaft. Die Streuung der kirchlichen und feudalen Zentren besaß zweifellos auf den allgemeinen kulturellen Aufschwung der Bevölkerung einen segensreichen Einfluß. Andererseits hatte das Überwiegen des Feudalelements im 18. Jahrhundert zur Folge, daß in den Städten keine eigenbürtige dem Adel konkurrierende bürgerliche Kultur wachsen konnte, derer sich große freie Städte Westeuropas rühmen konnten. Man wird weiter unten erfahren, daß beispielsweise seit dem Jahr 1732 in Brünn volle vier Jahre lang eine bekannte italienische Operngesellschaft für ein 'allen Ständen' erschwingliches Eintrittsgeld tätig war; allerdings laßen die Libretti ihrer Stücke deutlich erkennen, daß sie sich vor allem an den Adel und keineswegs an das Bürgertum wandte, das nur dazu diente, Lücken in der Theaterkasse auszufüllen.

Die erwähnten Monumentalbauten waren eine Art großartige, künstlerisch vollendete Kulisse, die eine Vorstellung der unerschütterlichen Macht ihrer Besitzer zu beschwören und sie zu idealisieren hatten. Obwohl alle an der Schaffung dieser Denkmäler beteiligten Künste und Handwerke in einer später niemals mehr wiederkehrenden, bewundernswerten Einheit die Formensprache der Zeit respektierten, handelte es sich im Grunde genommen um eine spielerische Illusion, die zwar noch tief in die zweite Hälfte des 18. Jahrhunderts dauern sollte, ihre ursprüngliche Begeisterung und den Glauben an die eigene Wahrheit jedoch bereits verloren hatte. Die Kunst dieser Zeit war ein Schauspiel, dem man eher glaubte als der erlebten Realität: die Begeisterung der Menschen für das Theater und die Oper spiegelte zweifellos eine Art Flucht aus der Wirklichkeit ...

Die Realität des Lebens war hart, der Unterschied zwischen den Lebensbedingungen des Adels und des Bürgertums bedeutend, zwischen den Lebensbedingungen des Adels und der Untertanen abgrundtief. Die Musik des 18. Jahrhunderts, die heute in Konzertsälen so viele Bewunderer findet, war ihrerzeit nur der Aristokratie zugänglich, die allein über die musikalischen Betriebsmittel verfügte. Die Bürger waren, abgesehen von der Hausmusik, im Grunde genommen auf die Routineproduktionen des Stadtturners angewiesen, der mit zwei bis vier Gesellen nur imstande war, Fanfaren, Märsche und Gesellschaftstänze zu spielen. Die Turmmusiker waren zwar vertraglich verpflichtet, in Kirchen auszuhelfen, jedoch der Kunstmusik im heutigen Sinn nicht gewachsen. Die Bauernmusik war eine andere Kategorie, unvereinbar mit der Musik des Adels. Es galt als unwürdig, sie als Adeliger anzuhören, es sei denn bei Faschingsunterhaltungen. In dieser Situation spielte die Kirchenmusik eine besondere Rolle, war sie doch allen Ständen zugänglich. Die Unterschiede zwischen der Musik in den einzelnen Kirchen waren von deren Reichtum und der Qualität der Musiker abhängig, die zur Verfügung standen. Die Kirchenmusik bot eine breite Skala verschiedener Stile und Genres, vom gregorianischen Choral über das geistliche Lied in der Nationalsprache bis zur mehrstimmigen, im Geiste der letzten Mode komponierten Musik. Nachdem die an den Residenzen des Hochadels gepflegte Musik als qualitativ beste galt, wurden ihre Ausdrucksmittel auch für den Gottesdienst geeignet befunden. So kann man erklären, weshalb es um das Jahr 1700 dem Ehrgeiz aller Kirchen entsprach, den Gottesdienst zumindest an den größten Kirchenfeiertagen mit Figuralmusik abzuhalten.

Die personellen und materiellen Möglichkeiten gestatteten es allerdings meist nicht allen Kirchen Figuralmusik zu betreiben, die vor allem geschulte Sänger und Instrumentalisten, besonders Streicher, und einen gebildeten *Regens chori* oder Organisten mit Kenntnissen aus der Komposition erforderte. An Orten, wo Adelsitze lagen, wirkten in der Kirche häufig dieselben Musiker mit, die am Schloß spielten. An Klosterkirchen betrieben die Figuralmusik besonders geschulte und zu diesem Zweck bestellte Musiker; an wichtigen Stadtkirchen versahen diese Aufgabe fest besoldete Musiker. Am flachen Land war der Figuralmusikbetrieb Sache der örtlichen Lehrer mit recht unterschiedlicher musikalischer Qualifikation, begabter Schüler und mancher Dilettanten.

In Städten halfen die Stadtturner aus. Volksmusikanten entbehrten meist die Grundvoraussetzungen des Musikbetriebs: sie beherrschten weder die erforderlichen Instrumente noch den Vortragsstil und konnten in der Regel nicht einmal Noten lesen.

Aus der ersten Hälfte des 18. Jahrhunderts blieben in Mähren überwiegend Denkmäler der Kirchenmusik erhalten, die verbreiteter war als die durch Liquidierung der Kapellen, Vermögensänderungen usw. stärker gefährdete Schloßmusik. Weder die Turmmusiker noch die Volksmusiker hinterließen in Mähren Quellendenkmäler. In beiden Fällen ging es nämlich um schriftlich nicht fixierte Musik oder Gebrauchsmusik, deren Aufzeichnungen gleich den Lautentabulaturen bei starker Abnützung als unbrauchbar weggeworfen wurden. Von der zeitgenössischen Volksmusik blieben nur einige stilisierte Tanzmelodien übrig; das Repertoire der tschechischen Kirchenlieder hat sich in gedruckten oder handschriftlichen Gesangbüchern erhalten. Nachdem die Quellen der einzelnen Musikinstitutionen recht ungleichmäßig erhalten sind, ist die Rekonstruktion des mährischen Musiklebens schwierig. Häufig muß man sich auf kurze oder mittelbare Berichte stützen und vermag dann erst nach Analogien mit Berichten über quellenmäßig reicher belegte Institutionen den einstigen Stand wiederherzustellen. Für manche Institutionen, die einst im mährischen Musikleben eine wichtige Rolle gespielt haben, blieben praktisch fast keine Quellen erhalten.

*   *   *   *   *

Die Adelskapellen

Als Zentren der weltlichen Kunstmusik gelten bei uns seit den zwanziger Jahren des 18. Jahrhunderts die Adelresidenzen. Trotzdem sind sich die Historiker darüber nicht einig, ob jeder Feudalherr an seinem Hauptsitz ein ständiges Musikensemble unterhielt. Nachdem es sich in Mähren vorwiegend um Kapellen handelte, die sich aus Dienstleuten zusammensetzten, welche an der Residenz verschiedene nichtmusikalische Funktionen bekleideten, enthält das Aktenmaterial nur sporadische Notizen. Andererseits berechtigt uns aber der Mangel an Berichten über diese Kapellen nicht dazu, in konkreten Fällen deren Existenz *a priori* zu verneinen. Immerhin ist es bekannt, daß die Musik, besonders die Orchester- und Opernmusik, ein Luxus war, der die Finanzen des betreffenden Hofs gehörig belastete. Deshalb war die Existenz einer Kapelle und die Intensität des Musikbetriebs vom persönlichen Interesse des regierenden Familienmitglieds abhängig und endete manchmal mit dessen Ableben. Besaß doch biespielsweise der bekannte Propagator der Oper in Böhmen Franz Anton Graf Sporck ein Ensemble, das bloß Gebrauchsmusik pflegte und höheren musikalischen Ansprüchen kaum Genüge leisten konnte. Es scheint auch, dass sich die dem Anhören gewidmete reine Instrumentalmusik im ersten Drittel des 18. Jahrhunderts in Mähren erst allmählich durchzusetzen begann.

Die zeitgenössische Gesellschaft verband die Auffassung der Musik immer mit außermusikalischen Funktionen. Typisch für den Adel Mährens ist im ersten Drittel des 18. Jahrhunderts das Interesse für die Oper und dramatische Musikformen. Die drei wichtigsten Kapellen Mährens pflegten zu dieser Zeit Opernmusik und die Orden der Jesuiten und Piaristen waren durch die Veranstaltung der sogenannten Schuldramen, meist mit Musik, berühmt. Deshalb bietet sich die Vermutung an, daß es die Oper und szenische Musik gewesen ist, die der Instrumentalmusik ohne die früher übliche Bindung an außermusikalische Funktionen den Weg gebahnt hat. Das Interesse des Adels für die Oper wurde meist durch Studienaufenthalte in der Fremde, besonders in Italien, oder 'Dienstreisen' an den Wiener kaiserlichen Hof angefeuert und schließlich durch die blendende Vorstellung von Fuxens Oper *Costanza e Fortezza* gekrönt, die im Jahr 1723 in Prag stattgefunden hat.

Die Kapelle des Olmützer Bischofs Kardinal Wolfgang Hannibal Schrattenbach (1711–1738) in Kroměříž (Kremsier).
Das Aktenmaterial bringt weniger Nachrichten über die Kapelle als über Kapellen anderer Olmützer Bischöfe, und auch im Kremsierer Musikarchiv hat sich aus dieser Zeit nichts erhalten. Der Kardinal war in den Jahren 1719–1722 Vizekönig von Neapel, wo er die Oper und das Oratorium Italiens kennenlernte. Nach seiner Rückkehr ließ er auf seinen Schlößern in Kremsier und Vyškov Opern aufführen, von denen nur gedruckte Libretti erhalten blieben, die erkennen lassen, daß es sich in den Jahren 1728–1735 um Opern von Bononcini, G. Giacomelli, V. Gurecký, J. A. Hasse, L. Leo, F. Peli, und N. Porpora[1] handelte. In Brünn ließ der Kardinal im Jahr 1730 *La caduta di Gerico* und *Morte e sepoltura di Cristo* sowie im Jahr 1731 *La passione di Gesù Cristo* von A. Caldara aufführen. In den folgenden Jahren waren es Oratorien von G. Costanzi, J. J. Fux, V. Gurecký, L. Leo, N. Logroscino, N. Porpora, C. Predieri, G. Reutter und D. Sarri.[2] Die Opernaufführungen organisierte in den Jahren 1722–1729 der *director musices* Abbate Leporati, den Schrattenbach nebst anderen Musikern aus Neapel mitgebracht hatte. Außer den Mitgliedern der Kardinalskapelle, deren Größe unbekannt ist, wirkten bei den Opernvorstellungen auch Zöglinge des Kremsierer Piaristenseminars mit, das damals P. David Kopecký leitete. Unter den Zöglingen dieses Seminars befanden sich die später berühmt gewordenen Brüder Carlo und Giuseppe Zuccari.[3] Bisher sind nur zehn Namen der Musiker des Kardinals bekannt.[4] Eine leitende Stellung nahm Václav Matyáš Gurecký (1729–1736) ein, nach ihm vielleicht Carlo Tessarini (1736–1738), der wohl in diesen Jahren dem Kardinal sein gedrucktes Opus 4 *La Stravaganza* widmete, wo er sich *Direttore della musica* des Kardinals nennt. Sonst blieben keinerlei Belege über Tessarinis Tätigkeit in Kremsier erhalten. Außer den bereits erwähnten italienischen Musikern sind die italienischen Kammermusiker Antonio Fornarini aus Urbino (1734–1738) und Philippus Regini (1731) bekannt. Anscheinend haben Schrattenbachs Nachfolger der Oper und dem Oratorium nicht mehr gehuldigt.

Die Kapelle des Grafen Johann Adam von Questenberg (1678–1752) in Jaroměřice nad Rokytnou (Südwestmähren).

Der Graf hat auf seinen Studienreisen in den europäischen Metropolen (1697–1698), vor allem in Italien (1699) und am kaiserlichen Hof in Wien die Oper und das Theater kennen und lieben gelernt. Er selbst war ein hervorragender Lautenspieler[5] und diese Eigenschaft hat ihn seinerzeit berühmter gemacht als sein Opernensemble. Questenbergs musikalische Begabung erbte seine Tochter Maria Karolina (geb. 1712, verehelichte Gräfin von Kuffstein), die Schülerin Theophil Muffats auf dem *Cembalo*. Manchen Anzeigen zufolge hat der Graf sogar Kontakte mit J. S. Bach angeknüpft.[6] Die engsten musikalischen Beziehungen unterhielt er jedoch mit Wien, wo er Mitglieder der Hofkapelle kannte. Zu seinen guten Bekannten gehörte vor allem A. Caldara, in dessen im Jahr 1724 zu Wien aufgeführter Oper *Euristeo* der Graf sogar als Theorbist mitwirkte. Im Jahr 1728 sandte er Caldara 250 fl. und Getreide aus Jaroměřice für eine nicht näher gennante Oper. Im Jahr 1730 wurde in Jaroměřice Caldaras Oper *Atalo ossia La verità nell'inganno* aufgeführt. Noch kurz vor Caldaras Tode im Jahr 1736 bemühte sich der Graf eine Abschrift des Oratoriums *La passione di Gesù Cristo*[7] zu erhalten, das im Jahr 1731 in Brünn aufgeführt worden war. Questenberg lud auch die Komponisten G. Bononcini und N. Porpora nach Jaroměřice ein.[8] Die eigene Kapelle begann er schon um das Jahr 1706 aus dem Kreis seiner Bediensteten in Wien aufzubauen. Nachdem sich der Graf ein Leben ohne Musik nicht vorstellen konnte, mußte ihn die Kapelle auch bei seinen Reisen auf die Güter Rappoltenkirchen (Österreich) und Bečov (Westböhmen) begleiten. In Jaroměřice schaltete Questenberg nicht nur seine Bediensteten sondern auch die Bewohner des Städtchens in seinen Theater- und Opernbetrieb ein. Im Jahr 1722 beendete er den Bau eines Theatersaals, in dem Opern, Oratorien, Kantaten und Singspiele aufgeführt wurden. Außer den Instrumentalisten standen ihm Sänger, Sängerinnen, Tänzer und ein Kinderchor, alle aus dem Kreis der örtlichen Bevölkerung, zur Verfügung. Die Dekorationen für das Theater von Jaroměřice entwarf der berühmte Giuseppe Galli Bibiena, der Jaroměřice in den Jahren 1735–1738 mehrmals besuchte.[9] Unermüdlicher *Maestro* der Kapelle war seit dem Jahr 1722 František Václav Míča (1694–1744), der nicht nur für den Opernbetrieb einschließlich der Notenabschriften, des Einstudierens und Dirigierens, sondern auch für die Bearbeitung der Partituren für das gräfliche Ensemble, die kompositorische Endfassung von Arien und Balletten, sowie die Komposition gelegentlicher Gratulationskantaten und Festopern zu sorgen hatte.[10] Die Intensität des Musikbetriebs in Jaroměřice bezeugt die Tatsache, daß Míča in den Jahren 1722–1744 mehr als 200 szenische Werke einstudiert und allein im Jahr 1738 zehn Opern und achtzehn Komödien zur Aufführung gebracht hat.[11] Es nimmt deshalb kaum wunder, daß eine derartige Arbeitsüberforderung Míčas Tod beschleunigt hat. Das Opernrepertoire von Jaroměřice stützte sich auf folgende Namen: E. Bambini, A. Brivio, A. Caldara, A. Constantini. F. B. Conti, I. Conti, B. Galuppi, G. Giacomelli, J. A. Hasse, L. Leo, M. Lucchini, G. B. Pergolesi, D. Sarri, L. Vinci. Míčas eigenes Schaffen spielte in diesem Repertoire nur eine untergeordnete, ergänzende Rolle. Seine Passions-Oratorien wurden aber auch außerhalb von Jaroměřice in Brünn, Olmütz u.a. aufgeführt.[12] Über die Aktivität der Questenbergschen Kapelle blieben relativ viele Berichte im Aktenmaterial erhalten, das Musikalienarchiv der Kapelle hinterließ dagegen nicht einmal ein Verzeichnis. Mehrere Kompositionen, einschließlich der Werke Míčas, die in Jaroměřice zur Aufführung kamen, gelangten in der Vergangenheit, unbekannt wie, in das Archiv der Gesellschaft der Musikfreunde in Wien. Hier und da blieben in Bibliotheken Libretti einiger Opern erhalten. Jedenfalls erscheint die Intensität des Opernbetriebs während der ersten Hälfte des 18. Jahrhunderts in einem weltabgeschiedenen Städtchen Südwestmährens heute unbegreiflich. Sie ist nur durch die leidenschaftliche Vorliebe Graf Questenbergs für die Oper zu erklären und war bloß in einer Zeit erklärlich, in der die Adeligen absolute Herren ihrer Dominien waren.

Die Kapelle des Grafen Franz Anton Rottal (1717–1762) in Holešov.
Auch Graf Rottal faßte um das Jahr 1730 eine Vorliebe für die Oper und pflegte sie in den Jahren 1731–1740. Die Dienerschaft wählte er bewußt aus musikalisch begabten Menschen, und die Oper stand in seinen Augen sehr hoch, daß er sogar seinen Töchtern gestattete, in ihr aufzutreten. Es ist allgemein bekannt, daß die Kapelle von Holešov in den Jahren 1737–1740 Ignaz Holzbauer leitete, der sich des in den böhmischen Ländern ungewöhnlich stolzen Titels 'componista ducalis' rühmen durfte. Weniger bekannt ist, daß in Rottals Kapelle in den Jahren 1736–1739 Ignác Mara und in den Jahren 1731–1736 Johann Georg Orsler (als 'aulae praefectus') spielte.[13] In den Jahren 1732–1736 traten in Holešov Mitglieder der Operngesellschaft Angelo Mingottis auf, die damals eine staggione in Brünn betrieb. In den Libretti dieser Jahre werden beispielsweise der Sänger und Komponist Giuseppe Niccolà Alberti, die Sängerinen Anna Cosmi, Laura Bambini, Giacinta Spinola, die Sänger Carlo Dardozzi, Domenico Battaglini u.a. gennant. Nach erhalten gebliebenen Libretti zu schließen[14] wurden in Holešov Opern von G. N. Alberti, E. Bambini, J. A. Hasse, I. Holzbauer und J. G. Orsler aufgeführt. In der Pfarrkirche zu Holešov erklang im Jahr 1736 das Oratorium *Santo Giovanni Battista* von Caldara.[15] Aus Holešov blieb weder Akten- noch Notenmaterial erhalten. Nach einem Bericht in der Chronik der Kremsierer Piaristen schenkte Gräfin Marie Therese Rottal im Jahr 1761 den Kremsierer Piaristen Theaterinventar und Notenmaterial.[16] Unter den erhaltenen Belegen der Piaristen von Kremsier ist allerdings keine Spur der Musikalien aus Holešov vorhanden.[17]

Im Falle Jaroměřice, Kremsier und Holešov handelte es sich um Opernvorstellungen, die nur einem engen Besucherkreis zugänglich waren. Im Herbst des Jahres 1732 kam jedoch nach Brünn die Operngesellschaft des Angelo Mingotti, die dreimal wöchentlich Opern 'mit pourlesque mittl Spillen für alle Stände' aufzuführen begann. Zuerst begnügte sie sich mit dem Saal der städtischen Reitschule, erbaute jedoch später ein hölzernes Theatergebäude und begann vom Jahr 1734 an in einem neuen gemauerten Theatergebäude, der sogenannten Taverne (an der Stelle des heutigen Redutentheaters) zu spielen. Nach den erhaltenen Libretti standen auf Mingottis Repertoire Opern von E. Bambini, A. Constantini, B. Galuppi, G. M. Orlandini, N. Porpora, D. Sarri, A. Vivaldi.[18] In den Sommermonaten gastierten Mitglieder der Operngesellschaft bei dem Grafen Rottal in Holešov. Am 27. Februar 1736 ersuchte A. Mingotti den Brünner Magistrat um ein Leumundszeugnis und ging dann laut E. H. Müller[19] nach Graz, um seinem Bruder Pietro beizustehen. Wir setzen voraus, daß die vierjährige Tätigkeit der Gesellschaft Mingottis tiefe Spuren in allen Schichten der Gesellschaft, vor allem bei den Musikern, hinterlassen hat, von denen manche sicherlich im Orchester aushalfen, obwohl sich der *impresario* offiziell vor allem an die Aristokratie wandte. Hoher Aufmerksamkeit erfreute sich die Oper unter den geistlichen Würdenträgern; der bereits erwähnte Kardinal Schrattenbach war also nicht der einzige, der ihr huldigte. Auch der Probst des Brünner Domkapitels Johann Mathias von Thurn und Vallessassina (1683-1746) mußte zu der dramatischen Musik enge Beziehungen hegen, denn in seinem Nachlaß wurden nicht weniger als dreizehn Opern (A. Bencini, S. Fiore, A. Fiorilli, A. Scarlatti, L. Vinci) und siebzehn Oratorien (F. Conti, M. Fini, Finazzoli, V. Gurecký, L. Leo, F. V. Míča, J. G. Orsler, G. B. Pergolesi, Camilla Rossi) entdeckt.[20] Ob der erwähnte Prälat Anteil an der Aufführung dieser Werke nahm oder sie nur aus Interesse sammelte, ist nicht bekannt. Von seiner Sammlung blieb nichts erhalten.

Die übrigen Adelskapellen Mährens, über die wir Nachricht besitzen, entstanden wohl erst an der Neige der Regierungszeit Karls VI. und pflegten nur Instrumentalmusik. In Betracht kommt hier vor allem die Kapelle des Grafen Anton Rombald Collalto (1681-1740) in Brtnice bei Iglau. Obwohl es über diese Kapelle keine Nachrichten gibt, hat sie wahrscheinlich existiert, weil sowohl Anton Rombalds Vorgänger Franz Rombald (1630-1696)[21] als auch sein Nachfolger Thomas Vinciguerra Collalto (1710-1769)[22] begeisterte Freunde der Musik waren (Abb. 1). In Velké Losiny (Gross Ullersdorf, Nordmähren) hatte Graf Johann Ludwig von Žerotín (1691-1761) wahrscheinlich eine Kapelle, und sein Vater Johann Joachim, der Erbauer des dortigen prachtvollen Schlosses, war ein Bewunderer der französischen Musik.[23] Offenbar unterhielt auch in Brünn Graf Johann Leopold von Dietrichstein (1703-1773) eine Kapelle, denn für die Jahre 1741-1747 wird als sein Direktor und Lehrer der Musik Joseph Umstatt genannt.[24]

Die Kirchen

Während die Zentren der Adelsmusik trotz ihres meist hervorragenden Niveaus episodischen Charakter trugen, wuchsen bei Kirchen seit dem 17. Jahrhundert Musikzentren beständigeren Charakters. Vom kirchenrechtlichen Standpunkt kann man Kirchen im bischöflichen Machtbereich und Kirchen der verschiedenen geistlichen Orden

CALDARA

Abbildung 1. Eintragungen der Messen Antonio Caldaras im Musikinventar von Brtnice
um 1750. (Cs-Bm: Sign: G84)
*Der Abteilung für Musikgeschichte des Mährischen Museums in Brünn ist
für die Reproduktionserlaubnis zu danken*

unterscheiden. Unter den erstgenannten nahmen die Kathedralen und Kirchen mit Kollegiatkapitel eine Sonderstellung ein. Es folgten die Pfarrkirchen, deren Bedeutung von ihrem Standort abhängig war. In den meisten wichtigeren Kirchen übten ständige, besoldete Musiker die Figuralmusik aus. Die Mittel ihres Unterhalts flossen entweder aus den Einkünften der betreffenden Stadt, beziehungsweise des betreffenden Klosters, oder aus den sogenannten Fundationen, d.i. Stiftungen von Kapitalsbeträgen an Kirchen oder Klöster durch Privatpersonen mit der Bestimmung, daß die Zinsen des in Wirtschaftsunternehmungen investierten Kapitals dem Unterhalt von Musikern einer bestimmten Kirche dienen würden.

Mähren war zur gegebenen Zeit eine Diözese und besaß deshalb eine einzige Kathedralkirche — die St. Wenzels-Kirche in Olmütz, in der die Figuralmusik und der Chorgesang von je einem Kapellmeister und Organisten, vier bis fünf Knaben-Diskantisten, acht Choralisten (die gleichzeitig das Instrumentenspiel, vor allem auf Streichinstrumenten beherrschten) und drei bis vier Turmmusikern bestritten wurde.[25] Das Repertoire der Kathedrale aus dieser Zeit ist unbekannt. In den Jahren 1691–1736 war hier Thomas Ignaz Albertini (geb. um 1660)[26] Kapellmeister, der mit seiner Stileinstellung noch der älteren Generation vor Fux angehörte. Im Jahr von Caldaras Ableben löste ihn der moderner orientierte Václav Matyáš Gurecký, der ehemalige Musikdirektor Kardinal Schrattenbachs, ab, der sich auf Empfehlung des Kardinals um das Jahr 1730 bei A. Caldara in der Komposition ausgebildet hatte. Nach einigen erhalten gebliebenen Werken können wir Gurecký als Komponisten charakterisieren, der sich vor allem auf einen frei imitierenden Kontrapunkt stützte. Diese Art des kompositorischen Denkens läßt sich am besten bei Gureckýs *Missa obligationis ex C* verfolgen, die anläßlich der Inthronisierung des Bischofs Jakob Ernst von Liechtenstein am 30. April 1740 in der Olmützer Kathedrale geschrieben wurde. Ihr Autograph blieb im Musikalienarchiv des Grafen Franz Erwein Schönborn in Wiesentheid erhalten, bei dem Václav Gureckýs Bruder Josef Gurecký in den Jahren 1735–1740 tätig war.[27]

Kirchen mit Kollegiatkapitel gab es in Mähren drei: St. Moritz in Kremsier, St. Peter in Brünn und St. Wenzel in Mikulov (Nikolsburg). Auch an diesen Kirchen bestand der Kern des Musikerensembles aus einer kleineren Zahl von Choralisten, dem Organisten und Regens chori, die von Leuten des örtlichen Turners verstärkt wurden. Außerdem halfen bei der Figuralmusik in Nikolsburg seit den dreißiger Jahren des 17. Jahrhunderts,[28] in Kremsier seit dem Jahr 1708[29] Zöglinge der örtlichen Piaristen aus. Zu A. Caldaras Zeiten wirkte bei St. Moritz in Kremsier als Chorleiter der Organist und Komponist Anton Bernkopf (geb. um 1675, gest. 1747)[30] bei St. Peter in Brünn Jiří František Slavíček (vom Jahr 1712 bis zu seinem Tod im Jahr 1746), ein seinerzeit ebenfalls beliebter Komponist,[31] und bei St. Wenzel in Nikolsburg Johann Georg Hinkemann (in den Jahren 1728–1759). Aus keiner der genannten Kirchen blieb eine vor das Jahr 1770 reichende Musikaliensammlung oder ein Inventar erhalten. Die *Missa in G* von A. Caldara (Sign. X C 40) in

Kremsier ist eine erst aus dem 19. Jahrhundert stammende Abschrift.
Man weiß nur, daß A. Bernkopf im Jahr 1731 für die St.-Moritz-Kirche
in Kremsier Kompositionen von Bachioni, G. B. Bassani, A. M.
Bononcini, Riccardo Broschi, G. B. Mazzaferrata, Peli von Modena, G.
B. Vitali,[32] also von Autoren gekauft hat, deren Werke (von M. A.
Bononcini abgesehen) noch im 17. Jahrhundert entstanden waren.
Dagegen kaufte J. F. Slavíček für die Peterskirche in Brünn in den dreißiger
Jahren bereits durchwegs gedruckte Werke seiner Zeitgenossen J. V.
Rathgeber, I. Bittinger, H. Peškovic, Oswald à s. Caecilia, K. Ritter,
M. Königsberger und I. Liechtenauer.[33]

Wenn man bedenkt, daß es unter Karl VI. außer den Sonntagen noch
40 Kirchenfeiertage gab, an denen jeder Gläubige verpflichtet war an
der Messe teilzunehmen, begreift man die Bedeutung der in Pfarrkirchen
aufgeführten Musik, in denen die Bewohner jeder Gemeinde regelmäßig
zusammentrafen. Am besten dotiert war begreiflicherweise die Musik in
Kirchen größerer Städte, wie Brünn, Olmütz, Iglau, Znaim, Boskovice,
Bystřice n. Pern., Hodonín, Hranice, Hustopeče u Brna, Ivančice, Litovel,
Mohelnice, Nový Jičín, Přerov, Svitavy, Šumperk, Telč, Trebíč, Uherský
Brod, Velké Meziříčí, Vizovice u.a. Auch bei Mangel an erhaltenen Quellen
kann man das Ausmaß und Niveau der Figuralmusik in den einzelnen
Kirchen nach der Größe der erhaltenen Orgel oder Berichten über den
Ankauf von Musikinstrumenten für den Chor indirekt beurteilen. An
manchen Orten wurde das hohe Niveau der Figuralmusik durch Musiker
der Obrigkeit gesichert, wie dies beispielsweise in Jaroměřice n. Rok.,
Holešov, Kvasice, Brtnice, Valašské Meziříčí und Velké Losiny der Fall
gewesen ist, oder durch Musiker des benachbarten Klosters, so daß die
Gläubigen auch in diesen entlegenen Städtchen Gelegenheit hatten, die
geistliche Musik ihrer Zeit kennenzulernen. Außerdem gab es eine Menge
kleiner Landkirchen, wo es dem örtlichen Lehrer (*ludirector*) nur zu
Weihnachten und Ostern gelang, ein Ensemble für die Figuralmusik
zusammenzustellen.

Einer Reihe weiterer Kirchen, zum Beispiel in den bergigen Gegenden
Ostmährens, standen nur Lehrer zur Verfügung, die es mit Müh und
Not zuwege brachten, die unumgänglichen Antwortpassagen an den
Priester zu singen und auf dem Orgelpositiv — sofern die betreffende
Kirche wenigstens über ein solches verfügte — tschechische geistliche
Lieder der Gemeinde zu begleiten. Im Hinblick auf die Tradition des
nichtkatholischen geistlichen Gesangs vor der Schlacht am Weißen Berg
und mit Rücksicht darauf, daß es unmöglich war, in armen Gegenden
den gregorianischen Choral und die Figuralmusik in den Kirchen
einzuführen, tolerierte die katholische Kirche in den böhmischen Ländern
das Singen tschechischer Lieder bei der Messe. Die Namen der
Chordirektoren und Organisten der Pfarrkirchen anzuführen, über deren
Wirken und Schaffen kaum etwas bekannt ist, hätte keinen Sinn.
Immerhin muß man anerkennen, daß auch diese vergessenen, elend
bezahlten Musiker echte Verdienste um die Hebung des musikalischen
Niveaus der Bevölkerung erworben haben. Leider wissen wir nicht einmal
allzuviel über die Musik großer Pfarrkirchen aus der ersten Hälfte des

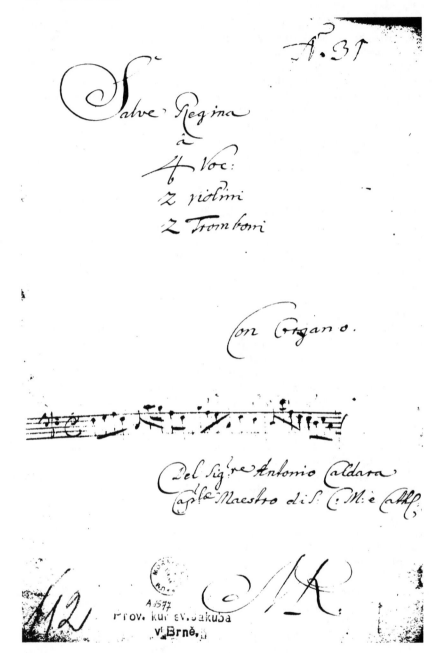

Abbildung 2. Titelblatt des *Salve Regina* von Antonio Caldara aus der Musiksammlung
der Stadtpfarrkirche St. Jakob in Brünn (Besitzer Kantor M. Rusman).
Abschrift vor 1750. (Cs-Bm: Sign: A1.577)
Der Abteilung für Musikgeschichte des Mährischen Museums in Brünn ist
für die Reproduktionserlaubnis zu danken

18. Jahrhunderts und verdanken es bloß dem glücklichen Zufall, daß die Musikaliensammlung der St.-Jakobs-Kirche in Brünn erhalten blieb, deren älteste Handschriften bis in die achtziger Jahre des 17. Jahrhunderts reichen.[34]

Schon um das Jahr 1720 zählte die Sammlung der St.-Jakobs-Kirche rund 1500 Kompositionen, die während seines Lebens Matthias Franz Altmann gesammelt hatte, der *Kantor* (so hiess der Chordirecktor bei St. Jakob) dieser Kirche in den Jahren 1715–1718. Von Altmans Musikalien sind heute nur 200 Exemplare erhalten. Die Musik der Zeit Karls VI. kennzeichnet ein Teil der Musikalien, die Matthäus Rusman, Kirchenkantor in den Jahren 1721–1762, gesammelt hatte. Weil Rusman in den Jahren 1716–1721 Choralist bei St. Michael in Wien war,[35] unterhielt er wahrscheinlich auch Beziehungen zu Hofmusikern. A. Caldara war in Rusmans Amtszeit offenbar der meistgespielte Autor bei St. Jakob, denn aus dieser Zeit blieben bis heute 41 Kompositionen Caldaras erhalten (A1556–1584, A 2127, A 2128 ?, A 2129, A 2138–2145), davon zwölf Messen oder Messeabschnitte, eine Litanei, fünf *Salve Regina* (Abb. 2) und fünf Vespergesänge. J. J. Fux war merkwürdigerweise nicht so populär, denn die Sammlung enthält nur sechzehn Kompositionen. Erst an der Neige der Ära Rusman wurde Caldara von Zechner mit mehr als fünfzig erhaltenen Kompositionen in den Schatten gestellt. Den Kern der Besetzung des St.-Jacobs-Chors bildeten der Kantor, der Organist, mehrere besoldete Tenoristen und Bassisten, in den Frauenstimmen Schüler der städtischen Schule und schließlich der städtische Turner mit seinen Leuten. Die Musiker von St. Jakob beherrschten alle Streichinstrumente ihrer Zeit, spielten Trombon, Zink, Klarine (höchst virtuos), Oboe und Querflöte.

Die einzige Repertoireprobe eines kleinen ländlichen Chors bietet die Musikaliensammlung der Kirche in Blížkovice (Südwestmähren). Die Sammlung entstand dank drei Chorleitern, die zugleich Lehrer waren — S. J. Weiser (1683–1756), A. S. Krimer (1700–1770?) und A. I. J. Krimer (1740–1797).[36] Die Tätigkeitszeit der einzelnen Lehrer am Chor läßt sich ebenso wenig eindeutig bestimmen wie die Entstehungszeit der einzelnen Handschriften. Aus den erhalten gebliebenen Musikalien geht nur hervor, daß man leichter zu spielende, einfachere Kompositionen wählte, mehr Musik zu tschechischen Texten pflegte als in den Stadtkirchen und daß das ländliche Repertoire im Vergleich mit dem städtischen als verspätet gelten konnte. Damit hängt auch der Umstand zusammen, daß zwar Caldara zugeschriebene Messen für den Chor wohl erst um das Jahr 1760 angeschafft wurden.[37] Woher sich die Musiker rekrutierten, die dem Chorleiter von Blížkovice aushalfen, wissen wir nicht. Trotzdem erweckt das Niveau des besprochenen Chors Respekt, denn die hier aufgeführten Kompositionen rechneten mit einem vier- bis fünfstimmigen Vokalensemble und einer Orgel, mit Streichinstrumenten, Trompeten (häufig auch Waldhörnern) und Timpani. Leider ist die Musikaliensammlung von Blížkovice die einzige so alte Sammlung einer kleinen Dorfkirche, die in Mähren erhalten blieb.

Die geistlichen Orden

Außer den Pfarrkirchen, die für die geistlichen Belange zu sorgen hatten, gab es damals in Mähren mindestens achtzig Kirchen der verschiedenen geistlichen Orden. In manchen wurde außer dem Gregorianischen Choral Figural- und Instrumentalmusik auf hohem Niveau betrieben, in anderen meist nur der Choral und geistliche Volksgesang. Zu den eifrigsten Pflegern der Figuralmusik gehörten die Piaristen, Jesuiten, Benediktiner, Zisterzienser, Prämonstratenser, die Beschuhten Augustiner, Mönchskanoniker des hl. Augustin, Minoriten und Barmherzigen Brüder.

Die Piaristen. Dieser Orden setzte sich die Erziehung der männlichen Jugend zum Ziel.[38] In Mähren hatten die Piaristen Trivialschulen und Gymnasien meist außerhalb der großen Siedlungszentren am Land: in Nikolsburg, Strážnice, Lipník, Kremsier, Příbor, Stará Voda und Bílá Voda. Die musische Erziehung war eine wesentliche Komponente ihres pädagogischen Systems. Außerdem stifteten Gönner oder Gründer mancher Kollegien in deren Rahmen Musikseminare (in Nikolsburg, Kremsier, Bílá Voda), in denen musikalisch begabte Knaben ärmerer Familien volle Verpflegung und intensive Musikausbildung genossen und dafür verpflichtet waren, in der Ordenskirche oder einer anderen Kirche nach Wunsch des Stifters zu musizieren. Weil das Musikstudium an diesen Seminaren nach einem Ausspruch des Bischofs Jakob Ernst von Liechtenstein im Jahr 1720 'tamquam perpetuum mobile' war, wuchsen aus den Seminaristen gute Berufssänger und -instrumentalisten, die sich später innerhalb oder außerhalb des Ordens als Lehrer, Chordirektoren, Organisten und Mitglieder von Schloßkapellen bewährten. Wenn man bedenkt, daß sich beispielsweise in Nikolsburg die Zahl der Piaristenschüler in der ersten Hälfte des 18. Jahrhunderts um 600, in Příbor um 250 und in Bílá Voda um 300 Jährlich bewegte, begreift man die hohe Bedeutung dieses Ordens für die Musikkultur Mährens. Außer der Kirchenmusik pflegten die Piaristen auch Instrumentalmusik und Musik zu den Schuldramen, die sie neben den Jesuiten am eifrigsten betrieben.[39] Die Schuldramen, in denen bis dreißig Mitwirkende auftraten, dauerten drei bis vier Stunden und waren der Öffentlichkeit zugänglich. Als künstlerisch reifstes gilt allgemein das piaristische Musikseminar in Kremsier, die Hauptstütze der Opern- und Oratorienproduktion in des Bischofs Residenz. Sein Leiter P. Jan Kopecký (Ordensnamen P. Davide a s. Joanne) komponierte sogar zwei italienische Opern, *Endymio* (1727) und *Yta innocens* (1728), die mit großem Erfolg am Hof des Kardinals aufgeführt wurden.[40] Belege über die Qualität der piaristischen Musiker gibt es auch aus anderen mährischen Kollegien,[41] die leider keine einzige Musikaliensammlung oder deren Verzeichnis hinterlassen haben. Man kann nur voraussetzen, daß das Repertoire der piaristischen Kollegien in Mähren ähnlich war wie in Böhmen, wo Inventare der Seminare aus Slaný[42] und Kosmonosy[43] erhalten blieben. Aus dem Piaristenorden kamen übrigens zahlreiche Komponisten. Die bekanntesten von ihnen, Antonín Brosman und Václav Kalous, gehören allerdings schon der Zeit nach dem Jahr 1750 an.

Die Jesuiten. Die Jesuiten widmeten sich ebenfalls der Schultätigkeit, hatten jedoch zum Unterschied von den Piaristen auch das Hochschulwesen in der Hand, waren vermögender, politisch aktiver als die Piaristen und hatten einen größeren Einfluss auf die herrschende Schicht ihrer Zeit. Ihre Kollegien lagen vor allem in den wichtigsten Städten des Landes, in Olmütz (seit dem Jahr 1581 auch eine Hochschule), Brünn, Iglau, Znaim, Troppau und Uherské Hradiště. Auch in ihrem pädagogischen System rechneten sie mit der Musik, die jedoch eher den augenblicklichen Bedürfnissen des Ordens untergeordnet war. In den Jesuitenkirchen musizierten Zöglinge der Seminare (in Olmütz, Uherské Hradiště und Brünn) oder Studenten. Nachdem die Jesuiten besonderes Gewicht auf eine musterhafte, prunkvolle Liturgie legten und in ihrem Orden strenge Disziplin herrschte, war auch die Musik in ihren Kirchen hervorragend. Die Zöglinge der Jesuitenseminare waren Anwärter auf das Priesteramt und widmeten sich in der Regel nach der Priesterweihe nicht mehr der Musik, falls dies die Vorgesetzten nicht ausdrücklich im Zusammenhang mit einer musikalischen Funktion bestimmt hatten. Auch die Jesuiten pflegten Schuldramen, aber zum Unterschied von den Piaristen weitaus prunkvoller, mit einer großen Zahl von Mitwirkenden und manchmal auf freien, der Öffentlichkeit zugänglichen Plätzen mit Tausenden von Zuschauern. Die Musikkomponente war oft so stark, daß das Spiel den Charakter einer Art Oper oder Oratorium annahm. In den Jahren 1723–1738 führten die Jesuiten in Olmütz alljährlich am Palmsonntag ein Melodrama mit Passionsthematik auf. Den Namen eines Autors, des Olmützer Domchoralisten J. R. Keller ausgenommen, sind weder die Komponisten noch die Musik dieser Melodramen bekannt. Im Hinblick auf die geschilderte intensive musikalische Tätigkeit wirkt der allgemeine Mangel an Belegen des Musiklebens der Jesuiten umso überraschender. Obwohl es unwahrscheinlich ist, daß die Musikalien der Jesuitenkirchen bei der Liquidierung des Ordens im Jahr 1773 kartiert wurden, blieben bis heute nur geringe Fragmente erhalten. Einzig und allein das Jesuitenseminar in Uherské Hradiště hinterließ ein Verzeichnis seiner Musikalien aus dem Jahr 1730,[44] in dem weder Caldara noch Fux mehr vertreten sind. Es überwiegen wenig bedeutende Komponisten aus dem Jesuitenorden (Václav Christen, Václav Majer), mährische Regionalkomponisten, Autoren deren Werke im Druck erschienen waren (besonders J. V. Rathgeber). Bemerkenswert schwach vertreten sind Wiener und italienische Komponisten. Aus Mangel an Vergleichsmaterial können wir nicht sagen, inwieweit das Jesuitenrepertoire aus Uherské Hradiště für die übrigen Seminare Mährens typisch war.

Die Benediktiner. Dieser Orden hatte seinen einzigen mährischen Sitz in Rajhrad bei Brünn. Seine Musiksammlungen blieben bis in unsere Zeit erhalten[45] und eine Reihe von Drucken aus der Renaissance beweist, daß die Benediktiner von Rajhrad schon am Ende des 16. Jahrhunderts Figuralmusik pflegten.[46] Aus dem Jahr 1725 stammt ein Musikinventar des Klosters,[47] das den starken Einfluß von Prager Komponisten erkennen läßt (28 Kompositionen von Brentner und 54 Kompositionen von G. Jacob

OSB). Die Komponisten des Wiener Hofkreises sind recht repräsentativ vertreten, unter ihnen Caldara mit drei Werken,[48] die in den Jahren 1726-1739 erworben wurden (meist dank dem Chordirektor P. Norbert Peschka), und vier *Salve Regina* (A 12.148), erst aus dem Jahr 1757. Insgesamt geht es um fünfzehn Kompositionen, davon sechs Messen und zwei Vespern. (Abb. 3). Die Benediktiner hielten in Rajhrad besoldete Musiker, Sänger und Laienorganisten aus (bis zum Jahr 1726 I.L.A. Beer, seit dem Jahr 1726 Jan Brixides — beide waren auch Komponisten).

Die Zisterzienser. Dieser Orden besaß in Mähren zwei große Klöster: in Žďár n.Sáz. und auf dem Velehrad. In der ersten Hälfte des 18. Jahrhunderts erleben beide Klöster ihre Blütezeit. In Žďár n.Sáz. war diese mit der Persönlichkeit des hochgebildeten und edlen Abtes Václav Vejmluva (1705-1738) verbunden, unter dem Konvent und Kirche von G. Santini im Geist der barocken Gotik umgebaut wurden und man im Kloster eine Akademie für die Erziehung junger Edelleute errichtete (1724-1740). Am 9. Mai, 1737, brannte das neu errichtete Kloster aus und fristete dann nur mehr bis zu seiner Liquidierung im Jahr 1784 ein kärgliches Dasein. Vielleicht auch deshalb blieb aus der ersten Hälfte des 18. Jahrhunderts weder eine Musikaliensammlung des Klosters noch deren Inventar erhalten. Die Musikaliensammlung in Žďár n.Sáz. besitzt eher eine Beziehung zur Pfarrkirche von Žďár als zum Kloster, und umfaßt in ihrer älteren Hälfte einige Kompositionen aus der Zeit um das Jahr 1700. Die ruhmreiche Vergangenheit der Musik unter dem Abt Vejmluva bezeugen nur die Orgel J. D. Siebers aus dem Jahr 1722 und die Libretti vierer Oratorien von J. F. Slavíček, die im Konvent Žďár in den Jahren 1734-1737 aufgeführt wurden.[49]

Über die Musik der Zisterzienser auf dem Velehrad sind wir leider noch weniger informiert. Bekannt ist nur, daß die Figuralmusik hier im letzten Viertel des 17. Jahrhunderts gepflegt wurde und unter dem Abt Josef Malý (1724-1748)[50] in der ersten Hälfte des 18. Jahrhunderts eine Blütezeit erlebte. Die in den Jahren 1745-1747 aufgestellte Orgel gehörte damals zu den größten Instrumenten Mährens.[51] Der Musikfond des Klosters verschwand nach dessen Auflösung im Jahr 1784 unbekannt wohin. Überraschenderweise nennt B. J. Dlabač,[52] der in seinem *Lexikon* den Zisterzienser-Musikern hohe Aufmerksamkeit widmet, aus der Zeit vor dem Jahr 1750 keinen einzigen aus Žďár und vom Velehrad.

Der Figuralmusik waren auch die Zisterzienserinnen ergeben, die Klöster in Altbrünn und Předklášteří bei Tišnov besaßen. Einige Nummern ihrer Musikalien aus der zweiten Hälfte des 18. Jahrhunderts blieben in der Sammlung der Brünner Augustiner erhalten, die im Jahre 1785 in ihr ehemaliges Kloster zu Altbrünn übersiedeln mußten. Die Figuralmusik war bei den Schwestern in Altbrünn so beliebt, daß der Visitator im Jahr 1727 ihre Verschränkung verlangte. Die Schwestern sangen nicht nur vorzüglich, sie spielten auch die verschiedensten Instrumente einschließlich der Trompete und des Waldhorns. Direktorin des Figuralchors war in den Jahren 1737-1755 Sapientia Michálková und die Kirchenorgel war das Werk des bekannten Abraham Starck aus Loket (Ellbogen).[53]

Abbildung 3. Caldaras Messen im Musikinventar der Benediktiner in Rajhrad aus dem
Jahr 1771. (Cs-Bm: Sign: G6)
*Der Abteilung für Musikgeschichte des Mährischen Museums in Brünn ist
für die Reproduktionserlaubnis zu danken*

Missa

S. Georgij
        à 4. Vocibus
    C. A. T. B.
    2. Violinis
    2. Clarinis
    Tympanis
    Con Organo.

Authore Sigß: Antonio
        Caldara.
    S: Cæs: Majes: Vice Cap: Magistro

Pro Choro Sacró = Montano.

A. 18. 583

B. V. 17.

Abbildung 4. Titelblatt der *Missa S. Georgii* von Antonio Caldara aus der Musiksammlung
    der Prämonstratenser in Kopeček. Abschrift aus den zwanziger Jahren des
    18. Jahrhunderts. (Cs-Bm: Sign: A18.583)
    Der Abteilung für Musikgeschichte des Mährischen Museums in Brünn ist
    für die Reproduktionserlaubnis zu danken

Die Prämonstratenser. In der ersten Hälfte des 18. Jahrhunderts besaß dieser Orden einen prächtigen Konvent in Hradisko bei Olmütz mit einer unweit gelegenen Abtei auf dem Kopeček (Heiligenberg) und Kanonien in Louka bei Znaim, Zábrodovice (heute ein Stadtteil Brünns) und Nová Říše. In allen Prämonstratenserklöstern pflegte man Figural- und Instrumentalmusik mit klostereigenen Musikern. Mit Ausnahme von Nová Říše wurden sämtliche Prämonstratenserklöster im Jahr 1784 aufgelöst, weshalb über ihre Musik nicht viel bekannt ist. Eine Musikaliensammlung blieb bloß in Nová Říše erhalten, deren älteste Handschriften jedoch nur in das Ende des 18. Jahrhunderts reichen.[54] Dank einigen Jahrgängen örtlicher Chroniken liegen die meisten Berichte über die Musik aus Hradisko bei Olmütz vor, aus denen hervorgeht, daß das Kloster ein Musikerensemble aus den Reihen der Schüler und Studenten (*alumni musici*) unterhielt und daß auch unter den Konventmitgliedern vorzügliche Musiker zu finden waren. In Hradisko und auf dem Kopeček wurden in den Jahren 1706 bzw. 1723–1725 drei schöne große Orgeln aufgestellt.[55]

Das lebhafte Musikleben auf dem Kopeček bezeugen Belege über die Liquidierung des Klosters, daß auf dem Kopecek 1700 Kompositionen gefunden wurden, von denen nur ein geringer Bruchteil in der Sammlung der Brünner Augustiner erhalten blieb. Es handelt sich um etwa neunzig Kompositionen, vorwiegend Messen und Litaneien aus den Jahren 1717–1780, u.a. ein Ensemble seltener Handschriften von Kompositionen J. J. Fuxens und A. Caldaras aus den Jahren 1717–1760. Caldara ist mit zwanzig Messen (Abb. 4), dem Psalm *Lauda Jerusalem*, ein Motette und zwei Offertorien vertreten, einer Zahl, die der großen Beliebtheit der Kirchenmusik dieses Komponisten in Mähren entspricht. Außerdem ist zu erkennen, daß sich die Kontakte der Prämonstratenser mit Wiener Musikkreisen, die Chroniken für das 17. Jahrhundert belegen, auch im 18. Jahrhundert fortgesetzt haben. Von Prämonstratenser-Musikern auf dem Kopeček kennen wir aus dieser Zeit nur den Laienorganisten Josef Kamenický. Auch in Louka war das Musikleben reich entwickelt, seit dem Jahr 1576 befand sich dort sogar eine vierjährige Gesang- und Musikschule, an der Musiker der kaiserlichen Kapelle unterrichteten und in den Jahren 1576–1579 Jacobus Gallus wirkte.[56] Dagegen liegen keinerlei Nachrichten über die Musik in Louka aus der ersten Hälfte des 18. Jahrhunderts vor. Unvollständig informiert sind wir auch über die Musik in der Kanonie von Zábrodovice, die bereits in der Neige des 16. Jahrhunderts durch das hohe Niveau der Musikkultur und die herzlichen Beziehungen der damaligen Äbte zum Komponisten Jacobus Gallus bekannt war.[57]

Die Minoriten. Sie besaßen Konvente in Brünn, Iglau, Krnov (Jägerndorf) und Opava (Troppau). Obwohl sie im Jahr 1784 von Josef II. nicht aufgelöst wurden, enthalten ihre Musikaliensammlungen nur jüngere Fonds aus der Neige des 18. und dem 19. Jahrhundert (Brünn, Troppau). Diese knüpfen allerdings zweifellos an bedeutend ältere Traditionen einer leider nicht konkret belegten Figuralmusik an, zumal aus dem Orden in der ersten Hälfte des 18. Jahrhunderts Kompositen wie Bernhard Artophaeus (1651–1721), Bohuslav Matěj Černohorský (1684–1742) und Česlav Vaňura (gest. 1736) hervorgegangen sind.

Beschuhte Augustiner. In Mähren besaß dieser Orden Klöster in Brünn und Jevíčko. Das Brünner Kloster bei St. Thomas gehörte seit dem 16. Jahrhundert zu den bedeutendsten Musikzentren der Stadt und seine im Jahr 1703 beendete Orgel war bis zum Jahr 1745 das größte und das einzige dreimanualige Instrument Mährens. In der erhalten gebliebenen Musikaliensammlung der Brünner Augustiner[58] fehlen jedoch gerade Musikalien aus der ersten Hälfte des 18. Jahrhunderts. Eine Art Vorstellung über die Musikaktivität der Augustiner bieten die summarischen Inventare aus den Jahren 1749 und 1754, laut denen dieser Orden im Jahr 1749 1156, im Jahr 1754 1288 Kompositionen einschließlich von Symphonien und Partiten für Blasinstrumente besessen hat. Den Kern des Musikensembles stellten acht bis zwölf Musiker, die aus einer besonderen Fundation (die später auch Leoš Janáček genossen hat) ausgehalten wurden, und eine nicht näher bekannte Zahl von Schülern oder Studenten (*alumni*), für deren Unterhalt das Kloster sorgte. Der Organist war meist ein Laie, in den Jahren 1735–1772 der ehemalige Organist von Rajhrad, Jan Brixides.

Als Chorleiter wurden in der Regel jüngere Priester nach Empfang der Weihe für relativ kurze Zeit bestellt. In der Zeit vom Jahr 1731 bis zum Jahr 1741 lösten einander in dieser Funktion Innozenz Tutsch, Michael Loserth und Hieronymus Haura ab, der einzige von ihnen, der auch Kompositionen schrieb.[59] Die Stellung eines Chordirektors war bei den Brünner Augustinern eher eine Organisations- als eine ausgesprochene Musikfunktion. Bescheidenere Figuralmusik betrieben die Augustiner auch in Jevíčko. Wie wir bereits erwähnten, blieb in der Musikaliensammlung der Brünner Augustiner ein Teil der Prämonstratenser-Sammlung von Kopeček erhalten, die wertvolle Quellen zum Schaffen A. Caldaras und J. J. Fuxens enthält. Wann und auf welche Weise diese Kompositionen nach Brünn gelangten, wissen wir nicht, jedenfalls waren sie gegen Ende des 18. Jahrhunderts noch nicht hier, weil sie das thematische Inventar der Messen aus dieser Zeit (siehe Abt. für Musikgeschichte des Mährischen Museums, G 295) noch nicht verzeichnet. Vorläufig nehmen wir an, der Augustinermönch und Komponist P. Pavel Křížkovský (1820–1885) aus Altbrünn habe sie erworben, als er im Jahr 1872 an die Olmützer Kathedrale berufen wurde, um dort eine Reform der Kirchenmusik vorzunehmen. Nachdem die Fürsprecher dieser Reform das Kirchenschaffen von Fux und Caldara für wertvoll hielten, ist es denkbar, daß P. Křížkovský die betreffenden Kompositionen der ursprünglichen Sammlung entnahm und seinem Konvent nach Brünn sandte.

Die Mönchskanoniker des hl. Augustin (Canonici regulares s. Patris Augustini). Dieser Orden besaß Klöster in Olmütz, Šternberk und Fulnek. Alle drei Klöster sorgten für den Unterhalt von Musikern, die Kirchen-

und Instrumentalmusik zu spielen hatten. Aus dem Kloster der Olmützer Augustiner sind sogar die Namen der Sänger bekannt, die in jesuitischen Melodramen auftraten, bzw. später andere Posten anstrebten. Es handelte sich durchwegs um hoch qualifizierte Musiker. Alle drei Klöster hat Kaiser Josef II. liquidiert und von ihren Musikalienfonds blieb nichts erhalten.

Serviten, Paulaner und Barmherzige Brüder. Nach der den Orgeln in ihren Kirchen gewidmeten Aufmerksamkeit zu schließen, waren die Serviten (Veselí, Jaroměřice n.Rok.) und Paulaner (Brtnice, Vranov bei Brünn, Mořice) auch der Figuralmusik geneigt. Nachdem aber alle Klöster unter Josef II. aufgelöst wurden, fehlen die Informationen über ihre Musikaktivität. Die Barmherzigen Brüder, die in der zweiten Hälfte des 18. Jahrhunderts durch glänzende Kirchenmusik bekannt waren und aus deren Reihen gute Komponisten hervorgingen, spielten zu Caldaras Zeit im Musikleben noch keine besondere Rolle, weil ihre Klöster damals in den Kinderschuhen steckten: in Prostějov 1733, in Brünn 1747 gegründet. Der im Jahr 1605 gegründete Konvent von Valtice gehörte damals nicht zu Mähren.

Bettelorden: Dominikaner (Olmütz, Brünn, Znaim, Uh.Brod, Iglau, Troppau, Boskovice, Šumperk), Franziskaner (Uh.Hradiště, Mor. Třebová, Kremsier, Dačice, Olmütz, Znaim, Troppau), Kapuziner (Olmütz, Brünn, Fulnek, Třebíč, Znaim, Nikolsburg, Kyjov, Prostějov, Iglau). Die genannten Orden hielten in der Regel keine ständigen Musiker, weil sie vor allem den Gregorianischen Choral pflegten und an hohen Feiertagen fremde Musiker zur Figuralmusik einluden. Alle Kirchen der erwähnten Orden besaßen Orgeln. Bei den Franziskanern und Kapuzinern handelte es sich meist um kleine, einmanualige Instrumente oder Orgelpositive. Bei den Dominikanern, die aus dem Mittelalter große gotische Kirchen erbten, welche im Laufe des 17. und 18. Jahrhunderts durchwegs barockisiert wurden, standen relativ große, zweimanualige Orgeln (z.B. in Brünn, Znaim, Olmütz, Uh.Brod). Die Brünner Dominikaner hatten einen Dauervertrag mit Musikern der städtischen Pfarrkirche und dem Stadtturner über die Aufführung von Figuralmusik in der Ordenskirche an Sonn- und Feiertagen.[60] Anscheinend war dies auch in Olmütz der Fall, wo in den Rechnungen im Zusammenhang mit der Musik an Sonn- und Feiertagen von Belohnungen externer Musiker die Rede ist. Zugleich werden regelmäßig ein Organist und drei Sänger genannt, die offenbar bei den üblichen Messen und Andachten geistliche Volkslieder vorzutragen hatten.[61] Von den Franziskanern und Kapuzinern ist bekannt, daß sie fremde Musiker zur Ausübung der Figuralmusik nur an den höchsten Feiertagen ihres Ordens (bes. am Fest der Portiunkula) einluden, die ohne Entgelt oder nur für die Bewirtung mitwirkten. Im Olmützer Franziskanerkonvent traten gelegentlich Jesuiten-Seminaristen und Musiker aus Hradisko auf.[62] Es war allgemein bekannt, daß diese Klöster arm sind und sich Bewirtungen nur an hohen Feiertagen dank den Spenden ihrer Gönner leisten können. Eine Art vereinfachte Figuralmusik bei den Franziskanern waren

einstimmige lateinische Ordinarien mit Orgelbegleitung, in denen sich
ein bestimmtes melodisch-harmonisches Modell mehrmals wiederholte,
dessen rhythmische Gliederung dem gegebenen Text angepaßt wurde.
Bei den Bettelorden sang man offenbar ziemlich oft geistliche Lieder
in der Nationalsprache, doch fehlen dafür nähere Belege.

*   *   *   *   *

Die hier skizzierte Übersicht des mährischen Musiklebens läßt deutlich
erkennen, daß die Kirchenmusik die am weitesten verbreitete Art der
Kunstmusik gewesen ist. Von Brünn abgesehen, wurde Opernmusik nur
an vier kleineren Orten als Ergebnis einer vorübergehenden Vorliebe
der örtlichen Herrschaft gepflegt. Eine künstlerisch anspruchsvollere Instrumentalmusik (die Turmmusiker betrieben damals reine Gebrauchsmusik) blieb einigen Adelsresidenzen und den Klosterrefektorien
vorbehalten. In manchen großen Kirchen wurde diese Musik aber auch
in der Funktion der *sonata da chiesa* gepflegt. Dem Großteil der
Bevölkerung vermittelten das Kennenlernen der Kunstmusik die
Pfarrkirchen, weil Klosterkirchen Laien nicht immer zugänglich waren
oder außerhalb größerer Städte lagen (Hradisko, Velehrad, Žďár, n.Sáz.,
Rajhrad u.a.). Pfarrkirchen gab es zur Zeit Caldaras in Mähren etwa
450, allerdings mit unterschiedlichen musikalischen Betriebsmöglich-
keiten. Die bisherigen Untersuchungen sprechen dafür, daß in Städten
mit mehr als 400 Häusern (d.i. mehr als 3000 Einwohnern) jeden Sonn-
und Feiertag Figuralmessen stattfanden, während das in kleineren Städten
mit 200–400 Häusern unregelmäßig der Fall war. In Siedlungen, die
weniger als 200 Häuser zählten, gab es Figuralmessen nur an den
Hauptfeiertagen, in Dörfern sehr selten oder überhaupt nicht. Ausnahmen
von dieser Regel existierten unter besonderen örtlichen Bedingungen.
Im großen und ganzen kann man sagen, das in Städten auf 2000
Einwohner acht bis zehn qualifizierte Musiker entfielen (Abb. 5).

Hochqualifizierte Musiker waren gesucht. Von den meisten Musikern
verlangte man, das sie imstande sind als Solisten aufzutreten, weil es
sich häufig als unmöglich erwies, manche Stimmen mit mehr als einem
Musiker zu besetzen, was eben hohe Anforderungen an die technische
Reife und Schlagfertigkeit des Interpreten stellte.[63] Nachdem aus
ehemaligen Diskantisten und Altisten nach dem Stimmbruch nur selten
gute Tenöre oder Bassisten wurden, war es leichter einen guten
Instrumentalisten zu finden, als einen guten Sänger. Außerdem gab es
nicht soviele Knaben, die Gelegenheit erhielten musikalische Bildung
an Kirchenschulen oder bei qualifizierten Chorregenten zu genießen, daß
man von einer musikalischen Massenerziehung sprechen könnte. Die
Musikbegabung erleichterte zweifellos Knaben aus bedürftigen Familien
den Weg zur Bildung, es war aber nicht leicht, von der Musik zu leben.
Stellen, deren Hauptaufgabe die Musik umfaßte, waren verhältnismäßig
selten. Bei den Lehrern beispielsweise war der Musikberuf nicht nur
mit dem Unterricht, sondern auch mit Kanzleiarbeiten und anderen, nicht
selten prosaischen Verpflichtungen (Aufziehen der Kirchturmuhr,

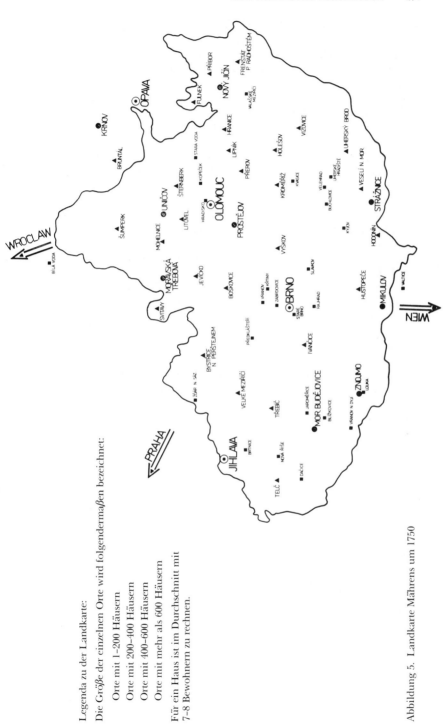

Legenda zu der Landkarte:

Die Größe der einzelnen Orte wird folgendermaßen bezeichnet:

Orte mit 1–200 Häusern

Orte mit 200–400 Häusern

Orte mit 400–600 Häusern

Orte mit mehr als 600 Häusern

Für ein Haus ist im Durchschnitt mit 7–8 Bewohnern zu rechnen.

Abbildung 5. Landkarte Mährens um 1750

Wetterläuten u.s.w.) verbunden. Die städtischen Musiker bildeten wohl eine Sonderkategorie, denn es ist nicht bekannt, daß ehemalige Studenten als solche verpflichtet worden wären. Der beste Posten für Berufsmusiker war die Stellung eines Kapellmeisters der Olmützer Kathedrale, dessen Grundgehalt zu Caldaras Zeit und im ganzen 18. Jahrhundert 300 fl. jährlich betragen hat, was annähernd den niedrigsten Entlohnungen bei der Wiener Hofkapelle der Jägerhornisten entsprach, wo die meisten Instrumentalisten jährlich 400 – 1400 Gulden und auch mehr erhielten.[64] Die Chorregenten und Organisten der übrigen Kirchen bezogen jährlich wesentlich weniger (100, 60, 40 und noch weniger fl.). Die Kapellmeister der Adelskapellen hatten zwar höhere Gehälter als 300 fl., außerdem freie Kost und Quartier, jedoch wurden diese Vorteile durch die unfreie, dienstbare Stellung und Existenzunsicherheit ausgeglichen. Deshalb war es keine Ausnahme, daß sich die meisten Kathedralen-Kapellmeister im 18. Jahrhundert aus ehemaligen Musikdirektoren der Adelsresidenzen zusammensetzten.[65]

Nach den relativ bescheidenen sozialen Bedingungen dieser Musiker darf man jedoch nicht etwa folgern, daß sie schlechte Musik produziert hätten. Schon ihr Repertoire bot den Beleg ihrer Qualitäten, denn es unterschied sich nicht wesentlich vom Repertoire der Hofkapelle und der Kathedralen in den Nachbarländern. Die meisten Musiker mußten sich damit aussöhnen, daß sie keine besondere Karriere gemacht hatten, denn gute Posten wurden nur selten frei und die übrigen waren, wie gesagt, durchschnittlich oder schlecht bezahlt. Es ist schwer, das Interpretationsniveau der einzelnen Kirchenchöre zu werten, weil zeitgenössische Zeugnisse fehlen oder zu allgemein lauten; als eine Art Richtschnur können die Informationen dienen, die wir in unserer Übersicht bei den einzelnen Musikinstitutionen geboten haben.

Das mährische Musikleben 273

Anmerkungen

[1] Jiří Sehnal 'Počátky opery na Moravě (Anfänge der Oper Mähren)' in *O divadle na Moravě* (Praha, 1974), S. 56-7.

[2] *Ibid.*, S. 61-2.

[3] Jan Bombera 'K významu Liechtenštejnova zpěváckého semináře v Kroměříži (Zur Bedeutung des Liechtensteinschen Sängerseminars in Kremsier)' *Hudební věda* XVI (1979) S. 329-37.

[4] Sehnal *op.cit.*, S. 63.

[5] Ernst Gottlieb Baron *Historisch-Theoretische und Praktische Untersuchung des Instruments der Lauten* (Nürnberg, 1727) S. 77; Johann Gottfried Walter *Musicalisches Lexikon* ... (Leipzig, 1732) S. 508; Bohumír Jan Dlabač *Allgemeines historisches Künstler-Lexikon* ... (Prag, 1815) 2.Teil, S. 526.

[6] Alois Plichta 'Johann Sebastian Bach und Johann Adam Graf von Questenberg' *Bach-Jahrbuch* (1981) S. 23-8.

[7] Vladimír Helfert *Hudební barok na českých zámcích (Der Musikbarock in den böhmischen Schlössern)* (Praha, 1916) S. 182-4.

[8] *Ibid.*, S. 188-9.

[9] Theodora Straková 'Jaroměřice nad Rokytnou a jejich význam v hudebním životě Moravy (Jaroměřice nad Rokytnou und ihre Bedeutung im Musikleben Mährens)' in *O životě a umění* (Jaroměřice, 1974) S. 400.

[10] Die Wertung Míčas als Komponisten siehe in Vladimír Helfert *Hudba na jaroměřickém zámku (Musik im Schloß Jaroměřice)* (Praha, 1924).

[11] Plichta *op.cit.*, S. 25

[12] Vladimír Telec 'Stará Libreta a míčovská otázka (Alte Libretti und Probleme um Míča)' *Opus musicum* II (1970) S.239-41; Jiří Sehnal 'Nové příspěvky k dějinám hudby na Moravě (Neue Beiträge zur Musikgeschichte Mährens)' *Časopis Moravského musea — vědy společenské* LX (1975) S. 176-7.

[13] Mehr über die Musiker des Grafen Rottal in Sehnal 'Počátky ... ' S. 66-7.

[14] Verzeichnis der erhaltenen Libretti aus Holešov siehe *ibid.*, S. 59.

[15] Jiří Sehnal, *Hudební literatura zámecké knihovny v Kroměříži (Die Musikliteratur der Schloßbibliothek in Kremsier)* (Gottwaldov, 1960) Libretto Nr. 381.

[16] Bombera *op.cit.*, S. 342.

[17] Antonín Breitenbacher *Hudební archiv bývalé piaristické koleje v Kroměříži (Das Musikarchiv des ehemaligen Piaristenkollegiums in Kremsier)* (Kroměříž, 1937).

[18] Sehnal 'Počátky ... ' S. 57.

[19] Erich H. Müller *Angelo und Pietro Mingotti* (Dresden, 1917) S. 13, XCI.

[20] Sehnal 'Nové ... ' S. 171-2.

[21] Theodora Straková 'Hudba na brtnickém zámku v. 17.století (Musik im Schloß Brtnice im 17.Jahrh.)' *Časopis Moravského musea — vědy společenské* L (1965) S. 188-9; dies., 'Hudebníci na collaltovském panství v 18. století (Die Musiker des collaltoschen Dominiums im 18.Jahrh.)' *ibid.*, LI (1966) S.231-68.

[22] Theodora Straková 'Das Musikalieninventar von Pirnitz (Brtnice)' *Sborník prací fil.fak.brněnské university* XIV (1965) F6, s. 279-87; dies., 'Brtnický hudební inventář' *Časopis Moravského musea — vědy společenské* XLVIII (1963) S.199-234.

[23] Jiří Sehnal 'Vývoj figurální hudby na chrámovém kůrn ve Velkých Losinách (Die Entwicklung der Figuralmusik auf dem Kirchenchor in Velké Losiny)' *Časopis Moravského musea — vědy společenské* LIII/IV (1968-9) S. 30-1.

[24] Tauf- und Traumatrikel der St.-Jakobs-Kirche in Brünn, Stadtarchiv Brünn.

[25] Jiří Sehnal, *Hudba a hudebníci olomoucké kapituly v 17. a 18. století (Musik und Musiker des Olmützer Kapitels im 17. und 18. Jahrh.)* im Druck.

[26] Jiří Sehnal 'Thomas Anton Albertini — kapelník olomoucké katedrály 1691-1736' (T. A. Albertini — Kapellmeister der Olmützer Kathedrale) in *Historická Olomouc* (1984). Im Druck.

[27] Fritz Zobeley *Die Musikalien der Grafen von Schönborn-Wiesentheid* 1 (Tutzing, 1967) S. XII.

[28] Josef Košulič 'Mikulov a počátky barokní hudby na Moravě (Nikolsburg und die Anfänge der Barockmusik in Mähren)' *Jižní Morava* (1973) S. 124.

[29] Anmerkungen aus den Erlebnissen des Liechtensteinschen Seminars. Bezirksarchiv Kroměříž: B-e 188-7.

[30] Matrikeln der Marienkirche in Kremsier im Staatsarchiv Brünn.

[31] Jiří Sehnal 'Hudba v Klášteře a městě Žďáru nad Sázavou (Musik in Kloster und Stadt Žďár nad Sázavou)' in *Dějiny Žďáru nad Sázavou* 3 (Brno, 1974) S. 298.

[32] Antonín Breitenbacher 'Hudební archiv kolegiátního kostela sv. Mořice v. Kroměříži (Das Musikarchiv der Kollegiatkirche St. Moritz in Kremsier)' Sonderbeilage der Z. *Časopis Vlasteneckého spolku musejního v Olomouci* 40 (1928) S. 10.

[33] Theodora Straková 'Hudba na Petrově v 17. a 18. století (Musik auf dem Petersberg im 17. und 18. Jahrhundert)' *Časopis Moravského musea — vědy společenské* LXVIII (1983) S. 109-10.

[34] Theodora Straková, Jiří Sehnal, Svatava Přibánová *Průvodce po archivních fondech Ústavu dějin hudby Moravského musea v Brne (Führer durch die Archivsammlungen des Instituts für Musikgeschichte des Mährischen Museums in Brünn)* (Brno, 1971) S. 25-7.

[35] Karl Schütz *Musikpflege an St. Michael zu Wien* (Wien, 1980) S. 67, 143.

[36] František Malý 'Bližkovická hudební sbírka (Die Musiksammlung von Bližkovice)' *Časopis Moravského musea — vědy společenské* LXX (1985).

[37] Es handelt sich um zwei anonyme Messen: *Missa S. Hieronymi* A 3824 und *Missa S. Hermenegildi* A. 3847. Auf ihren Titelblättern stand ursprünglich kein Autorenname. Von einem Unbekannten wurden sie später als Werke Caldaras bezeichnet.

[38] Die Hauptarbeit über die Piaristen in den böhmischen Ländern schrieb Antonín Neumann *Piaristé a český barok (Die Piaristen und der tschechische Barock)* (Přerov, 1933).

[39] Metoděj Zemek 'Školní divadlo u piaristů v Příboře (Das Schultheater bei den Piaristen in Příbor)' *Časopis Slezského musea* Serie B XV (1966) S. 50-8.

[40] Bombera *op.cit.*, S. 331-8.

[41] Košulič *op.cit.*, S.122-34; Rudolf Zuber 'Hudba v piaristické koleji v Bílé Vodě (Musik im Piaristenkollegium in Weißwasser)' *Slezský sborník* LX (1962) S.351-66; Jan Bombera 'Hudba v piaristické koleji v Lipníku n.b. v letech 1680-1780 (Musik im Piaristenkollegium in Lipník in den Jahren 1680-1790)' *Hudební věda* C (1973) S.111-25; ders., 'Záznamy o hudební činnosti ve Staré Vodě v 18.století (Nachrichten über das Musikleben in Stará Voda im 18.Jahrhundert)' *Hudební věda* XII (1975) S. 267-76.

[42] Dies Inventar wurde noch nicht herausgegeben. Es enthält 1439 Kompositionen aus den Jahren 1673-1756. Von Caldara sind dort im J. 1745 eine Messe, im J. 1751 zwei Messen und zwei Salve Regina, im J. 1752 eine Messe verzeichnet.

[43] Das Inventar stammt aus den Jahren 1707-1738 und enthält 720 Eintragungen (einschließlich der Musikinstrumente). Von Caldara ist merkwürdigerweise nur ein Kyrie und Gloria im J.1731 verzeichnet. Vgl. Zdeněk Culka 'Inventáře hudebních nástroju a hudebin piaristické koleje v Kosmonosích (Inventare der Musikinstrumente und Musikalien des Piaristenkollegiums in Kosmonosy)' *Příspěvky k dějinám české hudby* II (1972) S. 5-43.

[44] Jiří Sehnal 'Hudba v jesuitském semináři v Uherském Hradišti v roce 1730 (Musik im Jesuitenseminar in Uherské Hradište im J. 1730)' *Hudební věda* (1967) S. 139-47.

[45] Straková et al *Průvodce* ... S. 80-5.

[46] Theodora Straková 'Vokálněpolyfonní skladby na Moravě v 16. a na začátku 17.století (Vokalpolyphone Kompositionen in Mähren im 16. und am Anfang des 17.Jahrh)' *Časopis Moravského musea — vědy společenské* LXVIII (1983) S. 152 ff.

[47] Theodora Straková 'Rajhradský hudební Inventář z roku 1725 (Das Musikinventar von Rajhad aus dem J. 1725)' *Časopis Moravského musea — vědy společenské* LVIII (1973) S. 217-46.

[48] *Missa Spiritus sancti Italica; Missa S. Archangeli Michaelis Italica; Salve sponsa Christi.*

[49] Sehnal 'Hudba v klášteře ... ' S. 277-308.

[50] Rudolf Hurt *Dějiny cisterciáckého kláštera na Velehradě (Geschichte des Zisterzienserklosters in Velehrad)* (Olomouc, 1938) 2, S. 107-36.

[51] Jiří Sehnal 'Zur Geschichte der Orgel im Kloster Velehrad im 18.Jahrhundert' *Kirchenmusikalisches Jahrbuch* L (1966) S. 123-9.

[52] Dlabač *op.cit.*

[53] Rudolf Hurt 'Hudba u starobrněnských cisterciaček (Musik bei den Zisterzienserinnen zu Altbrünn)' *Opus musicum* VII (1974) S. 248-51.

[54] Věra Svobodová-Palečková 'Hudební sbírka premonstrátů v Nové Říši (Die Musiksammlung der Prämonstratenser in Nová Říše)' *Časopis Moravského musea — vědy společenské* XXXV (1951) S. 255-60.

[55] Zdeněk Fridrich 'On the History of the Organs at Kopeček and Hradisko, Czechoslovakia' *The Organ Yearbook* IV (1973) S. 31-8.

[56] Straková 'Vokálněpolyfonní ... ' S. 151.

[57] Rudolf Hurt 'Brno — Zábrdovice' *Opus musicum* I (1969) S. 214-5.

[58] Straková et al *Průvodce* ... S. 16-21; Bohumír Štedroň 'Hudební sbírka augustiniánů na Starém Brně (Die Musiksammlung der Augustiner zu Alt-Brünn)' *Věstník ČAVU* LII (1943) S. 1-29.

[59] Jiří Sehnal 'Hudba u brněnských augustiniánů v 18. století (Musik bei den Brünner Augustinern im 18.Jahrhundert)' *Hudební věda* XX (1983) S.227-41; Jiří Berkovec 'Pater Jeronym, regenschori u sv. Tomáše v Brne (Pater Jeronym — Regenschori bei St. Thomas in Brünn)' *Opus musicum* I (1969) S. 299-303.

[60] Staatsarchiv Brünn: E 12, kart.1, am 10.7. 1725.

[61] *Liber Confraternitatis S. Rosarii* im Staatsarchiv Olmütz: E 13, kart. 1-3.

[62] Z.B. im Olmützer Franziskanerkonvent traten gelegentlich Musiker des Jesuitenseminars, der St.Moritz-Kirche und des Klosters Hradisko auf. Vgl. *Archivum Conventus Olomucensis ad S. Bernardinum* ... im Staatsarchiv Brünn: E 21, kart 9.

[63] Jiří Sehnal 'Obsazení v chrámové hudbě na Moravě v 17. a 18. století (Die Besetzung der Kirchenmusik in Mähren im 17. und 18. Jahrhundert)' *Hudební věda* VIII (1971) S. 236-47; ders. 'Hudba u brněnských augustiniánů ... ' S. 237-40.

[64] Ludwig Ritter von Köchel *Die Kaiserliche Hof-Musikkapelle in Wien von 1543 bis 1867* (Wien, 1869) S. 72-81.

[65] Sehnal *Hudba a hudebníci* ...

Das Repertoire der Dresdner Hofkirchenmusik um 1720–1730 und die Werke Antonio Caldaras

Wolfgang Horn

Abstract

The repertoire of the *Hofkirche* at Dresden about 1720–1730, and the music of Antonio Caldara

It was only after 1720 that the continuous cultivation of Catholic church music at the Saxon court at Dresden began. The establishment of Catholicism at the court in 1697 had been a political move; and it was to remain a matter of the court, not of the Saxon population. The Catholic service, and especially the performance of Catholic church music was not rooted in a centuries-old tradition such as we find at Vienna.

Catholicism at Dresden was stabilized through the connection by marriage of the houses of Wettin and Habsburg in 1719. Throughout the 1720s the services became more festive and the necessary organisation established. It was the task of the *Kapellmeister*, Johann David Heinichen, and his assistant, Jan Dismas Zelenka (appointed *Kirchen-Compositeur* only in 1735) to build up the repertoire of Catholic church music.

Large numbers of the liturgical compositions by other masters which were performed under Heinichen and Zelenka — and frequently "adapted" by them to suit local circumstances — are still extant in the Sächsische Landesbibliothek, Dresden. Zelenka's own *Inventarium*, dating from 1726, in which he listed the church music in his private possession also is of great assistance. In the Dresden repertoire we find works by most of the composers who had made a name for themselves in Catholic church music of that time. Compositions by Antonio Caldara are prominent.

There was also a close connection between the Bohemian capital, Prague, and Dresden, and both cities engaged in regular interchange with Vienna. In an inventory made in 1728 of the music collection of the Loreto church in Prague we find many of the composers encountered at Dresden. This inventory again confirms the importance of Caldara's music and of his masses in particular, in the general church repertoire of the 1720s and 1730s.

The particular artistic quality of Caldara's church music is expressed by the music historian and collector, Franz Sales Kandler (1792–1831) when he terms Caldara a 'Harmoniker und Tonsetzer' whose importance equals that of the painter Raphael and the poet Klopstock.

Das Repertoire der Dresdner Hofkirchenmusik um 1720–1730 und die Werke Antonio Caldaras

*Wolfgang Horn**

IM JAHRE 1697 konvertierte der sächsische Kurfürst August der Starke zum Katholizismus. Zu einer Glaubensspaltung im Stammland der Reformation kam es jedoch nicht. Sachsen war und blieb evangelisch; erst im Jahre 1806 erfolgte die rechtliche Gleichstellung der sächsischen Katholiken. Der machtpolitische Hintergrund von Augusts Konversion ist bekannt; sie diente einzig und allein dazu, seine Bewerbung um die Krone des Wahlkönigreiches Polen zu ermöglichen, die seit dem Tod des Königs Jan III. Sobieski am 17. Juni 1696 vakant war. Weniger bekannt sind dagegen die Auswirkungen, die die Konstellation: katholisches Herrscherhaus — protestantisches Territorium für die Entwicklung des katholischen Kultus in Sachsen und insbesondere in Dresden hatte; sie seien im folgenden skizziert.[1]

Die sächsischen Landstände konnten dem Kurfürsten und König Geldmittel verweigern, deren er zur Verwirklichung seiner außenpolitischen Pläne dringend bedurfte. Dies zwang August den Starken zu größter Rücksichtnahme gerade auch in konfessionellen Fragen. Die Religionsgarantien, die er den Ständen wiederholt gab, sind daher nicht Ausdruck religiöser Toleranz, sondern Folge politischer Zwänge. Selbst in seiner eigenen Familie hatte sich August zunächst isoliert: seine Gemahlin, Christiane Eberhardine von Brandenburg-Bayreuth, blieb zeitlebens Protestantin,[2] und sein einziges legitimes Kind, Friedrich August II. (geboren 1696), trat erst nach langem Drängen zum Katholizismus über. Im November 1712 schwor er in Bologna dem lutherischen Glauben ab, doch wurde dieser Schritt zunächst geheim gehalten. Erst im Jahre 1717, als sich ein Erfolg des habsburgischen

* Ein Teil der folgenden Ausführungen beruht auf dem Studium der handschriftlichen Quellen aus den Beständen des Archivs der ehemaligen Katholischen Hofkirche zu Dresden, die sich heute in der Sächsischen Landesbibliothek Dresden befinden. Für freundlich gewährte Unterstützung habe ich Dr. Ortrun Landmann und Dr. Wolfgang Reich in Dresden sowie Dr. Thomas Kohlhase in Tübingen zu danken.

Eheprojekts abzeichnete, erfuhr die Öffentlichkeit vom Glaubenswechsel des Kurprinzen. Die Zweihundertjahrfeier der Reformation stand unmittelbar bevor; die Nachricht von der Konversion trübte die Festesfreude der sächsischen Protestanten erheblich.

In Dresden stand dem katholischen Gottesdienst zunächst kein repräsentativer Raum zur Verfügung. Sollte im Dresdner Schloß die Messe gelesen werden, so wurde der Audienzsaal provisorisch dafür hergerichtet. Ein festes Domizil erhielt der katholische Gottesdienst zunächst in dem einige Kilometer außerhalb Dresdens gelegenen Jagdschloß Moritzburg. Erst ein Jahrzehnt nach seiner Konversion ließ August das 1667 eröffnete Hoftheater umbauen; am Gründonnerstag des Jahres 1708 wurde es als katholische Hofkirche der Allerheiligsten Dreifaltigkeit geweiht.[3]

August erließ für die neue Hofkirche 'Reglements', die auch die Kirchenmusik betrafen. Denn er setzte Stipendien für Kapellknaben aus, die den erforderlichen Choral- und Figuralgesang ausführen sollten.[4] Zwar gibt es für die Zeit zwischen 1710 und 1720 nur wenige Zeugnisse über die katholische Hofkirchenmusik. Doch ist auch dies ein Indiz dafür, daß man bis um 1720 kaum von einer eigenständigen, quantitativ und qualitativ bedeutsamen Dresdner Kirchenmusik sprechen kann. So sind Dresden und Wien in dieser Hinsicht zunächst nicht zu vergleichen. Der Anstoß für den Aufschwung der Dresdner Kirchenmusik mußte von außen kommen. Er kam aus Wien: mit dem Einzug der Tochter des verstorbenen Kaisers Joseph I., der katholischen Habsburgerin Maria Josepha, die der Kurprinz im Jahre 1719 nach langer diplomatischer Vorbereitung geheiratet hatte, wurde der Katholizismus am Dresdner Hof fest verankert. Auch scheint der Kurprinz, anders als der Freigeist August der Starke, vom Katholizismus im Innersten ergriffen gewesen zu sein.

*   *   *   *   *

In den Jahren 1711–1719 bereiste der Kurprinz das katholische Europa; er weilte vornehmlich in Frankreich, Italien und schließlich in Wien. Man hat für seine Konversion auch die Bewunderung für die katholische Sakralkunst Italiens verantwortlich gemacht. Italien, insbesondere Venedig, prägte seinen musikalischen Geschmack entscheidend: er bevorzugte Komponisten wie Lotti und Heinichen, später dann den alle überstrahlenden Hasse, während er ein offenkundig geringeres Interesse an solchen Komponisten zeigte, die die strenge Arbeit mit mehreren Obligatstimmen pflegten. Ein unmittelbares Opfer dieser Haltung scheint Jan Dismas Zelenka geworden zu sein, dem die seiner Tätigkeit entsprechende Planstelle verweigert wurde. Auch Johann Sebastian Bach machte mit der Dedikation der *Missa h-Moll* im Jahre 1733 nicht jenes Glück, das er sich erhofft haben mag. Zwar erhielt er, wenn auch um Jahre verspätet, den gewünschten Titel, doch ließ der Hof offenbar keine Aufträge folgen, obwohl sich Bach ausdrücklich bereit erklärt hatte, sowohl für die Kammer als auch für die Kirche des Dresdner Hofes zu komponieren.[5]

Im Jahre 1716 hielt sich der Kurprinz in Venedig auf. Der venezianische Kaufmann Bianchi war vom sächsischen Hof beauftragt worden, an den 'königlichen Churprinzen, nachherigen König von Polen und Churfürsten von Sachsen, August II, die benöthigten Gelder auszuzahlen.'[6] Seine Gattin, Angioletta Bianchi, war im Ospedale degl' Incurabili erzogen worden und eine gute Sängerin und Cembalistin. Zu dem Künstlerkreis, der sich im Haus der Bianchis am Canale Grande nahe der Rialto-Brücke versammelte, hatte auch das sächsische Landeskind Johann David Heinichen (1683-1729) Zutritt.[7] Angioletta Bianchi scheint dessen Solokantaten besonders geschätzt zu haben, und so wurde der sächsische Kurprinz auf ihn aufmerksam. Mit Wirkung vom 1. August 1716 engagierte er Heinichen als Kapellmeister der sächsischen Hofkapelle neben Johann Christoph Schmidt bei gleichem Gehalt von 1200 Talern jährlich, nachdem er zuvor die Erlaubnis Augusts des Starken eingeholt hatte.[8] Nach etwa siebenjährigem Aufenthalt verließ Heinichen Italien und traf spätestens im Frühjahr 1717 in Dresden ein.

Mehr Aufsehen, aber auch erhebliche Unruhe unter den Kapellmitgliedern erregte die Gründung der italienischen Oper in Dresden. Zu diesem Zweck hatte der Kurprinz unter Zusicherung außergewöhnlich hoher Gagen in Venedig Antonio Lotti (1666/7-1740) als Opernkapellmeister gewonnen. Zusammen mit ihm wurden eine illustre Sängerschar, ein Operndichter und ein Kontrabassist engagiert, da Lotti den deutschen Kontrabassisten die richtige Begleitung eines italienischen Rezitativs nicht zutraute. August der Starke hat der Operngründung offenbar mit gemischten Gefühlen zugestimmt; jedenfalls verlangte er, 'que cela ne dérangera rien dans l'orchestre.'[9] Die Operisten erhielten lediglich Jahresverträge. Am 5. September 1717 brachen sie von Venedig nach Dresden auf.

In den Jahren 1717 bis 1719 scheinen die Aufgaben wie folgt verteilt gewesen zu sein: Johann Christoph Schmidt (1664-1728) versah wohl den evangelischen Hofgottesdienst in der Schloßkapelle; vielleicht unterstützte ihn Heinichen dabei.[10] Lotti schrieb die großen Opern — Heinichen kam hier vorerst nicht zum Zuge, und seine erste und einzige Dresdner Oper führte zum Fiasko — und sorgte zuweilen für die Aufführung von katholischer Kirchenmusik, wie sie in Dresden bislang noch nicht gehört worden war. Eine zeitgenössische Chronik der Dresdner Jesuiten bemerkt in diesem Zusammenhang für die Kartage 1718:

> Lamentationes, Psalmum Benedictus, ac miserere nescio ad luctum magis, an ad voluptatem sacram obstupescendo modulamine concinuêre Regij Phonasci Itali.[11]

> Die Lamentationes Jeremiae Prophetae, das Canticum Benedictus Dominus Deus Israel und das Miserere haben die königlichen italienischen Sänger mit staunenerregendem Wohlklang aufgeführt, so daß ich nicht sagen kann, ob dies mehr zur Trauer oder zur heiligen Lust gereichte.

Heinichen schließlich sorgte in erster Linie für Kantaten und Instrumentalmusik.[12] Jan Dismas Zelenka (1679-1745) spielte als

Komponist noch keine Rolle; er war in dieser Zeit auch zumeist in Wien, so daß es durchaus unsicher ist, ob er in größerem Maße Gelegenheit hatte, mit Lotti zu verkehren und von ihm zu lernen. Daß Lotti einen bedeutenden Einfluß auf Zelenkas Schaffen hatte, wie man gerne unterstellt,[13] wäre erst noch nachzuweisen.

Im September 1719 hielt die Habsburgerprinzessin Maria Josepha als Gemahlin des Kurprinzen ihren Einzug in Dresden, der mit ungeheurer Pracht gefeiert wurde.[14] Nun kulminierte die kurze Epoche der Dresdner italienischen Oper unter Lotti; zugleich fand sie damit ihr Ende, denn nach Abschluß der Feierlichkeiten ging Lotti nach Venedig zurück. Es ist fraglich, ob Heinichen die entstandene Lücke auf Dauer hätte schließen können. Die Ereignisse des Jahres 1720, die Hiller schildert, lassen Zweifel berechtigt erscheinen:

> Im darauf folgenden Jahre 1720 sollte noch eine von Heinichen ganz neu gesetzte Oper,[15] von eben dieser Gesellschaft aufgeführt, den Schauplatz in Dresden zieren. Allein der Castrat Senesino nahm, bey einer Probe, Gelegenheit, mit dem Kapellmeister, über eine für den Berselli gesetzte Arie, Streit anzufangen, und sich öffentlich sehr unanständig gegen ihn zu betragen. Dieser Vorfall wurde an den König nach Fraustadt in Polen berichtet. Es war zwar schon, durch einige Vornehme des Hofes, zwischen Heinichen und Senesino Versöhnung gestiftet worden: aber der König fand für gut, alle italiänische Sänger zu verabschieden. Heinichen blieb indeß, als nunmehr königlicher Kapellmeister[16] in Dresden; doch hatte er weiter keine Gelegenheit, theatralische Werke zu schreiben. Er arbeitete blos für die catholische Hofkapelle geistliche Musiken, wozu er um so viel mehr Gelegenheit hatte, da sein College im Kapellmeisteramte, Johann Christoph Schmidt, der zwar den Contrapunct gründlich verstand, sonst aber ein sehr trockener und unfruchtbarer Kopf war, wenig oder gar nichts mehr componirte.[17]

Nun konnte der schon einige Zeit schwelende Konflikt unter den Musikern beendet werden. Das Verhältnis von Italienern und Nichtitalienern war schon seit längerem gespannt, nicht zuletzt aufgrund von überdeutlichen Gehaltsunterschieden: der Kastrat Senesino erhielt jährlich 7000, Heinichen als Kapellmeister nur 1200 Taler.[18] Zudem war die Oper nach den Festlichkeiten des Jahres 1719 ein Luxus geworden, den man sich nicht länger leisten konnte oder wollte. So nahm August den Streit zum willkommenen Anlaß, sich eines wohl zunehmend lästigen Etatpostens zu entledigen. Aber auch die italienischen Sänger, zumindest die Spitzenkräfte unter ihnen, fielen keineswegs in den sozialen Abgrund. Hatte doch Georg Friedrich Händel bei seinem Dresdenbesuch 1719 versucht, einige von ihnen abzuwerben; diese nahmen nach ihrer Entlassung dann auch sogleich den Weg nach London.

Zurück blieben einige wenige Sänger, mit denen man keine großen Opern aufführen konnte, der alte Kapellmeister Schmidt, der offenkundig sein Gnadenbrot verzehrte, der 'moderne' Kapellmeister Heinichen, der keine Opern mehr zu komponieren brauchte, und ein Instrumentalensemble, das jedem Vergleich standhalten konnte: Die Geiger Volumier (auch Woulmyer geschrieben) und Pisendel, zunächst auch noch Veracini, die Flötisten Buffardin und später dann Johann Joachim Quantz, sowie der Lautenist Silvius Leopold Weiß gehörten unstreitig zu den ersten Virtuosen ihrer Zeit.

Der Opernkrach des Jahres 1720 schuf die organisatorischen Voraussetzungen für die Entstehung einer eigenständigen Dresdner Kirchenmusik. Denn nun war der Kapellmeister Heinichen — der stets Protestant blieb — für die katholische Kirchenkomposition frei geworden. Am Pfingstsonntag, dem 1. Juni 1721, erklang seine *Missa primitiva*[19] in der Hofkirche. Das Attribut hat einen doppelten Sinn: zum einen handelt es sich um Heinichens erste Messe, zum anderen eröffnet sie den Reigen festlicher katholischer Kirchenmusik, die von Bediensteten der sächsischen Hofkapelle von nun an kontinuierlich geschaffen wurde.[20]

Neben Heinichen wirkten auf diesem Gebiet in jenen Jahren vor allem Jan Dismas Zelenka, später auch Giovanni Alberto Ristori (1692–1753), von dessen Kirchenmusik leider nur wenig erhalten ist.[21] Dagegen scheint sich Johann Adolf Hasse in den Jahren vor Zelenkas Tod (1745) nur selten in der Dresdner Hofkirche präsentiert zu haben; zuverlässige Nachrichten fehlen allerdings. Zelenka war bereits über vierzig Jahre alt, als sich sein beharrlicher Lerneifer auszuzahlen begann, jedoch — wie es scheint — mehr für den katholischen Gottesdienst am Dresdner Hof als für ihn persönlich.

Offenbar hatte man zunächst die erforderliche Menge an Kirchenmusik nicht zur Verfügung; auch später konnte der Bedarf nie ganz mit Eigenproduktionen gedeckt werden. Man mußte, vielleicht zuweilen auch ohne genügende Rücksichtnahme auf die Qualität der Musik, ein Repertoire zusammenkaufen, von dem sich insbesondere der Anteil aus Zelenkas Besitz gut rekonstruieren läßt. Denn Zelenka hat in den Jahren 1726 bis 1739 kontinuierlich ein Inventar der *Rerum Musicarum Variorum Authorum Ecclesiae servientium* geführt.[22]

Aber auch Heinichen beschaffte Kopien von Werken anderer Komponisten, oder er kopierte solche Werke selbst. Da es jedoch kein Verzeichnis seines Notenvorrats gibt, ist man bei der Rekonstruktion auf mehr oder minder zufällige Quellenfunde angewiesen. Zu diesen Funden gehören auch drei Werke Antonio Caldaras, die Heinichen bearbeitet hat. Und hier ist generell festzustellen, daß die Bearbeitung fremder Werke, die in Dresden aufgeführt werden sollten, die Regel war. Viele Stücke mußten sich radikale Kürzungen gefallen lassen, die Instrumentation wurde bereichert und zuweilen wurden komplette Sätze ausgeschieden und durch andere, von den Bearbeitern komponierte Stücke ersetzt.

Im folgenden werden zwei Caldara-Bearbeitungen Heinichens kurz vorgestellt. Die Tendenzen dieser Caldara-Bearbeitungen gelten auch für einen Großteil der sonstigen Bearbeitungen im Repertoire der Dresdner Hofkirchenmusik.

Heinichen hat ein *Salve Regina in C* (D-ddr-Dlb: Mus. 2170-D-2, 2) und ein *Magnificat in C* (D-ddr-Dlb: Mus. 2170-D-2, 3) von Caldara bearbeitet; ihm lagen Abschriften beider Werke vor. In diese Partituren hat er nun seine Änderungen eingetragen: Hinweise zur Führung von Instrumenten mit den Singstimmen, Tempoangaben, Streichungen und Ergänzungen. Beim *Salve Regina*, einer kleinen Komposition für die Komplet, ging es ihm vor allem um Kürzungen. Sämtliche Textwiederholungen wurden geradezu gnadenlos eliminiert, in einer Arie tilgte er das gesamte einleitende Ritornell. Caldara schrieb das Stück für 'Violini unisoni, Canto solo, Organo'; Heinichen ergänzte durchweg auf einem zusätzlichen System eine Violetta-Stimme. Schrieben die Italiener gerne ohne Bratschenstimme — von Lotti wird überliefert, daß er die Ergänzung der Mittelstimmen seinem Kopisten überlassen habe[23] —, so war diese in Dresden ebenso üblich wie die Mitwirkung von Oboen im Orchestertutti und beim *colla-parte*-Spiel. Die Hinzufügung von Bratschen- und Oboenstimmen bzw. Angaben zur *colla-parte*-Führung gehören zum Grundbestand jeder Dresdner Bearbeitung.

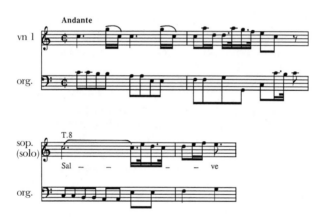

Interessanter ist Heinichens *Magnificat*-Bearbeitung; die folgende Tabelle soll einen Überblick vermitteln:

Tabelle 1. Magnificat *(Mus. 2170-D-2, 3)*

Caldara	Heinichens Bearbeitung
C-Dur; 2 Clarini, 2 Vl, Coro SATB, Soli SATB, Org	'Transponiert in d#' (Anweisung für den Kopisten; Grund: die in Dresden allein übliche D-Stimmung der Trompeten); zusätzliche Instrumente: Violetta, 2 Ob (vgl. Nr. 11)
1 'Magnificat anima mea' (C) 2 Cl, 2 Vl, Coro, Org	zusätzlich Violetta; fast vollständige Neufassung der Clarinpartien;
3/4: 18T.	3/4: 18T.
2 'Et exsultavit' (C) 2 Cl, 2 Vl, Coro, Org	zusätzlich Violetta; fast vollständige Neufassung der Clarinpartien;
₵; 14T.	₵ *allegro*: 14T.
3 'Quia respexit' (G) S, Org (Aria); C *adagio*: 20T.	keine Stimmen ergänzt; C *andante*; 14T: nur T. 1–2 von Caldara übernommen, T. 3–14 von Heinichen frei hinzukomponiert
4 'Quia fecit' (C) 2 Cl, 2 Vl, B, Org (Aria);	keine Stimmen ergänzt, ausdrücklicher Hinweis: 'Violetta tacet'; fast vollständige Neufassung der Clarinpartien;
3/8: 58T.	3/8: 58T.
5 'Et misericordia ejus' (a-E, dominantischer Halbschluß) SAT soli, Org;	keine Stimmen ergänzt;
₵: 6T.	₵; 6T: nur T. 1–3 von Caldara übernommen, T. 4–6 von Heinichen komponiert
6 'Fecit potentiam' (a-C) 2 Vl, Coro, Org 3/8 *(allegro)*: 16T. + C *adagio*: 2T. + 3/8 *allegro*: 12T. + C *adagio*: 2T. + C *allegro*: 9T. + C *adagio*: 2T.	zusätzlich Violetta und 2 Clarini; 16T. + 2T. (die folgenden 14 Takte wiederholen die Worte: 'dispersit superbos mente cordis sui', Heinichen hat sie gestrichen) + 9T. + 2T.
7 'Esurientes implevit bonis' (a) vni unis., T, Org (Aria); 3/4: 44T.	keine nennenswerten Änderungen; 3/4 *andante*: 44T.
8 'Suscepit Israel' (F) A, Org (Rez.); C: 8T.	keine nennenswerten Änderungen; C: 8T.
9 'Sicut locutus est' (C) SA, Org (Solo a due); C: 13T.	keine nennenswerten Änderungen; C *allegro*: 13T.
10 'Gloria Patri' (a-E, dominantischer Halbschluß) Coro, Org;	zusätzlich Violetta und *colla-parte*-Hinweis: 'li Violini unis: e sempre col Soprano' (wohl lediglich Verdeutlichung des auch von Caldara Gemeinten);
C *adagio*: 10T. 6 (T. 6–9: Textwiederholung)	C *adagio*: 6T. (T.1–5 und T.10)
11 'Sicut erat'-'Amen' (C) 2 Cl, Vni unis., Coro, Org;	zusätzlich Violetta; im 'Amen' der *colla-parte*-Hinweis: 'NB Viol. 1; Hautb. 1.2. col Soprano e il Violino 2. va con l'Alto'; Violetta 'sempre col Tenore'.
3/4 *allegro*: 13T. + C *presto*: 27T.	3/4 *allegro*: 12T. + C *presto*: 27T.
	Am Ende Angabe der Aufführungsdauer: '9 Min.'

Man darf diese Bearbeitungen nicht überwerten. Es handelt sich mehr um eine Einrichtung der Werke im Hinblick auf die Dresdner Aufführungsverhältnisse als um eine 'Verbesserung', aus der man künstlerische Absichten des Bearbeiters erschließen könnte. Neben Werken Caldaras hat Heinichen u.a. zwei Messen von Johann Friedrich Fasch und zwei Messen von Angelo Antonio Caroli bearbeitet (Quellen in der Sächsischen Landesbibliothek Dresden.)[24]

*   *   *   *   *

Wesentlich besser unterrichtet sind wir über die Bestände Zelenkas. Jan Lukás Zelenka wurde am 16. Oktober 1679 in der Kirche des böhmischen Dorfes Launowitz (Lounovice) getauft; den Namen Dismas hat er offenbar erst später angenommen. Zelenka erhielt seine höhere Schulbildung wahrscheinlich am Prager Jesuitenkolleg 'Clementinum'. Dort dürfte er neben Sprachen — in seinen Partituren begegnen v.a. lateinische und italienische, weniger französische und nur vereinzelt deutsche Vermerke — auch das Kontrabaßspiel erlernt haben, das ihn um 1710 in die Dresdner Hofkapelle brachte. Zuvor spielte Zelenka in der Prager Kapelle des Barons von Hartig, der kaiserlicher Statthalter in Böhmen war. Vielleicht war man auf Zelenka aufmerksam geworden, als man in böhmischen Jesuitenschulen nach Kapellknaben für das 1708 gegründete Institut an der katholischen Hofkirche suchte. Allerdings lassen sich keine Verbindungen Zelenkas zu diesem Institut nachweisen.

Das entscheidende Erlebnis im Leben des Komponisten Zelenka war ohne Zweifel der Unterricht bei Johann Joseph Fux in Wien. Fuxens *Gradus ad Parnassum* erschien zwar erst 1725, doch darf man die Maximen dieses Lehrbuchs getrost auch für den Unterricht Zelenkas in Anspruch nehmen. Dabei ist zu beachten, daß Zelenka wohl keinen Unterricht in den 'Species Contrapuncti' mehr nötig hatte. Eher dürfte Fux mit ihm die höhere Schule des Kontrapunkts, die Imitations- und Fugenlehre, durchgenommen haben: sei es, daß Zelenka Aufgaben löste, die Fux ihm vorgab, wobei das Ergebnis dann gemeinsam besprochen wurde, sei es, daß man gemeinsam mustergültige Werke der *auctores classici*, etwa Palestrinas oder Frescobaldis, im Hinblick auf Textbehandlung, Stimmführung, Dissonanzbehandlung u.ä. durchging. Vor allem diesen Bereich des Unterrichts dokumentieren Zelenkas *Collectaneorum Musicorum Libri quatuor* (D-ddr-Dlb: Mus. 1-B-98).[25] Dagegen ist die Zahl seiner eigenen in Wien entstandenen Werke recht klein. Sie lassen sich auch kaum mit dem Unterricht bei Fux in Verbindung bringen (sofern dieser nicht auch die Komposition im 'modernen Geschmack' einschloß).

Die Daten und der Verlauf des Wien-Aufenthalts lassen sich heute nicht mehr sicher rekonstruieren;[26] ein Abstecher zum Gefolge des Kurprinzen nach Venedig im Jahre 1716 ist wahrscheinlich, doch was Zelenka dort im einzelnen gemacht oder gelernt hat, kann man allenfalls vermuten. Es genügt hier jedoch die Feststellung, daß Zelenka in der ersten Hälfte des Jahres 1716 erstmals in Wien war, und daß er auch in den Jahren 1717 und 1718 dort weilte. Das letzte Wiener Datum gibt er in Buch IV der *Libri quatuor* mit 'à Vienna 1719 10 Febru:' an. Daß Zelenka in Wien Caldara und seine Musik kennengelernt hat, ist wahrscheinlich, wenn auch über persönliche Beziehungen nichts bekannt ist.

Zelenkas zweite und letzte größere Reise ermöglichte ihm ein Wiedersehen mit den Wiener Bekannten. Als sich Kaiser Karl VI. im Jahre 1723 zum böhmischen König krönen ließ, war dies der Anlaß für einen längeren Aufenthalt des Wiener Hofes in Prag. Dort fand am 28. August 1723, dem Geburtstag der Kaiserin Elisabeth Christine, die denkwürdige Aufführung von Fuxens Oper *Costanza e Fortezza* unter der Leitung Antonio Caldaras statt.[27]

Auch Zelenka leistete seinen Beitrag zur Huldigung (D-ddr-Dlb: Mus. 2358-D-2):

> MELODRAMA quod occasione Gloriosissimae inaugurationis in Regem CAROLI VI et In Reginam Bohemiae ELISAbethae CHRistinae, quaerente ita Caesareo et Academico Collegio Societatis Jesu Pragae ad Sanctum Clementem, in Musicam posuit et coram iisdem Caesareis Regiisque Maiestatibus et in Summa Veneratione direxit Augustissimi Poloniarum Regis et Electoris Saxo: FRIDERICI AUGUSTI à Camera Musicus Joannes Disma Zelenka Boemus Launowicensis A: D: 1723.

> Melodrama, welches anläßlich der rühmlichsten Erhebung Karls VI. zum König und Elisabeth Christines zur Königin von Böhmen auf Verlangen des Kaiserlichen und Akademischen Collegiums der Prager Jesuiten zum Heiligen Clemens in Musik gesetzt und vor den genannten Kaiserlichen und Königlichen Majestäten auch in höchster Verehrung dirigiert hat des hocherhabenen Königs von Polen und Kurfürsten zu Sachsen Friedrich August Kammermusikus Johannes Dismas Zelenka, Böhme aus Launowitz, im Jahre des Herrn 1723.

Den Rest seines Lebens verbrachte Zelenka offenbar in Dresden, sieht man einmal von einer Wallfahrt nach Graupen in Böhmen im Jahr 1725 ab. Jedenfalls ist über weitere Reisen nichts bekannt, und wenn er auf seinen datierten Kompositionen auch einen Ort nennt, so ist dies nach 1723 stets Dresden. Seine beträchtliche Sammlung an Kirchenmusik ist, von wenigen Ausnahmen abgesehen, nicht durch persönlichen Kontakt mit den Komponisten zusammengekommen.

Über Zelenkas Musikaliensammlung informiert das schon erwähnte weitgehend eigenhändig geschriebene

> Inventarium Rerum Musicarum Variorum Authorum Ecclesiae servientium Quas possidet Joannes Dismas Zelenka Augustissimi Poloniarum Regis et Electoris Saxoniae à Camera Musicus, (gestrichen: factum) inchoatum An: 1726. die 17. Janua:

> Verzeichnis der von verschiedenen Autoren stammenden und der Kirche dienenden musikalischen Werke, die der Kammermusikus des hocherhabenen Königs von Polen und Kurfürsten von Sachsen Johannes Dismas Zelenka besitzt, (gestrichen: erstellt) begonnen am 17. Januar 1726.

Das Inventar (D-ddr-Dlb: Bibl.-Arch. III H b 787d) ist in verschiedene Rubriken eingeteilt: Introitus, Missae integrae, Kyrie separata, Gloria, Credo, Sanctus, Agnus, Offertoria, Cantate (Rubrik später gestrichen), Arie, Hymni, Psalmi Vespertini, Antiphonae Alma, Ave Regina, Regina Coeli, Salve, Pro Defunctis, Quadragesimalia, Versus, Litaniae, Mottetti [sic], Te Deum laudamus. Auch Zelenkas eigene Kompositionen sind in dem Verzeichnis enthalten, das eine unschätzbare Hilfe bei der Klärung von Fragen der Zuweisung und der Datierung darstellt.

Das Verzeichnis wurde 1726 begonnen und wohl bis 1739 geführt; aus diesem Jahr nämlich stammt der letzte Messeneintrag, Zelenkas *Missa votiva* betreffend. Wenn es auch im einzelnen Unstimmigkeiten geben mag, so kann man insgesamt doch aus der Stellung eines Eintrags im Inventar das Datum der Komposition, wenn es sich um ein Werk Zelenkas handelt, oder des Erwerbs der Quelle eines fremden Werkes erschließen. Im Januar 1726 scheinen erst recht wenige Messen in Zelenkas Besitz gewesen zu sein; schon die zwölfte Eintragung nennt ein Werk Zelenkas, das nach diesem Datum entstanden ist, nämlich die im März und April 1726 komponierte *Missa Paschalis.*

Unter den elf ersten Messen finden sich drei Kompositionen Zelenkas,[28] vier Messen Palestrinas (die im dritten Buch der *Libri quatuor*, kopiert 1717, stehen), eine vierchörige Messe von Orazio Benevoli[29] (lediglich Besitzvermerk von Zelenkas Hand: 'à Zelenka Music: de S: M: Le Roy de Pologne Electeur de Saxe. 1719.'; D-ddr-Dlb: Mus. 1705-D-1) sowie zwei Messen von Fux — *Missa primitiva*[30] in C (K.26, D-ddr-Dlb: Mus. 2130-D-2) und *Missa canonica* in C (K.7, Dresden, 18.10. 1719)[31] – und schließlich eine *Missa quadragesimalis* von Georg Reutter d.Ä. (D-ddr-Dlb: Mus. 2979-D-9; Zelenkas Schriftformen deuten darauf, daß er diese Abschrift noch in Wien genommen hat).

Es fällt auf, daß unter den vor 1726 vorhandenen Werken keine Messe Caldaras vertreten ist. Man könnte daraus schließen, daß Zelenka sich erst Jahre nach seinem Wiener Aufenthalt mit der Musik Caldaras vertraut gemacht hat. Dabei scheint auf den ersten Blick die große Zahl von Werken Caldaras, die Zelenka später erwarb, dafür zu sprechen, daß er Caldara besonders geschätzt habe. Doch ist auch hier Vorsicht angebracht; denn der Anteil von Caldara-Messen in einem gleichzeitigen Prager Inventar (vgl. dazu unten) ist mindestens ebenso groß. Vielleicht war Caldara aufgrund seiner großen Produktivität auf dem Kopialienmarkt eben besonders gut vertreten.

Auch Zelenkas Bearbeitungen besagen wenig über seine persönliche Einstellung zur Musik Caldaras. Denn die Anpassung fremder Werke an die Dresdner Aufführungsbedingungen war der Normalfall. Dabei schützte auch ein großer Name nicht vor erheblichen Eingriffen. Die Bestimmung der Kirchenmusik als Gebrauchsmusik zeigt sich darin in doppelter Weise: Zum einen handelt es sich nicht um sakrosankte Werke, deren individuelles Wesen durch Kürzungen nennenswert berührt würde, zum anderen ist die Musik als Einkleidung des liturgischen Wortes offen gegenüber Bereicherungen.

Zelenkas Inventar verzeichnet etwa 85 Messen. Eine genaue Zahl läßt sich schwer angeben, weil manche Einträge überklebt, andere ausgestrichen sind. Hinzu kommt das Problem der Doppelverzeichnungen, die zuweilen sicher nachzuweisen sind, oft aber aufgrund der Unvollständigkeit der Angaben nur vermutet werden können. Die laufende Numerierung des Inventars reicht von 1 bis 68, doch weisen nicht alle Einträge eine Nummer auf (so die vier Palestrina Messen zwischen lfd. Nr. 6 und 7). Berücksichtigt man alle Eintragungen, unabhängig davon, ob sie gestrichen, überklebt oder mit dem Zusatz 'manca' (d.h. die Quelle fehlte schon zu Zelenkas Lebzeiten) versehen sind, so begegnen 25 Komponisten[32] und ein Anonymus (in der folgenden Aufstellung wurde die Orthographie der Namen normalisiert, Vornamen wurden ergänzt; die Zahl in Klammern nennt die Anzahl der im Inventar vertretenen Messen):

> Anonymus (1), Carlo Baliani (1), Orazio Benevoli (1), Antonio Bioni (2), Johann Michael Breunich (9, dabei wohl Doppelverzeichnungen), Antonio Caldara (10), Francesco Conti (2), Francesco Durante (1; die SLB besitzt heute jedoch zwei Messen Durantes aus Zelenkas Beständen), Johann Ernst Eberlin (1), Johann Friedrich Fasch (1), Johann Joseph Fux (3), Johann Gottlob Harrer (1), Gionelli (1; dieser Komponist nicht nachweisbar, weder Gonelli noch Jommelli scheinen in Frage zu kommen), Antonio Lotti (3), Francesco Mancini (2), Mathias Oettl (3), Palestrina (9), Franz Poppe (2), Anton Reichenauer (2), Johann Georg Reinhardt (2), Reutter d.Ä. und Reutter d. J. (zusammen 4), Domenico Sarri (3), Alessandro Scarlatti (1), Marcus Teller (5, dabei wohl Doppelverzeichnungen) und Jan Dismas Zelenka (18).

Die Italiener dominieren eindeutig; daneben aber ist der Wiener Kreis mit Fux, Reutter, Reinhardt, Oettl, Conti und Caldara gut repräsentiert. Antonio Caldara ist mit zehn Messen vertreten; dies ist die zweithöchste Zahl nach Zelenkas eigenen Werken. Es folgt eine Liste der Messen Caldaras mit Titel, Tonart, Besetzung (die Orthographie der Abkürzungen ist normalisiert, jedoch wurden Zelenkas zuweilen lückenhafte Angaben belassen), Angabe von Seitenzahl/laufender Nummer im Inventar und — falls die Quelle erhalten ist — Signatur der Sächsischen Landesbibliothek sowie dem vermutlichen Datum des Erwerbs der Quelle, das sich aus der Nachbarschaft der Inventareinträge zu datierbaren Messen Zelenkas ergibt:

Missa Providentiae (d) à 4 (SATB), 2 Vl, Va, Bc; Inv 5/10, Mus. 2170-D-7 (Credo von Zelenka komponiert); erworben um 1727.

Missa Divi Xaverii (C) à 4, Tr ex C et F, 2 Ob, 2 Vl, 2 Ve, Bc; Inv 6/
18, Mus. 2170-D-9 (Kyrie von Zelenka komponiert, fehlt jedoch in der
Quelle); um 1727.

Missa S. Caroli Borromei à 4, 2 Tr, Timp, 2 Vl, Va, Bc; Inv 6/19 (Eintragung
überklebt, Quelle nicht vorhanden); um 1727.

Missa Intende in adjutorium meum (D) à 4, Tr, 2 Vl, 2 Ve, Bc; Inv 6/
20, Mus. 2170-D-10 (Kyrie von Zelenka komponiert, fehlt jedoch in der
Quelle); um 1727.

Beginn des Chores von Zelenka komponiert

Missa brevis Vix orimur, morimur (D) à 4, 2 Ve *ad lib.*; Inv 7/23, Mus.
2170-D-13; um 1727/28.

Missa Mundata est lepra ejus (Matth. 8) (a) à 4, 2 Vl, Va, Bc; Inv 7/
28 (Zusatz: 'Caldara si verum est'), Mus. 2170-D-12; um 1729.

Missa Quia [?] mihi et tibi (A) à 4, 2 Vl, Va, Bc; Inv 9/37, Mus. 2170-
D-14; um 1730.

Missa Matris Dolorosae (h) à 4, 2 Vl, Va, Bç; Inv 8/34, Mus. 2170-D-4 (nicht identisch mit der *Missa dolorosa* in *DTO* XIII/1); um 1729 (Abb. 1).

Missa dicta Reformata (g) à 4 (keine weiteren Angaben), Inv 11/56, Mus. 2170-D-8; zwischen 1736 und 1739.

Missa (F) à 4 (keine weiteren Angaben), Inv 11/57, Mus. 2170-D-11; zwischen 1736 und 1739.

Des weiteren verzeichnet das Inventar zwei Vesperpsalmen Caldaras:

Laudate pueri (c) à 4, Canto praecinente, 2 Vl; Inv 35/6, Mus. 2170-E-3 (Partitur), Mus. 2170-E-10 (Stimmen).

Beatus vir (G) à 6: S, A concertati, SATB ripieni, Ob *ad lib*, 2 Vl; Inv 36/16, Mus. 2170-E-2, Mus. 2170-E-2a.

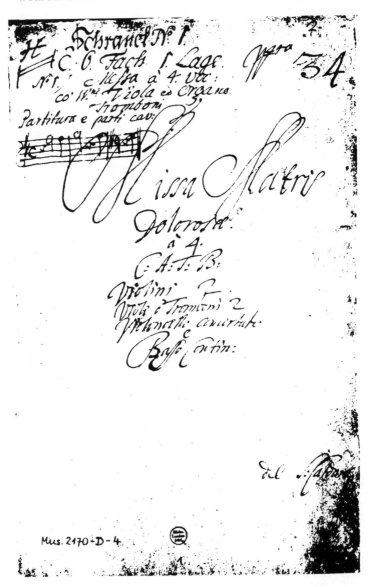

Abbildung 1. Caldara *Missa Matris Dolorosae*: Titelblatt. (Partitur von der Hand eines Dresdner Kopisten; D-ddr-Dlb: Mus. 2170-D-4).

Von Zelenkas Hand stammen die Tonartangabe 'h' (links oben) sowie der Titel, die Besetzungsangaben und der Name des Autors: 'Missa Matris / Dolorosae / à 4. / C: A: T: B: / Violini 2 / Viole ò Tromboni 2 / Violoncello concertato / e / Basso Contin: / del S: Caldara'. Rechts oben steht von der Hand Zelenkas 'N.ro 34' als Verweis auf das Inventar. Die Eintragungen links oben wie auch das Incipit stammen von einem späteren Schreiber; sie verweisen auf den Aufbewahrungsort der Quelle im Notenarchiv der Hofkirche.

Der Musikabteilung der Sächsischen Landesbibliothek Dresden ist für die Reproduktionserlaubnis zu danken

Ein Offertorium 'Perfice' (gressus meos?) in e-Moll für vierstimmigen Chor, 2 Vl, Va und Bc ist nicht erhalten. Dagegen besitzt die Sächsische Landesbibliothek über die Eintragungen des Inventars hinaus noch Caldaras *Miserere* in g-Moll, das Zelenka ebenfalls stark bearbeitet hat (Mus. 2170-E-4; dasselbe unbearbeitet: Mus. 2170-E-5, 1). Zelenkas Bearbeitung beschränkt sich hier auf die Ergänzung von Instrumenten (2 Ob, 2 Vl, Va); auf Änderungen in den Singstimmen und auf Kürzungen hat er verzichtet.

Wenn man die erschlossenen Daten des Erwerbs der Caldara-Messen betrachtet, so fällt auf, daß sie recht spät liegen. 1727 war Zelenka bereits 48 Jahre alt; seit mehreren Jahren komponierte er selbst größere Messen. Die Bekanntschaft mit Caldaras Musik konnte also kaum mehr auf so fruchtbaren Boden fallen wie ein Jahrzehnt zuvor der Unterricht bei Fux.

$$* \quad * \quad * \quad * \quad *$$

Auf den ersten Blick vermittelt Zelenkas Verzeichnis den Eindruck einer überwältigenden Fülle, doch sollte man die Einzigartigkeit des Dresdner Repertoires vorerst nicht zu sehr betonen. Denn es ist viel zu wenig bekannt, über welchen Notenvorrat andere katholische Hauptkirchen, die finanziell gut dotiert waren, in dieser Zeit verfügten. Die Rede ist hier nicht von Wien, dessen Repertoire gut erschlossen ist.[33] Hingewiesen sei vielmehr auf ein Prager Inventar aus den Jahren 1727 und 1728, dessen Repertoire mindestens ebenso reichhaltig ist wie das Dresdner. Es verzeichnet nur die innerhalb eines einzigen Jahres beschafften oder angefertigten Kopien, während Zelenkas Inventar das Ergebnis fast zwanzigjähriger Sammeltätigkeit dokumentiert.

Die 'Specification derer Musicalien welche von 2. Julj 1727. bis ultim: Junj 1728, ein gantzes Jahr zum nöthigen Brauch Bey Maria Lauretta seyndt Verphastet [?, zu lesen: 'Verschaffet'?] und abgeschrieben worden'[34] ist auch deshalb interessant, weil man an der Prager Loretokirche in einer ähnlichen Situation wie in Dresden war. Denn anders als in Wien, wo man auf eine kontinuierlich gewachsene Sammlung zurückgreifen konnte und darüberhinaus über etliche komponierende Kapellbedienstete verfügte, ging es in Dresden und Prag darum, ein Repertoire an katholischer Kirchenmusik, vorwiegend im neuesten Geschmack, überhaupt erst aufzubauen. In Prag hatte ein Streit zwischen den Kapuzinern, die die Loretokirche betreuten, und den dortigen Musikern, denen die Vernachlässigung ihrer Aufgaben vorgeworfen wurde, im Jahre 1726 zur Entlassung sämtlicher Musiker geführt. Ein neues Ensemble wurde zusammengestellt und ließ sich erstmals am Karsamstag 1727 unter Leitung des *Regens chori* Konstantin Antonius Taubner hören, der auch die 'Specification' anfertigte.[35]

Beschränken wir uns bei der Betrachtung auch hier auf die Messen, deren insgesamt 70 verzeichnet sind. Sie stammen von den folgenden Autoren:

Anonymi (17; bei zwei Messen Angabe 'Auth: Italo'), Arsler (1), S. Brixi
(1), Brustmann (1), Caldara (12), Contini (1), Cozzi (1), Einwaldt (3), Fago
(1), Fasch (1), Nic. Gratia (?, 1), Haas (1), Lotti (1), Jacobi (6), Mancini
(2), Oettl (3), Poppe (1), Porpora (1), Porsile (1), Rathgeber (2), Reichenauer
(4), Reinhardt (1), Ristori (2) und Roffeld (5).

Messen von italienischen Komponisten — mit Caldara an der Spitze
— überwiegen auch hier. Mit Caldara, Porsile, Oettl und Reinhardt sind
in Wien tätige Komponisten vertreten, Ristori stellt die Verbindung zu
Dresden her. Daneben begegnen einheimische Komponisten aus Böhmen
wie Simon Brixi, Karl Joseph Einwaldt oder Anton Reichenauer, die
auch in Zelenkas Inventar vertreten sind: Brixi mit den fünf Psalmen
der Sonntagsvesper und dem Magnificat, Einwaldt mit vier *Ave Maria*
und Reichenauer mit zwei Messen und einem *Salve Regina*. Simon Brixi
und Reichenauer wirkten als Organisten in Prag, Einwaldt war
Domorganist in Olmütz.

Die Zusammensetzung des Prager Repertoires stimmt in den
Grundzügen mit derjenigen von Zelenkas Dresdner Sammlung überein.
Dies ist kaum erstaunlich: Zum einen konnte man sich der allbeherr-
schenden italienischen Musik kaum entziehen, zum anderen bildeten die
Städte Wien, Prag und Dresden[36] die Eckpunkte eines damals noch
geschlossenen Kulturraumes. Zudem erhielt der in Dresden wirkende
Böhme Zelenka ja in Prag seine Schulbildung und erwarb sich dort in
der Kapelle des Barons von Hartig seine ersten musikalischen Sporen.
Schließlich dürfte auch der Umstand eine Rolle gespielt haben, daß der
Markt für zeitgenössische katholische Kirchenmusik, die den Anforderungen auch größerer Ensembles genügte, recht begrenzt war. So ist,
nimmt man alles in allem, in den Verzeichnissen Zelenkas und Taubners
fast jeder katholische Kirchenkomponist vertreten, der damals Rang und
Namen hatte.

*   *   *   *   *

Das häufige Auftreten eines Komponisten im Repertoire einer Kirche
muß keineswegs in erster Linie auf persönlichen Vorlieben des leitenden
Musikers beruhen; im Gegenteil dürfte die Brauchbarkeit der Musik
wichtiger gewesen sein als hoher künstlerischer Anspruch. Das bedeutet
nicht, daß man etwa Caldara als Vielschreiber abtun dürfte, dessen Werke
sich in der Erfüllung ihres Zweckes erschöpfen, mithin künstlerisch
belanglos wären. Im Gegenteil käme es darauf an, 'Brauchbarkeit' als
positive Kategorie der Kirchenkomposition des Spätbarock zu
formulieren: als die besondere Eigenschaft solcher Werke, die unter
vorgegebenen Bedingungen (welche gemäß den Anforderungen von
Liturgie und Aufführungspraxis zu bestimmen wären) aufgrund ihrer
Bindung an allgemein akzeptierte Kompositionsprinzipien (die auf einem
Konsens beruhen, der dem historischen Wandel unterworfen ist) die in
sie gesetzten Erwartungen angemessen erfüllen.

Diese Qualität ermöglicht einem Werk weite Verbreitung. So betrachtet,
erweist sich Caldara als ein Kirchenkomponist ersten Ranges. Dagegen

waren etwa Zelenkas letzte Messen, die 'Missae ultimae',[37] oder gar Bachs *h-Moll-Messe* unter dem Aspekt der 'Brauchbarkeit' sicher weniger lebensfähig, sieht man einmal von den äußeren Umständen ab, die ihre Verbreitung behinderten. Originalität, Einmaligkeit, Größe in Anspruch und Ausführung sind Kriterien, die das Interesse der Nachwelt beanspruchen dürfen, weit weniger aber das Wohlwollen der Zeitgenossen in der ersten Hälfte des 18. Jahrhunderts.

Wenn man das Typische wie auch das Besondere einzelner Werke der katholischen Kirchenmusik um 1720-30 erkennen will, dann muß man zunächst versuchen, das Umfeld zu rekonstruieren, in das sich die betreffenden Werke eingliedern oder von dem sie sich abheben. Nach Ausweis der Kirchenmusikpflege in Wien, Prag und Dresden spielten die Werke Antonio Caldaras in diesem Umfeld eine herausragende Rolle. Bereits aus diesem Grund kommt ihnen für die 'Geschichte der Kirchenmusik' eine besondere Bedeutung zu. Doch nicht nur für Historiker sind Caldaras Kirchenwerke von Interesse. So bekennt der renommierte Musikschriftsteller Franz Sales Kandler (1792-1831) einmal überschwenglich: 'Was Raphael als Mahler, Klopstock als Dichter, das ist mir Caldara als Harmoniker und Tonsetzer.'[38]

Anmerkungen

[1] Vgl. zum Folgenden die ausführliche Darstellung der politischen Zusammenhänge bei Wolfgang Horn 'Die Dresdner Hofkirchenmusik 1720-1745. Studien zu ihren Voraussetzungen und ihrem Repertoire' (D.Phil., diss. Universität Tübingen, 1986).
An Literatur sei hier nur genannt: Rudolf Kötzschke, Hellmut Kretzschmar *Sächsische Geschichte. Werden und Wandlungen eines Deutschen Stammes und seiner Heimat im Rahmen der Deutschen Geschichte* 2.Band: Hellmut Kretzschmar *Geschichte der Neuzeit seit der Mitte des 16. Jahrhunderts* (Dresden, 1935; Neudruck in einem Band: Frankfurt am Main, 1965) mit einem Verzeichnis der älteren Literatur; ferner die beiden Spezialstudien: Johannes Ziekursch 'August der Starke und die katholische Kirche in den Jahren 1697-1720' *Zeitschrift für Kirchengeschichte* XXIV (1903) S. 86-135 und 232-280, sowie Paul Franz Saft *Der Neuaufbau der katholischen Kirche in Sachsen im 18. Jahrhundert* (Leipzig, 1961) (*Studien zur katholischen Bistums- und Klostergeschichte* 2).

² Zu Christiane Eberhardine die beiden Biographien von Franz Blanckmeister 'Christiane Eberhardine, die letzte evangelische Kurfürstin von Sachsen, und die konfessionellen Kämpfe ihrer Tage' *Beiträge zur sächsischen Kirchengeschichte* VI (1891) S. 1–84, und Paul Haake *Christiane Eberhardine und August der Starke. Eine Ehetragödie* (Dresden, 1930).

³ Eine ausführliche Beschreibung der Räumlichkeiten bei Wilhelm Schäfer *Die Katholische Hofkirche zu Dresden … Nebst einer Einleitung: Die Geschichte der ersten katholischen Hofkapelle am Taschenberge* (Dresden, 1851) S. 1–15. Eine Abbildung des Theaters vor dem Umbau bei Moritz Fürstenau *Zur Geschichte der Musik und des Theaters am Hofe zu Dresden*, (Dresden, 1861–62/R Leipzig, 1971, 2. Auflage 1979), Erster Theil, nach S. 328 (das Datum 1664 bezieht sich auf die Grundsteinlegung); eine Abbildung des Theaters nach der Umwandlung in die katholische Hofkapelle bei Saft *op.cit.*, gegenüber S. 49. In der eigentlichen Schloßkapelle, in der Schütz und Bernhard musiziert hatten, wurde weiterhin der evangelische Hofgottesdienst abgehalten, bis sie 1737 einem Umbau zum Opfer fiel; vgl. Franz Blanckmeister *Der Prophet von Kursachsen. Valentin Ernst Löscher und seine Zeit* (Dresden, 1920) S. 130ff. Die berühmte katholische Hofkirche des Architekten Chiaveri wurde erst 1751 eingeweiht.

⁴ Vgl. die 'Reglements Du Roi pour l'Eglise et Chapelle Royale, ouverte aux Catholiques' mit speziellen Instruktionen für den 'Directeur de l'Eglise Royale', für die 'Chapellains', für die 'Clercs' (Kapellknaben) usw., abgedruckt bei Augustin Theiner *Geschichte der Zurückkehr der regierenden Häuser von Braunschweig und Sachsen in den Schoß der Katholischen Kirche im achtzehnten Jahrhundert, und der Wiederherstellung der Katholischen Religion in diesen Staaten* (Einsiedeln, 1843) Urkundenbuch, Aktenstück LXX, S. 75–87.

⁵ Zum Thema h-Moll-Messe und Dresden zuletzt Hans-Joachim Schulze *Johann Sebastian Bach: Missa h-Moll, BWV 232¹* Kommentar zum Faksimile des Originalstimmensatzes der Sächsischen Landesbibliothek Dresden (Leipzig, 1983).

⁶ Johann Adam Hiller *Lebensbeschreibungen berühmter Musikgelehrten und Tonkünstler, neuerer Zeit* (Leipzig, 1784/R1975) 'Heinichen-Biographie' S. 136. Der Name 'August II' ist ungenau: als sächsischer Kurfürst hieß der Sohn Augusts des Starken 'Friedrich August II.', als polnischer König dagegen 'August III'.

⁷ Heinichen stammte aus Krössuln nahe Teuchern, das zum Sekundogeniturfürstentum Sachsen-Weißenfels gehörte. Vgl. dazu die verläßlichste der Heinichen-Biographien von Gustav Adolph Seibel 'Das Leben des Königlich Polnischen und Kurfürstlich Sächsischen Hofkapellmeisters Johann David Heinichen nebst chronologischem Verzeichnis seiner Opern … und thematischem Katalog seiner Werke' (D.Phil., diss. 1912; gedruckt Leipzig, 1913) S. 3.

⁸ Vgl. die Anstellungsurkunde bei Seibel *op.cit.*, S. 19: 'Frédéric Auguste, Prince Royal de Pologne et Electoral de Saxe. Ayant le consentement de Sa Majesté le Roy mon Père, j'ay engagé à son [d.h. des Vaters!] service Jean David Heünichen [sic] pour maître de chapelle; c'est à dire pour composer en musique tout ce qui sera nécessaire, conformément aux obligations d'un maître de chapelle … et les appointements commenceront du mois d'Août 1716.' usw. Die Angaben bei Fürstenau *op.cit.*, Zweiter Theil, S. 102, sind nicht korrekt.

⁹ Vgl. zu den Vorgängen um die Gründung der italienischen Oper Fürstenau *op.cit.*, II, S. 99ff.

¹⁰ Von Schmidt gibt es u.a. einige wenige Kurzmessen: Kyrie und Gloria im alten Stil, die im lutherischen Gottesdienst verwendet werden konnten, sowie etliche deutsche Kirchenkantaten und lateinische Psalmen. Heinichens etwa 15 deutsche Kirchenkantaten, von denen keine im Autograph überliefert ist, dürften lange vor seiner Dresdner Zeit entstanden sein (die Quellen liegen in Berlin und Dresden; die Dresdner Bestände stammen aus der Fürstenschule Grimma, mit dem Dresdner Gottesdienst haben sie nichts zu tun).

¹¹ 'Historia Missionis Societatis Jesu Dresdae in Saxonia ab Anno Salutis 1708ᵛᵒ,' hs., S. 88. Quelle im Besitz des Bischöflichen Ordinariats des Bistums Dresden-Meissen. Zu Charakter und Inhalt dieser Quelle vgl. Saft *op.cit.*, S. 32. Die Tatsache,

daß die 'Phonasci Itali' in den Jahresberichten 1717-1719, also von der Ankunft
bis zur Abreise Lottis, mehrfach rühmend erwähnt werden, spricht dafür, daß *vor*
1717 höfisch-prunkvolle, vokal-instrumentale Kirchenmusik im italienischen Stil
wenn nicht ganz unbekannt, so doch keinesfalls die Regel war (die Kapellknaben
werden in erster Linie einfache Figuralmusik aufgeführt haben). Lotti scheint die
Noten nach Venedig mitgenommen zu haben. Ortrun Landmann hat die
Provenienzen der Dresdner Lotti-Quellen zusammengestellt; danach läßt sich keine
Quelle mit der genannten Aufführung in Verbindung bringen.

[12] Mit der hier gewählten Beschränkung auf die Kapellmeister ist die Vielfalt des
Musiklebens am Dresdner Hof nur unzulänglich beschrieben. Des weiteren wären
Namen wie Volumier (Woulmyer), Veracini, Petzold, später auch G. A. Ristori
und Pisendel zu nennen, die alle auch komponierten. Wie facettenreich das Bild
in jener Zeit war, dokumentieren die Arbeiten von Ortrun Landmann 'Zur
Standortbestimmung Dresdens unter den Musikzentren der ersten Hälfte des 18.
Jahrhunderts' *Studien zur Aufführungspraxis und Interpretation von Instrumentalmusik des 18. Jahrhunderts* (im folgenden abgekürzt: *StAI*) 8 (1979) S. 47-55;
dies., 'Dresden, Johann Georg Pisendel und der "deutsche Geschmack" ' *StAI* 13
(1981) S. 20-34; dies., 'Französische Elemente in der Musikpraxis des 18. Jahrhunderts
am Dresdener Hof' *StAI* 16 (1982) S. 48-56; dies., 'Einige Überlegungen zu den
Konzerten "nebenamtlich" komponierender Dresdener Hofmusiker in der Zeit von
etwa 1715 bis 1763' *StAI* 20 (1983) S. 57-73; sowie dies., 'Marginalien zur Dresdener
Höfischen Kammermusik zwischen 1720 und 1763' *StAI* 23 (1984) S. 11-18.

[13] Vgl. etwa Fürstenau *op.cit.*, II, S. 83: 'Kundige werden Zelenka dem großen
Harmoniker Antonio Lotti anreihen, dessen Einfluß auf unsern Meister, der ihn
1716 in Venedig und später in Dresden als Lehrer kennen und schätzen lernte,
nicht zu verkennen ist.' Ein Lehrer-Schüler-Verhältnis ist heute nicht zu belegen.

[14] Die eindrucksvollste Beschreibung bei Jean Louis Sponsel *Der Zwinger, die Hof-
feste und die Schloßbaupläne zu Dresden* (Dresden, 1924); vgl. auch Irmgard Becker-
Glauch *Die Bedeutung der Musik für die Dresdener Hoffeste bis in die Zeit Augusts
des Starken* (Kassel und Basel, 1951).

[15] Es handelt sich um die Oper *Flavio Crispo*; Seibel a.a.0., S. 38, bemerkt dazu:
'Die Partitur bricht im 3. Akt, in der 16. Szene, S. 131, plötzlich mitten im Rezitativ
ab und ist nicht zu Ende geschrieben; es sind noch ungefähr 30 leere Seiten in
dem Bande. Vielleicht hängt dies mit dem Streite zusammen?'

[16] Dies war Heinichen bekanntlich seit August 1716; vgl. Anm. 8.

[17] Hiller *op.cit.*, 'Heinichen-Biographie' S. 138f.; drastischer noch in der 'Quantz-
Biographie' S. 216.

[18] Vgl. Fürstenau *op.cit.*, II, S. 105f. und 134ff. (mit weiteren Angaben).

[19] Autograph in D-ddr-Dlb: Mus. 2398-D-5a; autograph datiert: 'Festo pentecost. 1721';
Wiederaufführung an Pfingsten 1724. Über Heinichens Messen vgl. Eberhard
Schmitz 'Die Messen Johann David Heinichens' (D.Phil., diss. Universität
Hamburg, 1967), mit gutem Katalog.

[20] Daß man die Geburtsstunde der autochthonen Dresdner Kirchenmusik mit
Heinichens erster Messe ansetzen darf, belegt eine Eintragung im (heute verlorenen)
handschriftlichen 'Diarium' der Dresdner Jesuiten, das Saft noch vor dem Zweiten
Weltkrieg exzerpiert hat: 'Zum Pfingstfest 1721 wird im Tagebuch *das erstemal*
(Hervorhebung W.H.) die Aufführung einer Messe erwähnt, was seitdem an allen
hohen Festtagen Brauch wurde' (Saft *op.cit.*, S. 42; zum 'Diarium' *ibid.*, S. 9 und
32). Heinichens Orchestermesse im modernen Stil muß den Zeitgenossen als etwas
Neues, Besonderes erschienen sein.

[21] Aufgrund der Kriegsverluste erhält die Arbeit von Curt Rudolf Mengelberg
'Giovanni Alberto Ristori. Ein Beitrag zur Geschichte italienischer Kunstherrschaft
in Deutschland im 18. Jahrhundert' (D. Phil., diss., Universität Leipzig, 1915)
trotz all ihrer Mängel zusätzliches Gewicht. Ein Mangel sei hier erwähnt: Mengelberg
hebt unter Ristoris drei Totenmessen eine hervor, 'die an musikalischem Wert
weit hervorragt' (S. 101 und ff.). Leider handelt es sich gerade hierbei keineswegs

um eine Komposition Ristoris, sondern um das *D-Dur-Requiem* Zelenkas für August den Starken (1733; Autograph: Mus. 2358-D-81), das Ristori, wohl für eine Aufführung unter seiner Leitung, bearbeitet hat. (Ristoris Partitur ist verschollen; Reste möglicherweise erhalten unter der Zelenka-Signatur Mus. 2358-D-41, Offertorium 'Domine Jesu Christe' in Hs. Ristoris). Die Reduktion der großen Bläserbesetzung von Zelenkas Original deutet auf eine Aufführung außerhalb Dresdens (in Polen?).

²² Das Inventar wird an anderer Stelle faksimiliert und ausgewertet: Wolfgang Horn, Thomas Kohlhase *Zelenka-Dokumentation. Quellen und Materialien zu Jan Dismas Zelenkas Leben und Werk* (masch. Ms. Tübingen, 1983; Druck i.V.). Eine Beschreibung und Bewertung des Inventars findet sich in der 'Einleitung' des Werkverzeichnisses: *Jan Dismas Zelenka. Thematisch-systematisches Verzeichnis der musikalischen Werke. Kleine Ausgabe* Zusammengestellt von Wolfgang Reich (Dresden, 1985) (*Studien und Materialien zur Musikgeschichte Dresdens* 6). Jaroslav Bužga hat Zelenkas Inventar beschrieben in seinem Aufsatz: 'Zelenkas Musikinventar aus der katholischen Schloßkapelle in Dresden' (*Fontes Artis Musicae* 31 (1984) S. 198–206). Bužgas Komponistenregister enthält zahlreiche Ungenauigkeiten und Irrtümer. Zelenkas Inventar ist oft schwer zu lesen, von vielen Komponisten wird nur der Nachname genannt. Daher ist es methodisch unerläßlich, Zelenkas Hinweise an den Quellen aus seiner Sammlung zu überprüfen, die in der Sächsischen Landesbibliothek Dresden in großer Zahl erhalten sind (vgl. dazu die in Anm. 1 genannte Arbeit des Vf.). Willkommen sind Bužgas Hinweise auf das Repertoire der Prager Kreuzherren. Dabei ist jedoch zu beachten, daß es sich nicht um Werk-Konkordanzen handelt.

²³ Vgl. Fürstenau *op.cit.*, II, S. 108.

²⁴ Die Staatsbibliothek Preußischer Kulturbesitz Berlin, Musikabteilung (D-brd-B), besitzt eine von Heinichen selbst revidierte Quelle aus der Sammlung Georg Poelchaus mit Caldaras 'Missa 2ª di Toson B.V. Mariae' in C-Dur (Signatur: Mus. ms. 2730).

²⁵ Eine ausführliche Darstellung des Inhalts der *Libri quatuor* enthält die in Anm. 22 genannte Materialsammlung.

²⁶ Den Wien-Aufenthalt erwähnt Zelenka auch in seinem Gesuch an König August III. vom November 1733, vgl. Hubert Unverricht 'Zelenka, Johann Dismas' *Die Musik in Geschichte und Gegenwart* (Kassel, 1968) 14, 1192–1198.

²⁷ Vgl. dazu die vorzügliche Einleitung zur Ausgabe der Oper: Egon Wellesz (Hg.) Johann Josef Fux *Costanza e Fortezza* in *Denkmäler der Tonkunst in Österreich* 34–35 (1910).

²⁸ Das bedeutet nicht, daß er vor 1726 nur drei Messen komponiert hätte, sondern lediglich, daß er die drei verzeichneten Messen für brauchbar hielt. Sein Erstling, die bereits erwähnte, vor 1712 entstandene *Missa Sanctae Caeciliae*, wurde erst nach dem Abschluß zahlreicher Revisionsdurchgänge um 1727 in das Inventar eingetragen.

²⁹ Die Eintragung ist gestrichen; ein solches Werk war wohl in Dresden kaum aufführbar, verlangte es doch neben entsprechend großzügigen Räumlichkeiten zumindest 16 Sänger, wobei fraglich ist, ob eine derart kleine Besetzung dem Werk angemessen wäre.

³⁰ Außer bei Heinichen ist mir der Terminus nur hier begegnet; sonst scheint er zur Bezeichnung von Messen ungebräuchlich. Bei Heinichen bezeichnet er das Erstlingswerk. Könnte Entsprechendes auch für die Fux-Messe gelten? Es wäre zu prüfen, ob der Titel original ist.

³¹ Diese Messe ist im Inventar als fehlend bezeichnet ('manca'). Heute ist die Quelle verschollen, doch kannte sie Köchel offenbar noch. Er schreibt: 'd) In der kön. Bibl. der Musik [also nicht unter den Beständen der Hofkirche, die die meisten Musikalien Zelenkas in Verwahrung hatte; W.H.] in Dresden (A. 112). Abschrift seines Schülers Joh. Dism. Zelenka, welcher am Schlusse schreibt: "Laus Deo et omnibus Sanctis ejus Dresdae 18. Oct. 1719" ' (Ludwig Ritter von Köchel *Johann*

Josef Fux, Hofcompositor und Hofkapellmeister der Kaiser Leopold I., Josef I. und Karl VI. von 1698 bis 1740 (Wien, 1872) Beilage X: Thematisches Verzeichnis, S. 12). Das Datum der Abschrift, kurz nach dem Ende der Einzugsfeiern, könnte darauf hindeuten, daß die Kopiervorlage gleichsam 'im Gefolge' Maria Josephas von Wien nach Dresden kam.

[32] Zahlreiche Komponisten sind im Inventar nur mit kleineren Kirchenwerken vertreten. Berücksichtigt man alle, so ergibt sich, neben den Anonymi, eine Zahl von 65 (inklusive Zelenka selbst).

[33] Insbesondere durch die Arbeit von Friedrich W. Riedel *Kirchenmusik am Hofe Karls VI. (1711–1740)* (München-Salzburg, 1977).

[34] Veröffentlicht in: *Catalogus Artis Musicae in Bohemia et Moravia Cultae. Artis Musicae Antiquioris Catalogorum Series* I./1: 'Domus Lauretana Pragensis. Catalogus Collectionis Operum Artis Musicae. Pars prima: Catalogus' Composuit Oldřich Pulkert (Prag, 1973) S. 41–60. Dazu: Pulkert 'Vorwort' (deutsche Fassung: S. 16–20); J. Křivka 'Loretokirche der Jungfrau Maria in Prag' (S. 21–25) und T. Volek 'Das Prager Loreto-Kloster als Musikinstitut' (S. 25–29). Die Quellen sind heute größtenteils verloren.

[35] Vgl. dazu die Ausführungen von Křivka und Volek *op.cit.*, Während des Prager Aufenthalts 1723 suchte auch die kaiserliche Familie die Loretokirche auf (Volek *ibid.*, S. 25).

[36] Beiläufig sei hier auf die wohl wertvollste Caldara-Quelle der Sächsischen Landesbibliothek Dresden hingewiesen: das Autograph Mus. 2170-D-1 mit neun *Salmi à otto voci* (doppelchörig), einem *Te Deum* und den *Litaniae Lauretanae*, datiert 'Milano 1711', sowie einer doppelchörigen *Messe in g-Moll*, nach dem *Credo* datiert 'Fine adi 18. Aprile 1712 à Vinn'. In der Dissertation von Elaine Raftery Walter 'The Masses of Antonio Caldara (1670–1736)' (Ph.D., diss. Catholic University of America, Washington, 1973) wird diese Quelle mit Zelenka in Verbindung gebracht und zum Anlaß genommen, über persönliche Beziehungen Caldaras und Zelenkas zu spekulieren (S. 71, Anm. 1). Doch diese Quelle hat mit Zelenka nichts zu tun: nicht nur fehlen Spuren seiner Handschrift gänzlich, sondern auch andere Indizien deuten auf einen wesentlich späteren Erwerb durch die Dresdner Bibliothek. Auf dem Vorsatzblatt der Quelle hat der als Hasse-Biograph auch heute noch bekannte Franz Sales Kandler (1792–1831) eine originelle Würdigung Caldaras eingetragen.

[37] Zelenkas drei erhaltene, von ihm selbst so genannte 'Missae ultimae' wurden offenbar zu ihrer Zeit nie aufgeführt; der Dresdner Hofkirchenkatalog (ca. 1760) verzeichnet für die um 1740 entstandenen Werke jedenfalls keine Stimmenmaterialien. Die Messen werden veröffentlicht in der Denkmälerreihe *Das Erbe deutscher Musik* 93 (1984), 100 und 101.

[38] In der Quelle D-ddr-Dlb: Mus. 2170-D-1.

Caldara, Borosini and the
One Hundred Cantici,
or some Viennese canons abroad

Glennys Ward

Zusammenfassung

Caldara, Borosini und die
One Hundred Cantici:
oder einige Wiener Kanons
im Ausland

Die *One Hundred Cantici in Italian ... collected by Sig^r Borosini ...*, herausgegeben von John Simpson in London in der Mitte des 18. Jahrhunderts, bringen einige Probleme mit sich. Die Identität des 'Sig^r Borosini' ist niemals schlüssig bewiesen worden, obwohl man ihn im allgemeinen mit dem Tenor Francesco Borosini (*c*1690–1754) gleichsetzt; man nimmt an, daß die undatierte Veröffentlichung 1746 oder1747 erschienen sei; kein Versuch wurde bislang unternommen, den Verfasser der Kanons zu identifizieren. Die Untersuchung des Verfassers kommt zu dem Ergebnis, daß Francesco Borosini in der Tat derjenige war, der sie zusammenstellte, und daß der Band im Februar 1747 veröffentlicht wurde. Ferner wurden zwei Nachdrucke hergestellt, der erste von A. Simpson, der zweite von Randall und Abell. Keiner von ihnen ist in der RISM *Recueils Imprimés XVIIIe Siècle* verzeichnet.

Äußerst wichtig ist die Identifizierung von fast neunzig Kanons als Werke Antonio Caldaras. Sie sind ein kleiner Teil jener etwa 700 Kanons, die er in Wien 1729 und 1730 komponierte. Es ist wahrscheinlich, daß Borosini an den Vorführungen am Kaiserhof teilnahm und wohl eine Anzahl für den Eigengebrauch vervielfältigte. Als er später in England war, schrieb er die *One Hundred Cantici* aus seinen eigenen Unterlagen.

Während der verbleibenden Jahre des 18. Jahrhunderts erschien eine kleinere Anzahl von Caldaras Kanons in verschiedenen Sammlungen in England veröffentlichter *Catches* und *Rounds*. Am Ende des Jahrhunderts wurde eine verbesserte Ausgabe der *One Hundred Cantici* in London durch Ann Bland herausgegeben. Alle diese Bände sind detaillierter im Aufsatz beschrieben, der auch die im Laufe der Überlieferung von Caldaras Kanons entstandenen Änderungen untersucht.

Caldara, Borosini and the *One Hundred Cantici,* or some Viennese canons abroad

Glennys Ward

Towards the end of the 1740s a volume entitled *One Hundred Cantici in Italian after the manner of English Canons and Catches* was published in London. According to the title-page, the *cantici* had been 'Collected by Sig.ʳ Borosini' who is assumed to have been the tenor, Francesco Borosini (c1690–1754).[1] This postulated identification seems to have led to the volume being assigned the publication dates of 'c1746' and 'c1747',[2] presumably on the basis that a singer named 'Borosini' appears among the performers listed for London's 1746–47 opera season. No attempt has been made either to substantiate Francesco Borosini as the collector, or even to identify the composer(s) of some or all of the *cantici* or vocal canons.[3]

This essay examines these unexplored areas and uses recent research to identify Antonio Caldara as the composer of the majority of the *cantici,* to provide evidence that confirms Francesco Borosini as the 'Sig.ʳ Borosini' of the title-page, to establish a precise date of publication, and to trace the subsequent history of the volume itself and some of its individual items. From this last it shall be seen that the *One Hundred Cantici* has figured quite prominently in the history of the publication of collections of canons and catches in England in the second half of the eighteenth century.

The composer of the vocal canons

No composer is mentioned in (presumably) the earliest entry for this volume in either a printed catalogue or bibliography — W. Barclay Squire's *Catalogue of Printed Music published between 1487 and 1800 now in the British Museum* (London, 1912). The entry in *The British Union-Catalogue of Early Music printed before 1801* (London, 1957) notes that 'A canon by A. Caldara is printed on the title-page' — no doubt an attribution based more on the recognition of the canon in question (*Questi son canoni*, incorporated into the ornate frontispiece — *not* the title-page — of the *One Hundred Cantici*, see Plate 1) in a twentieth-century publication of canons,[4] than on any systematic study of primary source materials. Neither does this identification appear to have prompted further study of the volume's contents. The same attribution is repeated but less specifically ('A. Caldara, Anon') in *Recueils Imprimés XVIIIᵉ Siècle*.

The only clear association of Caldara with a substantial portion of the *One Hundred Cantici* is the annotation 'wahrscheinlich alle von Caldara' that Eusebius Mandycewski (1857–1929), archivist of the Gesellschaft der Musikfreunde in Wien, made on the title-page of that institution's copy. No doubt Mandycewski knew many of the canons as Caldara's from his preparation of some of the composer's secular music for a volume in the series *Denkmäler der Tonkunst in Österreich*.[5] Only Mandycewski hints that the *One Hundred Cantici* may comprise Caldara's canons alone;[6] those entries in catalogues and bibliographies which mention Caldara by name imply that he was but one of several composers included in the volume. Certainly, no entry gives any indication of how many canons are his. (Neither is there mentioned anywhere the fact that 101 canons are printed but that three duplications are included in the total.) Now, however, almost ninety of the canons can be identified as Caldara's (Table 1), and even today this volume still presents the largest selection of his work in this genre ever to have appeared in print.[7]

Table 1. *The canons of the* One Hundred Cantici *and their appearance in major manuscript sources.*

One Hundred Cantici			Major manuscript sources of Caldara's canons			
No.	Title	DM	'Kandler'	'Stadler'*	B-Bc	I-PAc
1	Mia Clori addio	171	21	55	8	70
2	Quanto mi siete	135	22		14/30	65
3	Desto licor		23	82	10	
4	Che bel contento	166	26	57	33/42	
5	Chi viver vuol contento		7	51	31	
6	Chi mai d'iniqua stella		8		39	
7	Perchè vezzosi rai		9	52	4	
8	Comincio solo cantare		2	49	1	
9	Sò che vanti		5	50	23	
10	Se lontan ben mio		6		22	
11	Se un vero amante		12		6	
12	Se viver non poss'io		13		55	
13	Grand tormento d'un alma fedele		14		34	
14	Ah' ch'il destino	91	31		12	
15	Non più Clori	141	18	75	18	
16	Questi son canoni**	200	1	47	41	80

Table 1. (contd)

One Hundred Cantici		Major manuscript sources of Caldara's canons				
No.	Title	DM	'Kandler'	'Stadler'	B-Bc	I-PAc
17	Voi sole oh luci belle		3		65	
18	Di libertà son privo		4	48	29	
19	La sorte tiranna		10	53	27	
20	Se tu d'amor m'accendi		11		24	
21	Per voi mi struggo	145	19	72	45	14
22	Non mi sprezzar licori		15		11	
23	Mi giuri che m'ami		16		13	
24	Al povero d'amore	139	17	77	15/73	
25	Caro bell'idol mio	163	20	54	28	
26	Son stanca di sperar		40		58	
27	Che vi giova		45		60	
28	E non vuoi lasciarmi		46		61	
29	Non sò se sdegno			58	69	
30	E'troppo gran tormento		32		37	
31	Scieglier fra mille		36		52	
32	Di tanti miei tormenti		35		47	
33	Cosi canta nell				20	
34	Filen mio bene	142	27	61	7	
35	Crudel deh non resistere		28		2	
36	Alzate il fiasco		29		25	
37	Deh con me non		30	63	35/43	
38	Mi lagnerò tacendo					
39	Amo te solo		43		3	
40	Quel volto sereno				19	
41	Vuoi tu venir				21	
42	Lo sò che tiranna	[repeat of No 19 with alternative text]				
43	Di libertà son privo	[repeat of No 18]				
44	Ama mi pur o cara	266			'32	
45	Chi a ritrovar aspira		24		54	
46	Se penso a voi	147	25	56	9	5
47	A che mi vale		33		38	
48	Dal tuo gentil sembiante				48	
49	Sento da poco in quà				16	
50	Perchè mai ben mio		42	64	36	
51	Scioglierò le mie catene		39		51	
52	Ah che nel dirti addio				56	
53	Amor pietà mercede		41		57	
54	Che legge spietata		49		62	
55	In che t'offende				70	
56	Nacqui all'affanni in seno			60	68	
57	Sò che pietà			59	71	

Table 1. (contd)

One Hundred Cantici		Major manuscript sources of Caldara's canons				
No.	Title	DM	'Kandler'	'Stadler'	B-Bc	I-PAc
58	Benchè felice mi credi	138				
59	O care selve					
60	Lo sfacciato più fortuna	108				
61	Voglio che cantiamo	20				
62	Già che tu tremi					
63	Nel mondo denari	117				
64	L'ignoranza si vede	101				
65	Non sò se sdegno	[repeat of No 29]				
66	Bevete troppo	92				
67	Accende amore	249		78		
68	Lasciatemi in riposo	252				
69	S'egli è pazzo	258				
70	Che destino dispietato	192				
71	Figliuola tieni a mente	255				
72	Pensa che sei mortale	196				
73	La grand' Austriaca	87				
74	Andiamo a spasso	93		74		
75	Tutti di fedeltà	125				
76	Studiate ancora	1				
77	Tempo perduto	190				
78	Perchè se mio tu sei				66	
79	Chi vive amante			62	67	
80	Cerco ogn'or	119				
81	Movete via pietà	137				81
82	Un musico son io	83				
83	Poco ne san del'opera	85				
84	Caro con questi accenti					
85	Se la pietade è questa					
86	Rivolgi ad altro oggetto					
87	Ah, si ben mio ti credo					
88	Perchè si bella					
89	Ah, tu non sai cor mio					
90	Da labri tuoi					
91	Se dite mal di me	260				
92	Non mi l'an farti	22				
93	Istrioni, montinbanchi	102				
94	Sentir tacer tu dei in corte	3				
95	Chi non opera	188				
96	Che nobil diletto	72				
97	Se non chiedessi					
98	Fà il tuo dovere	131				88

Table 1. (cont'd)

One Hundred Cantici		Major manuscript sources of Caldara's canons				
No.	Title	DM	'Kandler'	'Stadler'	B-Bc	I-PAc
99	Senza di te ben mio					
100	Tu sei pazzo	129				67
101	Pour quoi toujurs [sic]					

*See Note 9   **Duplicated in Frontispiece.

From Table 1 it can be seen that only thirteen canons cannot as yet be attributed to Caldara but it seems most likely that with one exception these, too, will prove to be his. Music incipits for these canons, attributions, and manuscript sources are given in Appendix I.

Of the remainder, forty-one canons appear either in autograph manuscripts or in copies containing autograph corrections and additions:

> (i) I-PAc: CF-1-6 (35791). 'Divertimenti Musicali. / Canoni all'unisono à 3, 4, 5, e 6 Voci / di Antonio Caldara.'

This autograph now comprises the two outermost leaves of a gathering originally made up of five or six sheets of manuscript. It contains twenty-one of the original eighty-four canons.

> (ii) D-ddr-Dlb: 2170-H-2. 'Libro Primo. / Divertimenti Musicali, per Campagna. / Canoni all'unisono à 3, 4, 5, Sei e à nove Voci. / Con altri d'altro generi. / à 2, 3, e 4. / Composti in tempo che battea la luna / da / Antonio Caldara / 1729 / in Vienna.'

This is a fair copy, apparently based on the autograph at I-PAc, but including almost 400 canons. The manuscript contains autograph alterations and corrections of the copyist's work; autograph additions include the last five of a set of 'Do-re-mi' canons found towards the end of the volume. The volume seems to have been prepared for presentation and/or performance and the minor corrections may have been made while the volume was in use.[8]

Of the forty-four canons (three are duplicated) by Caldara in the *One Hundred Cantici* not found in these manuscripts, the majority appear in principal secondary sources:

> (i) A-Wgm: Q10514. 'Canoni e Passatempi / di Antonio Caldara'

A manuscript collection of fifty-two canons (all by Caldara) contained in a singer's 'pocket-book' dating from c1740–1750, and formerly in the possession of the cultured musical amateur and collector, Franz Sales Kandler (1792–1831). Forty-three of the canons in the *One Hundred Cantici* are in this manuscript (hereafter termed 'Kandler'); eleven of its canons are to be found in the *Divertimenti Musicali (DM)*.

> (ii) B-Bc: C14-980. 'Canoni. / à 3. et à 4. / Del Sign. Antonio Caldara / E di Diversi Autori.'

A manuscript collection of seventy-three canons, *c*1770. (A copy of this manuscript is at D-brd-B: 2782/2.) Four duplications within this collection suggest that it has been compiled from more than one source. Canons 56–73 make up a section labelled 'Diversi autori'; fourteen of these appear in the *One Hundred Cantici*. Six of the fourteen are attributed to Caldara in 'Kandler'.[9] Of the attributed group (canons 1–55), forty-three appear in the *One Hundred Cantici*; twelve of these are to be found in the *DM*. All the *DM* canons in 'Kandler' reappear in this manuscript, as well as *Ama mi pur o cara*. This manuscript also contains the eight canons of the *One Hundred Cantici* that are not confirmed in any other major source. Of these eight, three appear either unattributed or variously attributed[10] in minor sources dating from the late eighteenth or early nineteenth centuries:

Ah che nel dirti (OHC 52)	D-brd-DS: Ms567a, No. 8;
Perchè se mio (OHC 78)	GB-Lbl: Add 32035
Cosi canta nell (OHC 33)	D-brd-DO: 1377, No. 31;
	D-ddr-Dlb: 3403 C502, No. 6
	I-OS: 1605, No. 31; with the text 'Il mio grillo'
	Cs-N: HZJP-T 552 No. 4;

Francesco Borosini and Caldara

The establishment of nearly ninety per cent of the contents of the *One Hundred Cantici* as being by Caldara, combined with an examination of the career of Francesco Borosini, points very decidedly to the singer as the 'Sig^r Borosini', the compiler of the volume. Indeed, the close contact between these two eminent members of the *Hofkapelle* in Vienna and the ease of access Borosini must have had to Caldara's music strengthens such a conclusion.

Francesco Borosini was born in Italy (*c*1690), the son of Antonio Borosini (also a tenor) who spent the last years of his career (1692–1711) in the service of the Imperial court in Vienna.[11] Francesco appears to have been engaged in the *Hofkapelle* soon after his father's retirement.[12] His initial salary of 1080 fl. ranked him about the middle of the *Kapelle's* tenors but two petitions (30 July, 1716 and 18 April, 1719) raised his remuneration to 1800 fl.[13] The increase not only made Borosini the highest-paid tenor at the court (a ranking he shared with Gaetano Borghi after 1720) but also confirmed *Kapellmeister* Fux's assessment of him as 'ein sehr gutter Virtuos ... und in Teatralsachen sich sonderbar distinguiret ... '[14]

Between 1715 and the second petition, Borosini had performed in six dramatic works by Fux alone — four operas and two oratorios. His connection with Caldara began with that composer's first oratorios and opera for the Imperial court, *Santa Ferma* (February, 1717), *Cristo condannato* (March, 1717) and *Cajo Marzio Coriolano* (August, 1717). It was a connection that was to continue almost to Borosini's last years of service. He made his final appearance in an oratorio by Caldara in *Gionata* (March, 1728) and in an opera in *Cajo Fabbricio* (November, 1729).

Naturally, Borosini was among the august company of performers, described by J. J. Quantz as 'die meisten berühmten Virtuosen aus Europa', who took part in the spectacular production of Fux's *Costanza e Fortezza* in Prague in August, 1723. On the basis of that appearance Quantz considered Borosini 'ein lebhafter Tenorist und auch geschickter Acteur'.[15] It may well have been in Prague that arrangements were concluded for him to appear in London at the King's Theatre for the 1724-25 opera season,[16] and he made his English debut as Bajazet in Handel's *Tamerlano* on 17 October, 1724.[17] He subsequently performed in *Artaxerxes, Giulio Cesare, Rodelinda, Darius* and *Elpidia.* Borosini must have returned more or less directly to Vienna at the end of the season[18] and apparently remained there until he retired (*jubilato*) on 20 May, 1731.[19] His name continues among the *Hof-Statt* in the *Hof- und Ehren-Calender* until his death in 1754.

When Borosini first performed in England, London was 'the operatic centre of the world'.[20] There could scarcely have been a greater contrast than the situation he found on his return more than two decades later. Handel had withdrawn from the operatic scene; for several seasons a succession of relatively minor composers,[21] excepting only Gluck, had provided the operas. The current singers, with little talent among them, seemed to underline the decline from the 1720s — the decade of the virtuosi. Lord Middlesex (Charles Sackville) the director of the operas at the King's Theatre in the Haymarket (perhaps in association with Heidegger, the aged impresario[22]) struggled to maintain full seasons. Opera performances in particular had been affected by the Jacobite rebellion of 1745 with the theatre remaining closed. The 1745-46 season did not open until 7 January, 1746, and despite its extension to 24 June, the opera company was unable to give the fifty performances promised to subscribers.[23] Middlesex's problems for the 1746-47 season were compounded by Gluck's return to the Continent.[24] Only on 22 September, 1746, could he announce, in the *General Advertiser*:

> HAYMARKET. WHEREAS, from Various Accidents and Disappointments the Undertaking an OPERA for the next Year was resolv'd upon too late in the Season to permit of solliciting the Subscriptions in the usual Manner; and as the Proposals for the ensuing Year are of a different Nature, and, as it is presumed, much more to the Advantage of the Subscribers than any hitherto offered, it has been thought proper to take this Method of informing the Publick, that Attendance will be given at the Opera-Office in the Hay Market ... in Order to shew the Proposals, take in Subscriptions...

Middlesex had greatest need of a manager.[25] Borosini, that long-experienced singer, with an extensive knowledge of dramatic production, an acquaintance with the English stage, for some years from 1728 co-director of the Kärntnertor theatre in Vienna and, no doubt, even in his retirement, still in contact with opera singers (some of whom might be enticed to a new situation), would have been an admirable choice for this position. It must have been in this capacity, and not as a singer, that he was engaged for London in 1746.[26] Although he did appear in minor roles throughout the season these probably were additional duties, stop-gap measures to cover deficiencies in the Theatre's casts.[27] It is clear that the 'Sig[r] Borosini' of the title-page of the *One Hundred Cantici* implies a person easily identified and of some standing. Such would have been Francesco Borosini, the 'Manager of the Opera', not Francesco Borosini, an elderly, retired singer, past his prime and scarcely, if at all, remembered from one season of twenty years ago.[28]

It was during this second sojourn in England that Borosini compiled the *One Hundred Cantici* for publication. He must have made a prompt start, for John Simpson announced the volume in the *General Advertiser* on Saturday, 28 February, 1747:

> NEW MUSICK. / This Day is Published, / ONE Hundred celebrated Italian Canticis / or Catches. Collected by Signor BOROSINI. / Printed for J. Simpson in Sweetings Alley, opposite the East-Door of the Royal-Exchange. / By whom it is published, Price 3s.

He readvertised the volume two months later (23 April, 1747), altering the wording — and the price!

> NEW MUSICK. / ... Price 4s. / ONE Hundred of the most celebrated Italian Catches, compos'd by the greatest Masters in Italy. / Collected and publish'd by / Signor BOROSINI, / Manager of the Operas in London.

An early beginning also is suggested by the publication of the *One Hundred Cantici* on a subscription basis. The subscription list may well have closed by the end of 1746; certainly, some of the subscribers, especially those in diplomatic service,[29] were in England only for a short time or at irregular intervals. Their Royal Highnesses, the Prince and Princess of Wales, headed a list that included many of rank and importance, in particular from among the aristocracy with connections of service to the Royal family, and as mentioned, from diplomatic circles. The quality of the list is remarkable for a volume of what, after all, are minor compositions. If the subscriptions were solicited only by Borosini, they suggest an unusually open access to the very highest circles of English society. As 'Manager of the Opera' Borosini may have had this entrée; as a mere singer his task would have been much more difficult. It cannot, of course, be determined to what extent subscriptions were expedited by Middlesex, with his aristocratic connections, or even by Heidegger, well-versed as he was in matters of this kind and with a wide range of contacts built up over many years.[30]

Borosini's sources for the *One Hundred Cantici*

No trace has yet been found of any manuscript collection of canons that can be linked directly with Borosini — a collection that he might have taken to England and there, abstracted from it the canons making up the *One Hundred Cantici*. The most likely source would be a collection written out as a singer's 'pocket-book' or, possibly, 'books'. Such a source (perhaps very similar in format to the 'Kandler' manuscript) may have been compiled at one time or over a period of several years, with Borosini entering favourite canons as they came to his attention.

Borosini lived and worked at a court that held contrapuntal writing in high esteem. The prevailing style, in sacred and secular music alike, reflected Charles VI's well-known partiality for counterpoint, and it seems that he was especially fascinated by the intricacies of canonic composition.[31] Caldara apparently provided the court with its repertoire of vocal canons, and on the evidence of the manuscripts described above, turned out at least 600 canons in 1729–30. Doubtless, the bulk was used for intimate, convivial entertainments at the court. Having regard to the esteem in which both Caldara and Borosini were held, it may be assumed that both were present, even participating in such amusements. It may well have been that Borosini wrote out his smaller, more practical pocket-books at this time, selecting canons from the bulky fair copy of the 'Libro Primo' of the *DM* and, as seems likely, from similar copies (unfortunately no longer extant) of the missing second, third and fourth books. Certainly, a source such as a singer's pocket-book would explain Borosini's ready access in 1746 to quantities of Caldara's canons. His access to such material may have been severely curtailed by his retirement in 1731;[32] after Caldara's death, his opportunities to copy further material may have ceased completely.

The contents of *One Hundred Cantici* are curious on three points: the duplication of three canons; the considerable number of canons which appear in very few manuscript sources; and the twenty-one canons which have quite different texts from those found in the extant manuscripts.

The duplication of *La sorte tiranna* (*OHC* 19 and 42), *Di libertà son privo* (*OHC* 18 and 43) and *Non so se sdegno* (*OHC* 29 and 65) may have resulted from the haste with which Borosini probably compiled his volume — presumably the selection of the hundred canons rested with him. One portion of the volume may even have been with the engraver(s) while the other was being copied out. However, the duplications may also indicate that Borosini was working from multiple sources (that is, two or more pocket-books) — a likely explanation at least for the duplication of *La sorte tiranna*, which has a variant text at its second appearance:

> *OHC* 19: 'La sorte tiranna mi niega il tuo affetto ... '
> *OHC* 42: 'Lo sò che tiranna disprezzi il mio affetto ... '

The rarity with which the canons comprising the second half of the *One Hundred Cantici* appear in manuscript sources (see Table 1) suggests that Borosini had privileged access to private material; that is, to manuscripts that had a very limited circulation (presumably the court copies) and which after the death of Caldara, or Charles VI, were completely withdrawn from use. No other sources are known for twenty-four of the twenty-nine canons that come from the 'Libro Primo' of the *DM* and which fall in the second half of the *One Hundred Cantici*. The remaining five are to be found only in single sources. In contrast, the twelve of the thirteen canons from the 'Libro Primo' which appear in the first half of the *One Hundred Cantici*, are widely reproduced — *Non più Clori*, for example, appears in ten primary and secondary manuscripts. Perhaps they become 'common property' through their inclusion in the 'Kandler' manuscript.[33] Apparently unrestricted in circulation, this brought at least a few of Caldara's canons into the public domain.

Twenty-one of the canons in *One Hundred Cantici* which come from the 'Libro Primo' appear with texts different from those given in the manuscript source (Table 2).

Table 2. *Canons from the* Divertimenti Musicali *included in the* One Hundred Cantici *with alternative texts.*

Divertimenti Musicali	One Hundred Cantici
O caro amigo	14 Ah' ch'il destino
Guardato intorno	58 Benchè felice
Voglio che femo	61 Voglio che cantiamo
Giudicio ci vuole	63 Nel mondo
Mi duole i denti	66 Bevete troppo
Il dio d'amore	67 Accende amore
Assae m'have	68 Lasciatemi in riposo
Una volta pur	69 S'egli è pazzo
Vedo che il mondo	70 Che destino
L'è cosi amabile	73 La grand' Austriaca
Dileto in verità	75 Tutti di fedeltà
Penso e ver	80 Cerco ogn'or
Mi voglio andar	82 Un musico son io
Nu semo tre	83 Poco ne san del'opera
A forza de conossi	91 Se dite mal
Nol ghi ne sa	92 Non mi l'an farti
Cochien vetterini	93 Istrioni, montinbanchi
V'è sè burlà	94 Sentir tacer
Che affano	96 Che nobil diletto
Ama chi t'ama	98 Fà il tuo dovere
Voglio dire	100 Tu sei pazzo

Borosini himself may have provided some of these alternatives but there is evidence, too, that Caldara equipped a number of canons with dual texts. In the autograph manuscript (I-PAc) of the canons of the 'Libro Primo', *L'orbo non canta* is provided with an additional text 'Libero ho il core'. The first text is retained in the fair copy (*DM*); the other disappears. On the other hand *Se non vi piacciono* has only the one text in the autograph yet it becomes *Questi son canoni* in the fair copy, and is printed as such in the *One Hundred Cantici* (16). That the version with the I-Pac text, as well as 'Libero ho il core', may have gone into one of the other 'Libri' is a possibility raised by *Ah' ch'il destino* (*OHC* 14). This canon appears only as *O caro amigo* in the 'Libro Primo'. The presence of the *One Hundred Cantici* text in the 'Kandler' manuscript (which it has been suggested, derives from Borosini's own pocket-book(s)), implies that Borosini had copied this version from a source other than the 'Libro primo' (presumably one of the other Books) and, further, that Caldara allowed the repetition of canons but with different texts in at least two fair copies. The text of *La grand'Austriaca (OHC* 73), which may possibly have been concocted by Borosini in tribute to England's support of the Empress, Maria Theresa, in her embattled position in enforcing the Pragmatic Sanction, probably has a more prosaic origin — as an alternative text (in another 'Libro') for the canon *L'è cosi amabile* in the 'Libro Primo'.[34]

It is unlikely that Borosini published the *One Hundred Cantici* with the permission either of Caldara's widow, or of the Imperial court which may still have exercised some claim over the compositions of a deceased employee. Perhaps it is of considerable significance that the volume appeared in England, the furthest extreme from Vienna, whence news of such a publication or even a copy, would penetrate only slowly, if at all. Perhaps, too, the inference in the title that the contents had their origins in Italy and had been appropriated from among several composers, is not insignificant. The reworded second advertisement which describes the catches as 'compos'd by the greatest Masters in Italy' seems an almost deliberate attempt to mislead. It is as if Borosini, in receipt of a pension from the court, realised that his publishing venture had placed him in an equivocal position.

Borosini can scarcely have published the *One Hundred Cantici* to take advantage of any wide-spread and immediate demand for vocal canons. Indeed, the appearance of his collection seems to anticipate rather than confirm the English taste for canon writing as it was not until the advent of the metropolitan and provincial catch-clubs in the 1760s that the great vogue for the composition and performance of canons developed. As the Preface to one of the many late-eighteenth-century collections pointed out:

> No progress seems to have been made in the composition of *Catches* and *Rotàs* from the beginning, till the middle of the present century . . . [when] the CATCH-CLUB at the Thatched-house (St Alban's Tavern) London was instituted in 1762, and was well-supported by many of the nobility, gentry, and professors.[35]

Certainly, England had a long tradition of catches and canons. They had been published from Thomas Ravenscroft's *Pammelia. Musicks miscellanie; or, Mixed Varietie of pleasant roundelayes and delightful catches . . .* (1609) and the companion volume, *Deuteromelia: or the second part of Musicks melodie . . .* (1609), up to the time of the *One Hundred Cantici* — and Borosini pays tribute to them in his title. Nevertheless, volumes of comparable extent had not appeared with any regularity. The *Catch that Catch can, or The Musical Companion,* first published by John Playford in 1667 and frequently reissued in altered and expanded versions by Henry Playford, William Pearson and John Young, up to the 1740s, Walsh's similarly-titled *The Catch Club or Merry Companions* (c1725/1733) and Michael Broome's *The Catch Club* (c1740), each containing upwards of 100 canons, appear to have been the only sizeable collections preceding the *One Hundred Cantici*. Borosini's volume may have owed its immediate success (it was reprinted within four years) to the still fashionable taste for things Italian, whether language, composers or performers. However, when placed in historical perspective it may be seen standing in the forefront of, and perhaps stimulating, a form of musical activity that was to continue with unabated vigour for nearly one hundred years.

The editions of the *One Hundred Cantici*

Contrary to the entry in *Recueils Imprimés XVIIIe Siècle*, there were three printings of the *One Hundred Cantici*.[36] However, as the original plates were reused for the later, undated issues, some general observations can be made about all three.

All editions retain the original folio format, c32.5 cm x 23.5 cm. Vagaries of trimming have produced individual differences in overall dimensions but all extant copies have generous margins beyond the plate impressions. The handsome volume is well-printed and remarkably free of errors. The title-page is neatly engraved but not excessively ornate in design; the punching of the publisher's imprint is commendably regular. The music notation combines punched and engraved work; the texts of the canons and other working have been punched throughout. The canons are set in 'linear' format, not in 'score' — a layout only adopted in many later publications of canons and catches.[37]

The volume lacks boards and is stitched as one gathering of 18 sheets. The title-page/cover and its engraved reverse, and the rear leaf are unnumbered; pagination (1–31), runs from first to last pages of score. Each canon is numbered in Roman numerals, except the last (*Pour quoi toujurs*), which probably was inserted by the publisher to complete the final page. All canons start at the left margin, with the first line of each indented for numbering; there is no infilling of uncompleted lines with shorter canons. In each canon the entries of the voices after the first are indicated with Arabic numerals and pause signs. The number of voices involved (à 3, à 4) is given at the head of each canon.

As noted earlier, the first edition was published by John Simpson 'at the Bass Viol and Flute in Sweetings Alley opposite the East Door of the Royal Exchange', his address since 1734.[38] His major publication, the *Thesaurus Musicus* (1745) in which he brought together much of his previously published sheet music, is incorporated in the imprint of the *One Hundred Cantici* (Plate 2).

'A List of the Subscribers' appears only in the first edition and ... no longer extant in all copies (see Table 3). This may indicate that it was inserted loose (as a single sheet, with the names typeset only on the recto)[39] into copies distributed among the subscribers. The remaining copies presumably were for sale to the general public.

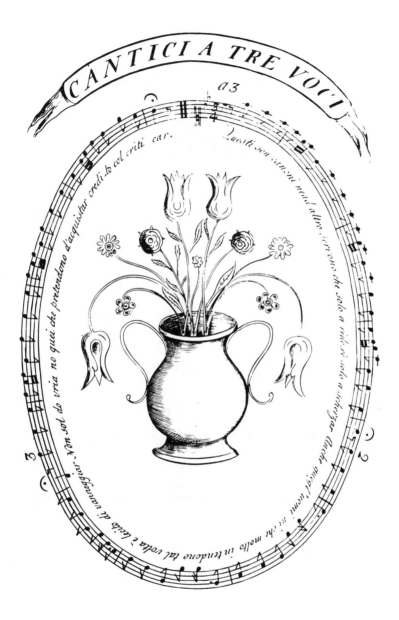

Plate 1. *One Hundred Cantici*: frontispiece. This engraving, incorporating the canon *Questi son canoni*, appeared in all three printings of the collection. (GB-Ge: Euing Music Collection R.X. 44)
Reproduced by permission of Glasgow University Library

One Hundred

Cantici

In Italian after the manner of English Canons & Catches

Collected by

Sig^R Borosini

LONDON Printed for J. Simpſon at the Baſs Viol and Flute in Sweetings Alley
oppoſite the Eaſt Door of the Royal Exchange ,

of whom may be had

THESAURUS MUSICUS a Collection of the Choiceſt & moſt favourite two, three, and
four Part Songs, ſeveral of them never before Printed To which are added, ſome Choice
Dialogues, ſet to Muſick by the moſt Eminent MaſtersViz . D.ᵣ Blow, Henry Purcel ,
D.ᵣ Croft, Handel, D.ᵣ Green, Morley, Hicks, Dan.ˡ Purcel, Eccles, Weldon, Travers, Corfe, Hayden,
Leveridge, Lampe, Carey &c The whole Reviſd carefully corrected & figur'd by a Judicious Maſter
in 2 Vollumes Price of each 5.ˢ

Plate 2. *One Hundred Cantici*. Title-page of the first printing. (GB-Ge: Euing Music
Collection R.X. 44)
Reproduced by permission of Glasgow University Library.

In the first edition all canons are notated in the soprano clef and are unchanged from the keys in which they are set in the manuscript sources. Variations in notation throughout the volume suggest that several engravers were involved.[40] At least three varieties of the soprano clef can be seen, the Roman numerals vary in size and shape, and both single and double hyphens are used for syllabification. Throughout, key signatures show expected vagaries in spacings between the individual sharps or flats. The variety of punches is obvious in sharp signs that are elongated (canons 1–12), truncated (13–38) and (from canon 42) squat and diagonally placed. Flat signs are long and pointed (1–13), rather more ornamental (14–39) and pronouncedly shorter and rounded from canon 44. A variety of punches also can be observed among the time signatures. For example, three distinct C signs appear — in canons 1–12 and 13–40, and from canon 41. That the majority of these changes of punches coincide (at canon 13 and again at canon 40) indicates an apportioning of the work-load — perhaps among two or three principal engravers, perhaps between an engraver and his apprentices.[41]

Apart from the substitution of the initial 'A' for the 'J' of J. Simpson in the imprint, the title-page of the second edition is identical. This change denotes Ann Simpson, who upon the death of her husband, John, in 1749, took over the business until her remarriage in 1751, after which the imprint was further altered. This second edition, therefore, was brought out during the three-year period, 1749–1751. The plates of the first edition have been reused but the soprano clef has been replaced throughout by the more modern treble clef. However, as the notes themselves have remained unchanged, the effect of this alteration has been to transpose each canon a third higher. This not only has resulted in an uncomfortably high *tessitura* in many instances, but also has necessitated new key signatures and the alteration of accidentals. Many of the new key signatures have been cramped into spaces never intended for such a purpose; for example, canons originally in C major are now in E major. On the whole these alterations have been neatly done, but some of the canons reveal traces of the reworking process.[42] Alterations have not extended to the few errors of omission found in the first edition: the lower figure is still missing from the time signature in Canon 10, as is the 'à' from 'à 3' in Canon 45 and the designation 'à 3' from Canon 54. However, the previously unnumbered final canon has become No. 'CI', the punches differing markedly from those used for the Roman figures in the first printing.

The third printing of the *One Hundred Cantici* was brought out by Randall and Abell, 'Successors to the late Mr Walsh in Catherine Street in the Strand.'; apart from the completely new imprint, it is identical with Ann Simpson's version. The reuse of the amended plates suggests that they had been purchased either by Randall and Abell or, earlier, by their predecessor, Walsh. As Randall and Abell published from Catherine Street from 1766 until July, 1768, when the partnership was dissolved at Abell's death, this third printing appeared about 20 years after the original edition. Possibly the publishers found the burgeoning interest in canons and catches in the 1760s made reprinting an attractive proposition, especially as much of the material in the volume was not widely known and had not been in print for about fifteen years.

Table 3. *The present location of copies of the* One Hundred Cantici

First printing (J. Simpson)	Second printing (A. Simpson)	Third printing (Randall and Abell)
GB-Lbl (5 copies; 3 with subscribers' lists)	GB-Er	US-Pu
GB-Ge (2 copies; one with subscribers' list)	GB-Lam	
A-Wgm (lacks subscribers' list)	US-Wc	
I-Fc (lacks title-page, and pp. 1-4; unidentified by title in library catalogue)		

The reuse of canons from the *One Hundred Cantici*

While the first printings of the *One Hundred Cantici* had few companions in the late 1740s and early 1750s, from the 1760s they were to become a source that provided a thread of continuity for Caldara's canons in numerous collections of catches and canons published in England in response to the upsurge of interest in this genre and the rapid growth in the number of clubs in which they might be sung. Three of the earliest publications to have recourse to the *One Hundred Cantici* were:

(i)   A COLLECTION of / Catches Canons and Glees / FOR / *Three, four, five, six and nine Voices* / never before published / Selected by / *Thomas Warren* / Printed for the EDITOR ... London, [1762–63]

(ii)   *A Second Collection of* / CATCHES / *By the Following Masters* /

D.ʳ ARNE	Sig.ʳ GIARDINI
M.ʳ BAILDON	M.ʳ LAMPE
M.ʳ BATTISHILL	M.ʳ TRAVERS
M.ʳ BERG	M.ʳ WOODWARD &
Sig.ʳ COCCHI	OTHERS

Price 2.ˢ 6.ᵈ

LONDON Printed by WELCKER in Gerrard Street S.ᵗ Ann's Soho / Where may be had the first Collection Price 2.ˢ 6.ᵈ likewise 8 Books of Catches Canons and / Glees in Score Printed by Permission of the Hon.ᵇˡᵉ Members of the Catch Club ...

(iii)   THE / ESSEX HARMONY: / Being an Entire New / COLLECTION / of the most Celebrated / SONGS and CATCHES, / CANZONETS, / CANONS and GLEES, / FOR / TWO, THREE, FOUR, FIVE and NINE VOICES. / From the WORKS of the most eminent MASTERS. / ... VOL II. / By JOHN ARNOLD, Philo-Musicae. / Author of the COMPLEAT PSALMODIST, / And CHURCH MUSIC REFORMED, / LONDON: / Printed by R. and M. BROWN, and sold by L. HAWES, and Co. / J. BUCKLAND, and S. CROWDER, all in Paternoster-Row. / MDCCLXIX / [Price Bound Two Shillings and Six Pence.] /

All three share the same canon which is distinguished by being the first of Caldara's canons to be given an English text. *Perchè vezzosi rai (OHC 7)* becomes 'O beauteous eyes, discover'.[43] It continued to be associated with this text in most of its subsequent appearances and became, despite or perhaps because of its totally uncomplicated nature (melodically, harmonically and rhythmically), the most frequently reproduced of all the canons which were abstracted from the *One Hundred Cantici* (see Appendix II).

If, as Emanuel Rubin proposes, Warren's *Collection* was based on the repertoire of the Noblemen and Gentlemen's Catch Club, the appearance of Caldara's canon (unattributed) in the first (1762) issue of the thirty-two-volume series, suggests that at least some of the contents, if not a copy of the *One Hundred Cantici* formed a corner-stone of that institution's library.[44] It may even have been a member of the Catch Club who provided the English text. Peter Welcker, who worked at Gerrard Street from *c*1762 until his death in 1775, became the publisher of Warren's *Collection,* reissuing the first books and borrowing heavily from the *Collection* for his *A Collection of Catches...(c1763–64)* and *A Second Collection...(c1770).*

The most curious version of *Perchè vezzosi rai* was its instrumental arrangement[45] (Ex. 1), entitled 'O Beateous [sic] Eyes', in:

> *A Choice Collection of / CATCHES and GLEES / Adapted for a / Violin and Violoncello / ... Humbly inscribed to / George Tate Esq! / By / JOSEPH AGUS. / Price 6? / N.B.: These Catches and Glees may be played on / the Harpsichord or Piano Forte. / LONDON / Printed & Sold at Fentum's N° 78 Corner of Salisbury S¹ Strand / ...*

Example 1. *O Beateous Eyes* arranged for violin and cello in Joseph Agus's *A Choice Collection of Catches...*

On the basis of the address given in the imprint, this volume was published between 1781 and 1784.

John Sibbald's rather more orthodox collection of vocal compositions:

> *A Collection of* / Catches, Canons, Glees, Duettos, &c / *Selected from the Works of the most eminent Composers* / *Antient & Modern* / Edinburgh / Vol. I. / *Printed for* J. SIBBALD & Co. *and Sold at their Circulating Library Parliament Square.*

can be dated precisely. The editor's dedication 'To the Catch Club instituted at Edinburgh June 1771', which is dated 'Edin. June 1780', makes this one of Sibbald's earliest publications[46] (he was active from 1780 to 1803), and demonstrates further the widespread and continuing support for this repertoire. In the first volume of the two volume set, *Perchè vezzosi rai*, again unattributed, is reunited with its original text. The return of the Italian text implies that in this instance the canon was taken directly from an issue of the *One Hundred Cantici*[47] — a conclusion borne out by the appearance of another canon from Borosini's collection in the second volume. This, however, has had its Italian text removed. The substituted English text, 'Oh that the salvation' (verse 7 of Psalm 53 'Dixit insipiens' — 'The foolish body hath said'), certainly cannot have been meant as a translation for *Comincio solo* (*OHC* 8). Perhaps the rather severe *da cappella* appearance of this canon suggested it as suitable for a sacred text[48] (Ex. 2).

Example 2
(a) *Comincio solo* (*OHC* 8)
(b) *Oh that the salvation* (*A Collection* of *Catches* ... Sibbald, [1780])

(a)

(b) ·

Robert Bremner published music in both London and Edinburgh over a long period — from 1754 until his death in 1789. In 1779 he purchased plates from Welcker's widow, Mary, but the canon by Caldara which appears in the second issue of his monthly publication:

THE / VOCAL HARMONIST'S MAGAZINE / *being a Collection of* / CATCHES, GLEES, CANONS, / and / CANZONETS. / *Selected from the best Authors both Ancient and Modern.* / Number II [added] / LONDON. / Printed and Sold by R: BREMNER, facing Somerset-House in the STRAND.

is not that of Welcker's volume. Bremner, in fact, worked from his Strand address from 1762 and this early issue of *The Vocal Harmonist's Magazine* may well predate the Welcker purchase. Certainly Bremner's choice of the chromatic *Mia Clori addio*, the first canon in the *One Hundred Cantici* and arguably one of Caldara's most elaborate settings, demonstrates some discernment and, possibly, an independent examination of that volume.

The widest selection of canons from the *One Hundred Cantici* is to be found among the many volumes (often interrelated) of canons and catches, produced between 1778 and 1795 by that prolific London publisher, John Bland. Most of Bland's collections of canons were issued as separate books of about ten to fifteen pages, within a series. However, a series could undergo a title change mid-way; its contents could be transferred to another concurrent series which used the same plates but continuous pagination; and a series could be reissued in 'volume' format, with a number of 'books' incorporated in a single volume. The situation was further complicated through the short-titles used to describe both the books/volumes and their contents in the advertisement pages which usually served as rear covers of so many of Bland's publications.

The mainstay of Bland's collections of canons and catches was his:

A / Collection / of / Catches Glees / &c &c / *Selected from the Works* / of the most / *Eminent Composers* / Price 1ˢ / LONDON / *Printed by J. Bland Nº 45 Holborn.*

With Book 5 its title changed to '*Bland's* / *Collection*...' All the canons by Caldara used by Bland appear (unattributed) in Books 2, 3, 6 and 8 in this series:

Book 2: *Perchè vezzosi rai*
          O beauteous eyes
Book 3: *Senza di te*
          Comincio solo
          Chi mai d'iniqua stella
Book 6: *Sò che vanti*
Book 8: *Tu sei pazzo*

They also reappear in:

The / LADIES COLLECTION / OF / *Catches, Glees, Canons,* / CANZONETS, MADRIGALS, &c. / SELECTED from the WORKS of the MOST / *Eminent Composers.* / *By John Bland* / *and Sold by him at his Music Warehouse.* / Nº [blank] — Nº 45. HOLBORN. — Pr.1s/ 6ᴅ. / NB. *These Numbers will be Continued* / at least Four in a Year.

which uses the same plates, but which was issued in 'book' and then 'volume' form, the first twelve books comprising the first volume. Two further canons *Poco ne san del'opera* and *Che bel contento* appear in the second and third volumes of *The Ladies Collection* respectively. There is no evidence to show that the contents of these ever appeared as individual 'books'.

In all, Bland brings a further six of Caldara's canons before a late-eighteenth-century public, apparently having made more extensive use of the *One Hundred Cantici* than any of his rival publishers. That Bland took most of his material direct from Borosini's collection seems confirmed not only by his use of *Poco ne san del'opera* and *Tu sei pazzo*, which are not to be found with these texts in any other source, but also by the general agreement of the keys used with those of the first edition of the *One Hundred Cantici*. *O beauteous eyes*, however, is reproduced in Warren's 1762 version; yet at the same time Bland further modifies its original, *Perchè vezzosi rai*.

In the midst of Bland's activities, his namesake (but unrelated?), Ann Bland, published:

> One Hundred / CANTICI or CATCHES / for 3 and 4 Voices / *Selected from the Works of the best* / ITALIAN MASTERS. / Price 5s / LONDON: / *Printed for A. Bland N.º 23, Oxford Street.*

As the familiar wording of the title suggests, this was yet another version of Borosini's compilation. However, an examination of this significant volume must be briefly delayed while those end-of-the-century publishers who continued to include some of Caldara's canons in their volumes are considered. They abstracted their examples from either the *One Hundred Cantici* or the publications already listed, and not from Ann Bland's volume.

One of the last provincial publications to retain a canon by Caldara was:

> A Collection of / DUETS, ROTAS, CANONS, CATCHES & GLEES / *Selected for, and most respectfully inscribed* / *To the Members of the* / Bristol Catch Club, / and the / CECILIAN SOCIETY, / by the *Editor.* / 1795. /

The 'Editor', who signed himself 'R.B.' at the conclusion of the Preface in which he discussed the progress of canon writing in England throughout the eighteenth century (and which has been quoted above), probably was Robert Broderip (1758–1808), a Bristol organist and composer. The Caldara canon is again *Perchè vezzosi rai*, and again it appears with its English text. This time the canon is attributed to Geminiani, suggesting that Broderip obtained it from a manuscript source[49] and not from one of the earlier publications.

Between 1776 and 1782 James Longman and Francis Broderip published:

> Amusement / *FOR THE* / LADIES / being a Selection of Favorite / Catches Glees and Madrigals / *Several of which have gained the* PRIZE

MEDALS / Composed by / Dr *Arne* Dr *Hayes* Dr *Cooke* / Mr *Webbe* Mr *Smith & Mr Battishill &c* / Vol [1–111] Pr. 10^{sh} 6^d / London / *Printed by* LONGMAN *and* BRODERIP N.^o *26 Cheapside* / . . .

Caldara's *Sò che vanti,* unattributed (and possibly 'borrowed' from one of John Bland's publications) appeared in the third volume. The firm's borrowings became more pronounced in two later publications. The contents of:

A Collection / OF / CATCHES, CANONS, GLEES, / DUETS &c / *selected from the works of the most* / Eminent Composers / *Antient & Modern* / VOL. I. / *London, Printed by* LONGMAN & BRODERIP, N.^o *26 Cheapside, & N.º 13 Haymarket.* / . . .

match those of Sibbald's 1780 issue. Indeed, this publication, which dates from between 1782 and 1798, is distinguished only by the altered imprint and the omission of the dedication to the Edinburgh Catch Club. It would seem that Longman and Broderip purchased the plates from Sibbald and reprinted without altering either the arrangement of the contents or pagination. Thus the familiar *Perchè vezzosi rai* reappears in the first volume, and in the second *Oh that the salvation* is reprinted for the first time. About 1780 the firm assumed publication of Warren's *Collection* and throughout the decade also reissued the early volumes using Welcker's plates and again altering only the imprint. In this way *O Beauteous Eyes* made yet another appearance — and in a volume whose title-page still read 'never before published'.

Longman and Broderip were adjudged bankrupt in 1798. Broderip, however, went into partnership with C. Wilkinson and up to 1807 the pair reissued many of the original firm's publications including, in a revised format:

AMUSEMENT / *for the* / LADIES, / *being a Selection of the Favorite* / CATCHES, CANONS, GLEES, and MADRIGALS, / *as performed at the* / Noblemen & Gentlemen's Catch Club / *Including the most popular which have gained the Prize Medals* / Composed by / *the following Eminent Authors* / LORD MORNINGTON / DOCTORS - ARNE - ARNOLD - ALCOCK - COOKE - DUPHIS - HAYES - & HARRINGTON. / Messrs - ATTERBURY - CALLCOTT - DANBY - NORRIS - PAXTON - SMITH - STEVENS - & WEBBE / VOL: [blank] PRICE [blank] / *Entered at Stationers Hall* / *London, Printed by* BRODERIP & WILKINSON N.^o *13 Haymarket,* / . . .

In this reissue, the three volumes of the earlier version were labelled 'Books' and brought together as Volume I. Pagination was altered to run continuously; *Sò che vanti* now appeared in Volume I, Book III.

John Bland's *Ladies Collection* was also subjected to the reissuing process at the end of the century. Some time before 1819, Robert Birchall 'at his Musical Circulating Library 133 New Bond Street.' reprinted the two-volume version:

> *The* / LADIES COLLECTION / OF / *Catches, Glees, Canons,* /
> CANZONETS, MADRIGALS, &c. / SELECTED from the WORKS of
> the MOST / Eminent Composers. / *By John Bland.* / Continued / *And*
> *Sold by R.! Birchall* ...

Finally, there is the undated volume published at Thompson's Music
Warehouse:

> APOLLONIAN HARMONY: / *a Collection of scarce & celebrated* /
> GLEES, CATCHES, MADRIGALS, / CANZONETS, ROUNDS,
> & CANONS, / *Antient & Modern, with some Originals* ... /
> LONDON. / Published at THOMPSON's Music Warehouse.

This contains *Senza di te* in Volume 6, unattributed and now termed
a 'ROUND'. In all probability the compilers had worked from one of
John Bland's collections.

When set alongside all of these volumes, the majority with only one
or two canons by Caldara, there can be little doubt that Ann Bland's
One Hundred Cantici or Catches is a major late-eighteenth-century source
of Caldara's canons in England.[50] Neither can there be any doubt that
this edition was based on the first printing of the *One Hundred Cantici*.
Whether or not Ann Bland was aware of the two subsequent reprintings,
almost certainly she was aware that very few of the canons in Borosoni's
collection had been in print at all in the intervening period. To her,
the *One Hundred Cantici* was a volume that not only matched
contemporary tastes but also provided, ready-made, a sizeable addition
to the current repertoire. As such it could be used to commercial advantage.
Sometime between 1784 and 1792 Ann Bland produced a corrected,
reorganized, modernized and well-printed version of the original *One*
Hundred Cantici (Plate 3).

In format, Bland's oblong volume (15 cm x 23.2 cm) is more practical
than its forebear, and with one to three (but usually two) canons per
page, is visually more appealing — an appeal enhanced by the
presentation of the canons in 'score' (Plate 4). The most significant feature,
however, is Bland's restoration of the canons to the pitches of the 1747
print but without a return to the soprano clef. For the first time in
nearly fifty years the canons were again available in their original and
practical *tessiture*. Bland dispenses with the engraved frontispiece of the
One Hundred Cantici and also with one of the three canons duplicated
in Borosini's volume. John Simpson's addition, *Pour quoi toujurs* (*OHC*
101), likewise is dropped, but Bland adds a new canon, *Beviam godiam*,
to maintain the total at one hundred (see Appendix I). Like all the
others in the volume, the newcomer is unattributed, but stylistically it
appears to post-date Caldara, being closer in character to the canons
of the last decades of the century and especially similar to those of Vincenzo
Martini (1754–1806). Despite this addition there is nothing to indicate
that Bland was working from a source other than the *One Hundred*
Cantici — although there is the slender chance that she may have had
access to Borosini's own pocket-books. All canons for which alternative
texts exist, appear with those given by Borosini.

Plate 3. *One Hundred Cantici or Catches:* title-page. Ann Bland's revised version of Borosini's *One Hundred Cantici.* (US-CA: Mus 516.5)
Reproduced by permission of the Edna Kuhn Loeb Music Library, Harvard University

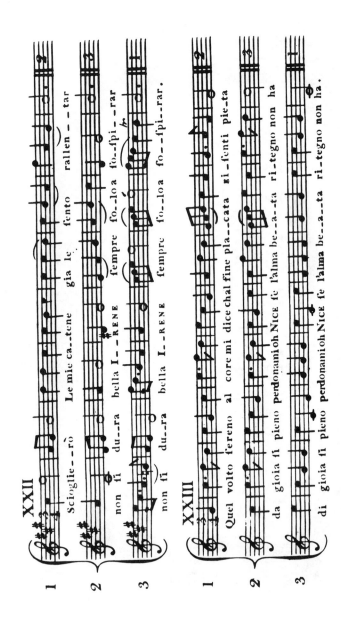

Plate 4. *One Hundred Cantici or Catches*. The 'score' layout of Bland's publication.
(US-CA: Mus. 516.5)
Reproduced by permission of the Edna Kuhn Loeb Music Library, Harvard University

Although Bland does not retain exactly Borosini's sequence of canons, her ordering is founded on that of the earlier publication just as the overall layout of her volume owes much to Simpson's design. For example, twenty-three of the thirty-two canons which head a page in the first *One Hundred Cantici* occupy the same position in Bland's volume. In other instances small groups of two to ten canons in Bland can be readily identified in Borosini.

Table 4. *Similarities in the ordering of canons in Bland's and Borosini's* One Hundred Cantici

Bland		Borosini
Page	Canon	Canon
1	1-2	13-14
6	14-15	1-2
11	19-20	23-24
15	26	45
16	27	46
20	33-34	16-17
26	43-44	54, 53
27	45-46	55-56
28	47-48	57-58
33	55-56	62, 64
34	57 [occupies ½ page]	63
36	60-62	72, 86, 73
37	63-64	74-75
38	65-66	83, 76
39	67	78
40	68	79
41	69-71	80, 77, 99
42	72-73	81-82
47	80	89
48	81	90
54	94-95	67-68

Bland did not merely reproduce the canons as they appeared in the *One Hundred Cantici*. On the contrary, the many editorial changes (fifty-seven canons show some alteration) suggest that she closely scrutinised her source. Her alterations and corrections fall into several categories.

Slur markings are changed in twenty-one canons. The majority are additions (usually to indicate that two or more notes are to be sung to the one syllable) but occasionally a slur is discarded when Bland's rearrangement of text underlay removes the elision of syllables so typical of Italian texts (Ex. 3) also. Other alterations of notation also arise from changes in text underlay: a tie is removed in *Studiate ancora* (Ex. 4); another is added in *Se viver non poss'io* (Ex. 5).

Alterations have been made to cadences in fourteen canons so that, as in *Non più Clori* and *Crudel deh non resistere*, the second or third voices now rise a fourth in the cadential progression instead of falling a fifth (Ex. 6 and 7).

Six canons show slight alterations to their original rhythms. In each, Bland brings uniformity to the voices by repeating a figure used elsewhere

Example 3. *Perchè vezzosi rai* (voice 3)

(a) *OHC* 7

mai   chi   v'a – mi al

(b) Bland 82

mai   chi   v'a - mi   al

Example 4. *Studiate ancora* (voices 2 and 3)

(a) *OHC* 76

voi   sie – te un paz-zo e un   fioc - co

stu – dia – te an – co - ra un   po – co

(b) Bland 66

voi   sie – te un paz-zo e un   fioc - co

stu – dia – te an – co - ra   un   po –   co

Example 5. *Se viver non poss'io* (voice 1)

(a) *OHC* 12

Se   vi – ver   non   pos – s'i – o

(b) Bland 16

Se   vi – ver   non   pos –   so

Example 6. *Non più Clori* (voice 2)

(a) *OHC* 15

[cate-] ne, le mie ca - te – ne.

(b) Bland 11

[cate-] ne, le mie ca - te – ne.

Example 7. *Crudel deh non resistere* (voice 3)

(a) *OHC* 35

per te non hò cor.

(b) Bland 32

per   te non ho cor.

in the canon. She also displays a tendency to smooth out rhythms evidently considered to be 'irregularities' (Ex. 8). Allied with these amendments is her rebarring of all five 12/8 metre canons in 6/8.

Example 8. *Se lontan ben mio* (voice 1)

(a) *OHC* 10

mi – o   tu   se – i

(b) Bland 8

mi – o   tu   se – i

Caldara's melodic shapes are also subject to alteration. Again a similar principle is applied: the flow of the music is to be enhanced by removing awkward or extreme leaps. Bland appears to act with considerable licence although her 'improvements' now provide an insight into contemporary taste. Intervals of an octave or more, usually are reduced through an octave displacement — a ninth to a second in *Che legge spietata* (Ex. 9), an octave to a unison in *Cerco ogn'or* (Ex. 10). In *Amor pietà* the awkward but effective and expressive drop of a seventh is reversed, the note rising by step to a resolution an octave higher and then falling the easier octave interval (Ex. 11).

Example 9. *Che legge spietata* (voice 2)

(a) *OHC* 54

d'un   al – ma pia – [gata]

(b) Bland 43

d'un   al – ma pia – [gata]

Example 10. *Cerco ogn'or* (voice 2)

(a) *OHC* 80

non   so,   non   so

(b) Bland 69

non   so,   non   so

Example 11. *Amor pietà* (voice 3)

(a) *OHC* 53

(b) Bland 44

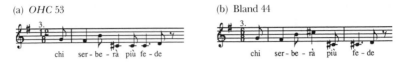

Sometimes alterations of the melodic line will result in alterations of the harmonic progressions. In *Mi giuri* the attempt to remove a discordant clash at the cadential progression comes close to introducing parallel fifths (Ex. 12). A more extreme case is the substantial reworking of the opening of *Se penso a voi* (Ex. 13). The entry of the second voice is converted to a unison with the first; the third voice probably was altered to move in melifluous thirds with the first and also to avoid what appear to be parallel fourths with the same voice on the third and fourth beats. However, Borosini's version has followed Caldara's autograph in every particular: in the manuscript at I-PAc he has rewritten the third voice part from e^{II} d^{II} c^{II} to e^{II} e^{II} f^{II}.

Example 12. *Mi giuri* (voices 1, 2 and 3)

(a) *OHC* 23

(b) Bland 6

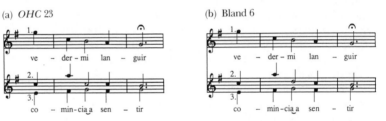

Example 13. *Se penso a voi* (voices 1, 2 and 3)

(a) *OHC* 46

(b) Bland 47

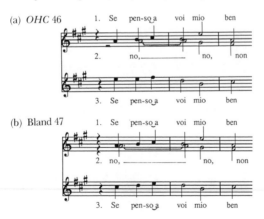

Changes to ornamentation are few. Bland omits the original ornaments from two canons but adds ornamentation in two others (Ex. 14, 15).

Example 14. *Che bel contento* (voice 3)

(a) *OHC* 4

ch'u - ni – ti   stan.

(b) Bland 9

ch'u - ni – ti   stan.

Example 15. *Scoglierò le mie catene* (voice 3)

(a) *OHC* 51

so – spi – rar.

(b) Bland 22

so – spi – rar.

Despite the obvious care taken with this publication, it is not entirely free from error. The omission of a tie at bars 17–18 in *Studiate ancora* leaves the placing of the second syllable of 'poco' open to question. The lower figure of the time signature of *Se lontan ben mio* is still missing, and an engraver's error in *In che t'offende* seems to have compounded the difficulties of Caldara's melodic line (Ex. 16).

Example 16. *In che t'offende* (voices 1–2)

(a) *OHC* 55

a-mor l'ac - cen-de s'o - [diar]

que-sta so - gna-ta fe - [licità]

(b) Bland 45

a-mor l'ac - cen-de s'o - [diar]

que-sta so - gna-ta fe - [licità]

Although many of the alterations that appear in Bland's version of Borosini's *One Hundred Cantici* are slight, they combine to produce a subtle change in the overall impression made by the volume. Much of the strength and musical interest in Caldara's canons has been weakened by the smoothing of the melodic lines and rhythmic patterns, by the softening of final cadences and by the removal of discords. Borosini, whether he had any right to Caldara's canons or not, at least remained faithful to the originals. Nearly fifty years later, the music which had very largely inaugurated a movement, was adapted and reduced to the style of its successors. Borosini claimed the *One Hundred Cantici* to be 'after the manner of English Canons and Catches'; Bland converted the claim into reality.

*   *   *   *   *

The thread of continuity of Caldara's canons in English publications which began with Borosini's edition, moves into the nineteenth century with the reappearance of a substantial number of his canons in Novello's *Sixty Italian Rounds* (*c*1840). But it finally breaks some ten years later. The inclusion of *O beauteous eyes* in the mid-century publication *The British Minstrel, and Musical and Literary Miscellany* is an anachronism, a curiosity from an age in which preferences in vocal music differed markedly from those of its successor.

Although Borosini's *One Hundred Cantici* contained only a small portion of Caldara's immense output of canons, it transferred some of this from the composer's immediate circle to a wider audience than Caldara could ever have imagined. As a source, both direct and indirect, for subsequent publications of canons, the *One Hundred Cantici* was before the public far longer than Borosini might have anticipated. But most curious of all, thanks to the processes of transmission described here, the *One Hundred Cantici* became both a stimulus to, and an integral part of, a national amusement which in nearly every respect was far removed from the courtly *milieu* for which the canons originally had been intended.[51]

Notes

[1] Winton Dean '(2) Francesco Borosini' *The New Grove Dictionary of Music and Musicians* (London, 1980), 3, pp. 63–4.

[2] W. Barclay Squire *Catalogue of Printed Music published between 1487 and 1800 now in the British Museum* (London, 1912/R1968) I, p. 176: '[1747?]'; Edith B. Schnapper (ed.) *The British Union-Catalogue of Early Music printed before the year 1801* (London, 1957) I, p. 126: '[1746]'; RISM *Recueils Imprimés XVIIIe Siècle* (München, 1964) BII, p. 125: '[c.1746]'.

[3] Dean states ' ... a collection of *One Hundred Cantici* ... is attributed to him [Francesco Borosini]' *op.cit.,* pp. 63–4.

[4] Probably Karl Geiringer (ed.) *Antonio Caldara, Kammermusik für Gesang, Kantaten, Madrigale, Kanons, Denkmäler der Tonkunst in Österreich* 75 (1932). *Questi son canoni* is the first of 35 canons published here.

[5] Band 75. Karl Geiringer completed the preparation of this volume after Mandycewski's death. Geiringer's 'Revisionsbericht' makes no reference to any printed source and fails to mention the *One Hundred Cantici.*

[6] The wording of the annotation suggests that he did not undertake an exhaustive analysis of the contents. If, in fact, he did do so, evidence of such a study has not been located.

[7] Fritz Jöde (ed.) *Antonio Caldara: Das Do-Re-Mi, Spielcanons I* (Wolfenbüttel, 1928), containing 24 canons, and his *Der Kanon* (Wolfenbüttel – Berlin, 1929) with its 34 canons by Caldara were the next most substantial representations. They were followed by the *DTÖ* volume (see Note 4), and Karl Geiringer (ed.) *Ein Madrigal und achtzehn Kanons, Das Chorwerk* 25 (1932). Several canons are duplicated among these publications which still only present a small portion of Caldara's output. In association with Brian W. Pritchard, the present writer has compiled a thematic index of canons (à 3 to à 9) by Caldara.

[8] The 'Libro Primo' of the title-page also is an autograph addition. In 1730 Caldara completed a further volume of some 220 canons entitled: 'Il Quinto Libro de Canoni all' Uni.^{no} / a $\underline{3}$ Voci, Composti in tempo che battea la luna / da Ant? Caldara / nell'Anno 1730 Nel Mese / di Aprile' (D-ddr-Dlb: Mus. 2170-H-1). This suggests that around 1730, Caldara ordered his volumes of canons and added 'Libro Primo' to the *Divertimenti*. No intervening *libri* have been found. It may be that the subdivisions within the *Divertimenti*, such as the 'Do-re-mi' canons, were intended as separate books. On the other hand, several of the manuscript sets of canons by Caldara now extant, could have been compiled from one or several of the 'missing' books (see Note 33).

[9] A further four are attributed to Caldara in a manuscript set of 85 canons (*c*1760) formerly in the possession of Therese Stadler (subsequently the wife of the minor composer Wenzel Trnka, 1739–1791): 'Canoni del Sig^{re} Antonio Caldara' (A-Wgm: Q4635). This set, one of the most important of the 'corroborating sources', is duplicated in D-brd-B: Mus 2782 (*c*1780-1800). The contents of the 'Stadler' manuscript also reappear in three manuscript books of canons in the Musikarchiv of the Minoritenkonvent in Vienna (Ms. 768a–c).

[10] The misattribution of canons by Caldara in many manuscripts cannot be discussed here, but it should be noted that the subsequent attribution of many of the canons in the *One Hundred Cantici* to composers such as Michael Haydn, Martini and Geminiani, and even to Metastasio, is demonstrably false. At least in part, the attribution to Metastasio arises from the texts of some of the *One Hundred Cantici* being taken from his *Strofe per Musica da cantarsi à canone*. Charles Burney points out the connection in a statement otherwise imprecise: 'These [the *Strofe*] amount to Thirty-five, many of them appear in the Italian Collection of Catches, Rounds and Canons, brought to England by Borosini, and published by Walsh, about the year 1748.' *Memoirs of the Life and Writings of the Abate Metastasio* (London, 1796/R1971) III, p. 347.

[11] Winton Dean '(1) Antonio Borosini' *The New Grove Dictionary of Music and Musicians* (London, 1980) 3, p. 63. Ludwig Ritter von Köchel gives his appointment as '1. Jän 1710 – 1 Oct. 1711 pens.' *Johann Josef Fux, Hofcompositor und Hofkapellmeister der Kaiser Leopold I., Josef I. und Karl VI. von 1698 bis 1740* (Wien, 1872) p. 359.

[12] Köchel *op.cit.*, pp. 320 and 365.

[13] *Ibid.*, pp. 380, 385 and 365. Hermine Williams's study of the *Hof-Protocol* records confirms Francesco's appointment and initial salary. He is listed in January, 1713 'in simili als Tenorist mit Jahrlisten 1080 fl.' I am indebted to Hermine Williams, Hamilton College, Clinton, N.Y., for this further information.

[14] Köchel *op.cit.*, p. 385.

[15] 'Herrn Johann Joachim Quantzens Lebenslauf, von ihm selbst entworfen' in Friedrich Wilhelm Marpurg *Historische-kritische Beyträge zur Aufnahme der Musik* (Berlin, 1754–78) 1, p. 218.

[16] Handel may have approached Borosini in 1719 when he visited the continent in search of opera singers for the newly-formed Royal Academy of Music's undertakings. At the end of July he was at the Electoral court in Dresden waiting 'for the engagements of Senesino, Berselli and Guizzardi to be concluded'. In August the Electoral Prince (Friedrich August) married the Archduchess, Maria Josepha, in Vienna, uniting the Viennese and Dresden courts. The marriage was celebrated by a performance of Caldara's *Sirita*, and at the end of the month, Fux's *Elisa* was performed on the Empress's birthday. Borosini sang in both operas. On the return of the Electoral Prince to Dresden, a new opera house was opened with singers from the Habsburg court assisting. There seems little doubt that Handel had opportunity to contact Borosini. At present this cannot be documented but Dean notes that 'there was talk of Borosini's engagement for London in 1719' (*op.cit.*, p. 63). Further evidence of Handel's contact with singers at the Imperial court appears in the Minutes of the Royal Academy of Music (27 November, 1719) '... that he [Handel] bring with him [to England] the proposalls of all the Singers he has treated with, particularly Cajetano Orsini.' The castrato Orsini (usually named 'Gaetano' in cast lists) was first engaged at the Habsburg court in 1699; he too sang in the opera performances of 1719 (see Köchel *op.cit.*, pp. 359 and 365, and Beilage X, p. 138; Otto Erich Deutsch *Handel, a documentary biography* (London, 1955) pp. 90–6; and H. C. Robbins Landon *Handel and his world* (London, 1984) pp. 97 ff.).

[17] Handel went to considerable trouble to accommodate his new tenor, rewriting the part of Bajazet in *Tamerlano*, and then Sextus in *Giulio Cesare*, to take full advantage of Borosini's exceptionally wide range (nearly two octaves) and interpretative powers. (Conti, for example, used both tenor and bass clefs in notating Borosini's parts. Information from Hermine Williams.)

Borosini's arrival in England was noted in the *Weekly Journal* (17 October, 1724):

'We hear that there is a new Opera now in Practice ... called *Tamerlane*, the Musick composed by Mynheer Hendel, and that Signior Borseni [sic], newly arrived from Italy, is to sing the Part of the Tyrant Bajazet. *N.B.* It is commonly reported this Gentleman was never *cut out for a Singer*.'

Uncomplimentary though it seems, the final comment is more likely an allusion to Borosini as a male Italian singer with a natural vocal range instead of that more common (and derided) phenomenon in England, the imported castrato.

Lady Bristol remarked on the performance of *Tamerlano* that 'the new man takes extremely'. Deutsch (*op.cit.*, p. 174) regards this as a reference to the alto castrato, Pacini, an opinion shared by Winton Dean. Landon, however, conjectures otherwise: 'The new castrato, Andrea Pacini, had the title role, but the sensation of the evening was the new tenor, Francesco Borosini.' (*op.cit.*, p. 105). It might be expected that Handel's bold writing for Borosini would have had a more immediate impact on the audience than the limited range of Pacini's arias. According to Paul Henry Lang 'Handel was entirely successful in portraying Bajazet, a noble hero who dominates the opera; his antagonist Tamerlano, sung by a new alto castrato, Pacini, is not nearly so convincing.' *George Frideric Handel* (London, 1966) p. 182.

[18] He did not appear in the revival of *Elpidia* which opened the 1725-26 season (30 November, 1725).

[19] Köchel *op.cit.*, p. 365; but '20. März' in his *Die Kaiserliche Hof-Musikkapelle in Wien von 1543 bis 1867* (Wien, 1869) p. 74.

[20] Landon *op.cit.*, p. 102.

[21] The succession of 'resident' composers at the King's Theatre included Baldassare Galuppi, 1741-42 and 1742-43 seasons; Giovanno Battista Lampugnani, 1743-44 season, but possibly longer; Christoph Willibald Gluck, 1745-46 season; Domingo Terradellas, 1746-47 season; and Domenico Paradies, 1746-47 season, but who continued to reside in London. As well as supplying their own operas, these composers also concocted *pasticci* to augment the seasons. In early 1744 two operas by Francesco Veracini 'Leader of the opera band' were performed. See also the respective entries in *The New Grove Dictionary of Music and Musicians* (London, 1980) and Charles Burney *A General History of Music* ed. Frank Mercer (London, 1935) pp. 838-47.

[22] Johann Jakob Heidegger had been associated with the management of the King's Theatre since 1713. In 1741 he was granted a licence good for four years at the theatre and let it to Lord Middlesex for operas. It is not clear when he finally abandoned the theatre. See Winton Dean 'Heidegger, Johann Jakob' *The New Grove Dictionary of Music and Musicians* (London, 1980) 8, p. 433, and Philip H. Highfill, Kalman A. Burnim and Edward A. Langhans *A Biographical Dictionary of Actors, Actresses, Musicians, Dancers, Managers, and other Stage Personnel in London, 1660-1800* (Carbondale, 1982) 7, p. 240.

[23] For a detailed coverage of each season, see Arthur H. Scouten (ed.) *The London Stage 1600-1800. Part 3: 1729-1747* (Carbondale, 1961).

[24] Although because of the delayed start of the 1745-46 season Gluck's first opera (*La caduta de'giganti*) was not performed until January, 1746, he brought new distinction to the King's Theatre. 'The operas flourish more than in any latter years; the composer is Gluck, ... ' (Horace Walpole to Horace Mann, 28 March, 1746 OS). Gluck's departure probably was unexpected. It may have resulted from Middlesex's tardiness in paying his musicians. In August, 1746, Walpole told Mann 'Lord Middlesex ... has paid nobody; ... to the composer [Gluck?] his Lordship gave a bad note, not payable in two years, besides amercing him entirely three hundred pounds ... ' (12 August, 1746 OS).

Lord Middlesex's leading role (and ill-success) as the principal and, occasionally, sole director of the opera at the King's Theatre is graphically depicted in Horace Walpole's letters. 'There is to be a fine opera in England next year; Lord Middlesex the chief undertaker' (27 December, 1740 NS); 'The music displeases everybody, ... I am quite uneasy about the opera, ... I fear they [the directors] will lose considerably' (5 November, 1741 OS); ' ... the Duke of Dorset has set himself strenuously to oppose it [the opera], as Lord Middlesex is the impresario, and must ruin the house of Sackville by a course of these follies. Besides what he will lose this year, he has not paid his share to the losses of the last, and yet is singly undertaking another for next season, with the almost certainty of losing between four or five thousand pounds, to which the deficiencies of the opera generally amount now.' (4 May, 1743 OS); 'We have operas, but no company at them: the Prince [of Wales] and Lord Middlesex impresarii.' (5 December, 1746 OS). See also Lang *op.cit.,* pp. 420 and 459-60.

25 Middlesex had employed the Abbé Francesco Vanneschi 'first as poet, and then as assistant manager' upon assuming the directorship of the theatre. Vanneschi was heavily involved in the opera in 1741 and 1742, but his connection over the next few years is less clear. Walpole (a subscriber to the 1742-43 season) noted that 'We [the subscribers] shall discard Mr Vanneschi' (3 March, 1742 OS). In April, 1743, he implied that Vanneschi was no longer associated with the opera 'I really don't know whether Vanneschi be dead' and spoke of 'Lords Middlesex and Holderness, the two sole managers' (14 April, 1743 OS). Vanneschi resurfaced at least by early 1747 when he supplied the libretto for Paradies's *Fetonte* and inscribed a prefatory *A Discourse on Operas* to Lord Middlesex. Eventually he became manager of the opera from 1753 (perhaps as early as 1748) to 1756 when he absconded (Burney *A General History* ... pp. 839 ff.).

26 Winton Dean (*op.cit.,* p. 63) appears to be the first writer to have noted Francesco Borosini's return to England. Burney (*A General History* ... p. 846) lists a 'Borosini' among the singers of the 1746-7 season but offers no further identification. The statement that 'The names of Borosini ... are not found again in England after 1725.' (J[ulian] M[arshall] 'Borosini, Francesco' *Grove's Dictionary of Music and Musicians* (London, 1889) 1, p. 261) is omitted in the fifth (1954) edition. It cannot now be determined who engaged Borosini. Possibly Heidegger made the suggestion; Vanneschi who was in Italy engaging singers and dancers for the 1741-42 season may have contacted Borosini. Middlesex himself had visited Italy (and Austria?) by early 1743 (Walpole to Mann, 5 November, 1741 OS and 14 April, 1743 OS). The term of Borosini's engagement is unknown; perhaps it was for the one season only. However, the other singers of that season appear to have been retained for the next. The 1746-47 season was the usual financial disaster, though that can scarcely have been Borosini's fault.

27 The season comprised the pasticcio *Annibale in Capua* (4 November, 1746); Terradellas's *Mitridate* (6 December, 1746); Paradies's *Fetonte* (17 January, 1747); Lampugnani's *Roxana* (24 February, 1747); and Terradellas's *Bellerofonte* (24 March, 1747). There was a revival of *Mitridate* at the close of the season (9 May, 1747). The principal male singer, the castrato Nicolo Reginelli, was past his best; 'the rest of the singers of this season were not captivating' (Burney *A General History* ... p. 846).

28 Burney's remark that the male singers, including Borosini, had 'never been possessed of the powers of pleasing;' (*ibid*) suggests the total eclipse of Borosini's earlier success in England. Obviously his return stirred no memories, at least not among those with whom Burney might have had contact.

29 Among the diplomats appearing in the subscribers' list were M. de Wasnar, Count de Haslang, M. de Champigny, and Chevalier Osorio. They can be identified respectively as 'Minister Plenipotentiary of their Imperial Majesties'; 'Minister Plenipotentiary of his Most Serene Highness the Elector of *Bavaria*'; 'Minister of his most Serene Highness the Elector of *Cologne*'; and 'Envoy Extraordinary from the King of *Sardinia*' and were described as 'Ministers of the several Roman Catholick Princes and State residing here'. All were signatories to letters protesting about discrimination against Roman Catholics in England; see *The London Magazine and Monthly Chronologer* January, 1746, pp. 19-20. The subscribers' list also includes 'The Venetian Ambassador'. He can be identified as 'Signor Capello' through the letters of protest.

30 That Heidegger should be the only professional musician identifiable among the subscribers lends weight to his probable involvement in the affair. Naturally, Lord Middlesex was among the subscribers.

31 J. J. Fux's renowned canonic mass (K.7) of 1718 (entitled *Messa di San Carlo* in honour of the Saint of the Emperor's name-day) is dedicated to Charles VI, and it is no coincidence that Fux's famous treatise *Gradus ad Parnassum*, in which

the virtues of a good contrapuntal technique were extolled, was published with the Emperor's patronage. A number of *quasi*-canonic masses in the *stil antico* were written by both Fux and Caldara, and many other liturgical compositions feature movements in the strict (*da cappella*) style. The Emperor's liking for canons is noted by J. J. Rousseau in his *Dictionnaire de Musique* (Paris, 1768) p. 72: 'L'Empreur Charles VI, qui étoit grand Musicien & composoit très-bien, re plaisoit beaucoup à faire & chanter des *Canons* ... ' Ursula Kirkendale notes 'Nichts is wahrscheinlicher, als daß Caldara diese Divertimenti [the 'Libro Primo' and *Il Quinto Libro*] für den kaiserlichen Kanonfreund geschrieben hat.' *Antonio Caldara: Sein Leben und seine venezianisch-römischen Oratorien* (Graz-Köln, 1966) p. 86.

[32] It would seem that Borosini's access even to the *DM* was limited. The last canon from this set which he included in the *One Hundred Cantici* is No. 266 — that is, none comes from among the final 150 canons in the manuscript. Moreover, Borosini used no canons at all from *Il Quinto Libro*. He may never have had any access to this collection. It may also be that Borosini's departure from the court brought the vogue for canon composition and performance to a halt. No canons by Caldara can be dated with any certainty beyond *Il Quinto Libro* of 1730.

[33] It is not impossible that the 'Kandler' manuscript represents a selection made from the proposed fair copies of the 'missing' books of canons (see Note 8). It contains 31 of the 59 canons of the *One Hundred Cantici* that are not from the *DM*. On the other hand, 'Kandler' could also represent a condensed version of a more extensive pocket-book (or books) compiled directly from the fair copies. That it may even have been compiled from Borosini's own books is perhaps borne out by similarities between the ordering of the canons in 'Kandler' and the *One Hundred Cantici*: nine groups of two, three or four consecutive canons correlate, for example *OHC* 1–3 = 'Kandler' 31–33, and *OHC* 5–7 = 'Kandler' 7–9. There are also two pairs of reversed numbers, for example *OHC* 27–28 = 'Kandler' 46–45. In all, 28 canons are involved in such groupings. Their relationship surely indicates a close relationship between Borosini's source for the *One Hundred Cantici* and the 'Kandler' manuscript.

[34] Certainly the sentiments of the text seem better suited to the glorious age of the Habsburg empire under Charles VI.

[35] Robert Broderip, editor of *A Collection of Duets, Rotas, Canons, Catches & Glees* ... [Bristol], 1795 (see above p. 322). For further on the Noblemen and Gentlemen's Catch Club, see Henry Raynor 'London, VI, 4: Concert life – Organizations – *Catch Club' The New Grove Dictionary of Music and Musicians* (London, 1980) 11, pp. 193–4, and Emanuel Rubin's 'Introduction' to the facsimile edition of *A Collection of Catches Canons and Glees* (Wilmington, 1970) 1.

[36] The holding institutions are listed correctly but the entry gives the imprint only of the first publication.

[37] 'Canons, rounds, and catches were never published in score till after the institution of the present CATCH-CLUB in 1762; and, therefore, *one line* often contained the whole composition; ... ' (Burney *A General History* ... p. 279n). The first publication with canons in score may have been the initial (1762) volume of *A Collection of Catches Canons and Glees ... Selected by Thomas Warren* (London).

[38] For further on publishers and printers mentioned here, see Charles Humphries and William C. Smith *Music Publishing in the British Isles* (Oxford, 1970) and Frank Kidson *British Music Publishers, Printers and Engravers* (London, 1900/ R1967).

[39] I am indebted to Sheila M. Craik, Assistant Librarian, Humanities Division, Glasgow University Library, Glasgow, for this information. I also wish to acknowledge the generous assistance of Michael Anderson, Music Librarian, Reid Music Library, Edinburgh University Library, Edinburgh; Norris L. Stephens, Music Librarian, University of Pittsburgh Libraries, Pittsburgh; O. W. Neighbour, Music Librarian, and Nicholas Chadwick, Research Assistant, The British Library, London; Rosalind Cyphus, Library Assistant, Royal Academy of Music, London;

Rodney H. Mill, Music Specialist, Music Division, The Library of Congress, Washington, D.C., and Michael Ochs, Librarian, Eda Kuhn Loeb Music Library, Harvard University, Cambridge, MA.

[40] It would seem that each engraver had his own punches. Perhaps he had to make these as part of his trade. It is unlikely that a publisher supplied a range of punches from which engravers could choose at random. See Donald Burrows 'Walsh's editions of Handel's Opera 1-5: the texts and their sources' *Music in Eighteenth-Century England, Essays in memory of Charles Cudworth* ed. Christopher Hogwood and Richard Luckett (Cambridge, 1983) p. 80.

[41] Burrows cites instances of two or three engravers working on one publication. Of particular relevance is the division of labour he deduces for Handel's Op. 1-3 (*ibid.*, pp. 81 ff.).

[42] This included the 'infilling' of some of the original stave lines, and the punching and smoothing of the reverse of the plate, prior to the punching of the new clef and time signatures.

[43] In addition to sharing the English text, all three are set in A major (B-flat major in the *One Hundred Cantici*) and have the same additional ornamentation. However, only in Warren's *Collection* is the canon printed in score format.

[44] For further about this important series which continued to 1793, see Rubin *op.cit.*

[45] Such instrumental arrangements of catches and canons were rare, although an early eighteenth-century example was John Walsh's *Catches for Flutes or A Collection of the best Catches contriv'd and fitted for 1:2:3: or 4 Flutes ...* [c1711]. Agus's arrangement represents a move away from the popular 'gentleman's' instrument of the first half of the eighteenth century. It is also noteworthy for its accommodation of the three voices on two instruments. A number of Caldara's canons appeared in instrumental arrangements in the present century.

[46] A reissue bears a slightly altered imprint '*Printed for* J. SIBBALD *Parliament Square, and / Mess.rs* CORRI & SUTHERLAND *Music / Sellers to* HER MAJESTY.'

[47] The copy of the *One Hundred Cantici* now in the Reid Music Library, Edinburgh, has the hand-written inscription 'Presented to the Catch Club by Mr John Lumsdaine.' Unfortunately, neither the identity of the club nor the date of the donation is known. If, however, the club was that at Edinburgh, it may be that Sibbald had access to this copy. Sibbald prints the canon in B-flat major, although it is in D major in the Edinburgh copy (A. Simpson print) of the *One Hundred Cantici*. Possibly Sibbald realised the cause of the high *tessitura*, and if he did use the A. Simpson print as a source, his experience as a printer would have made him aware of the nature of the typographical changes visible on the printed page.

[48] Although attributed to Caldara in four major manuscript collections and existing in his own hand (but without text) at I-Bc: DD226, f4b, it cannot be his own composition. It appears, textless, in Athansius Kircher *Musurgia universalis* (Roma, 1650) p. 384.

[49] There is little doubt about the authenticity of this canon, but numerous minor and late eighteenth-century sources attribute it variously to Gassman, Martini, Michael Haydn, Geminiani and Bernasconi, among others. However, Broderip's is the only publication which attributed this canon to a particular composer.

[50] US-CA: Mus. 516.5; the only copy listed in *Recueils Imprimés XVIIIᵉ Siècle.* I am indebted to the Library of Harvard University for supplying a microfilm copy.

[51] Apart from those used as examples in treatises (Johann Albrechtsberger *Gründliche Anweisung zur Composition* (Leipzig, 1790) and J. Müller-Blattau (ed.) *Die Kompositionslehre Heinrich Schützens in der Fassung seines Schülers Christoph Bernard* (Leipzig, 1926), no canon by Caldara was in print on the continent until present century.

Appendix I

Of the thirteen canons of the *One Hundred Cantici* that cannot as yet be attributed to Caldara, seven are to be found in minor manuscript sources:

OHC 84 *Caro con questi* I-Fc: D232, No. 87.

OHC 86 *Rivolgi ad altro* D-brd-DS: 567a, No. 9.

OHC 87 *Ah, si ben mio* I-Fc: D232, No. 50; GB-Cfm: Ms 22.

OHC 88 *Perchè sì bella* I-Fc: D232, No. 47.

OHC 89 *Ah, tu non sai* I-Fc: D232, No. 36.

OHC 90 *Da labri tuoi* I-Fc: D232, No. 52.

OHC 99 *Senza di te* Cs-N: HZJP-T 552 ('Heiden'); D-ddr-Dlb: Mus 3403-c-502, 8 ('M. Haydn').

Sen – za   di   te   ben   mi – o

The other six canons are not known in any manuscript source.

OHC 38 *Mi lagnerò tacendo*

Mi   la-gne – rò ta – cen-do del –   la mia sor – te a – va – ra

OHC 59 *O care selve*

O   ca – re   sel – ve,   o   ca – ra

OHC 62 *Già che tu tremi*

Già che tu   tre – mi   al – lor che pen – si, al – lor che   pen-si

OHC 85 *Se la pietade*

Se   la   pie – ta – de è   que – sta.

OHC 97 *Se non chiedessi*

Se non chie – des – si,   non chie – des – si a – mo – re

OHC 101 *Pour quoi toujurs*

Pour quoi tou – jurs   tou – jurs far – dez tou – jurs

The canon *Beviam godiam* No. 100 in Bland's *One Hundred Cantici or Catches*

Be – viam   go – diam,   go – dia – mo a – mi – ci

Appendix II

Different versions of Caldara's canon *Perchè vezzosi rai:*

(1) *One Hundred Cantici* (J. Simpson, 1747); reappears in *One Hundred Cantici or Catches* (A. Bland, [c1784-92])

*added in Bland

(2) *A Collection of Catches ... selected by Thomas Warren* [1762]; reappears in *A Second Collection of Catches ...* (Welcker, [c1762-78]); *The Essex Harmony ... By John Arnold* (R. & M. Brown, 1769); and *A Collection of Catches ... and The Ladies Collection of Catches ...* (J. Bland, [c1778-85])

(3) *A Collection of Catches* ... (J. Sibbald, [1780]); reappears unaltered in *A Collection of Catches* ... (*Longman & Broderip,* [c1782–98])

(4) *A Collection of Catches* ... and *The Ladies Collection of Catches* ... (J. Bland, [c1778–85])

(5) *A Collection of Duets, Rotas* ... ([Robert Broderip] 1795)

Aspekte der Bühnenbildentwicklung in Italien bis zum Beginn des 18. Jahrhunderts

Frauke Gerdes

Abstract

Aspects of stage development in Italy up to the beginning of the eighteenth century

Baroque stage settings were an essential part of contemporary opera productions which were staged at considerable personal and especially financial expense. The baroque principle of peep-show stage, wings, and gallery-box system for an auditorium still exists today.

The rediscovery of classical writers and architectural theoreticians, especially Vitruvius, led to a lively debate and fruitful discussion on the method of stage engineering. The static style of scene of the Renaissance (Serlio) followed the three stage-set types (tragedy, comedy, satire) of Vitruvius, and the architectonic *scaenae frons* of Roman theatre lived on in the Teatro Olimpico of Palladio.

Towards the end of the sixteenth century the changed production conditions of musical *intermezzi*, which had been inserted into the plays in Florence, led to a change in stage engineering. Choruses and dances required more room than the actors, and the mythological subjects, with manifestations of gods, etc., required certain stage machinery and many changes of scenery. The periaktoi stage of Greek theatre was recalled, and, together with early baroque opera developing out of the Florentine *intermezzi*, began its conquest of Italy and the rest of Europe.

Up to the last years of the seventeenth century the stage set remained firmly based on a central perspective, and was characterised by surprising transformations and set changes, and spectacular mechanical effects. The optical attraction was uppermost.

The designs of Ferdinando Galli Bibiena (1656-1743) broke this pattern with oblique positionings of the rooms being presented. These stage sets in the 'maniera di verde le scene per angolo' had several vanishing points running out from the sides of the scene. The sections being shown could be extended beyond the stage in the viewer's imagination. The power of the set was enhanced thereby, even though the actual stage space became smaller, since the oblique positioning limited it in depth. Filippo Juvarra (1678-1736), who like Ferdinando was also active as an architect, developed this principle further.

Antonio Caldara's association with the Bibiena family of stage designers began with his early Italian operas. A closer connection was formed with Ferdinando Galli Bibiena at Barcelona in 1708 when both were involved in *Il più bel nome* performed to celebrate the marriage of Charles III. Later, the composer was reunited with the Galli Bibienas at the Imperial court in Vienna, working with Francesco (1659-1737) and Antonio (1697-1744?). The operas produced there represent their greatest accomplishments in their respective fields.

Aspekte der Bühnenbildentwicklung in Italien bis zum Beginn des 18. Jahrhunderts

Frauke Gerdes

D IE HAUPTROLLE IN der barocken Theaterszene spielte das *dramma per musica* — die Oper, die sich, von Florenz ausgehend, schnell über ganz Italien und das übrige Europa ausbreitete. Die Bühnenbilder, mit ihren prachtvollen Ausstattungen, ihren überraschenden Maschineneneffekten, ihren verblüffenden Verwandlungen, waren nicht nur schmückendes Beiwerk, sondern wesentlicher Bestandteil barocker Opernaufführungen. Zahlreiche Augenzeugenberichte[1] zeigen uns, daß oft in erster Linie die Ausstattung und die Effekte einer Aufführung gewürdigt wurden. Auch die Librettisten und ihre Texte fanden Beachtung, während von den Komponisten und der Musik seltener die Rede ist.

Oft ist es heute nicht mehr möglich, die Opern zu überlieferten Bühnenbildern zu identifizieren, weil sie vergessen wurden. Die Auswertung von Archivalien, insbesondere von Rechnungsbüchern u.ä., italienischer Höfe[2] macht deutlich, welcher personelle und vor allem finanzielle Aufwand getrieben wurde, um die Aufführungen, die an den Höfen meist zu dynastischen Festen (Hochzeit, Taufe usw.) und ausländischen Besuchen (befreundete Herrscher, Diplomaten u.ä.) stattfanden, so prachtvoll wie möglich auszustatten.

Eine umfangreiche Darstellung zum Thema 'Bühnenbild im Barock' würde den Rahmen eines Aufsatzes sprengen, denn in jedem Land fanden, trotz gemeinsamer Grundtendenzen, örtlich und zeitlich unterschiedliche und eigenständige Entwicklungen statt,[3] die eine genaue Untersuchung der jeweils vorliegenden Voraussetzungen und Bedingungen erfordern würde. Deshalb möchte ich mich, auch im Zusammenhang mit den Opern Caldaras, auf Italien beschränken, zumal die wichtigsten Impulse zur Gestaltung der barocken Bühnendekoration von hier ausgingen und durch italienische Künstler über ganz Europa verbreitet wurden[4]. Um die Wende vom 17. zum 18. Jahrhundert wurde eine Änderung der Raumauffassung in der szenischen Gestaltung der Bühne deutlich, speziell in den Arbeiten Ferdinando Galli Bibienas (Abb. 1) und, in der Folge, Filippo Juvarras, die beide u.a. auch frühe Opern Antonio Caldaras ausgestattet haben (s. Anhang). Um herauszufinden, in welchen Punkten sich die Bühnenraumgestaltung um 1700 ändert, ist es nötig, festzustellen, wie sie vor den Arbeiten z.B. der Bibienas aussah. In die Jahre um 1700 fiel auch die Librettoreform Zenos und Metastasios[5] und begann der Siegeszug der *opera seria*. Es wird also auch im literarischen und musikalischen Bereich eine neue ästhetische Auffassung deutlich.

Bei der Fülle des Materials ist es demnach nur möglich, einige Aspekte der Bühnenbildentwicklung in Italien zu beleuchten.

In den Jahren zwischen 1689 (*L'Argene*, Venedig) und 1714 (*Tito e Berenice*, Rom), also in der Zeit vor seiner festen Anstellung am habsburgischen Kaiserhof in Wien, komponierte Caldara zahlreiche *drammi per musica*, Pastoralen und andere Werke für die Bühne.[6] Bis auf einen kurzen Aufenthalt in Barcelona,[7] wo 1708 sein *componimento da camera, Il più bel nome* als Festoper bei den Feierlichkeiten zur Hochzeit des spanischen Thronfolgers Karl III. — er ging 1711 als Kaiser Karl VI. nach Wien — mit Elisabeth Christine von Braunschweig aufgeführt wurde, arbeitete Caldara in diesen Jahren in Italien. Fest angestellt war er in Mantua, am Gonzaga-Hof Ferdinando Carlos (1699–1707) und am Hof des Prinzen Ruspoli in Rom (1709–1716). Außerdem komponierte er für Theater in Venedig, Bologna, Ferrara usw.[8] und den Kaiser in Wien, wohin er 1712 reiste, um sich um die Stelle als Hofkapellmeister zu bewerben.[9]

Über die Dekorationen zu seinen Opern informieren uns in erster Linie die überlieferten, gedruckten Libretti,[10] in denen, wie es damals üblich war, die Bühnenbilder aktweise angegeben sind. In einigen der erhaltenen Partituren[11] finden sich ebenfalls Angaben zu Bühnendekoration, oft ergänzt durch genauere Beschreibungen und Regieanweisungen. Die Bühnenbildner sind leider nicht in allen Fällen genannt.

Die Auswertung dieses Materials ergibt, daß neben den Brüdern Ferdinando (1656–1743) und Francesco (1659–1737) Galli Bibiena und Filippo Juvarra (1678–1736) auch Giuseppe (? — ?) und Pompeo (1677–1735) Aldovrandini, sowie Antonio Mauri (? — ?), um nur die bekannteren Bühnenbildner zu nennen, Aufführungen von Opern Caldaras ausstatteten.[11] Für die Dekorationen zur Oper *L'inimico generoso* (Bologna, 1709) arbeitete Ferdinando Galli Bibiena mit seinem Schwager, dem Maler Giovacchino Pizzoli (1651–1733) zusammen[12] (Abb. 2).

Die Auswertung der Bühnenbildangaben *(Mutazione delle scene)* der Libretti und Partituren ergibt u.a. folgende Gruppen:

1) innen: z.B. Sala Regia, Appartimenti, Galleria, Prigione
2) außen: z.B. Landschaft, Wald
3) außen, kombiniert mit Architektur: z.B. Straße, Platz, Palastgarten, Hof

Abbildung 1. Ferdinando Galli Bibiena (1656–1743). Mitarbeiter Caldaras in Italien, der das Bühnenbild der Oper zu neurer Vollendung führte.

SCENE [5]

Nell' Atto Primo.

Campo di Perfiani con regio Padiglione d' Isdegarde.

Logge interne nella Reggia di Bizanzio, che introducono à diverfi Appartamenti.

Padiglione di Berenice fituato nel Campo Perfiano.

Atrio di Fontane corrifpondente agli Appartamenti di Pulcheria.

Nel Secondo Atto.

Viale di Verdura vicino al Campo Perfiano.

Sala con Trono, ove fi riduce il Senato.

Borgo dirupato dal fuoco, e dalla guerra.

Camera negli Appartamenti di Pulcheria.

Nell' Atto Terzo.

Suburbj di Bizanzio colla veduta della Porta della Città.

Camera negli Appartamenti di Pulcheria.

Reggia di Bizanzio.

La Mufica è del Sig. Antonio Caldara.

Le Scene Invenzione, e Pittura del Sig. Ferdinando Bibiena, e del Sig. Giovachino Pizzoli Bolognefi.

A 3   AT-

Abbildung 2. Die Veränderungen der Schaubühne durch Ferdinando Galli Bibiena und Giovacchino Pizzoli anläßlich einer Vorführung von Caldaras *L'inimico generoso* in Bologna, 1709.

Diese Grundtypen sind z.T. genauer beschrieben und werden durch Zusätze erweitert, z.B. 'Sala Regia, in cui alzandosi un pareto, si apre una stanza lugubre colla statua del morto Rè Sancio, preparato pell'arresto di Fernando'[13] oder 'Bosco con veduta di Campagna'[14] oder 'Piazza con un tempio d'Apollo da un lato'.[15] Im Durchschnitt enthält jeder Akt zwei oder drei Szenenwechsel (d.h. 3-4 verschiedene Bühnenbilder). Das trifft insbesondere für die als *dramma per musica* bezeichneten Stücke zu. Die pastoralen Opern, wie z.B. *Paride sull'Ida*[16] oder *La costanza in amor vince l'inganno*[17] haben meist nur einen Bühnenbildtypus. Im Fall der *La costanza* handelt es sich um den Typ 'bosco', der aber vielfältig variiert wird: 'Bosco con veduta in lontano di Fiume, e sorgente d'aqua vera, che forma un ruscello per pescare' (*La costanza* I/1) und 'Bosco areccia folta, dove siegue la Caccia' (*La costanza* II/1).

An Bildmaterial zu den frühen Opern Caldaras sind nur die Entwürfe und Aquarelle Juvarras zu den Opern *Giunio Bruto*[18] und *Tito e Berenice*[19] überliefert. Die zahlreich erhaltenen Entwürfe der Bibienas sind bislang für Opern Caldaras nicht eindeutig identifiziert worden.[20] Einige Librettoillustrationen zeigen eine wichtige Szene der jeweiligen Oper.

An dieser Stelle sei eine kurze Anmerkung zum dokumentarischen Wert der überlieferten Bildquellen im allgemeinen erlaubt. An Bildmaterial zur Barockoper stehen uns heute, neben den Librettoillustrationen und Titelkupfern, Kupferstiche zu Festaufführungen und natürlich die große Zahl der Originalentwürfe der Bühnenbildner zur Verfügung. Die Titelbilder der Libretti sind eine freie Wiedergabe des Bühnengeschehens (sie wurden schon vor der Aufführung gedruckt) und oft frei erfunden. Nach Wolff[21] ist hier ein genauer Vergleich mit den szenischen Angaben und Regieanweisungen des Librettos oder der Partitur nötig, um Fehlerquellen auszuschließen. Besonders das Hochformat der Libretti verfälscht den Eindruck des eigentlichen Bühnenraumes.[22] Kupferstiche, die zu Festaufführungen hergestellt wurden, geben Bühnenbilder und Kostüme ziemlich genau wieder, sind aber, laut Wolff,[23] nicht kennzeichnend für den Durchschnitt der Bühnenausstattungen, da sie zu besonderen Gelegenheiten angefertigt wurden und meist prächtiger ausfielen als das Original.

Dokumentarisch bedeutsam sind in erster Linie die Originalentwürfe der Bühnenbildner, da sie sich mit den Gegebenheiten vor Ort auseinandersetzen mußten. Nach ihren Zeichnungen und technischen Einzelheiten wurden die Entwürfe ja in die Realität der jeweiligen Bühne umgesetzt.

*   *   *   *   *

Das Bühnenbild bzw. die Ausgestaltung des Bühnenraumes ist keine Erfindung der Neuzeit, sondern hat eine lange Tradition. Ihre Geschichte begann bei den 'Erfindern' des europäischen Theaters, den Griechen[24]. Die frühe Tragödie, aus religiösen Wurzeln entstanden, kam ohne festes Bühnenhaus aus. Der Begriff 'skene' geht auf die aus Holz gezimmerten Umkleidehäuschen der Schauspieler zurück. Diese Bretterbuden wurden später teilweise mit bemalten Stoffbahnen oder Holztafeln verkleidet und dienten so, als Felsen, Häuser, Stadtmauern u.ä., zur Dekoration des jeweiligen Stückes. Aus der Zeit des Aischylos ist der erste Bühnenbildner namentlich bekannt. Vitruv schrieb ihm, Agatharchos, ein heute verschollenes Traktat über die Skene zu, das um 430 v. Chr. entstanden sein soll.

Ab ca. 450 v. Chr. gab es dann ein erstes festes Bühnenhaus (unter Perikles in Athen), das die Voraussetzungen bot, die das griechische Theater jetzt für die Ausgestaltung des Bühnenraumes und die Erweiterungen der szenischen Aktionen benötigte. Die Front des Bühnenhauses hatte drei Auftrittstore und zwei seitliche Anbauten, die Paraskenien. Das Dach des Skenebaues wurde als Theologeion (Ort der Götter), bei Bedarf, in das Spiel mit einbezogen. Perspektivisch bemalte Stoffbahnen oder Holztafeln schufen in den Toren des Bühnenhauses dreidimensionale Ein-und Durchblicke. Bestandteil der Aufführungspraxis für Tragödien war die sogenannte Ekkyklema, eine kleine Sonderbühne, die, auf Rollen laufend, aus dem Tor der Haus- oder Palastdekoration herausgeschoben werden konnte. Sie diente zur Darstellung der dramatischen Szenen (z.B. Mord, Tod u.ä.), die sich eigentlich hinter der Bühne abspielten. Die 'charontische Stiege', eine aus dem Hintergrund heraufführende Treppe, bot den aus der Unterwelt emporsteigenden Personen einen effektvollen Auftritt. Ein Kran, der einen Korb hinter dem Bühnenhaus hervorschwenkte, ermöglichte Göttererscheinungen, die, insbesondere in den Stücken des Euripides, als *deus ex machina* in das Bühnengeschehen eingriffen. Die Bühnentechniker, die mechanopoioi, waren auch für die Geräuscheffekte, wie Donner, Erdbeben usw., zuständig, die durch Steine in Holz- oder Metalltrommeln erzeugt wurden.

Das römische Theater orientierte sich in der Dichtung am griechischen Vorbild,[25] doch waren Theaterbau und Ausstattung diesem Vorbild in keiner Weise adäquat. Die ersten Bühnen waren die viereckigen Bretterpodien der Possenspieler, mit einem weißen Hintergrundvorhang und einer seitlichen Holztreppe. Das Publikum stand um dieses Provisorium, das, je nach Bedarf, auf- und abgebaut wurde. Später kamen dann Holzbuden als Umkleideräume für die Schauspieler dazu.

Die szenischen Bedingungen der Autoren Plautus und Terenz führten dann zur Vorstufe der *scaenae frons*, die später den griechischen Skenebauten entsprechen sollte.

Eine aus Holz gezimmerte Bühnenwand wurde mit Dach und Seitenwänden versehen. Sie erhielt drei Auftrittstore, die mittlere 'Porta Regia' und die beiden seitlichen 'hospitaliae'. Später kamen seitlich noch je eine weitere Auftrittsmöglichkeit dazu. So entstanden die 'fünf Häuser', die für die Straßenszenen in den Stücken von Plautus und Terenz notwendig waren.[26] Ca. 155 v. Chr. errichtete der Censor Cassius Longinus das erste Bühnenhaus mit säulengeschmückter scaenae frons, das jedoch wie alle römischen Theaterbauten der Zeit, nach den Aufführungen wieder abgerissen werden mußte. Die Verwendung gemalter Dekorationen ist umstritten. Evtl. wurde ab ca. 99 v. Chr. die Bühnenwand mit naturalistisch bemalten, verschiebbaren Holzwänden verkleidet, die in der Mitte geteilt waren und nach beiden Seiten weggezogen werden konnten. Nach Angaben Vitruvs sind Seitendekorationen ca. 79 v. Chr. von den Brüdern Lucius und Marcus Lucullus eingeführt worden. Später wurden dann die, aus Griechenland übernommenen, Periakten verwendet — dreiseitig mit bemalter Leinwand oder Holztafeln versehene Prismen, die auf Stiften drehbar und perspektivisch angeordnet waren. Durch Dritteldrehung konnten sie dem wechselnden Hintergrund angepaßt werden. Die Türen neben den Periakten hatten ihre bestimmte, dem Publikum bekannte, Bedeutung: links auftretende Personen kamen aus der Fremde, wer von rechts auftrat, kam aus der nahen Stadt.

Bewegungs- und Flugapparate fanden nur noch im Circus Verwendung.

Erst in der Kaiserzeit, unter Pompejus, erhielt Rom seinen ersten festen Theaterbau. Die architektonisch gestaltete Bühnenwand, die säulenge schmückte *scaenae frons*, verdrängte endgültig die gemalten Dekorationen.

Unsere Kenntnisse über Bau und Ausstattung des antiken Theaters verdanken wir dem römischen Architekturtheoretiker Pollio Vitruvius, dessen zehnbändiges Werk *De Architectura* ca. 25 v. Chr., unter Verwendung griechischen Materials, entstand. Er teilte die Bühnenbilder in drei Kategorien ein: Ausstattung für Tragödie, Komödie und Satyrspiel. Jeder dieser Typen charakterisiert in seiner Dekoration die Umwelt, in der die jeweilige Handlung spielt. Auf der tragischen Bühne führt die Palastarchitektur in die Welt von Königen und Helden. Die Komödie spielt in der Welt der Bürger und 'kleinen Leute', in ihrer städtischen Umgebung mit gewöhnlichen Häusern und Plätzen. Die Bühne des Satyrspiels versetzt die Zuschauer in Wälder und ländliche Gegenden.

Die Wurzeln des modernen Theaters reichen zurück bis ins 15. und 16. Jahrhundert. Die humanistischen Grundideen der Renaissance führten u.a. zu einem enormen Aufschwung des weltlichen Theaters, während im vorangegangenen Mittelalter das religiöse Theater, das Mysterienspiel, dominiert hatte. Dessen theatergeschichtliche Errungenschaften, wie Simultanbühne u.ä., wurden in der Frührenaissance mit Elementen des antiken Theaters kombiniert. Der Wunsch nach Wiederbelebung des antiken Dramas führte auch zu Rekonstruktionsversuchen des dazugehörigen Bühnenraumes.

Die Bücher des Vitruv waren 1414 wiederentdeckt worden und wurden zum Vorbild für Theater und Architektur. Zahlreiche Autoren gaben sie neu heraus, kommentierten und interpretierten sie, wie z.B. Leon Battista Alberti (1404-1472) und Sebastiano Serlio (1475-1554).

Bei der weiteren geschichtlichen Betrachtung der Bühnenbildentwicklung ist zu bemerken, daß sich die Dekorationssysteme nicht chronologisch ablösten, sondern zeitweilig nebeneinander weiterbestanden, immer abhängig von Aufführungspraxis und örtlichen und zeitlichen Strömungen. So bestand neben der barocken Kulissenbühne die manieristische Periaktenbühne zunächst ebenso weiter, wie der Einfluß der antiken römischen Architekturbühne in der Weiterentwicklung Palladios im Teatro Olimpico in Vicenza.[27]

Die Bühne der Renaissance kann als Bild-, Winkelrahmen- und offene Reliefbühne bezeichnet werden, d.h. der Raum der Handlung wurde bildartig, mit Hilfe von auf Winkelrahmen reliefartig abgebildeten Häusern, Palästen u.ä. dargestellt.

1508 führten Girolamo Genga und Giovanni da Udine die Zentralperspektive zur Gestaltung des Hintergrundprospektes ein. In der Malerei wurde der zentralperspektivische Bildraum schon früher angewendet. Als Vater der Zentralperspektive gilt Filippo Brunelleschi (1377–1446), während Alberti in seiner 1436 erschienenen Schrift *Della pittura* die theoretischen Grundlagen formulierte und die genauen mathematischen Berechnungen, die zur Konstruktion eines zentralperspektivischen Raumeindruckes nötig sind, darlegte.

Im Theater wurde die zentralperspektivische Illusionsmalerei auf die Stoffbahnen des rückwärtigen Bühnenabschlusses übertragen. Die vollständige Wirkung des Bühnenbildes und seiner Perspektive hatten nur die Zuschauer, die in der Mittelachse saßen, wo sich die Fürstenplätze befanden.[28]

1519 verwendete Raphael für eine Aufführung von Ludovico Ariostos *I suppositi* in Rom ein einheitlich zentralperspektivisches Bühnenbild mit einer Stadtansicht Ferraras im Hintergrund. Ein Bühnenbildentwurf Perruzzis (1481–1536) erregte Anfang des 16. Jahrhunderts Aufsehen beim Publikum. Die Bühne bestand aus Vorderbühne (Terenzbühne) und perspektivisch gestalteter Hinterbühne, wo die reliefartig dargestellten Häuser nicht nebeneinander, wie bei der Simultanbühne, sondern perspektivisch hintereinander gestaffelt angeordnet wurden.

Das wichtigste Merkmal der Renaissancebühne ist ihre Unveränderlichkeit, d.h. ein Stück wurde in einem einheitlichen Bühnenbild aufgeführt, dessen Typisierung man von Vitruv übernommen hatte.

Sebastiano Serlio beschreibt im 2. Buch seines Werkes *De Architettura* (1545) genau die Bühne seiner Zeit und bildet die drei Typen auf Holzschnitten ab. Die Bühne stand auf einem hölzernen Podest und war aufgeteilt in Spiel- und Bildbühne. Vorn sollten die kleineren Gebäude stehen, die größeren hinten. Die Häuser wurden mit Rahmen angefertigt und mußten, ebenso wie z.B. Balkone u.ä., auf die Perspektive ausgerichtet sein. Die plastisch perspektivischen Winkelrahmen stießen in stumpfem Winkel aneinander und standen auf soliden, festen Basen. Außerdem wurde ein perspektivisch bemalter Hintergrundprospekt verwendet, der je nach Art des Stückes (Tragödie, Komödie, Satyrspiel) in den drei Kategorien Vitruvs gestaltet wurde.

Spiel- und Bildbühne wurden auf unterschiedliche Art und Weise beleuchtet, wobei die Bildbühne magisch-unwirkliches Licht erhielt. Die Szene sollte von der Mitte aus beleuchtet werden. Scheinbares Seitenlicht entstand durch einheitlich gemalte Schatten und unsichtbare Lichtquellen in der Mitte. Die Schmuckscheiben der Fenster waren durchsichtig und konnten von hinten erhellt werden. Das künstliche Oberlicht entstand durch hängende Fackeln über der Bühne. Darüber befanden sich Gefäße, die mit Wasser und teilweise mit Kampfer gefüllt waren und so schönes Licht und angenehmen Duft verbreiteten. Fackeln vor der Bühne dienten ebenfalls zur Beleuchtung der Szene. Die Spiel- oder Vorderbühne war nicht auf den Hauptperspektivpunkt ausgerichtet. Diese Art der Renaissancebühne stellte sich dem Zuschauer als Bild dar.

Zur Triebfeder der Entwicklung von der unbeweglichen Winkelrahmenbühne der Renaissance, mit ihren drei Bildtypen, zur beweglichen, tiefen Kulissenbühne des Barock wurden die Intermedien des Manierismus und später die Oper.

In die Komödien der Hoffeste der Spätrenaissance, die in Winkelrahmenbühnen aufgeführt wurden, wurden, zuerst in Florenz, musikalische Intermedien eingeschoben, in denen Tanz- und Chorgruppen auftraten, die mehr Platz brauchten als die Darsteller der Komödien. Die Intermedien spielten in antiken mythologischen Gefilden und verlangten nach prächtigeren Dekorationen und Maschinen für Verwandlungen und Göttererscheinungen. Man besann sich auf die dreiseitig bemalten, drehbaren Prismen der antiken Theaterdekorationen, und es entstand die Periaktenbühne des Manierismus.

Bernardo Buontalenti (1536–1608) stattete die Intermedien von 1585 und 1589[29] in Florenz mit einer Periaktenbühne aus und führte sie in der Folge zu ihrem Höhepunkt.

Die Humanisten der Renaissance bemühten sich, neben der Rekonstruktion des antiken Theaterraumes auch den Geist und die Aufführungspraxis des antiken Dramas wiederzubeleben. Aus einer Kombination dieser Bestrebungen mit Elementen der höfischen Renaissancefeste und ihren musikalischen Intermedien, sowie den neuen musikalischen Möglichkeiten der Monodie, entstand in Florenz ein neues musikalisches Genre, das später Oper genannt wurde. Sie erfreute sich schnell großer Beliebtheit und übernahm mit Begeisterung die Errungenschaften der Bühnengestaltung, die bald zu einem der wichtigsten Bestandteile der Aufführungen wurde und immer neue Impulse aus den Ansprüchen an Verwandlungsmöglichkeiten erhielt.

Hans Tintelnot[30] beschreibt die Oper als 'Synthese von Dichtung, bildender Kunst, Allegorik, von Symbol und dynastischer Idee'. Die antike Mythologie diente der frühen Oper als Stoffquelle. Szene und Bühnenbild waren auf Stilisierung und Überhöhung ausgerichtet und strebten Symbolik und Intensivierung an. Bewußte Unwirklichkeit und Überwirklichkeit (z.B. Verzerrung und Übersteigerung der Affektdarstellung, Traumszenen u.ä.) und Verwandlungen[31] waren wichtige Kriterien. Grundelemente manieristischer Kunst waren Überraschung und Wunder. Und so verlangte das bildhafte Sehen nach Bewegung, Abwechslung und Überraschung, alles Bedingungen, die die Weiterentwicklung der Bühnentechnik förderten. Bühnengeschehen und Bühnenbild waren primäre Faktoren der Aufführungen.

Giulio Parigi (1571–1635) etablierte die Periaktenbühne in Florenz und Sabbatini befaßte sich 1638 im 2. Band seiner Schrift *Pratica di fabbrica scene e machine* mit der Möglichkeit der Koppelung von je zwei Periakten.

Auch der Prospekt konnte verwandelt werden — entweder war er in Rinnen seitlich auseinanderzuziehen,[32] oder als vierteiliger Rahmen, zu je zwei Teilen in Angeln hängend, seitlich zusammenzufalten oder auf einer Walze nach oben zu ziehen.

Die Periaktenbühne verbreitete sich von Florenz aus schnell über ganz Europa, obwohl in der Zwischenzeit schon das Kulissensystem erfunden worden war.

1606 entwarf Giovanni Battista Aleotti für die 'Accademia degli Intrepidi' in Ferrara ein Theater mit gerahmter Kulissenbühne, die im Gegensatz zur offenen Reliefbühne der Renaissance eine gerahmte Tiefenbühne war, deren Tiefe durch Öffnung der Bühnenrückwand noch zu erweitern war. Technisch funktionerte das neue Kulissensystem (von frz. couler-gleiten) folgendermaßen:[33] Der Bühnenboden steigt in einem Gefälle von 1:9 nach hinten an. In Schlitzen im Bühnenboden (tagli), die in Gruppen (canali) angeordnet waren, liefen sogenannte Kulissenwagen oder Kulissenschlitten (carretti), die von Riemen über eine Winde auf die Bühne und wieder zurück gezogen werden konnten. Das ermöglichte Verwandlungen bei offener Bühne. Auf den Kulissenwagen wurden Holzrahmen oder Leitern befestigt, die mit Leinwand bespannt waren. Die seitlichen Kulissen (telari), waren perspektivisch bemalt und ergaben, in perspektivischer Anordnung, einen dreidimensionalen, zentralperspektivischen Raumeindruck. An den Leitern der Kulissenwagen konnten auch senkrechte Beleuchtungsrinnen befestigt werden. Einzelne Kulissenteile (spezzati), die Einzelelemente des Bühnenbildes darstellten (Felsen, Brunnen usw.), konnten unabhängig von den telari bewegt werden. Soffitten, gesteifte Leinwandbahnen, die von einer Bühnenseite zur anderen gespannt wurden, sollten den Zuschauern den Einblick in die Oberbühne verwehren. Sie wurden, wie die Kulissen, perspektivisch bemalt und stellten Baumkronen, Decke, Himmel, Wolken u.ä. dar. Der Prospekt (fondali) füllte die gesamte Bühnenbreite — im Gegensatz zur Renaissancebühne — und lief in Rinnen im Bühnenboden. Die horizontal beweglichen Kulissen wurden von einer Maschinerie bewegt, die sich in der Unterbühne befand, während hängende Kulissenteile (arie) vom Schnürboden aus bedient wurden. Maschinen, die Göttererscheinungen, schwebende Wolken oder Erscheinungen aus der Unterwelt ermöglichten, waren ebenfalls Bestandteile dieser neuen Art der Bühnenraumgestaltung.

Die Umrahmung der Bühne versteckte die Technik vor den Blicken der Zuschauer. Diesen Proszeniumsbogen könnte man als erweiterte 'porta regia' der antiken scaenae frons bezeichnen.

Diese neue Kulissenbühne erwies sich für die Oper, deren Bühnenmaschinen immer komplizierter wurden, als geeigneter als das Periaktensystem.

Zur allgemeinen Ausstattung der barocken Bühne gehörte, neben den Kulissen, der in Einklang mit diesen zu wechselnde, perspektivisch bemalte Prospekt, der entweder hochgezogen oder versenkt wurde. Der hintere Bühnengraben, in dem z.B. Schiffe und Seeungeheuer bewegt werden konnten, gehörte ebenso dazu wie die durch Kurbeln zu drehenden

Spiralen zur Darstellung von Wellen. Lampen und Kerzen wurden für die Beleuchtungseffekte benötigt, wie z.B. Sonnenunter- und Sonnenaufgänge, bei denen die Kerzen entweder nacheinander verdeckt bzw. die Abblendungen nacheinander entfernt wurden. Blitze konnte man z.B. darstellen, indem blitzförmige Ausschnitte im Prospekt beleuchtet wurden. Außerdem gehörten Flugmaschinen zur Standardausrüstung.

Zu den typischen Szeneneffekten gehörten die schnelle Verwandlung des gesamten oder von Teilen des Bühnenbildes, die Verwendung von Ober- und Unterbühne ebenso wie die von Vorder- und Hinterbühne, das Hereinschweben von Wolken und deren Teilung, das Erscheinen von Göttern und Geistern und ihr Auf- und Abschweben.[34]

Die Reihenfolge der verschiedenen Schauplätze und die technischen Überraschungen waren eine Grundlage für die Anlage eines Librettos. Wichtig waren dabei die Kontraste der Schauplätze, z.B. folgte auf eine liebliche Landschaft eine Höllendarstellung. Auch der Wechsel von kurzer und langer Bühne gehörte dazu.

In den einzelnen Opernzentren, wie z.B. Rom und Venedig, wurde das Kulissensystem den jeweiligen Bedingungen entsprechend weiterentwickelt.

Die volle Ausbildung der Kulissenbühne und des Logen-Rang-Systems des Zuschauerraumes erfuhr die Oper in Venedig. Hier wurde 1637 das erste öffentliche Opernhaus (S. Cassiano) eröffnet. Damit standen nun die kommerziellen Interessen der jeweiligen Betreiber im Vordergrund, die vom zahlenden Besucher abhingen. Dessen Ansprüche wurden damit ausschlaggebend. Das Publikum wurde hauptsächlich von den sensationellen Verwandlungsmöglichkeiten der Bühne angelockt. Die ca. achtzehn Opernhäuser Venedigs versuchten, sich gegenseitig an prunkvoller Ausstattung und spektakulären Maschineneffekten zu übertreffen.

Giacomo Torelli (1608–1678) ist als der Hauptbühnenbildner der venezianischen Maschinenoper zu bezeichnen. Er leistete u.a. einen wichtigen Beitrag zur Weiterentwicklung der Bühnentechnik. 1641 führte er im Teatro Novissimo die zentrale Steuerung des Bühnenbildwechsels ein, der nun mit Hilfe eines einzigen Gegengewichtes durchgeführt werden konnte. Dadurch wurden schnellere und überraschendere Szenenwechsel möglich. In seinen Entwürfen wurden bestimmte Bühnenbildtypen ausgebildet, wie z.B. Ruinenlandschaft, Colonnaden, Wolkensäle, Theater auf dem Theater u.ä. Für die drei Akte der venezianischen Oper waren im Durchschnitt zwölf verschiedene Dekorationen üblich. Die einzelnen Grundtypen, Garten, Straße, Platz, Saal, Hof, Kerker, Fluß (Hafen), Wolken, Treppen, Grotten, Turm, Schlafzimmer,[35] wurden einzeln verwendet, konnten aber auch miteinander kombiniert werden. Gleiche Dekorationen wurden oft (wohl hauptsächlich aus finanziellen Gründen) für mehrere Opern verwendet und durch individuelle Ausstattung mit Requisiten dem Charakter des jeweiligen Stückes angepaßt.

Der venezianische Dekorationsstil verbreitete sich im Laufe der Zeit rasch im übrigen Verbreitungsgebiet der italienischen Oper, z.B. bis Wien oder München.

In Bologna erschien 1672 die erste Schrift, die sich ausschließlich mit den Problemen der perspektivischen Gestaltung der Kulissenbühne beschäftigte. Der Verfasser, Giulio Troili, beschreibt darin u.a. das Distanzpunktverfahren: der Abstand der Kulissen voneinander ist nach hinten zu verringern, damit die Zuschauer zusammenhängende Linien und Flächen wahrnehmen können. Troili beschäftigte sich auch schon theoretisch mit dem Problem der schräggestellten Kulissen, die Einblicke in die seitlichen Gassen verhindern sollten. In Bologna gab es bis dahin schon eine lange Tradition in der perspektivischen Malerei.[36]

In Wien entstand, neben Venedig, ein neues Zentrum der italienischen Oper. Der Venezianer Ludovico Ottavio Burnacini (1636-1707) prägte hier statt der venezianischen Maschinenoper den Typus der höfischen Prunkoper. Damit ergab sich ein neuer Ausgangspunkt für die Weiterentwicklung der Kulissenbühne. Burnacini lockerte die starre Raumgliederung auf, die noch für die Entwürfe Torellis charakteristisch war. Der zentralperspektivische Gesamteindruck blieb erhalten. Burnacini teilte die Bühne in drei 'Räume' ein, von denen zwei bespielbar und einer nur gemalt war.[37] Praktisch stellte sich das folgendermaßen dar: nach fünf Kulissenpaaren kam ein kleiner Zwischenraum, dann eine schmalere Gruppe von ebenfals fünf Kulissenpaaren und nach einem weiteren Zwischenraum der Prospekt. Diese Art der Gestaltung der barocken Tiefenbühne kam auch der neuen Art der Chorbehandlung zugute, denn der bewegte sich jetzt, laut Stadler,[38] axial von hinten nach vorn. Stadler charakterisiert die Wiener Variante der Bühnengestaltung u.a. unter folgendem Aspekt: 'Im übrigen ist hier jegliche Realität zugunsten phantastischer Bildwirkung aufgegeben'.[39]

Ein typisches Beispiel der Arbeiten Burnacinis für Wien sind die Entwürfe zu *Il pomo d'oro*.[40] Die Handlung, das Urteil des Paris, wurde zur Staffage für die 24 Bühnenbilder deren Berühmtheit sich bis heute erhalten hat – die Musik Cestis ist heute nahezu vergessen. Nach der Uraufführung für den Hof fanden zahlreiche öffentliche Vorstellungen statt, sodaß sich ihr Ruhm weit verbreitete.

Ein besonderes Handikap für die Bühnenbildner war die räumliche Beschränkung der Bühne, die der Phantasie oft praktische Grenzen setzte. Die Dualität von gemalter und natürlicher Perspektive konnte auch Burnacini nur in seinen Freilichtaufführungen überwinden.

1693-1700 erschien die Schrift des Jesuiten Andrea Pozzo *Tractatus perspectivae pictorum et architectorum*, in der er die Entwicklung der zentralperspektivischen Kulissenbühne theoretisch abschloß. Folgende Punkte charakterisieren die barocke Bühne in diesem Stadium der Entwicklung:

> das Orchester hat seinen Platz endgültig vor der Bühne
>
> der Fluchtpunkt der Perspektive liegt in der Mitte der Bühne (der Saalwand), hinter dem Schlußprospekt

der Augenpunkt befindet sich an der gegenüberliegenden Rückwand, d.h. der vornehmste Platz ist nicht mehr im Parkett, sondern endgültig in der Mittelloge

das Problem der Schrägkulissen ist jetzt auch praktisch gelöst.[41]

'In der malerischen Durchdringung der Perspektive liegt die große, oft allzu sehr unterschätzte und auf die Illusionsbühne des Spätbarock vorweisende Bedeutung von Pozzo'.[42]

Trotz der zahlreichen Verwandlungsmöglichkeiten blieb das Bühnenbild bis zu diesem Zeitpunkt (also fast 200 Jahre hindurch) streng zentralperspektivisch und lief Gefahr, z.B. durch bevorzugte und ständig wiederholte Motive, wie Baumalleen, Straßenfluchten, Colonnaden u.ä., in Schematismus zu erstarren.

Ferdinando Galli Bibiena durchbrach mit seinen Entwürfen dieses Schema. In seinem 1711 erschienen Traktat *L'Architettura civile* nannte er seine neue Art der Bühnenraumgestaltung 'vedere le scene per angolo' und erläuterte die mathematischen und theoretischen Bedingungen (Abb. 3).

Statt eines zentralen Fluchtpunktes, der den zentralperspektivischen und in die Unendlichkeit reichenden Raumeindruck entstehen ließ, haben seine Entwürfe mehrere Fluchtpunkte, die seitlich aus dem Bild herausführen. Die über Eck gestellten Bühnenbilder zeigen nur den Ausschnitt eines Raumes und beflügeln so die Phantasie des Zuschauers, der die Räume in Gedanken über den Bühnenausschnitt hinaus erweitern kann. Die Mächtigkeit der dargestellten Räume wird erhöht, obwohl der Bühnenraum selbst nicht vergrößert wird.[43] Die Spielfläche wird sogar kleiner, da die diagonalperspektivische Gestaltung die Bühnenraumtiefe verringert.

Dem 1711 erschienenen Traktat sind zahlreiche praktische Arbeiten vorausgegangen, mit denen Ferdinando den Ruhm seiner Familie begründete. Schon 1690 erregten seine Entwürfe Aufmerksamkeit und verschafften ihm Anstellungen in Parma und Piacenza. 1708 bekam er den Auftrag, die Festlichkeiten zur Hochzeit des spanischen Thronfolgers auszustatten. In der Folge wurde er dann, als Karl III. Kaiser geworden war (1711), am Hof in Wien angestellt. Doch er war nicht nur als Bühnenbildner berühmt, sondern auch als Architekt[44] und war ab 1716 als Lehrer an der Accademia Clementina in Bologna tätig.[45] In seinen theoretischen Schriften[46] gab er sein Wissen weiter.

Die Ähnlichkeit der Karrieren Ferdinando Galli Bibienas und Caldaras ist deutlich erkennbar. Beide erlangten den Gipfel ihrer Berühmtheit im Dienste des kaiserlichen Hofs in Wien, des einen Kunstform ist eng mit der des anderen verbunden. Beide verbrachten ihre vorbereitenden Jahre in Italien und beide machten die erste nahe Bekanntschaft mit dem andern und ihrem gemeinsamen späteren Dienstherrn in Barcelona. Vielleicht von grösserer Bedeutung ist die Tatsache, dass beide Künstler den höchsten Grad einer alten Tradition herbeiführten und eine neue Tradition einleiteten. In Italien führte Caldaras und Ferdinandos Einfluß zu jahrzehntelangen sogar jahrhundertelangen Errungenschaften auf den

Abbildung 3. Ferdinando Galli Bibiena — Studie für ein Bühnenbild 'per angolo'.

Gebieten der Oper und der Bühnenraumgestaltung. In Wien gaben die neuen dramatischen Möglichkeiten der 'per angolo'-Gestaltung und die neuen Reformlibretti Zenos und Metastasios Caldara die Gelegenheit, diese neuen Richtungen in seinen Opern weiter zu entwickeln.

Ferdinandos Bruder Francesco und sein Sohn Giovanni wurden ebenfalls berühmte Bühnenbilder. Es ist heute schwierig, die zahlreichen unsignierten Entwürfe den einzelnen Familienmitgliedern immer genau zuzuordnen. Außerdem ist es bis heute noch nicht gelungen, von wenigen Ausnahmen abgesehen, alle Opern, für die Ferdinando die Ausstattung entworfen hat, zu identifizieren.[47]

Die Bühnenbilder 'per angolo' traten ihren Siegeszug durch Europa an, verbreitet durch die Mitglieder der Familie Galli Bibiena[48] und zahlreiche Schüler.

Obwohl bei den Entwürfen Ferdinandos immer deutlich auch Elemente aus seinem Schaffen als Architekt zu erkennen sind (z.B. 'Freie Säulen'), waren seine Bühnenbauten reine Phantasie und wären als reale Bauten nicht auszuführen gewesen.

Anders die Entwürfe Filippo Juvarras, der ebenfalls als Architekt und Bühnenbildner tätig war. Die Bauten, die er für die Bühne entwarf, wären auch in der Realität zu bauen gewesen. Seine Entwürfe greifen das Prinzip des 'vedere per angolo' auf, doch die Bühne erhielt einen anderen Charakter. 'Hierbei konnte erstmals die Durchbrechung der seitlichen Kulissenstellung durch frei über die Bühne verteilte Kulissenteile nachgewiesen werden'.[49]

Die Änderung der Bühnenraumgestaltung muß auch im Zusammenhang mit einer veränderten Aufführungspraxis gesehen werden. Die Librettoreform Zenos und Metastasios führte zur Entstehung der *opera seria*. Die Personenzahl der Stücke wurde reduziert, die dramatische Handlung von Nebenhandlungen befreit und die komischen Rollen eingeschränkt. Die Szenen wurden dramaturgisch durch Rezitativ und Abgangsarie schematisiert. Die Arien — von der Strophenarie zur *da capo*-Arie, mit von den Sängern virtuos gestaltetem *da capo* entwickelt- rückten in den Mittelpunkt des Zuschauerinteresses. Für die Aufführungen dieser 'Arienopern' benötigte man weniger Platz, was der Ausstattung in der 'maniera per angolo' entgegenkam, denn hier geht Raum durch die Schrägstellung verloren. Die Arien wurden an der Rampe gesungen.[50] Die Dynamik der Aktionen im Bühnenraum, z.B. durch Flugmaschinen usw., wurde ersetzt durch eine Dynamisierung des Raumes selbst. Die räumliche Einheit, die durch die Zentralperspektive zwischen Bühne und Zuschauerraum gegeben war, wurde wieder aufgehoben. Die Zuschauer sind dadurch nicht mehr so intensiv in das Bühnengeschehen einbezogen, sie werden wieder zu reinen Betrachtern.

*   *   *   *   *

Ein kurzer Vergleich zwischen den Bühnenbildern der verschiedenen Entwicklungsphasen macht deutlich, daß sich Raumauffassung und Charakter der Bühnenräume im Laufe der Zeit immer wieder verändert haben. Diese Veränderungen geschahen aber nicht isoliert, sondern müssen immer auch im Zusammenhang mit allgemeinen Strömungen in allen künstlerischen Bereichen gesehen werden.

Die Bildbühne der Renaissance war statisch und fassadenähnlich aufgebaut. Der Raum war unveränderlich, und Dynamik, Bewegung entstand durch die Aktivitäten der Darsteller. Eine gewisse Strenge, verbunden mit klaren Linien und Raumaufteilungen, läßt sich auch in Architektur und Malerei der Renaissance wiederfinden. Die Fassaden, z.B. von Kirchen, geben keinerlei Aufschluß über den nachfolgenden Raum. Sie werden vorgeblendet und dienen als Selbstzweck, als beeindruckendes Schaubild. Der Mensch der Renaissance stand, mit seinem aus humanistischen Ideen und naturwissenschaftlichen Errungenschaften gewachsenen Selbstbewußtsein, der Welt aktiv gegenüber.

Die aus der Renaissancemalerei auf die Bühne übertragene Zentralperspektive führte dort zu einer Raumgestaltung, die den Zuschauer mit einbezog. Die optischen Begrenzungen der Bildbühne der Renaissance wurden aufgehoben und der Raum der barocken Kulissenbühne scheinbar ins Unendliche erweitert. Die Bühne ist nicht mehr Schaufront, sondern der Bühnen*raum* wird gestaltet, gegliedert und, etwa durch Flugmaschinen, nicht nur optisch erlebbar. Dieses Raumerlebnis ist auch für die barocke Architektur charakteristisch. Kirchenkuppeln z.B. wurden durch Illusionsmalerei optisch in die Unendlichkeit geöffnet. Auch die klaren Linien und Raumaufteilungen wurden abgelöst, beispielsweise durch ineinandergreifende quer- und längsovale Kuppeln und Gewölbe.

Der Mensch stand damit in der Unendlichkeit und war ihr und dem Raum ausgeliefert, hing ab vom göttlichen Willen. Er empfand sich als Figur im 'göttlichen Welttheater' und wurde, auch wenn er im Theater, der Oper saß, in den unendlichen Raum einbezogen. Der Fluchtpunkt der zentralperspektivischen Bühne reicht in die Unendlichkeit und damit in göttliche Bereiche. Genau gegenüber, im Augenpunkt und durch den Mittelstrahl mit dem 'göttlichen' Fluchtpunkt verbunden, hatte der Fürst seinen Platz, der in der absolutistischen Regierungsform des Barock seine Legitimation und Herrschaft als von Gott gegeben ansah.

Mit den über Eck gestellten Bühnenbildern Bibienas und Juvarras wird der Zuschauerraum optisch wieder von der Bühne getrennt, und der Besucher wird wieder zum bloßen Betrachter. Auch die durch den zentralperspektivischen Mittelstrahl gegebene Verbindung zwischen göttlichen Bereichen und den Fürsten wird damit aufgehoben.

Zusammen mit einer immer größeren bürgerlichen Zuschauergemein-schaft, lassen sich hier vielleicht schon frühe, noch unbewußte Hinweise auf das kommende Zeitalter der Aufklärung finden?

Anmerkungen

[1] z.B. die Reiseberichte des Freiherrn von Uffenbach (Universitätsbibliothek Göttingen, Cod.Uff.29/11), u.ä.

[2] Für Rom s. z.B.: Ursula Kirkendale *Antonio Caldara: Sein Leben und seine venezianisch-römischen Oratorien* (Graz-Köln, 1966) S. 44
Für Turin, z.B.: Mercedes Viale-Ferrero "Die Bühnenausstattung des 'Teatro Regio di Torino' (1667-1740)" *Hamburger Jahrbuch für Musikwissenschaft* 3 (1978) S. 239-72.

[3] In Frankreich z.B. überwog im Theater klassizistische Strenge, und am Beispiel der Arbeiten Joseph Furrtenbachs, der noch 1620, in Ulm, am Periaktensystem festhält, läßt sich unterschiedliche zeitliche Entwicklung feststellen.

[4] Torelli entwarf 1647 Bühnenbilder für Paris, Francesco Santurini ging 1650 nach München, Domenico und Gasparo Mauro arbeiteten ebenfalls in München, Alessandro Mauro ging nach Dresden, Giuseppe Galli-Bibiena arbeitete, außer in Venedig, auch in Wien, Dresden, München, Prag, Bayreuth, Berlin.

[5] Zur Librettoreform: Robert S. Freeman *Opera without Drama; Currents of Change in Italian Opera, 1675-1725*, (Ann Arbor, 1981).

[6] Ein ausführliches Werkverzeichnis (mit Arienverzeichnis und Inhaltsangaben) ist Bestandteil meiner, sich in Arbeit befindlichen, Dissertation mit dem Thema 'Die frühen szenisch-dramatischen Werke Antonio Caldaras'.

[7] Kirkendale *op.cit.*, S. 39 (dort auch weitere Literaturhinweise zu diesem Problem).

[8] Angaben in den Libretti

[9] Kirkendale *op.cit.*, S. 65

[10] Die genauen Quellenangaben und Fundorte werden ebenfalls dem Werkverzeichnis zu entnehmen sein.

[11] s. Anhang

[12] s. Anhang

[13] *L'Anagilda* Rom, 1711, 1.Akt

[14] *La costanza in amor vince l'inganno* Rom, 1711, 1. und 2. Akt.

[15] *La promessa serbata al primo* Venedig, 1697.

[16] Mantua, 1704, Libretto.

[17] Rom, 1711, Libretto.

[18] Prachtpartitur für den Wiener Hof (A-Wn: Mus.Hs.16692); abgebildet, zusammen mit Entwürfen, in: Mercedes Viale-Ferrero *Filippo Juvarra, scenografo e architetto teatrale*, (Turin-New York, 1970).

[19] Entwürfe *ibid.*

[20] Entwürfe und Abbildungen in:
(a) Elena Povoledo und Maria Teresa Muraro *Disegni teatrali dei Bibiena, Catalogo della mostra* (Venezia, 1970);   (b) Franco Mancini, Maria Teresa Muraro, Elena Povoledo, u.a. *Illusione e pratica Teatrale, Catalogo della mostra* (Venezia, 1975);   (c) Mario Monteverdi und Ercolano Murani *I Bibiena. Disegni e incisioni nelle collezioni del Museo Teatrale alla Scala* (Milano, 1975).

[21] Hellmuth Christian Wolff *Oper – Szene und Darstellung von 1600–1900, Musikgeschichte in Bildern* IV (Leipzig, o.d.) S. 7.

[22] Ausnahmen hiervon sind die Entwürfe Juvarras für das Teatro Ottoboni in Rom, das eine hochformatige Bühne hatte.

[23] Wolff *op.cit.,* S. 8.

[24] Margot Berthold *Weltgeschichte des Theaters* (Stuttgart, 1968) S. 105ff.

[25] *ibid.,* S. 133ff.

[26] In ihrer gedrängtesten Form war diese Art der Bühne noch im 16. Jahrhundert im Schultheater der deutschen Humanisten in Gebrauch.

[27] Das Teatro Olimpico wurde 1585 von Scamozzi nach Plänen Palladios fertiggestellt.

[28] Edmund Stadler 'Raumgestaltung im barocken Theater' *Kunstformen des Barock, Vierzehn Vorträge* hrg. Rudolf von Stamm (München–Berlin, 1956) S. 191.

[29] 1589 zur Hochzeit des Großherzogs Ferdinando de'Medici mit Christine von Lothringen. Abb. in Berthold *op.cit.,* S. 207 (Kostümentwürfe).

[30] Hans Tintelnot *Barocktheater und Barocke Kunst* (Berlin, 1939) S. 54.

[31] Die Zauberin Alcina war in diesem Zusammenhang ein beliebtes Sujet.

[32] Das erinnert an die Dekorationen des römischen Theaters. s. vorliegende Arbeit, S. 3–4.

[33] Berthold *op.cit.,* S. 303ff. und Viale-Ferrero 'Die Bühnenausstattung … ' *op.cit.,* S. 239ff.

[34] Wolff *op.cit.,* S. 9.

[35] Die Intimität von Schlafzimmerszenen war, lt. Wolff *op.cit.,* S. 9, eine Besonderheit der Venezianischen Oper.

[36] s. Anmerkung 20(b)

[37] Erinnerung an Serlios Spiel- und Bildbühne?

[38] Stadler *op.cit.,* S. 217.

[39] *Ibid.,* S. 218.

[40] Abb. in Mancini *et al, op.cit.*

[41] s. auch Viale-Ferrero 'Die Bühnenausstattung … ' *op.cit.,* S. 240.

[42] Stadler *op.cit.,* S. 222.

[43] Das macht dieses Prinzip auch heute noch für kleine Bühnen interessant.

[44] Beispiele in Mancini, Muraro, Povoledo *op.cit.,* s. Anmerkung 20(b).

[45] Ein Augenleiden zwang ihn, seine Arbeit einzuschränken. Er nahm Urlaub aus Wien und ging nach Bologna zurück.

[46] *L'Architettura civile preparata su la geometria, e ridotta alle prospettiva* (Parma, 1711). *Direzioni ai giovani Studenti nel disegno dell'Architettura civile* (Bologna, 1731–32).

[47] Neben den Katalogen s. auch Franz Hadamowsky *Die Familie Galli Bibiena in Wien* (Wien, 1962).

[48] *ibid.*

[49] Wolff *op.cit.*, S. 11.

[50] Pierluigi Petrobelli 'Lo spazio e l'azione scenica nell'opera seria settecentesca' *Illusione e pratica Teatrale* ... S. 25ff.

Anhang

Bühnenbildner der frühen Opern Antonio Caldaras

Francesco Galli Bibiena Ferdinando Galli Bibiena	*L'oracolo in sogno*	Mantua	1699
Ferdinando Galli Bibiena	*Il più bel nome*	Barcelona	1708
Ferdinando Galli Bibiena	*L'Atenaide*	Wien	1714
Ferdinando Galli Bibiena Giovacchino Pizzoli	*L'inimico generoso*	Bologna	1709
Pompeo Aldovrandini	*L'onesta nelli amori*	Genua	1705
Giuseppe Aldovrandini	*L'Arminio*	Genua	1705
Giovanni Speziga	*Paride sull'Ida*	Mantua	1704
Antonio Mauri	*La Partenope*	Ferrara	1709
Filippo Juvarra	*Giunio Bruto*	Wien	1711
Filippo Juvarra	*Tito e Berenice*	Roma	1714

L'Irene in Venice and Naples: tyrant and victim, or the *rifacimento* process examined

Olga Termini

Zusammenfassung

L'Irene in Venedig und Neapel: Tyrann und Opfer, oder der Rifacimento-vorgang untersucht

Als eine der Reformopern zeigt Frigimelica Robertis *L'Irene*, 1695 in Venedig mit Musik von Carlo Francesco Pollarolo uraufgeführt, eine ernste, einheitliche Handlung, psychologisch motivierte Charaktere, eine mäßige Anzahl von Arien, sehr wenige *ariosi, arie à 2*, und Duette, und nur ein Ensemble auf. Als die Oper 1704 für Neapel bearbeitet wurde, fiel das Libretto dem lokalen Geschmack und der offiziellen Theaterpolitik zum Opfer: komische Rollen in eingeschobenen Szenen wurden hinzugefügt, Rezitativzeilen ausgelassen und viele Arien hinzugefügt während die Intermezzi wegfielen. Die Musik wurde von Domenico Scarlatti, damals im frühesten Stadium seiner Laufbahn, bearbeitet und erweitert. Jedoch ein ins Einzelne gehender Vergleich der venezianischen Partitur mit der erhaltenen Ariensammlung vom neapolitanischen *Rifacimento* zeigte, daß Pollarolo auch einen bedeutenden Beitrag zu der Bearbeitung leistete: nicht nur wurden mehrere Arien beibehalten, sondern er komponierte auch Ersatzarien für die neue Besetzung. Ausserdem waren einige Scarlatti-arien Pollarolos venezianischen nachgebildet. Der *Rifacimento*-Vorgang selbst erwies sich als komplex und vielseitig, neben der Streichung und Beibehaltung schliesst er Revidierung, Neukomposition der vorherigen Texte, Ersetzung neuer Texte und Musik, Wiedereinsetzung von Texten, die in der venezianischen Partitur unterdrückt waren, und Hinzufügung neuer Arien, besonders für die neuen Rollen, ein.

L'Irene in Venice and Naples: tyrant and victim, or the *rifacimento* process examined

Olga Termini

T HE OPERAS OF Carlo Francesco Pollarolo (*c*1653–1723) — who, as an older contemporary of Antonio Caldara, undoubtedly was a model for the fledgling opera composer[1] — are inextricably tied to the so-called 'first reform'[2] of the late seventeenth-century opera libretto. For example, Apostolo Zeno's first libretto, entitled *Gl'inganni felici* (1695), was originally set to music by Pollarolo for the Venetian stage,[3] although an earlier opera on a libretto by Domenico David, *La forza della virtù* (1693), was perhaps the first in which Pollarolo showed reform tendencies.[4] One of the central figures of this reform was Girolamo Frigimelica Roberti (1653–1732), a Paduan librettist, librarian, architect and magistrate who supplied opera composers with libretti from 1694 to 1708.[5] His very first libretto, *Ottone* (1694), was set to music by Pollarolo for one of the most prestigious theatres in Venice, the Teatro San Giovanni Grisostomo. Among the six further settings by Pollarolo of Frigimelica Roberti's texts which were performed at the same theatre[6] was *L'Irene*, presented in 1694–95.[7]

Nine years later this opera was revived in Naples at the Teatro San Bartolomeo. The fact that Domenico Scarlatti contributed music to this production together with the survival of an Aria Collection containing examples by both Scarlatti and Pollarolo, has attracted some attention to the Neapolitan version.[8] There are thirty-two arias and one duet by Scarlatti, and twenty arias, two arias *à 2* and one duet by Pollarolo in this manuscript, located at the Conservatorio San Pietro a Maiella in Naples: MS A 512 'Arie con stromenti, / Dell'Irene / [crossed out: Musica degli Sigri Carlo Francesco / Pollaroli e] di Domenico Scarlatti'. Despite the change made to authorship in the title, the composers of these arias were nonetheless identified on the basis of the Naples libretto which calls the attention of the reader to the specific designation of the composer:

> Sappi intanto, che per non defraudare alla lode (che degnamente è dovuta al Sig. Gio. Battista Pullaroli [sic] primo compositore della Musica) si segneranno l'Arie del medesimo col segno § . Tutte l'altre sono del Sig. Domenico Scarlatti.[9]

It seems to have been a Neapolitan practice during this period to give credit to the composers of a *rifacimento*.[10] Needless to say, this identification of authorship is an invaluable aid to studies of operatic revisions such as the present one although, as we shall see, it does not tell the whole story.[11]

Until a few years ago the score of the original production of *L'Irene* in Venice was thought to be lost, but it is now preserved in Prague where it had been transferred after World War II from the archive of the Schwarzenberg Castle at Český Krumlov in Bohemia.[12] From a comparison of these manuscripts and libretti it is now possible to see just how 'drastically [Scarlatti] rewrote Pollarolo's *Irene*' for the Neapolitan stage.[13] Above all, we must consider what happened to Frigimelica Roberti's reform libretto when it was revived in Naples nine years after the Venetian première and what factors influenced the textual and musical changes made to the score. (See also the summary listing of the arias of the Venetian and Neapolitan versions given in the Appendix.)

L'Irene at Venice (1694-95)

Frigimelica Roberti's libretto is based on an old story from Matteo Bandello's *Novelle* first published in 1554.[14] After his conquest of Constantinople, the Sultan Mahomet falls in love with Irene (a captured Greek princess) to such an extent as to forget his duties as a ruler. The indignation of the janissaries almost leads to a rebellion. Finally, Mustapha, the Sultan's friend, dares to reproach him. Mahomet orders a meeting of the Grand Advisers and introduces his beloved to them. They are charmed by her beauty and ready to forgive Mahomet his weakness. But in order to show that nothing can keep him from defending the greatness of the empire, the Sultan decapitates the beautiful Irene before the assembled nobles.

The heroic-cruel motif was doubtlessly invented in the time of the Turkish danger to the Venetian Empire.[15] However, it certainly would not do for a late seventeenth-century Venetian opera with its mandatory *lieto fine*. In his *Argomento Istorico* the librettist explains that the Sultan (here called Memete), when faced with the reproaches of his nobles and the whole army, resolves to deprive himself of his beloved and generously steps aside in favour of Demetrio, Irene's fiancé. The Sultan carries out this resolution 'con modo impensato, e ferocemente generoso.'[16]

As is customary in Venetian operas of this period, the heroine (Irene) is paired with a lover (Demetrio) whom she was to marry with the approval of the Sultan prior to the latter's infatuation. A second pair consists of the Sultan's friend (Solimano) and Irene's sister (Deianira) who is, however, in love with Demetrio. Two further characters are Hali, grand vizier and confidant to Memete, and Olobolo, a servant. The plot of the opera consists of Irene's rejection of the Sultan's love by posing a condition which she thinks would be impossible for him to accept, namely to make her queen.[17] To her horror the Sultan accepts her condition, compelling Irene to reject him openly. Solimano's and Deianira's efforts to save Irene and her fiancé from the wrath of the spurned monarch seem in vain: the Sultan condemns the lovers to slavery, but in the end relents, renounces love, and chooses instead the road to glory ('della gloria il gran cammino').[18]

Frigimelica Roberti's concept of the drama is based on the Aristotelian *Poetics* as explained in the earlier libretto of *Ottone*, his first work for Venice. The success of this work encouraged the author to believe that good taste was not lost in Venice (' ... che in Venezia regna il buon gusto della Drammatica Poesia').[19] L'Irene is, according to Frigimelica Roberti, a 'simple' tragedy in which all the action is motivated by human passion ('la forza delle Passioni') rather than by external factors or unrecognized persons.[20] The plot is unified, involving all characters with increasing intensity as the play goes on. Throughout the five acts, Frigimelica Roberti's customary organization, Irene and Demetrio run the gamut of emotions, from joyful anticipation of their wedding, to despair at Memete's intentions, mutual reproaches and reaffirmations of their love, contemplation of suicide, hopelessness, death wishes and final rejoicing.

Although Frigimelica Roberti usually is preoccupied with the so-called three unities in his libretti, in L'Irene his interpretation of the unity of place is rather loose — the action shifts from the Imperial Palace of Constantinople to the Turkish camp outside the city. This, the librettist admits, is a concession to the importance of stagecraft (' ... per dare maggior comodo alla magnificenza delle Apparenze').[21] The unity of time is better preserved. The action takes place on the day of the 'Bairano', the Turkish Easter holiday, which gives rise to the festivities acted out in the *intermezzi*.

One important reform trait, the absence of comedy, is conspicuous in this opera. The tone is serious throughout. Even the most light-hearted character, Deianira, turns from frivolity to self-sacrifice and resignation. The only lower-class character in the opera is the servant Olobolo and his part is very small. He acts as adviser, messenger, and sounding board to Deianira, even criticizing her kind for spurning a faithful suitor in favour of some adventurous infatuation:

> Questo è il brutto di tutte le Belle
> Che l'ardor di conquiste novelle
> Le fa sprezzar chi l'ama
> Ed amar gl'incostanti, crudeli ... [22]

Frigimelica Roberti observes the *liaison des scènes*, another trait of the reform libretto,[23] rather carefully: there are only three breaks without set changes, one in Act I, between Scenes 5 and 6, one in Act II, between Scenes 2 and 3, and one in Act IV, between Scenes 2 and 3.

There are thirty-five arias in the libretto of *L'Irene*. The score contains thirty-three, all of which probably were sung in the production of 1694.[24] This relatively small total fits the pattern of a steady decline in the number of arias in Venetian operas in general and in Pollarolo's in particular, whether or not the libretti were written by reform-minded authors.[25] Most arias are exit-arias. Two notable exceptions are those opening Acts I and III — the arias for Hali which serve as introductions to the entrance of Memete.[26] In addition, there are three *arie in duetto* (that is, a strophic aria shared by two singers in succession, also known as an *aria à* 2), four actual duets, two *ariosi*, and one ensemble (the finale to the opera).

When *L'Irene* was premièred in Venice, Pollarolo was at the height of his popularity as a composer, producing a steady stream of opera scores for San Giovanni Grisostomo. His musical style was elaborate, especially in orchestration and in the aria structures.[27] Indeed, his *Prachtstil* coincided with his collaboration with the reform-librettists, especially Frigimelica Roberti.[28]

The cast for whom Pollarolo wrote *L'Irene* was the same as that of *Il pastore d'Anfriso*. Some of the singers had also appeared in *Ottone* in the preceding year. One of them, Tommaso Boni, who sang the small part of Olobolo in *L'Irene*, appeared in similar roles throughout the 1690s at that theatre.[29] The composer must have been thoroughly familiar with the singers' capabilities and tailored their parts to suit. For example, the castrato contralto, Francesco Ballarini, famous for his portrayals of tyrant roles, was perfectly cast as Memete.[30] Evidently a master of the 'rage-and-revenge' *aria agitata*, his arias in *L'Irene* (such as 'Guerra, guerra, voglio guerra' Act I, Scene 3) closely resemble those in *Ottone* (such as 'Terra, terra, che non t'apri' Act V, Scene 7) in vehemence, agitated *presto*-style and use of *coloratura*.[31] Ballarini's voice must have been powerful, for the orchestral accompaniments are quite full: solo trumpet, two oboes, timpani and five-part strings are called for in 'Guerra, guerra'. In addition, a sustained pedal in the voice part in this aria indicates some of the demands made on Ballarini's breath control. In view of all this, it is surprising to find the range of his arias rather narrow: in 'Guerra, guerra' it is limited to a ninth (a^I–b^{II}). In his second act aria 'Vincitor, terror del mondo', another *aria agitata* with *coloratura* featuring thirty-second runs and with an accompaniment of violins and violas doubling the bass-line, the range is only a minor seventh (d^I–c^{II}).

The title role was sung by Antonia Merzari, a young soprano who would have been at the beginning of her career, for Quadrio lists her as 'emerging in the 1690s'.[32] She also sang the leading parts in *Ottone* and *Il pastore d'Anfriso* and later appeared in Naples in *Tito Manlio* (by Pollarolo?) and in *Il prigioniero fortunato* (A. Scarlatti), both performed in 1698, as well as in Luigi Manzo's *La Partenope* (1699).[33] Her arias in *L'Irene* indicate that she had a flexible voice with a working range at least to g^{II} and that she was capable of varied expression from the lyric to the dramatic. Her partner was Valentino Urbani, '*musico* del Duca di Mantova',[34] who sang in Handel's operas in London (1711–13) and subsequently appeared again in Venice at least until 1719.[35] Although sometimes called an alto, Urbani definitely sang in a soprano range up to g[II]. In style and *tessitura*, his arias (notated in the soprano clef) are quite analogous with Merzari's with whom he also had duets in Acts I (*aria in duetto*), II, III (*aria in duetto*), and IV.

One of the most renowned singers in the cast was Diamante Maria Scarabelli who, according to Quadrio, was a '*Virtuosa del Duca di Mantova e degnamente celebrata*'.[36] Her appearance as Deianira in *L'Irene* must have come early in her career and was followed by innumerable engagements in Venice alone throughout the first two decades of the eighteenth century. Some of her arias in *L'Irene* place considerable demands on the singer — such as the extensive *coloratura* and widely-ranging lines of 'Gran tormento' (Act IV, Scene 10) (Ex. 1). The part of Solimano was sung by the alto castrato, Vincenzo Dati, '*Virtuoso dei Serenissimi di Mantova, e di Parma*'[37] who had appeared in two earlier Pollarolo operas, *La pace fra Tolomeo e Seleuco* (Piacenza, 1691) and *La forza della virtù* (Venice, 1693).[38] Dati's arias, like Ballarini's, tend to be narrow in range (a seventh or octave) and generally lie between c[I] and c[II]. Contrary to Memete's character, Solimano's calls for lyrical expression and the *parlando* style, and only rarely for dramatic force. The minor part of Hali (four arias in all) was sung by the bass, Giacomo Filippo Cabella, a singer from San Petronio, Bologna,[39] who had appeared in Legrenzi's opera *Eteocle e Polinice* (Milan) as early as 1684.[40]

Example 1. Pollarolo 'Gran tormento' Venice, Act IV, Scene 10

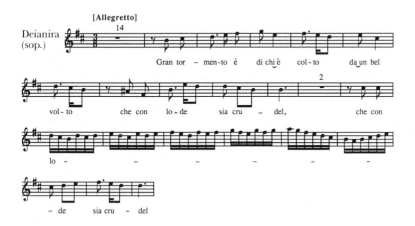

Venice was known for its love of the stage spectacle. Sumptuous sets and numerous set changes were *de rigueur*. As we have seen, Frigimelica Roberti used this necessity as an excuse for his loose interpretation of the unity of place in *L'Irene* and specified in his libretto that the action occur in:

Act I: Scenes 1-4:
                Great loggia of the Imperial palace with Turkish-style throne, completely illuminated. View of the similarly illuminated city.
                Scenes 5-8:
                A sumptuously furnished room.

Act II: Shaded garden of the Imperial palace.

Act III: Scenes 1-2:
                Coast of Constantinople; on one side the infantry, on the other the naval forces on the point of formal departure. The ship's stern changes into a richly decorated bridge above which a triumphal arch is erected.
                Scenes 3-8:
                Imperial gallery partly destroyed by the war.

Act IV: A building of beautiful design in the Imperial palace.

Act V: Scenes 1-3:
                Great pavilion in the Turkish camp.
                Scenes 4-6:
                The pavilion opens to reveal the entire camp with pavilions and tents. The throne for Irene's coronation.
                Scene 7:
                The encampment is removed to make room for the departure of the army, led by the great Ruler.[41]

These detailed descriptions, paraphrased in part in the above translation, stress the emphasis placed on the richness of the decorations, lighting effects, picturesque sets such as ruins and gardens, and on grand vistas or panoramic views. A favourite effect was the stunning transformation on the open stage: thus the ship's stern became a bridge with triumphal arch in Act III, while in Act V two such *coups d'oeil* climaxed the whole opera. This elaborate staging together with the four lavish between-acts ballet-*intermezzi* in which the Turkish theme was acted out in pantomime dances,[42] must have made this opera a spectacular visual entertainment, ensuring its success with the Venetian public. Yet with only two mid-act scene changes, the flow of the action within acts was scarcely interrupted by these visual extravaganzas. The *intermezzi*, being wordless pantomime dances, were not part of the drama nor, in all probability, of the librettist's design for his 'semplicissima' Irene.[43]

L'Irene at Naples (1704)

L'Irene was not the first opera by Pollarolo to be remade for Naples. *Tito Manlio*, performed there in 1698, was probably a *rifacimento* of the Pratolino version of the work.[44] In the following year Pollarolo's *Creonte, tiranno di Tebe*, and *Gl'inganni felici*[45] as well as a new version of *La forza della virtù*[46] were also presented at San Bartolomeo in Naples. Neither was *L'Irene* Domenico Scarlatti's first Neapolitan *rifacimento*.

Maometto in costante.

L'IRENE

DRAMA PER MUSICA

Da rapprefentarfi nel Teatro di
S. Bartolomeo. di Napoli

DEDICATO

All'Illuftrifs.ed Eccellentifs.Sig.

IL SIGNOR

D. MERCURIO ANTONIO

LOPEZ, FERNANDEZ, PACECCO, A CUGNA, GIRON, E PORTOCARRERO,

Conte di S. Stefano de Gormaz,&c. Maeftro di
Campo,&c. Capitano delle Guardie Alema-
ne , Figlio dell' Eccell. Signor Duca d'
Afcalona, Marchefe di Vigliena,&c.
Vicerè, e Capitan Generale in
quefto Regno di Napoli.

IN NAPOLI 1704.
Per il Parrino , & il Mutio.

Con Licenza de' Superiori .
Si vende nella Stampa di Michele Luigi Mutio
fotto l'Infermaria di S.M.la Nova.

Plate 1. Title-page of the libretto for the *rifacimento* version of *L'Irene*, Naples, 1704.
(US-Wc: Schatz 9539)
Reproduced by permission of the Music Division of The Library of Congress, Washington

He had tried his hand earlier with *Ottavia restituita al trono* (San Bartolomeo, 1703) and *Il Giustino* (Palazzo Real, 1703), tasks entrusted to him during the absence of his father, Alessandro.[47] During this period Domenico was hoping (in vain, as it proved) to be elected *primo maestro* at the Neapolitan court, and his musical style, as we find in his early sonatas, was very much in agreement with his Italian contemporaries. Pestelli speaks of an 'archaic patina' which adhered to his music at this time and which in no way suggested the direction or the greatness of his future career as a keyboard composer.[48] Thus it was a relatively inexperienced nineteen-year-old who was assigned to adapt the veteran composer's score for the Neapolitan stage.

It is not certain who revised Frigimelica Roberti's libretto for Naples[49] but it must have been done in some haste. Nicola Barbapiccola, the impresario who mounted the performance, dedicated the libretto to the current 'tyrant' of Naples, the Viceroy Don Mercurio Antonio Lopez, and in it he refers to 'qualche alteratione della sua prima forma' that had been necessary in order to produce the opera in a short period of time.[50]

Among the most striking changes are the reorganisation of the five-act structure into three acts and the introduction of comic characters and scenes. The changes in the number of acts is somewhat superficial; the original scenes are, for the most part, kept intact in the new organisation. The addition of three characters of servant status represents a more drastic move. Of these, Lesbia, as lady-in-waiting to Irene, is not a comic character *per se* and therefore is well integrated into the basic plot. However, the other two, Dori, a maid, and Nuto, the gardener, are a comic pair and the protagonists of a mini sub-plot, such as it is. With the scenes newly written for these characters added to the opera, the redistribution of the acts and scenes of the Venetian original became:

Table 1. *Redistribution of acts and scenes*

| Venice | | Naples | Interpolated scenes | |
			Lesbia & Irene	Dori & Nuto
Act I, Scenes 1–8	=	Act I, Scenes 1–8		
Act II, Scenes 1–2	=	Act I, Scenes 9–10		
			Act I, Scene 11	
				Act I, Scene 12
Act II, Scene 3	=	Act II, Scene 1		
			Act II, Scene 2	
Act II, Scenes 4–6	=	Act II, Scenes 3–5		
				Act II, Scene 6

Table 1. (contd)

Venice		Naples	Interpolated scenes	
			Lesbia & Irene	Dori & Nuto
Act III, Scenes 1-8	=	Act III, Scenes 7-13 (omits Scene 6 of Venice)		
Act IV, Scenes 1-8	=	Act II, Scenes 14-15 Act III, Scenes 1-6		
Scenes 9-10	=	Scene 7		
				Act III, Scenes 8-9
Act V, Scenes 1-7	=	Act III, Scenes 10-16		

We see from this that the scenes of the comic sub-plot have been placed either at the end of an act, as for Act I, or at the point corresponding to the end of an act in Frigimelica Roberti's Venetian libretto. Thus even these interpolated scenes form less of an interruption of the original scheme of action than might be expected. Indeed, Scene 9 in the third act forms a subtle bridge to Scene 10 (originally the beginning of a new act) by means of the parallelism in the situation between Dori and Nuto, and Deianira and Solimano, respectively. The parodistic intent is clearly reflected even in the specific words of advice given by the two women to their respective lovers:

Act III, Scene 9	Act III, Scene 10
Dori: Servimi, e spera, ch'io Desio d'amata esser così.	Deianira: Se tu speri che un dì t'ami O contenta pur mi brami Servi, servi, e poi chi sa.[51]

In terms of the amount of added material, these six new scenes consist of nine arias and 156 lines of recitative.[52] However, not counting replacements or substitutions, other additions or interpolations bring the total to twenty-four arias and 169 lines of recitative — a sizeable expansion of the Venetian original.

This new material is distributed rather unevenly among the characters. The part of the servant, now named Alete, is increased by five arias (Act I, Scenes 5 and 10; Act II, Scenes 9 and 11, and Act III, Scene 11) and a few lines of introductory recitative. As the part was sung by an unnamed '*Virtuoso Napoletano*' this expansion was due more, perhaps, to a local interest in the delineation of lower-class characters than to the specific status of the singer. The other characters who received additional arias were Demetrio (in Act I, Scenes 4 and 10; Act II, Scenes 9 and 11, and Act III, Scene 11), Irene (in Act I, Scene 11, and Act III, Scenes 6 and 13), Deianira (in Act I, Scene 9, and Act III, Scene 10), Solimano (in Act II, Scenes 4 and 8, and Act III, Scene 15), Halì (in Act I, Scene 2, and Act III, Scene 14), Lesbia (in Act I, Scene 11;

Act II, Scene 2, and Act III, Scene 8), Dori (in Act I, Scene 12; Act II, Scene 6, and Act III, Scene 8) and Nuto (in Act I, Scene 12, and Act II, Scene 6).

In some instances these new numbers[53] were created by the conversion of existing *ariosi* into arias. One example of this procedure is Deianira's 'Ogni amante ha un bel momento' which as an *arioso* in the Venetian score (Act III, Scene 7), consisted of three lines of text. In the Neapolitan libretto (Act II, Scene 12) this text was expanded into a four-line aria, the extra line being required by the conversion of the third line into a conditional clause.

Venice	Naples
Ogni amante ha un bel momento	Ogni amante ha un bel momento
Se nol coglie, è per sua colpa	Se nol coglie, è per sua colpa
Che mai più non sia contento.	Se mai più non sei contento
	Non già me, te stessa incolpa.

The musical expansion, however, is much more extensive: the four bars of *arioso* are replaced by a *da capo* aria with violin obbligato. Although the aria is of modest proportions (*A*-section: 22 bars, *B*-section: 14 bars), the instrumental introduction and interlude, the musical elaboration of repeated text phrases within each section, and, of course, the return of the *A*-section, all elevate the four lines to new importance and independence (Ex.2).

It is obvious that such substantial additions added considerably to the total length of the opera. Some compensation came through the omission of the *intermezzi* but primarily through extensive cuts in recitative lines. A total of 209 lines are deleted throughout the opera to produce a more action-oriented drama.

Seldom are passages of fast exchange-dialogue omitted, even in long recitative scenes.[54] But descriptions of varying emotions, vacillations between different moods, evocations of memories, suggestions of larger historical issues, explanations of a character's motivation, further argumentations — all are curtailed to streamline the play or simply to make room for the above-mentioned additions.

Many historical references are dropped, such as Memete's lines in which he compares himself with Caesar and Alexander the Great who were lovers as well as heroes (Act I, Scene 2). Elaborations of a given statement, especially those cast in poetic effusions replete with metaphors, in the Venetian original, vanish from the Neapolitan revision. Referring to his impending wedding day, Demetrio says 'Giorno beato! O fortunato giorno!' in the condensed Neapolitan revision. In Venice he went on: 'Bell'espero seren de'miei tormenti, Aurora e primo sol de'miei contenti.'[55] Moreover, the broad generalisation to which Frigimelica Roberti frequently leads a character from the contemplation of a specific situation is often deleted from the Neapolitan version. For example, in Act II, Scene 13, in a monologue which follows his foolhardy promise to Deianira to save Irene from the love or wrath of the tyrant, Solimano considers his folly with the words: 'Ahimè che feci? Ahimè che dissi? O amore

Example 2
(a) Pollarolo 'Ogni amante' Venice, Act III, Scene 7
(b) Scarlatti 'Ogni amante' Naples, Act II, Scene 12

(a)

(b)

no sei no cieco tu, ma gli altri acciechi.' He then sings an aria expressing essentially the same lament, 'Crudo tiranno amore'. However, in Venice, he continued thinking over his situation, coming to the general conclusion:

> Non è più tempo di mutar pensiero
> Troppo, troppo m'ho aperto.
> Quando il riparo è incerto,
> Rimedio è de l'error seguir l'errore[56]

His subsequent aria text, 'Grand'amante è grand'imprudente'[57] (not used in either Venice or Naples), was a further generalization applying to both himself and the Sultan.

At times these omissions also affect the characterisations, especially that of the Sultan. In the Venetian libretto which plays on the audience's animosity towards the Turks, Memete is seen as a personification of Turkish cruelty. The Neapolitan libretto tones down this aspect of the tyrant by omitting such lines as:

Act I, Scene 7	Act I, Scene 8
Solimano: Impune non s'offende Amor così potente ... Deh, non aspetta Che Memete ti mostri Quante' è forte il suo Ardor con la vendetta.	Demetrio: Anime disperate Nel vivo orror de la Tartarea morte ... [58]

The pronounced trend towards a personalised or first-person approach in the new aria texts in the Neapolitan libretto brings a more intimate 'directness' to the opera. For example, Solimano's 'Chi non può vincere amore' (Venice, Act I, Scene 4) is replaced with 'Per godere il mio tesoro' (Naples, Act I, Scene 4):

Venice	Naples
He who cannot vanquish love Should try to win his lover ...	To enjoy my treasure for whom I long and die ...

Sometimes a simple reversal of the position of juxtaposed words or images in two aria texts of related content could result in radically different aria types, textually as well as musically. In the Venetian version, Pollarolo gave Memete's aria text 'Guerra, guerra' (Act I, Scene 3) an *agitata* setting which highlighted the keyword 'war'. What was basically the same sentiment but voiced in reverse order, generated music of a quite opposite character in the aria added for Halì in the Neapolitan libretto ('Amante, e insiem guerriero, esser ben puote un cor' Act I, Scene 2). The word 'lover', now coming first, elicited a more lyrical setting in a flowing 12/8 metre from the composer, Domenico Scarlatti. Through this reversal of keywords the librettist was able to manipulate the aria types to accord with those favoured and desired by the local audiences and, at the same time, provide for dramatic and musical variety in otherwise very similar texts (Ex. 3).

Example 3
(a) Pollarolo 'Guerra, guerra' Venice, Act I, Scene 3
(b) Scarlatti 'Amante, e insiem guerriero' Naples, Act I, Scene 2

It is difficult to assess the role of the staging in the Neapolitan version of *L'Irene*. The 'locations' are the same as in Venice but they are much more briefly described. While this may be a quirk on the part of the librettist, it may also indicate a reduction of those stage effects so dear to the hearts of the Venetian audiences.

The Neapolitan production was prepared, of course, for a new set of singers, most of whom had appeared in other operas there, and almost all in *Il Giustino*. Perhaps the most interesting feature is the casting of a woman in the role of the tyrant Memete. She is listed as *'La Signora Angiola Magliani Romana, Virtuosa dell'Eminentiss. Cardinal dei Medici'*.[59] Evidently male parts were her specialty for she sang Anastasio in *Il Giustino*[60] and Tolomeo in *Il più fedele tra Vasalli* (1705).[61] The changes in her arias indicate that, compared to Francesco Ballarini, her voice and style were not quite so *fiero*. The *aria agitata* from the Venetian score, 'Vincitor, terror del mondo' (Act II, Scene 5) which with its dotted rhythms and *coloratura* in thirty-second runs clearly was crafted for Ballarini, reappears substantially revised in the Neapolitan collection (Act II, Scene 4). The opening, now in even *parlando* rhythm, has lost its bite, *coloratura* is reduced, and complex rhythms are eliminated from the vocal line. Pollarolo must have altered this aria deliberately to accommodate Magliani's limitations, for he retained most other characteristics of the original version such as key, form, length, bass pattern and unison-orchestration[62] (Ex. 4).

Example 4
(a) Pollarolo 'Vincitor, terror del mondo' Venice, Act II, Scene 5
(b) Pollarolo 'Vincitor, terror del mondo' Naples, Act II, Scene 4

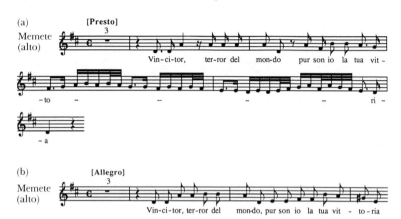

In other instances, Pollarolo seems to have accommodated Magliani by reducing the instrumentation of her arias. Whereas in Venice 'Il mio amore ti fa regina' (Act V, Scene 4) had a five-part accompaniment, Pollarolo set its replacement for Naples (Act III, Scene 13) with a lighter instrumentation featuring a violin obbligato. However, according to the libretto, Magliani was still expected to sing the bravura aria 'Guerra, guerra' of the Venetian version[63] and her first-act aria 'Sento una forza' with *basso continuo* was left nearly unchanged.[64]

Maria Angelica Bracci, also employed by the Cardinal dei Medici, sang the part of Irene. This singer appeared in at least six other operas in Naples[65] and Venice from 1710.[66] There seem to be few, if any, singer-induced changes in her arias, suggesting that her voice was comparable to Antonia Merzari's. The Neapolitan Demetrio was an unidentified '*virtuoso*' of the court chapel while Deianira was sung by Vittoria Nassinbene from Mantua. Her voice must have lain considerably higher than Diamante Scarabelli's, her Venetian counterpart, as her first act aria 'Non ha pena l'amor più crudele' is transposed up a minor third (from A to C major) which extends its range to a top a^{II}. When the librettist replaced her Venetian aria 'Non chiedo amor non più' with 'Più non voglio il cor amante' (Act II, Scene 9), Scarlatti wrote a quite different, more ambitious composition. An opening ricercar motive, a polyphonic texture, an expanded vocal range (up to b^{II}), an enlarged form and extensive *coloratura*, all give a new dimension to the character of Deianira as she renounces her love for Demetrio with a dramatic gesture (Ex. 5).

Example 5
(a) Pollarolo 'Non chiedo amor' Venice Act III, Scene 3
(b) Scarlatti 'Più non voglio' Naples, Act II, Scene 9

(a)

Deianira
(sop.)

Non chie-do a-mor non più, di-man-do cru-del - tà

(b)

[Allegro]

Deianira
(sop.)

Più   non   vo – glio   il cor a – man – te

The revision of Solimano's part for Giovanni Rapaccioli, '*Virtuoso dell'Eccellentis. Sig. Principe di Montesarchio*',[67] presents a somewhat puzzling picture. Scarlatti wrote his five new arias for this singer in the soprano clef.[68] Yet two of Pollarolo's original alto arias are also retained in the Aria Collection. Moreover, one of the two new arias Pollarolo wrote for Naples ('Mal resiste la beltà' Act 1, Scene 7) is in the alto clef with the same narrow range as the corresponding Venetian aria (d^I–c^{II}), while the other (L'amore oltraggiato' Act III, Scene 4) is in the soprano clef with a range from g^I to f^{II}. If the singer was capable of spanning both ranges, we would expect the new arias to do likewise instead of lying in one or the other narrow *tessitura*. Perhaps the most plausible explanation is that Pollarolo still thought in terms of an alto for the part, that Scarlatti wrote for the soprano Rapaccioli, and that 'L'amore oltraggiato' has been misattributed. Even so, the question remains: if the alto arias were retained only for the Collection and not for the performance, what did Rapaccioli sing in their stead?

The part of Halì was sung by Domenico's uncle, Tommaso Scarlatti, a tenor who sang many serious and comic parts in Naples, from about 1703 to 1740. All three arias allotted Halì were newly composed by Domenico Scarlatti[69] as was all the music for Alete. This latter part, however, moves downward from the alto range of Tommaso Boni to the tenor range of the unidentified Neapolitan singer.[70] Since Olobolo, the servant in the Venetian version had no arias to sing, the assignment of a tenor to the expanded servant role represents some balancing of the increasingly top-heavy vocal ranges of the cast. The trend toward higher *tessiture* is especially noticeable in the parts for Deianira, Solimano, and Halì (see Table 2). Although Giacomo Filippo Cabella, the Venetian Halì, is sometimes described as a tenor, his arias are appreciably lower in *tessitura* than those of Tommaso Scalatti. Perhaps it is significant that no Venetian arias notated in the bass clef (that is, Halì's arias) have been included in the Aria Collection. The Neapolitan *L'Irene* reflects the contemporary move of Italian opera into the high vocal ranges.

Table 2. *Alterations of vocal ranges*

	Venice	Naples
Irene	soprano	soprano
Demetrio	soprano	soprano
Memete	alto castrato	female alto
Deianira	soprano	high soprano
Solimano	alto	soprano
Halì	bass	tenor
Olobolo/Alete	alto	tenor

Rifacimento techniques: *L'Irene* remade

Except for the cuts discussed above, the recitative texts in the two libretti correspond very closely to each other. Naturally, new recitative had to be composed for the six added scenes and for the few lines interpolated here and there, and cadences had to be adjusted at places of deletion. We might be tempted to assume, however, that the music for the bulk of the unchanged text was left intact in the revision of the score. This was probably not the case. Musical recomposition was likely to be fairly extensive, primarily because the vocal ranges or *tessiture* of four singers in the Neapolitan cast were different (see Table 2). Their lines would have been rewritten or transposed. In scenes of dialogue, the other characters' responses also would have been changed in order to dovetail with the new recitative lines. Moreover, a new aria in a different key or with an altered modulatory scheme would have necessitated changes in the preceding recitative because the old cadence would no longer fit. Unfortunately, in the absence of the Neapolitan full score, we cannot tell to what extent the recitatives were revised.[71] We do know, however, that the arias received a tremendous amount of attention. It was not simply a question of dropping some and writing new ones. To be sure, new arias were added but a comparison of the Venetian score and the Neapolitan Aria Collection shows that procedures of deletion, retention, revision, substitution, restoration and addition were all involved in the remodelling of *L'Irene*.

Deletion. If we understand this to mean the omission of an aria without a replacement, we can say that according to the libretto, there are no deletions. In the Aria Collection, however, two of Memete's arias, two for Halì and one for Deianira[72] are dropped. We also find one duet between Irene and Demetrio ('Fuggo/Fuggi' Act IV, Scene 1, in Venice) deleted from the Neapolitan libretto and replaced by an aria for Demetrio (Act II, Scene 14).[73] One other duet, between Solimano and Halì ('Su, su s'armi' Act V, Scene 4 in Venice), is omitted from the Collection but not from the libretto (Act III, Scene 13 in Naples). And among the lines deleted from the original Act III, Scene 4, is 'Siamo ben miseri', a short *arioso* for Irene.

Retention. Eight arias, two *arie in duetto* and one duet were taken over from the Venetian score without any change whatsoever except for slight differences in notation. These represent a little more than one fourth of the vocal numbers.[74] Deianira's aria 'Non ha pena' (Act 1, Scene 5 in Venice; Act I, Scene 5 in Naples), the only example of a simple transposition, may also be included here.

Revision. Here we encounter the greatest diversity. Pollarolo's substantial modification of 'Vincitor, terror del mondo' for Angiola Magliani has already been described (see Ex. 4) but in her 'Su presto a godere' (Act IV, Scene 5 in Venice; Act III, Scene 3 in Naples) he was content only to remove the tenor viola.

In some cases it is difficult to understand the reason for a revision. The Venetian and Neapolitan settings, both by Pollarolo, of 'Sperar degg'io, sì o nò' are so similar to each other that we may wonder why he bothered to revise the aria. Both versions are in A major, in 4/4 metre, and are identical in range (e^I–f-sharp^{II}) and in form. The revision is shorter (twenty rather than thirty-one bars) and has a different bass-line, a *quasi*-ostinato figure instead of a line which anticipates the opening phrase of the melody, but the theme retains its original shape even though its *parlando* flow gives way to a slightly more march-like motive:

Example 6
(a) Pollarolo 'Sperar degg'io' Venice, Act IV, Scene 2
(b) Pollarolo 'Sperar degg'io' Naples, Act II, Scene 15

Scarlatti revised Pollarolo's aria for Demetrio, 'Si viva, si mora' (Act I, Scene 8 in both versions), along similar lines. Again the basic melodic shape is retained but the short-winded *parlando* becomes a more flowing, if rather four-square, theme in ₵ time:

Example 7
(a) Pollarolo 'Si viva, si mora' Venice, Act I, Scene 8
(b) Scarlatti 'Si viva, si mora' Naples, Act I, Scene 8

Ex. 7 (contd)

(b)

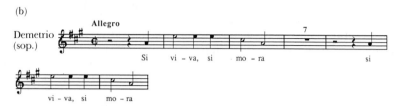

However, in the curtailing of the *coloratura* patterns and the thinning of the accompaniment from five to three parts, we find changes that may have been occasioned by the singer's abilities. Both versions have the usual sustained note on the word 'costanza', but in Venice Pollarolo obviously expected Valentino Urbani to sing a long *fioritura* leading into the pedal note and to follow it with an elaborate cadential finish:

Example 8
(a) Pollarolo 'Si viva, si mora' bars 18–45
(b) Scarlatti 'Si viva, si mora' bars 15–22

(a)

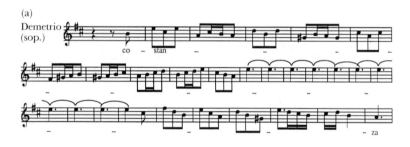

(b)

Substitution. As we would expect in a *rifacimento*, aria substitution is the most prevalent practice. We can distinguish six procedures among the twenty examples the two composers contributed to this category: aria replacing aria on the same text, aria with a new text replacing aria, aria replacing *arioso*, aria replacing recitative, aria replacing a duet, and duet replacing duet.

Table 3. *Aria substitution in* L'Irene

(1) Substitution with the same text
  'Mal resiste la beltà'
  'Il far schiavo'
  'Misero amante core'
  'Il mio amore'
  'Belle catene/Dolce
    piacere (*aria à 2*)'
	Pollarolo

'Su, di metalli'*
  'Per lei caro'
  'Sii pur fedele'
  'Vivi, o caro'*
	Scarlatti

(2) Substitution with a new text
  'Per godere'
  'Più non voglio'
  'Crudo tiranno amore'
  'Ciò nol concedo'
	Scarlatti

(3) Aria replacing *arioso*
  'Il mio contento'
  'Ogni amante'
  'Non più amore per me')
	Scarlatti

(4) Aria replacing recitative
  "Perchè sprezzar
    chi t'ama'
  'Del destino gl'eventi'
	Scarlatti

(5) Aria replacing duet 'Dimmi s'havrà mai fin'	Scarlatti
(6) Duet replacing duet 'Io t'amo/Tu m'ami'	Scarlatti

* Close to being revisions

In replacing his 'Belle catene', an *aria in duetto*, with another on the same text (Act I, Scene 6, both versions), Pollarolo retained the musical structure, vocal range, accompaniment type (*basso continuo* only), and general style of the original. But he changed the key from C major to c minor, and the modulatory scheme from an extremely simple tonic-dominant-tonic progression to a more varied movement to the relative major and its dominant. The original melody, reflecting the chain-image of the text, revolved around the tonic; it was replaced with a soaring line in a *quasi-sarabanda* rhythm (Ex. 9).

Example 9
(a) Pollarolo 'Belle catene' Venice, Act I, Scene 6
(b) Pollarolo 'Belle catene' Naples, Act I, Scene 6

(a)

Demetrio
(sop.)

Bel - le   ca – te - ne_____   co - stan   so - spi – ri

(b)

Demetrio
(sop.)

Bel - le   ca   - te - ne   co - stan   so   -   spi – ri

The bass, too, was changed from cadential support to a line that moved in similar and contrary motion and in rhythmic counterpoint to the melody.

One reason for the change in tonality may lie in the new musical context. In Venice the previous scene had ended with Deianira's A major exit aria 'Non ha pena'. But in the Neapolitan version, with this aria transposed to C major and followed by a new aria for Alete, also in C major, the selection of a key *other* than C major for 'Belle catene' became essential. The choice of the minor mode in such circumstances seems a characteristic of the revised opera. Scarlatti's use of a minor for his new version of Demetrio's 'Per lei caro' (Act II, Scene 9) links it to, while contrasting it with, Irene's substituted aria in C major in the preceding scene. In the Venetian score both arias were in B-flat major.

Of Scarlatti's four arias on new texts which replace other arias and their texts, two are for the soprano Rapaccioli who sang Solimano's part. The replacement of 'Non chiedo amor non più' with 'Più non voglio' for Vittoria Nassinbene (discussed above) represents his most independent work in the adaptation of the opera (see Ex. 5).

There are three places where *ariosi* in the Venetian score (Act II, Scene 1; Act III, Scene 7; Act IV, Scene 8) are replaced with arias, two of these utilizing the original texts (see Ex. 2). Some of the deleted recitative is replaced with arias. For example, Olobolo/Alete's generalization 'Questo è il brutto' (Act II, Scene 2 in Venice) is replaced by an entrance aria with words to the same effect 'Perchè sprezzar chi t'ama' (Act I, Scene 10 in Naples).

Restoration. We find several aria texts which were suppressed or replaced in the Venetian production[75] restored in the Neapolitan version. 'Piangete, occhi, piangete', replaced in the Venetian score by 'A morire', resurfaces in a setting by Pollarolo in the Neapolitan score (Act III, Scene 7). The vehement, desperate *affetto* of 'A morire' gives way to the melancholy and lyrical — as death gives way to love. While the two texts show this transformation within a closely parallel structure:

Venice	Naples
A-section	
A morire, a morir	Piangete, occhi, piangete
ne'mali estremi	stillate in lagrime
è il sol rimedio	sia tutto pianto
il disperar.	chi è tutto amor.
B-section	
Nel gran dividersi	Nel gran dividersi
d'alma con alma	d'alma con alma
non sa più vivere	sia tutto pianto
chi seppe amar.	chi è tutto amor.

the musical settings differ considerably. The aria type, determined by the keywords of the first stanza, is radically altered by the move away from 'morir', 'estremi', and 'disperar' in the Venetian version to 'piangete', 'lagrime', and 'piano' in the Neapolitan (Ex. 10). The four-part orchestration (with alto and tenor viola parts) of 'Piangete' may indicate that the music originally had been composed for the Venetian production but was dropped for the sake of the singer. (Scarlatti's four-part accompaniments invariably feature two violin parts, one viola part in the alto clef, and bass.) This aria, Pollarolo's 'Misero amante core' (Act II, Scene 8) and Scarlatti's setting of 'Vivi, o caro' (Act III, Scene 11) are the only extant arias that replaced settings originally given smaller instrumentations.[76]

Example 10
(a) Pollarolo 'A morire, a morir' Venice, Act IV, Scene 9
(b) Pollarolo 'Piangete, occhi, piangete' Naples, Act III, Scene 7

(a)

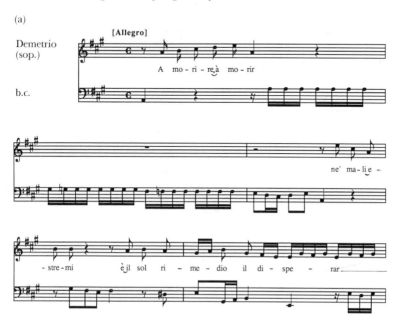

Ex. 10 (contd)

(b)

Ex. 10 (contd)

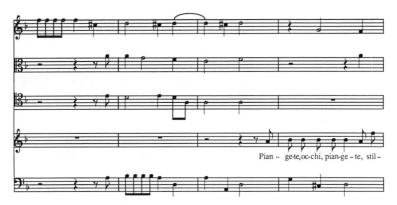

Scarlatti provided the music for 'Vo'dividere il mio affetto', restored in Act II, Scene 7 of the Neapolitan libretto after being replaced by 'Con la gloria', an aria for Ballarini, in Venice. He set the text *alla francese*, conspicuous in the dotted rhythms of the accompaniment, and with a slightly higher *tessitura* for Angiola Magliani (Ex. 11).

Addition. The interpolated scenes in the Neapolitan libretto provide for nine new arias, one *aria à 2*, and three duets,[77] but of these only six arias appear in the Aria Collection.[78] Interestingly, all the extant arias for the added characters, Lesbia and Dori, are in minor keys and in 12/8 or 6/8 metres with flowing rhythms *alla siciliana* (Ex. 12).

Likewise, the ten arias which Scarlatti supplied for lines added or inserted into *existing* scenes[79] for a variety of characters,[80] emphasize compound metres and minor tonalities.

Example 11. Scarlatti 'Vo'dividere il mio affetto' Naples, Act III, Scene 7

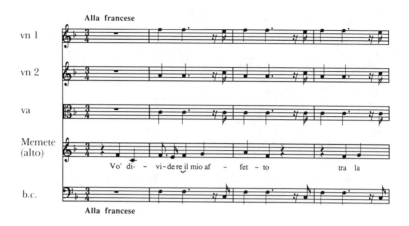

Example 12. Scarlatti 'Quanto è grato' Naples, Act I, Scene 11

Patterns of stylistic change in the *rifacimento*

First, the opera increased in the number of arias, decreased in recitative, and eliminated most *ariosi*. The time gained through the omission of the *intermezzi* was re-allotted not only to the interpolated comic scenes but also to additional arias for the regular cast. *L'Irene* moved from stage spectacle to stage concert. If all the arias in the Neapolitan Collection or in the libretto actually were performed, the numbers compare as follows:

Table 4. *Totals of closed forms*

	Venice score	Venice libretto	Naples collection	Naples libretto
Arias	33	35	52	60
Arie à 2	3	3	2	4
Duets	4	4	2	7
Ensembles	1	1	0	1
Totals	41	43	56	72

A comparison of the placement of the solo arias in the Venetian and Neapolitan libretti reveals a larger proportion of mid-scene arias in the *rifacimento* (Table 5). Only slightly more than half of its arias come at the end of a scene. In this respect the *rifacimento* is more conservative than the original. However, in both libretti, eight of the end-of-scene arias are not true exit arias because the character singing does not leave the stage.[81]

Table 5. *Aria distribution in scenes*

	Venice	Naples
Entrance arias	3 = 9%	5 = 8%
Mid-scene arias	5 = 14%	22 = 37%
End-of-scene arias	27 = 77%	33 = 55%
Exit arias (included in the preceding)	19 = 54%	25 = 42%
Totals	35	60

Second, the arias most frequently revised or replaced were those with fast *parlando* themes in a more or less martial style, such as 'Non chiedo amor non più' (see Ex. 5), 'A morire' (both replaced) or 'Si viva, si mora' (revised). The *parlando* theme seems admissable in Naples only in a slower tempo and a more lyrical style or when associated with a lilting dance rhythm, as in 'Il mio contento dal suo dipende' (Act I, Scene 9), a new aria by Scarlatti which replaced a short *arioso*.[82] Throughout the Neapolitan version of the opera there is a decided emphasis on the *cantabile* style with its lyrical, ingratiating, tuneful melody. In the revised arias this is usually achieved by the note values of a theme being lengthened and the phrase structures regularised (see Ex. 9).

Third, there has been a marked shift in the rhythmic basis of the arias of *L'Irene*. Thanks almost entirely to Scarlatti's efforts, compound-metre arias amount to one-third of the Neapolitan version, shattering the near total dominance of the simple metre aria in the Venetian original (Table 6). Moreover, these 6/8 or 12/8 metre arias usually display the rapidly intruding *cantabile* melodic lines, their flow enhanced by Scarlatti's diverse combinations of the basic   ♩ ♪ ♫   rhythm. His avoidance of dotted rhythms in his other arias makes their appearance in the specifically-designated *alla francese* 'Vo'dividere il mio affetto' even more effective.

Table 6. *Metre in closed forms*

	Venice (Pollarolo)	Naples (Pollarolo)	Naples (Scarlatti)
4/4	24	14	9
3/4	7	5	4
¢	6	1	4
3/8 or 6/8	4	0	5
12/8	0	2	11
2/4	0	2	0

Fourth, there is the obvious preference of the minor mode for lyric expression (Table 7). Indeed, this is the most striking tonal feature of the Neapolitan revision — something which not only Scarlatti but, to some extent, Pollarolo also observes in his substituted areas.

Table 7. *Mode in closed forms*

	Venice (Pollarolo)	Naples (Pollarolo)	Naples (Scarlatti)
Major	32	16	11
Minor	9	7	22

Within the arias themselves, the simplistic tonic-dominant movements have been replaced by a wider variety of modulatory schemes (Table 8). Even in short *ABA* structures, the *B*-section provides some tonal contrast, as in 'Belle catene' where it is in the relative major.

Table 8. *Modulatory scheme of selected arias*

Venice	Naples
'Belle catene' (Act I, Scene 6) by Pollarolo sections: ‖:a :‖:b :‖ bars: 4 4 keys: C – G G – C	'Belle catene' (Act I, Scene 6) by Pollarolo ‖:a :‖:b :‖ 8 8 c — E♭ E♭– B♭ – c
'Vincitor, terror del mondo' (Act II, Scene 5) by Pollarolo sections: A B (*da capo*) bars: 15 7 keys: D D - G	'Vincitor, terror del mondo' (Act II, Scene 4) by Pollarolo A B (*da capo*) 16 8 D – A – D e – f♯
'Sii pur fedele a me' (Act III, Scene 7) by Pollarolo sections: A B (*da capo*) bars: 27 12 keys: B♭ g – c – B♭	'Sii pur fedele a me' (Act II, Scene 12) by Scarlatti A B (*da capo*) 16 7 c – E♭ – c c – B♭ – g

As noted above, the extant arias for the added characters are sentimental rather than humorous and invariably in the minor mode (see Ex. 12).

Fifth, our two versions reveal few changes in the formal structure of the arias. The *da capo* pattern survives unchallenged. It is, perhaps, surprising that the majority of the revisions of nine years later show only slight increases in their dimensions; some are about the same in length, some are even briefer than their Venetian forebears (see Table 8).

Sixth, changes in the orchestration of the Neapolitan version almost invariably brought about a reduction of the instrumental forces. Without exception, all arias with five or more parts in the accompaniments in the Venetian version have been either omitted, revised or replaced in Naples so that four-part accompaniments became the maximum.[83] These reductions may have been related to the strengths (or weaknesses) of individual singers,[84] but in general they seem to have resulted from the pronounced preference for two-part or three-part accompaniments (one or two melody-instruments plus continuo) noticeable throughout the *rifacimento*. *L'Irene* certainly was made lighter, if not better, through this conversion to contemporary taste.

Table 9. *Accompaniments in closed forms*

	Venice (Pollarolo)	Naples (Pollarolo)	Naples (Scarlatti)
b.c.	22	10	11
à 2	5	6	11
à 3	1	3	7
à 4	4	3	4
à 5	6	1	0
à 6	1	0	0
à 7	1	0	0
à 9	1	0	0

The violin, of course, was the most favoured melody instrument. The disappearance of wind parts from the accompaniments parallels the reduced emphasis on the military aspects of plot and character in the Neapolitan libretto (Table 10). In fact, the only appearance of a wind instrument in the Neapolitan Collection is inspired by a textual allusion. Not unexpectedly, Scarlatti's 'Su, di metalli, e di feroci trombe' is scored for trumpet and strings, four parts altogether. In Pollarolo's seven-part Venetian setting trumpets and oboes doubled the two top parts. In the duet 'Su, contro i furori' (Act II, Scene 7 in Venice; Act II, Scene 5 in Naples) where the original five-part orchestration is retained in the *rifacimento*, the instruction in the Venetian score ' ... con Istrom[enti] tutti d'Arco, ed da Fiato' is left out of the Aria Collection.

Table 10. *Instruments in accompaniments*

	Venice (Pollarolo)	Naples (Pollarolo)	Naples (Scarlatti)
Strings only	9	8	10
Strings & winds	6	0	1
Obbligato:			
violin	3	1	11
viola	1	1	0
cello	0	0	1
Total	19	10	23

Table 10 does not include those *basso continuo* arias which have directions for doubling the bass-line by strings or other specified instruments. Pollarolo, for example, has 'tutti istrom[en]ti' play the bass-line of 'Vincitor, terror del mondo' (Act II, Scene 4 in Naples) and Scarlatti assigns a solo cello to the bass part of 'Più non voglio' (Act II, Scene 9 in Naples).

Very occasionally a replacement aria at Naples brought about an increase in instrumentation. In addition to Pollarolo's four-part 'Piangete' which replaced the continuo-aria 'A morire',[85] there is Scarlatti's aria for Deianira, 'Vivi, o caro', which replaced Pollarolo's aria on the same text. This new setting also has a four-string accompaniment; again, the original was scored for continuo only. In 'Misero amante core' Pollarolo replaced an aria with a violin and bass accompaniment by a setting scored only for two violins and viola (marked *violette* in the score) — that is, without a true bass.

*   *   *   *   *

This comparison of the extant music of the two versions of *L'Irene* has shown that the *rifacimento* process was rather complex. Before becoming acquainted with the Venetian score, I had assumed that Pollarolo's arias in the Neapolitan collection were simply those taken over from the Venetian production while Scarlatti's represented the substitutions. As it turns out, Pollarolo must have participated in the revision, for many of his arias in the Neapolitan collection are replacements or modifications of the Venetian ones. Moreover, the patterns of stylistic change in his arias point in the same direction as those in Scarlatti's music and reflect the local partiality for tuneful, lilting, melancholy and harmonically colourful music — an indication that Pollarolo, too, was well aware of the *gusto locale* of Neapolitan audiences. The earlier *rifacimenti* of 1698 and 1699 must have stood him in good stead in 1704.[86]

Indeed, in the move to Naples *L'Irene* became localized. To be sure, some of the revisions of the music were motivated by the requirements of a new cast. Others, such as the near elimination of *ariosi*, the upwards movement of the vocal ranges employed, the reduction of the instrumentation to four or fewer parts, and the flowing rhythms and regular phrases of the new arias, were signs of at least a limited modernization. But all of these were tempered by the overwhelming emphasis on the *cantabile* aria, especially the *siciliano* type, which serious and comic characters alike constantly sang — an almost complete capitulation to local taste.

Although represented in the Aria Collection by thirty-three arias to Pollarolo's twenty-three, Domenico Scarlatti does not appear as the dominant partner. Indeed, he seems to have been rather timid in his revisions. Several of the arias attributed to him are only his modifications of Pollarolo's music, not entirely new pieces. Some of Scarlatti's original settings certainly are forward-looking but he does not move appreciably beyond the older composer's concept of the aria as it appeared in the Venetian score of 1694. There is as yet no sign of the large-scale *da capo*, the sweeping melodic line or the enhanced vocal virtuosity of the eighteenth-century aria. Thus it seems to me that Domenico Scarlatti's revisions of *L'Irene* can be regarded as 'drastic' only in terms of the sheer amount of modified and new music incorporated into the 1704 production — and some of this is by Pollarolo, not Scarlatti.

While the original composer had a hand in the revision, the original librettist definitely did not. Nine years after the original production, this 'reform' libretto fell victim to the *rifacimento* process and, like the music, to the dictates of the *gusto locale*. Several of Frigimelica Roberti's principles were sacrificed in the Neapolitan *L'Irene*. The five-act structure, presumably 'Aristotelian', gave way to the conventional three acts, the *semplicità* to additional characters extraneous to the story, the unity of plot to interpolated scenes carrying a 'sub-plot', and the clarity and flow of action to multiple cuts in the recitative and a plethora of added aria texts. Together with the introduction of a substantial comic element, these changes demonstrate the strong preferences of Neapolitan taste which, no doubt, helped retard the trend toward 'reform' in that city by several years.[87] Certainly they point in a direction opposite to that indicated by the changes made in Stampiglia's libretto for *La Partenope* when it travelled *from* Naples in 1699 *to* Venice, among other places, in 1708. Its comic scenes were eliminated and the servant Beltramme was reduced to a humourless role with only a few dozen lines of recitative, much like Olobolo in the Venetian *L'Irene*.[88] In Naples, at any rate, the day of *opera seria* had still to dawn.[89]

The transplanted and adapted Venetian opera theatre which reigned in Naples during this period and which was best represented by Alessandro Scarlatti, was part of the official vice-regal policy.[90] In plot after plot there is a concentration on the figure of the monarch, portrayed as a tragic character forced into a hopeless situation by love and war and from which only his magnanimity could save him.[91] In *L'Irene* Memete fits this image perfectly, since the happy outcome for the other characters hinges entirely on the selfless resignation of the hero. This transformed character was probably one of the reasons why the subject was deemed suitable for the Kingdom of Naples where the magnanimous tyrant may have appeared on stage more often than in other Italian cities.[92] In its revised state *L'Irene* must have pleased both official propaganda and popular taste even as its 'reform' libretto and its music became a victim of both.

Notes

[1] At least two of Pollarolo's operas had been performed in Venice by the time Caldara's first opera *L'Argene* was produced there in 1689 at the Teatro alli Saloni. He had long dominated the Venetian opera houses when Caldara's next opera *La promessa serbata* (1697) and the collaborations *Il Tirsi* (1696) and *L'oracolo in sogno* (1699) were produced. The latter composition was shared by Caldara, Quintavalle and Pollarolo. It was well possible that Caldara was employed as a cellist in the orchestras for the performances of some of Pollarolo's work. Their paths definitely crossed at San Marco where Caldara served as instrumentalist (even before his regular employment in 1694) during Pollarolo's tenure as Second Organist and *Vice-maestro*.

[2] A term employed by Patrick Smith to distinguish the reform efforts along the lines of the Arcadians and other seventeenth-century librettists from the Metastasian reform. See Patrick Smith *The Tenth Muse* (New York, 1970) p. 63ff. It is understood that this 'first reform' was part of a general literary trend. See Robert Freeman 'Apostolo Zeno's Reform of the Libretto' *Journal of the American Musicological Society* XXI (1968) pp. 321–341.

[3] See Nathaniel Burt, 'Plus ça change: Or, The Progress of Reform in Seventeenth and Eighteenth Century Opera as Illustrated in the Books of Three Operas' *Studies in Music History: Essays for Oliver Strunk* ed. Harold Powers, (Princeton, 1968) p. 332ff.

[4] See Nathaniel Burt 'Opera in Arcadia' *The Musical Quarterly* XLI (1955) p. 156ff.

[5] Karl Leich 'Girolamo Frigimelica-Robertis Libretti (1694–1708)' *Schriften zur Musik* 26 (1972) p. 10ff.

[6] *Il pastore d'Anfriso* and *Rosimonda* were also performed in 1695, *Ercole in cielo* in 1696, *La fortuna per dote* in 1704 and *Il Dafni* in 1705. See Leich *op.cit.*, p. 18ff and p. 95ff.

[7] Not at the theatre San Giovanni e Paolo, as listed in Lorenzo Bianconi *Funktionen des Operntheaters in Neapel bis 1700* Sonderdruck (Tutzing, n.d.) p. 104. The première actually took place on 26 December, 1694.

[8] Ralph Kirkpatrick *Domenico Scarlatti* (Princeton, 1953) p. 18.

[9] US-Wc: Schatz 9539. Libretto: 'L'IRENE / DRAMA PER MUSICA / Da rappresentarsi nel Teatro di / S. Bartolomeo di Napoli … IN NAPOLI 1704. / Per il Parrino, & il Mutio.'

[10] Claudio Sartori cites aria identifications for *Il Giustino* (Naples, 1703) in 'Gli Scarlatti a Napoli' *Rivista Musicale Italiana* XLVI (1942) p. 376 and Graham Hardie for Leonardo Leo's *La finta frascatana* (Naples, 1745) and for the collaboration *Il trionfo del valore* (Naples, 1741) by Porpora, Palella, Di Domenico and Signorile in 'Neapolitan Comic Opera, 1707–1750: Some Addenda and Corrigenda for *The New Grove*' *Journal of the American Musicological Society* XXXVI (1983) p. 127.

[11] There is at least one error in the identification: 'Al mio core' (Act III, Scene 12) should have been attributed to Pollarolo.

[12] Cs-K Pracoviště Statního Archívu Třeboň (Český Krumlov Archive). I gratefully acknowledge the aid of Dr Gary Cohen, Professor of History at the University of Oklahoma, in obtaining microfilms of the score.

[13] Joel Sheveloff '(Giuseppe) Domenico Scarlatti' *The New Grove Dictionary of Music and Musicians* (London, 1980) 16, p. 568.

[14] Elizabeth Frenzel *Stoffe der Weltliteratur* (Stuttgart, 1962) p. 301.

[15] *Ibid.*

[16] US-LAu: uncatalogued. Libretto: 'L'Irene … ' *Raccolta de'Drammi* Vol. of 1694, p. 12. A collection of Venetian libretti in chronological order, 1637–1797, one volume per year. The year is the only designation for an individual volume.

[17] Frigimelica Roberti refers to a law prohibiting sultans from marrying. US-LAu: Libretto, p. 13.

[18] *Ibid.* p. 68.

[19] *Ibid.* p. 7

[20] For a detailed discussion of Frigimelica Roberti's libretto see Leich *op.cit.*, pp. 27–35.

[21] US-LAu: Libretto, p. 14.

[22] *Ibid.*, p. 29.

[23] For a discussion of Arcadian reform traits see Robert Freeman 'The Travels of Partenope' *Studies in Music History: Essays for Oliver Strunk* ed. Harold Powers (Princeton, 1968) p. 357ff.

[24] The libretto, p.11, announces three aria substitutions 'per dare maggior comodo ad alcune voci': Memete's 'Con la gloria' for 'Vo'dividere' (Act III, Scene 1), Solimano's 'Ne l'amante' for 'Grand'amanta' (Act III, Scene 8), and Demetrio's

'A morire' for 'Piangete, occhi, piangete' (Act VI, Scene 9). In addition there are a few suppressed aria texts (see Appendix).

[25] See Olga Termini 'Stylistic and Formal Changes in the Arias of Carlo Francesco Pollarolo (c. 1653–1723)' *Current Musicology* 26 (1978) p. 113.

[26] There are only six mid-scene arias in the libretto, five of these appear in the score. These are placed in structures such as R-A-R or R-A-R-A (Act I, Scene 2; Act II, Scene 5; Act III, Scene 3; Act III, Scene 4, not in score; Act IV, Scene 2, and Act V, Scene 4). See also Table 5.

[27] See Olga Termini 'Carlo Francesco Pollarolo: Follower or Leader in Venetian Opera?' *Studi Musicali* VIII (1979) p. 242ff.

[28] According to documents published by Remo Giazotto, Pollarolo received over 2000 ducats for *L'Irene, Ottone, Il pastore d'Anfriso* and *Rosimonda*. See 'La guerra dei palchi' *Nuova Rivista Musicale Italiana* I (1967) p. 496.

[29] See cast lists in Simon P. Towneley Worsthorne *Venetian Opera in the Seventeenth Century* (Oxford, 1954) pp.172–175. Boni first appeared in Venice in 1678.

[30] Francois Raguenet *Parallèle des Italiens et des Français en ce que regarde la musique et les opéras* (1702); trans. by J. E. Gaillard (?) as *A comparison between the French and Italian Music* (1709), and reprinted in *The Musical Quarterly* XXXII (1946) p. 432.

[31] When the Venetian opera houses were closed during the Christmas season a number of singers were engaged for special Christmas services at the Basilica of San Marco. Ballarini appeared there in 1690, 94, 95, and 96. See Olga Termini 'Singers at San Marco in Venice — The Competition between Church and Theatre (c. 1675–c. 1725)' *RMA Research Chronicle* 17 (1981) p. 89. For details of Ballarini's later career see Wulf Arlt 'Zur Deutung der Barockoper: *Il Trionfo dell'Amicizia e dell'Amore* Wien 1711' *Musik und Geschichte* (Köln, 1963) pp. 105–109, 116–117.

[32] *Della Storia e della Ragione d'ogni Poesia* (Milan, 1744) III, Part 2, p. 574. However, she appeared in Venice as early as 1683 in Pallavicino's *Il re infante*. See Worsthorne *op.cit.*, p. 171.

[33] F. Florimo *Scuola musicale di Napoli e i suoi conservatorii* (Naples, 1881) 4, pp. 7 and 9.

[34] Quadrio *op.cit.*, p. 528.

[35] His first operatic appearance that I know of was in 1690, in Perti's *Brenno in Efeso*, where he is called 'Udinese' (Worsthorne *op.cit.*, p. 172). Angus Heriot judges him inferior to Nicolini (*The Castrati in Opera* London, 1956/R1975, p. 125).

[36] Quadrio *op.cit.*, p. 535.

[37] *Ibid.*, p. 528.

[38] I-Mb: Brera *Racc. Dramm.* 6102: Libretto, and Worsthorne *op.cit.*, p.173, respectively.

[39] Quadrio *op.cit.*, p. 529.

[40] Stephen Bonta 'The Church Sonatas of Giovanni Legrenzi' (Ph.D., diss. Harvard University, 1964) p. 355.

[41] US-LAu: Libretto, pp. 15–16.

[42] *Ibid.* At the conclusion of Act I: Mute servants of the Sultan talk to Turkish ladies in sign language; Act 2: Eunuchs, Moors, and Turks with Turkish instruments celebrate the 'Bairano'; Act 3: Slaves and Moors dance in the ruins of the gallery; Act 4: Janissaries and Moors perform a war game to the sound of trumpet and drum.

[43] Smith (*op.cit.*, p. 65) criticizes Frigimelica Roberti for not practising what he preaches by including ballets and machines. However, the librettist probably had little control in this area of operatic production.

44 According to Bonlini, *Tito Manlio* was given first at Pratolino in the summer of 1696. It was repeated 'in qualche parte variato, e ristretto' at Venice in 1697 (*op.cit.*, p.128). The libretto for the Venetian performance (US-LAu: uncatalogued. *Raccolta de'Drammi* Vol. of 1697) identifies the composer; that for the Neapolitan performance (I-Bl: 7230) refers to both productions. A collection of arias from the Naples production is preserved at I-Nc: Ms 33.6.28.

45 Bianconi *op.cit.*, p. 97, gives Alessandro Scarlatti as the composer.

46 I-Fm: 1.00X.90. Libretto, pp. A2–A2 verso: ' … fu veduto con sommo piacimento ne'primi Teatri d'Italia intitolata *La Forza della Virtù*.' Bianconi (*op.cit.*, p. 97) suggests S. De Luca as composer but with a question mark.

47 Claudio Sartori 'Gli Scarlatti … ' *op.cit.*, p. 379. Perhaps *Ottavia* was entirely his (see Bianconi *op.cit.*, p. 103).

48 Giorgio Pestelli *Le Sonate di Domenico Scarlatti* (Turin, 1967) p. 100. Kirkpatrick, too, finds the early sonatas 'curiously lacking in exuberance and vitality'. (*op.cit.*, p. 103).

49 Perhaps Giulio Convò, see Pestelli *op.cit.*, p. 104.

50 US-Wc: Libretto, p. A3.

51 *Ibid.*, p. 43.

52 Only six arias appear in the aria collection.

53 These figures do not include the additional arias generated by the restoration of aria texts omitted from the Venetian score, because they are not a result of changes in the libretto as such.

54 For example, of the 56 lines of recitative in Act II, Scene 3, only five are deleted and none from the 47 lines in Scene 5. See US-LAu: Libretto, pp. 31–2 and 35–6 and US-Wc: Libretto, pp. 16–17 and 19–21, respectively.

55 US-LAu: Libretto, p. 22.

56 *Ibid.*, p. 47.

57 *Ibid.*, p. 48.

58 *Ibid.*, p. 25. On the other hand, certain cuts in Act III, Scene 13 made Memete's call for Irene's head come about even more abruptly. See US-Wc: Libretto, p. 47.

59 US-LAu: Libretto, p. 25.

60 Sartori *op.cit.*, p. 379.

61 Florimo *op.cit.*, p. 11.

62 There is, however, more harmonic variety in the Naples version, the *B*-section being in e minor and modulating to f-sharp minor instead of beginning in the tonic key and moving to G.

63 The aria is omitted from the Collection. In the absence of a full score it is impossible to determine what prompted omissions from the anthology. Most likely, arias thought to be appealing and technically manageable for non-professionals were included.

64 The Aria Collection omits all *ritornelli* which are independent in the *basso continuo* arias.

65 Florimo *op.cit.*, pp. 11 and 35.

66 Taddeo Wiel *I Teatri musicali veneziani nel Settecento* (Venice, 1897) pp. 25–6 and 35.

67 According to Robert Lamar and N. R. Weaver *A Chronology of music in the Florentine Theatre, 1590–1750* (Detroit, 1978) p. 339, Rapaccioli served the King

of Spain and died in 1756 at the age of 67. But then he would have been only 15 years old in 1704!

[68] According to Wiel (*op.cit.*, p. 60) he was indeed a soprano.

[69] One of Scarlatti's arias ('Su, di metalli') (Act II, Scene 7) could be considered a revision of Pollarolo's counterpart (Act III, Scene 1), its rhythmic scheme being almost identical.

[70] Of the three added characters, Lesbia was sung by Angiola Catarina Liuzzi, soprano, and Dori by Pompilia Pozzi, soprano. The latter also sang the role of Brillo in *Il Giustino*. Neither arias nor duets for Nuto appear in the Collection although the libretto allots him two arias, one *aria à 2* and three duets. The singer is only identified as '*un'altro virtuoso della Real Cappella di Napoli*'. (Libretto, p. A5)

[71] Comparison of the 1716 and 1718 versions of Pollarolo's *Ariodante* (both scores are extant) has shown that the composer tended to recompose rather than simply transpose recitatives, altering melody and bass-line, as well as harmonic progressions, more than rhythmic patterns. In the case of *Ariodante* there was even a distinct tendency to change the cadential patterns before arias in different keys.

[72] 'Se in amor' is deleted as part of a short scene (Act III, Scene 6 in Venice).

[73] 'Dimmi s'havrà mai fin' which features extreme tempi in juxtaposition.

[74] These include three arias for Irene, two each for Memete and Solimano, and one for Demetrio. The duet is for Demetrio and Irene. As no characters are indicated in the Aria Collection the *aria à 2* 'La speranza/Vuol ch'io goda' appears to be an aria with two stanzas. The other *aria à 2* 'Bella mia/Ogni amor' is actually notated as two arias (nos. 10 and 11) in the Collection. Memete's 'Son vindicato, sì' was retained according to the Neapolitan libretto but it does not appear in the Collection.

[75] See Note 24.

[76] See p. 394. 'Piangete' also became a mid-scene, instead of an exit-aria. See Powers 'Il Mutio tramutato' *Venezia e il Melodramma nel Seicento* (Florence, 1976) p. 231 for a similar case of 'restored' aria texts in a later collection.

[77] These include three arias each for Lesbia and Dori, two for Nuto and one for Irene. All duets and the *aria à 2* are for Dori and Nuto.

[78] Lesbia's three arias, two for Dori and one for Irene.

[79] Two are mid-scene arias, eight are added at scene ends.

[80] All of these are extant: two arias for Halì, four for Alete, three for Solimano, and one for Deianira.

[81] In Venice these eight are located in Act II, Scene 3, Act III, Scenes 3 and 6, Act IV, Scenes 3, 4 and 7, and Act V, Scenes 2 and 3; in Naples in Act II, Scenes 1, 9 and 14, and Act III, Scenes 1, 2, 5, 12 and 15.

[82] For an exception, see Example 4, p. 380.

[83] Pollarolo's 'Su, contro i furori', a duet between Irene and Deianira, (Act II, Scene 6 in the Venetian score; Act II, Scene 5 in Naples) is the only example retained with an unaltered five-part accompaniment.

[84] See p. 380. However, strategically placed rests in many accompaniments in the Venetian score show that Pollarolo was adept at avoiding any smothering of the singer by the thicker orchestration.

[85] See p. 386-7

[86] There is no indication in the extant biographical documents that he actually went to Naples. The only requests for leaves-of-absence from his position as *vice-maestro*, albeit *giubilato*, at San Marco date from 1708 (to Vicenza) and 1709 (to Rome). Termini 'Carlo Francesco Pollarolo: Follower or Leader . . . ' *op.cit.*, p. 223.

87 For example, for Alessandro Scarlatti's *La principessa fedele* produced in Naples in 1710, two comic characters and several comic scenes were added to Piovene's libretto set for Venice in the previous year by Gasparini. See Donald J. Grout *Alessandro Scarlatti: An Introduction to his Operas* (Berkeley, 1978) p. 79. Of course comedy had been part of Venetian opera especially from *c*1650 to *c*1690. See Thomas Walker 'Opera II, 1: Italy — Origins to Scarlatti' *The New Grove Dictionary of Music and Musicians* (London, 1980) 13, p. 553.

88 Freeman 'The Travels of Partenope' *op.cit.*, pp. 366-7.

89 Walker *op.cit.*, p. 554-5.

90 Bianconi *op.cit.*, p. 33 and p. 116.

91 *Ibid.*, p. 35.

92 Grout *op.cit.*, p .9.

Appendix

Arias in the Venetian and Neapolitan versions of *L'Irene*

LEGEND

x = same title, same words as in Venetian score (left column)	Dei = Deianira
	D = Demetrio
o = omitted	I = Irene
DS = Domenico Scarlatti, composer	O = Olobolo
CFP = Carlo Francesco Pollarolo, composer	A = Alete
	L = Lesbia
M = Memete	Dor = Dori
H = Hali	N = Nuto
S = Solimano	

ARIAS IN THE VENETIAN

	Acts & Scenes (VENICE)	Score by C.F. Pollarolo — Arias		Acts & Scenes (NAPLES)	Venetian arias retained in Naples libretto	with Venetian music	with new music	
VENICE			NAPLES					
	I, 1	'Primo Cesare Ottomano' (H)		I, 1	x			
	I, 2	'Sento una forza' (M)		I, 2	x	x		
	I, 2			I, 2				
	I, 3	'Guerra, guerra' (M)		I, 3	x			
	I, 4	'Chi non può vincere' (S)		I, 4	o			
	I, 5	'Non ha pena l'amor' (Dei)		I, 5	x	x		
	I, 5			I, 5				
	I, 6	'Belle catene/Dolce piacere' aria à 2 (D & I)		I, 6	x		x (CFP)	
	I, 6	'La speranza d'un core ardente' (I)		I, 6	x	x		
	I, 7	'Mal resiste la beltà' (S)		I, 7	x		x (CFP)	
	I, 8	'Si viva, si mora' (D)		I, 8	x		x (DS)	
	II, 1	'Bella mia/Ogni amor' aria à 2 (Dei & S)		I, 9	x	x		
	II, 1	['Non voglio, non amo' arioso] (Dei)		I, 9	o			
	II, 1	'Se vuoi ch'io serva' (S)		I, 9	x	x		
	II, 2	['Questo è il brutto' recitative (0)]		I,10	o			
	II, 2	'Il far schiavo' (Dei)		I,10	x		x (CFP)	
				I,11				
				I,11				
				I,12				
				I,12				
				I,12				
	II, 3	'Godrò, si, si' (I)		II, 1	x	x		
				II, 2				

AND NEAPOLITAN VERSIONS OF L'IRENE

Aria texts restored (omitted in Venetian score)	New aria texts with new music	Aria Collection	Treatment in Naples *rifacimento*
		o	According to libretto DS
		I, no.1	Only ritornello omitted
	'Amante, e insiem guerriero' (H)	I, no.2	Added aria
		o	According to libretto CFP
	'Per godere il mio tesoro' (S) DS	I, no.3	Aria replaces aria
		I, no.4	Transposed for new singer
	'Non sarebbe l'amare' (A) DS	I, no.7	Added aria
		I, no.8	No characters indicated in collection (aria)
		I, no.5	Retained unchanged
		I, no.9	
		I, no.6	Revision
		I, nos.10,11	Notated as 2 arias; ritornello omitted
	'Il mio contento' (Dei) DS	I, no.12	Aria replaces *arioso*
		I, no.13	Retained unchanged
	'Perchè sprezzar chi t'ama' (A) DS	I, no.14	Aria replaces recitative
		I, no.15	
	'Quanto è grato' (L) DS	I, no.17	Interpolated scene & aria
	'Chi tanto l'alma' (I) DS	I, no.16	Interpolated scene & aria
	'O se qui trovassi' (Dor) DS	I, no.18	Interpolated scene & aria
	'Per due poma' (N)	o	According to libretto DS
	'O brutto/Son forte' *duet* (Dor & N)	o	According to libretto DS
		II, no.1	Retained unchanged
	'Un cor lungi dal volto' (L) DS	II, no.2	Interpolated scene & aria

VENICE

Acts & Scenes	Score by CFP: Arias
II, 5	'Vincitor, terror del mondo' (M)
II, 5	'Non sa chi ben non ama' (M)
II, 5	
II, 6	'Su contro i furori' *duet* (Dei & I) (II,7 in libretto)
III, 1	'Su, di metalli, e di feroci trombe' (H)
III, 1	'Con la gloria e con l'amor' (M)
III, 2	
III, 2	'Misero amante core' (I)
III, 3	'Per lei caro m'è ogni duolo' (D)
III, 3	'Non chiedo amor non più ' (Dei)
III, 3	
III, 4	
III, 4	'La speranza/Vuol ch'io goda' (*aria à* 2) (D & I)
III, 5	
III, 6	'Se in amor sempre non si gode' (Dei)
III, 7	['Ogni amante ha un bel momento' *arioso* (Dei)]
III, 7	'Sii pur fedele a me' (Dei)
III, 8	'Ne l'amante son' (S)
IV, 1	'Fuggo/Fuggi' *duet* (Dei & D)
IV, 2	'Sperar degg'io, si o nò ' (I)
IV, 2	'Finche sei cara/Finche sei caro' *duet* (D & I)
IV, 3	

NAPLES

Acts & Scenes	Venetian arias retained		
	in Naples libretto	with Venetian music	with new music
II, 4	x		x (CFP)
II, 4	x	x	
II, 4			
II, 5	x	x	
II, 6			
II, 6			
II, 6			
II, 7	x		x (DS)
II, 7	o		
II, 8			
II, 8	x		x (CFP)
II, 9	x		x (DS)
II, 9	o		
II, 9			
II,10			
II,10	x	x	
II,11			
o	o		
II,12	x		x (DS)
II,12	x		x (DS)
II,13	o		
II,14	o		
II,15	x		x (CFP)
II,15	o		
III, 1			

Aria texts restored (omitted in Venetian score)	New aria texts with new music	Aria Collection	Treatment in Naples *rifacimento*
		II, no.14	Revision
		II, no.15	Retained almost unchanged
	'Giubila il seno mio' (S) DS	II, no.16	Added aria
		II, no.17	Retained unchanged
	'O se tu dicessi il vero' (N)	o	Interpolated scene & aria; DS?
	'Tu mi piaci' (Dor) DS	II, no. 4	Interpolated scene & aria
	'Te lo credi/Questo a me' *duet* (Dor & N)	o	Interpolated scene & aria; According to libretto DS
		II, no. 5	Elements of revision
'Vo'dividere il mio affetto' (M) DS		II, no. 6	
	'Del destino gl'eventi' (S) DS	II, no. 7	Aria replaces recitative; mid-scene
		II, no.18	
		II, no.19	
	'Più non voglio' (Dei) DS	II, no.20	Aria replaces aria
	'A vincere te stessa' (A) DS	II, no. 8	Added aria, end of scene
'Vuoi ch'accetti' (I) DS		II, no. 9	Restored text slightly modified
		II, no.2i	No characters indentified; appears as aria
	'Non puo far dono' (A) DS	II, no.10	Interpolated aria
		o	Scene omitted in N libretto
		II, no.22	Expanded *arioso* text = aria
		II, no.11	
	'Crudo tiranno amore' (S) DS	II, no.23	Text replaced both in V and N
	'Dimmi s'havrà mai fin' (D) DS	II, no. 12	Aria replaces duet
		II, no.13	Revision
	'Io t'amo/Tu m'ami' (D & I) DS	II, no.24	Duet replaces duet
'Chi è più in alto' (M) CFP		II, no. 3	

VENICE

Acts & Scenes	Score by CFP: Arias
IV, 4	'Ama un bene' (H)
IV, 5	'Su presto a godere' (M)
IV, 6	
IV, 7	'Se mai dolce' (I)
IV, 7	'Sia pur morta la speranza' (D)
IV, 8	['Non più amore per me' *arioso* (I)]
IV, 9	'A morire, a morir' (D)
IV,10	'Gran tormento è di chi e colto' (Dei)
V, 1	
V, 1	'Se mi condanni' (S)
V, 2	'Vivi, o caro' (Dei)
V, 2	
V, 3	'Al mio core' (D)
V, 4	'Su, su s'armi' *duet* (H & S)
V, 4	'Il mio amore ti fa regina' (M)
V, 4	
V, 5	'Son vendicato, sì'(M)
V, 5	
V, 6	
V, 7	'Guerra, guerra' ensemble

NAPLES

Acts & Scenes	Venetian arias retained in Naples libretto	with Venetian music	with new music
III, 2	x		
III, 3	x	x	
III, 4			
III, 5	x	x	
III, 5	o		
III, 6	x		x (DS)
III, 7	o		
III, 7	o		
III, 8			
III, 8			
III, 9			
III, 9			
III,10			
III,10	x	x	
III,11	x		x (DS)
III,11			
III,12	x	x	
III,13	x		
III,13	x		x (CFP)
III,13			
III,14	x		
III,14			
III,15			
III,16	o		

Aria texts restored (omitted in Venetian score)	New aria texts with new music	Aria Collection	Treatment in Naples *rifacimento*
		o	According to libretto DS
		III, no.10	Revision: only tenor viola part ommitted
'L'amore oltraggiato' (S) CFP		III, no. 1	
		III, no. 2	Retained unchanged
	'Ciò nol concedo' (D) DS	III, no.11	Aria replaces aria
		III, no. 3	Expanded *arioso* text = aria
'Piangete, occhi, piangete' (D)CFP		III, no.12	
	'Cruda guerra è nel mio core' (Dei)	o	Aria replaces aria; DS (libr.)
	'Quel primo amore' (L) DS	III, no. 4	Interpolated scene & aria
	'Io che son donna sagace' (Dor)	o	Interpolated scene & aria; DS? (libr)
	'Credimi/Tu dici' *aria à 2* (Dor & N)	o	Interpolated scene & aria; DS? (libr)
	'Ti servirò /Servimi' *duet* (Dor & N)	o	Interpolated scene & aria; DS? (libr)
	'Se tu speri' (Dei) DS	III, no. 5	Added aria, mid-scene
		III, no.13	Retained unchanged
		III, no. 6	Elements of revision
	'Voler cedere il suo bene' (A) DS	III, no. 7	Added aria, end of scene
		III, no.14	Retained unchanged
		o	According to libretto CFP
		III, no.15	
	'Potrai far ciò che vuoi' (I)	o	According to libretto DS; added aria
		o	According to libretto CFP
	'Corro veloce e spero' (H) DS	III, no. 8	Added aria, end of scene
	'Perdona, si, perdona' (S) DS	III, no.16	Added aria, end of scene
	'Suoni pur per ogni riva' ensemble	o	Ensemble replaces ensemble; DS?(libr.)

Index

by John M. Jennings

This *Index* is of names, titles, compositions, venues and institutions (but not towns, cities or countries) mentioned in the text. Unless otherwise indicated, names are of composers. Pages which include **musical examples** are shown in **bold** type; pages which include *plates of photographic reproductions of manuscripts or publications* are shown in *italics*.

Contributors

Lawrence E. Bennett received his Ph.D. from New York University in 1980. He is Associate Professor of music at Upsala College in East Orange, New Jersey. Dr Bennett is a specialist in Baroque and early American music, has edited two books of vocal music and has contributed articles to *The New Grove Dictionary of Music*, *Notes* and *The Journal of Popular Culture*. A tenor and founding member of 'The Western Wind' vocal sextet, he has recorded often and toured internationally with this *a cappella* ensemble.

A. Peter Brown is Professor of musicology at Indiana University. He has published a number of studies and books on Joseph Haydn and on composers at the Viennese court during the eighteenth century, including a thematic catalogue of the compositions of Carlo d'Ordonez.

Robert N. Freeman received his training in musicology at the University of California, Los Angeles. He is presently Associate Professor of music at the University of California, Santa Barbara, specializing in music at the Austrian abbeys in the eighteenth century.

Frauke Gerdes was born in Bremen. Since 1976 she has studied musicology and the history of arts at the University of Hamburg, working on her dissertation 'Die frühen szenisch-dramatischen Werke Antonio Caldaras'.

Wolfgang Horn studied musicology and Germanistics at Tübingen University. From 1981–83 he was assistant editor for the series *Das Erbe deutscher Musik* and from 1983 Assistant in the Department of musicology at Tübingen University. He has completed his doctoral dissertation on *Die Dresdner Hofkirchenmusik 1720-1745* and has published several editions of Catholic church music of the eighteenth century.

Andrew D. McCredie is Professor of musicology at the University of Adelaide. He studied in Australia and Europe (D.Phil., Hamburg) specializing in the development of the orchestra and instrumental music in the eighteenth century. Awarded the Royal Musical Association's Edward J. Dent medal in 1974, he was made a Fellow of the Australian Academy of the Humanities in 1975, and Member, Order of Australia in 1984. He holds positions on several international bodies and is general editor of *Miscellanea Musicologica* (Adelaide) and *Paperbacks in Musicology* (Heinrichshofen Verlag, Wilhelmshaven).

Reinhard G. Pauly was appointed Professor of music at Lewis and Clark College, Portland, Oregon in 1948, and in 1972 became Director of the College's music school. He received his musical education at Columbia and Yale universities and throughout his career has specialized in opera and the sacred music of the eighteenth century. His publications include books and articles, and editions of music.

Brian W. Pritchard, Senior lecturer in musicology at Canterbury University, Christchurch, New Zealand, has undertaken extensive research into the music of Antonio Caldara. His editions of Caldara's music (operas, church and instrumental compositions) have been used in performances in England and the Continent. Currently he is completing a thematic catalogue of Caldara's output and has instituted (with an international advisory panel) a Centre for Caldara Studies.

Jiří Sehnal, CSc. studied musicology and aesthetics in the Faculty of Philosophy at Palacký University, Olomouc, ČSSR. He has been a member of the staff of Department for music history of the Moravské Muzeum in Brno since 1964, and Director of the Department from 1978. His speciality is the music history of Moravia, and he has published extensively on this subject. His editions of early music have appeared in the series *Denkmäler der Tonkunst in Österreich* and *Musica Antiqua Bohemica*.

Eleanor Selfridge-Field has been extensively involved in examining the history of instrumental music. She is the author of *Venetian Instrumental Music from Gabrieli to Vivaldi* (1975) and *Pallade Veneta: Writings on Music in Venetian Society, 1650–1750* (1985) as well as numerous articles in journals and encyclopediae. Currently, she is completing a thematic index of the music of Bernedetto Marcello. She works for the Centre for Computer Assisted Research in the Humanities in Menlo Park, CA.

Hisako Serizawa, studied at the Kunitachi Music College in Tokyo from 1964 to 1970 and subsequently undertook musicological research in Europe. At present she is Associate Professor at the Osaka University of Arts and a member of the Japanese Musicological Society.

Olga Termini, a native of Hamburg, Germany, earned her Ph.D. from the University of Southern California, with a dissertion on Carlo Francesco Pollarolo. She is now Professor of music at California State University, Los Angeles, and continues to investigate aspects of Venetian opera.

Glennys Ward specializes in archival and documentary studies. She has been involved in the preparation of the thematic catalogue of Caldara's music and is Research Associate for the newly-established Centre for Caldara Studies.